INTIMATE LIVES OF THE
ANCIENT GREEKS

INTIMATE LIVES OF THE
ANCIENT GREEKS

Stephanie Lynn Budin

Intimate Lives of the Ancient Peoples
Kevin M. McGeough, Series Editor

 PRAEGER

AN IMPRINT OF ABC-CLIO, LLC
Santa Barbara, California • Denver, Colorado • Oxford, England

Library of Congress Cataloging-in-Publication Data

Budin, Stephanie Lynn.
  Intimate lives of the ancient Greeks / Stephanie Lynn Budin.
    pages cm. — (Intimate lives of the ancient peoples)
  Includes bibliographical references and index.
  ISBN 978–0–313–38571–1 (hardcopy : alk. paper) — ISBN 978–0–313–38572–8 (ebook)
  1. Greece—Civilization—To 146 B.C. 2. Greece—Social life and customs. I. Title.
DF91.B84   2013
938—dc23   2013012035

ISBN: 978–0–313–38571–1
EISBN: 978–0–313–38572–8

17 16 15 14 13   1 2 3 4 5

This book is also available on the World Wide Web as an eBook.
Visit www.abc-clio.com for details.

Praeger
An Imprint of ABC-CLIO, LLC

ABC-CLIO, LLC
130 Cremona Drive, P.O. Box 1911
Santa Barbara, California 93116-1911

This book is printed on acid-free paper ∞

Manufactured in the United States of America

Contents

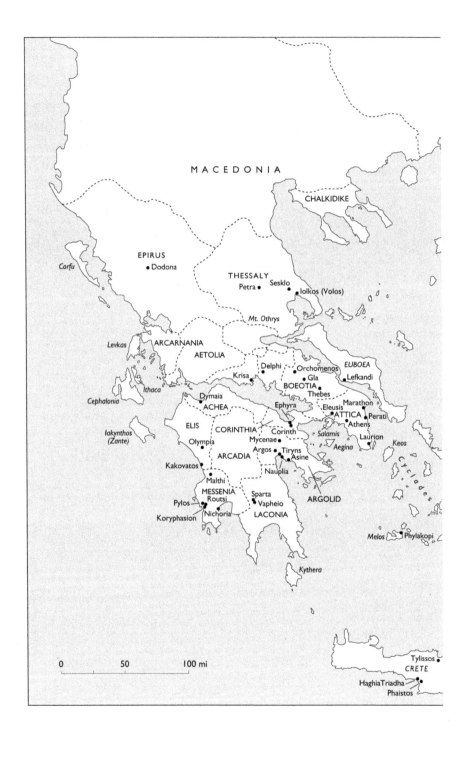

MACEDONIA

CHALKIDIKE

EPIRUS

Corfu

• Dodona

THESSALY

Petra • • Sesklo

• Iolkos (Volos)

Mt. Othrys

Levkas

ARCARNANIA

AETOLIA

EUBOEA

Delphi • • Orchomenos

• Gla • Lefkandi

Krisa •

BOEOTIA

Ithaca

Dymaia •

• Thebes

Cephalonia

ACHEA

Ephyra •

Marathon •

• Eleusis

ATTICA • Perati

• Athens

Iakynthos
(Zante)

ELIS

CORINTHIA

• Corinth

Salamis

Laurion •

Olympia •

Mycenae •

Keos

ARCADIA

Argos • • Tiryns

Asine

Aegina

Cyclades

Kakovatos •

• Nauplia

• Malthi

MESSENIA

Routsi

Sparta •

• Vapheio

ARGOLID

Pylos •

• Nichoria

LACONIA

Koryphasion

Melos

• Phylakopi

Kythera

Tylissos •

CRETE

HaghiaTriadha •

Phaistos

0   50   100 mi

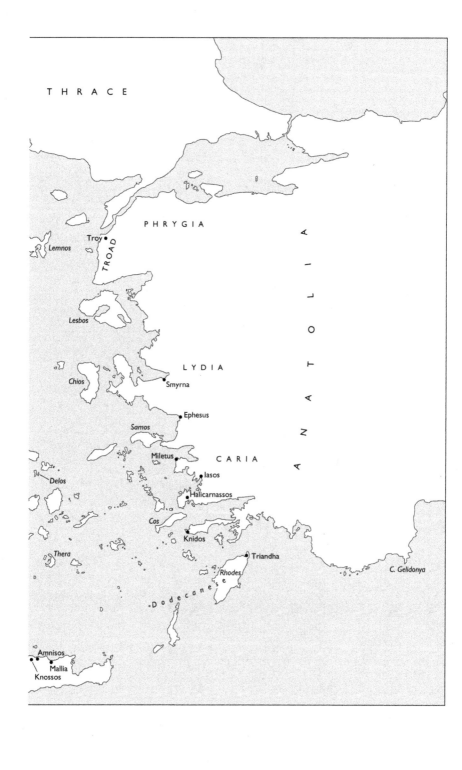

THRACE

PHRYGIA

Lemnos

Troy

TROAD

Lesbos

Chios

LYDIA

Smyrna

Samos

Ephesus

Miletus

CARIA

Iasos

Delos

Halicarnassos

Cos

Knidos

ANATOLIA

Thera

Triandha

Rhodes

Dodecanese

C. Gelidonya

Amnisos

Mallia

Knossos

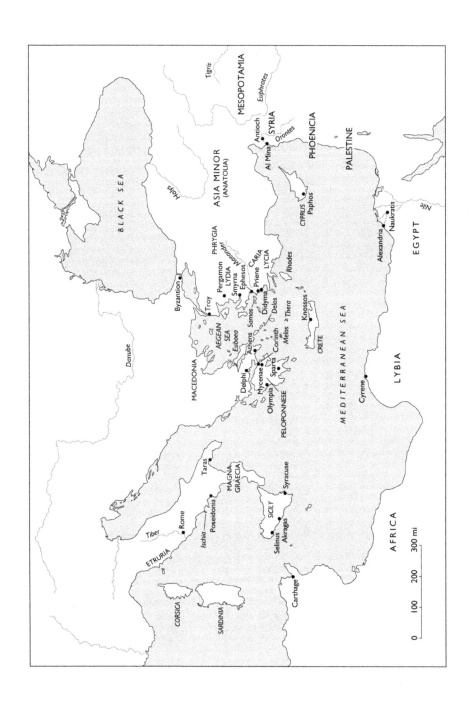

MESOPOTAMIA

Tigris

Euphrates

SYRIA

Antioch

Orontes

Al Mina

PHOENICIA

PALESTINE

BLACK SEA

ASIA MINOR
(ANATOLIA)

Halys

CYPRUS

Paphos

Nile

Alexandria

Naukratis

EGYPT

PHRYGIA

Pergamon

LYDIA

Maeander

Smyrna

CARIA

Priene

LYCIA

Ephesos

Didyma

Rhodes

Troy

Byzantion

Samos

Delos

AEGEAN
SEA

Athens

Euboea

Corinth

Thera

Knossos

Melos

CRETE

Danube

MACEDONIA

Delphi

Mycenae

Sparta

Olympia

PELOPONNESE

MEDITERRANEAN SEA

Cyrene

LYBIA

Taras

MAGNA
GRAECIA

Syracuse

Rome

Tiber

Poseidonia

SICILY

Selinus

Akragas

Ischia

ETRURIA

Carthage

AFRICA

CORSICA

SARDINIA

0   100   200   300 mi

Preface

One of our goals, as ancient historians, is to lessen the gap between our experiences today and those of the people of the ancient world. We want to get to know these people who lived centuries ago and to understand them as fellow human beings. We want to understand their thoughts, beliefs, and feelings. We want to understand their relationships: husbands and wives, parents and children, siblings, neighbors, friends, and enemies. How did they feel as members of a community and as members of a greater world? How did they relate to their environment and to their divinities?

So, for example, what did it feel like to be an ancient Greek? Stephanie Budin has written a lively overview of what we know about the intimate lives of the ancient Greeks. Given the sources that have survived from ancient Greece, she has been creative in her use of various types of literary and archaeological evidence to reconstruct how the ancient Greeks felt and thought about themselves and others. Stephanie has succeeded remarkably well and what follows represents a major contribution to our thinking about ancient intimacy, a contribution that is free of scholarly jargon but based on scholarly rigor.

Of all the people who helped bring this project to fruition, none deserves more thanks than Simon Mason. Simon was responsible for the foundational work that made this volume possible. He identified the major questions that nonspecialists have about ancient intimate lives and conceptualized a means to organize answers to those questions in an accessible manner. Without Simon's initial work, this book would not have been possible. Additional thanks are also due to the team at Praeger who have helped make this book a reality.

Kevin M. McGeough
Department of Geography (Archaeology)
University of Lethbridge

Introduction

It isn't all that easy to write a book about the intimate lives of the ancient Greeks, a book about what they thought and how they viewed the world and their place in it. The problem is the lack of sources. At first, sure, it certainly seems like there are plenty of pictures and stories relating the day-to-day lives of the ancient Spartans, Sybarites, Athenians, and Massiliots. We have transcripts from legal cases, cooking wares, poetic complaints about love sickness, medical records, business contracts, even graphic pictures of full-scale sexual orgies. (For graphic pictures of full-scale sexual orgies, go to Chapter 2.) But closer examination inevitably gives a sense of what is lacking, and where the weaknesses are. Does the lifestyle presented in the Athenian legal speeches reflect life for anyone outside of fourth-century Athens? Were those lovelorn lyricists really writing from personal experience, or were they merely following the conventions of the day, like when Elvis insisted that "You were always on my mind"? Why do the sources tell us so much about upper-class men's sex lives and so little about women's? And should we really take Euripides's word for it when one of his female characters insists that she would rather stand in battle three times than give birth once? Sometimes it seems like we get very explicit glimpses of very tiny fractions of the personal lives of the ancient Greeks, and more often than not they are glimpses of elite Athenian men, occasionally elite Spartan men. Everything else requires considerable digging and inevitable speculation to some degree.

There is also the problem that ancient Greece did not often preserve the sources that revealed the Greeks' intimate lives. For example, by way of contrast, we have many personal letters from the Roman Empire. An entire hoard of letters came to light at the Roman outpost of Vindolanda, just south of Hadrian's Wall in Great Britain. One soldier wrote home complaining about the cold and asked his family to please send socks. Just about everything that has ever been produced in ancient Egypt is still preserved. At least it feels that way sometimes. We have ancient Egyptian bed sheets, household murals, sandals, personal finance accounts—we have 3,000-year-old ancient Egyptian underwear! (When the End of Days comes, Egypt is going to have the most spectacular garage sale.)

Oftentimes, ancient Greek materials got preserved in Egypt, especially from the Hellenistic period, after the conquests of Alexander the Great in the late fourth century, when Egypt became a Greek kingdom. Thus we have preserved the marriage contract of Heraklides and Demetria of Kos, who married in 311 BCE, wherein all parties agreed that Heraklides was *not* allowed to have children with another woman, and he was certainly not allowed to bring home another wife. We have a letter sent by a travelling husband back home to his pregnant wife, telling her to keep the child if it's a boy but to expose it if it's a girl. But these documents pertain to only a specific fraction of the Greek population, now outside of Greece, late in Greece's history when its culture was very much in flux. So once again, we are left frustrated by our lack of sources.

Nevertheless, in this book I have attempted to cobble together the ancient written, inscribed, painted, and excavated sources in order to present a kind of daily-life portrait of the ancient Greeks. More often than not, I tried to let the Greeks "speak for themselves" by presenting the primary sources directly (texts, images, and so on from Greece itself). There are, of course, some difficulties with this method, the first and foremost of which is that they are all in ancient Greek, so a lot of translation was necessary. And while I may sound like I'm joking (and I am a bit), this notion of translation pertains to more than just the language: The culture also needs to be translated. Let me give you an example.

In Homer's *Odyssey*, Odysseus winds up on the island of Skheria, where the goddess Athena, disguised as a little girl, tells Odysseus the history of the royal family, King Alkinoös and Queen Aretê (*Od.* 7, 61–68):

> Poseidon mingled with Periboia and sired a son,
> Great-hearted Nausithoös, who ruled the Phaiakians,
> Nausithoös engendered Rhexenor and Alkinoös.
> Silver-bowed Apollo shot Rhexenor—sonless—
> A bride-groom in his chamber, having such an only child—
> Aretê. Alkinoös made her his wife
> And he honors her as no one on earth honors another,
> Of as many wives who now keep house for their husbands.

So what did you notice about the king and queen? They are married, of course, but you should also note that they are uncle and niece. Yes, Alkinoös married his niece Aretê.

At this point you might be cringing and muttering something about incest and wondering what the hell is the matter with these people, but this is where the cultural translation comes in. You see, in ancient Greece it was very important for property to be handed down father to son. If a family had a daughter but no sons, the ideal solution was to marry off the daughter to her closest male relative on her father's side of the family, be that an uncle or a first cousin. Aretê, as an only child, made a perfect match by ancient Greek standards, but it's not the sort of thing one might realize on a first or twelfth reading.

For the most part, this book focuses on Greece from the Archaic Age to the end of the Classical period, that is to say, from the age of Homer in the eighth century until the death of Alexander the Great at the end of the fourth (all dates BCE unless otherwise noted). But there are some exceptions. While many sources are roughly contemporary with the events they describe, other sources come from much later periods. The geographer Strabo, the travel guide writer Pausanias, the biographer and moralist Plutarch, and the academic dilatant Athenaios all lived and wrote in the Roman period, but often they give testimony to the old times in ancient Greece. And while they may have been several centuries removed from the period about which they wrote, they are still millennia closer to those events than we are. So they are useful.

Geographically, my ideal was to treat as much of the ancient Greek world as possible, from Spain in the west to the Ukraine in the east. I was, of course, delusional. I'd say that at any given time, about half of this book deals with classical Athens. It can't be helped. Athens is kind of like the Egypt of ancient Greece—the vast majority of our stuff comes from there. But to one extent or another, most of the rest of Greece is touched upon, be that trade contracts with the Etruscans in southern France or the domestic architecture of the Ukraine.

Finally, and you probably noticed this already, I aimed to write a *casual* book about ancient Greece. I tell jokes. I relate personal anecdotes. I can be terribly opinionated. Part of this was just to help me write the book. As I said at the beginning of this introduction, it isn't easy to write a book on the intimate lives of the ancient Greeks. The task was daunting. But I found that if I let myself embrace and channel and even highlight all the little absurdities that constitute daily life, it made the writing easier. When Klio, muse of history, balked at this project, Thalia, muse of comedy, paved the way.

I also felt that it was appropriate that a book on intimate lives should have an element of the personal in it. It seemed fair that if I was going to expound upon the somewhat ridiculous nature of the ancient Greek notions of ethnicity, I should at least mention how much my own Italian heritage revolved around *The Godfather*.

Ultimately, I hope that you *enjoy* reading this book, as well as learning something from it. And in the hopes that I do not offend, either by the subject matter or my treatment of it, let me offer the following advice: If you will be easily offended by pictures of people masturbating, just close this book right now. (For pictures of people masturbating, go to Chapter 2.)

Stephanie Lynn Budin
December 2012

1

Peri Tês Autês: On the Self

AGE

The life of the human body shows a continuous process of change, staring with birth, proceeding through growth, puberty, the finding of our first grey hairs and screaming, and death. In ancient Greece, as now, there was a need to subdivide and categorize this continual process. At its simplest, the ancient Greeks recognized three ages of life—youth, adulthood, and old age—divisions attested as early as Hesiod and continuously through the Classical period. Plutarch relates that in Sparta, choruses of men were so grouped, with the *gerontes* (old men) singing first, then the *akmazontes* (men at their peak, literally "acme"), and finally the *paides*, or boys (Garland 1990, 4–5). By contrast, a philosophical school called the Pythagoreans identified four ages, parallel to the four seasons. For them, there was childhood, like spring; youth, like summer; adulthood, like autumn; and old age, like winter (Garland 1990, 6). Such divisions, with or without the seasonal speculations, clearly influenced the common way of thinking: At the Nemean, Isthmian, and Panathenaic games, males competed according to the age grades of children, youths, and full-grown men, with the elderly males seated comfortably in the stands (see Chapter 4 sidebar IG II^2 2311). Likewise, there were three divisions of female competitors at the Heraia festival: girls, maidens, and young women, with the older women serving as organizers (Calame 2001, 28). At its most elaborate, life had seven stages, each composed of seven years. The Athenian statesman and poet Solon claimed (fr. 27):

> A young child still growing first loses baby teeth at seven years.
> When indeed god might complete seven additional years the signs of full youth become manifest.
> In the third, limbs still growing, the chin becomes downy, changing the bloom of his skin.
> In the fourth seven, all are best in strength, and men have signs of excellence.

The fifth is the season for a man to think of marriage and producing children to
   follow after him.
In the sixth the mind of man is educated in all things, he wishes as well not to
   work at impractical tasks.
At seven sevens he is best in mind and speech; as well as at eight—fourteen
   years for both.
In the ninth he is still capable, but his speech and wisdom are softer in matters
   of great virtue.
In the tenth, if one should arrive at this completed measure, he'll have his
   portion of death not out of season.

Infants and Toddlers

The Greek neonate was not considered to be a social human, and as a
result there were no ethical or legal prohibitions on killing one's own new-
born. Thus at birth, there was a decision as to whether to keep the child. In
most parts of Greece, the father made this decision, although in Sparta it
was a council of elders who chose whether the infant was a "keeper." Our
information from Plutarch's *Life of Lykourgos* tells us that the *gerousia*
(Council of Old Men) examined boys to see if they would make fit soldiers;
if not, they were abandoned. There is no comparable evidence for girls, and
thus we do not know if they went through the same process of "eugenics"
(Pomeroy 2002, 34ff.). However, girls were more likely to be abandoned in
other parts of the Greek world, up to 20 percent in Classical Athens (Golden
1981 passim). Even in Hellenistic Egypt, where infanticide appears to have
been less common than elsewhere, a letter from Hilarion to his wife Alis dated
to the first century BCE states: "If—good luck to you—you bear offspring, if it
is male, let it live; if it is a female, expose it" (Lefkowitz and Fant 1992, 187).

Except for Astyanax, son of Hektor, who was thrown from the walls of
Troy (an extreme scenario, to put it mildly), exposure was the main form of
infanticide, as no one had to take responsibility for actively killing the child.
A baby could be left in a public place with hopes of being adopted. Or the
gods could take pity on it and rescue it themselves, as did Apollo for his
own exposed son Ion in Euripides's play of that name. By the Hellenistic
period, some *poleis* tried to curb infant exposure. In Thebes, it became illegal.
Should a father claim dire poverty, he could give up a child to the local magistrates, who then sold/adopted off the child. In Ephesos, infant exposure was
permissible only in cases of severe famine, when there was little hope of the
child surviving anyway (Garland 1990, 93).

If the father/family chose to keep the baby, it was brought into the family
through religious rituals. As ever, our best information comes from Athens.
Here, the father carried the child around the household hearth, thus putting
the child under the protection of Hestia, the goddess of hearth and stability.

This not only "humanized" the infant, but also inducted him/her formally into the household. A similar ritual was conducted when admitting new slaves or brides. The technical name for this ritual is the *amphidromia*, literally "running around," and one has to wonder how well Mom might have taken to the idea of Dad running around a fire with their new kid in his arms.

The literary evidence suggests that newborns were wrapped in swaddling clothes. The Archaic *Homeric Hymn to Apollo* notes that right after bathing the baby, the attending goddesses "swaddled you in a soft, new cloth and wrapped gold bands around you" (ll. 120–122). The Spartans, by contrast (because the Spartans did everything by contrast) reared their children without swaddling bands, believing that the limbs developed better when they could move freely. Nevertheless, a terracotta from Taras, a Spartan colony in southern Italy, shows a swaddled child lying in a cradle, which gives some archaeological evidence for this practice (Garland 1990, 103).

Around the tenth day after birth (the *dekatê*), the child was named. This involved a party to which relatives were invited and brought gifts for the baby, something like a postnatal baby shower. According to the comic playwright Ephippos, the celebration could be quite considerable, with a feast where one would: "toast hunks of Chersonese cheese, boil cabbages gleaming in olive oil, bake fat breasts of lamb, pluck the feathers of doves and thrushes and finches all at the same time, nibble squid with cuttlefish, tenderize the tentacles of many octopodes, and drink many goblets of minimally diluted wine" (Garland 1990, 94). Meat-eating was comparatively rare in ancient Greece and usually associated with religious rituals, so to consume so many animals at once was quite the social event.

Provided the child did not die (and infant mortality could be very high, up to 20 to 25%), the lives of infants appear to have been peaceful and enjoyable. Most babies were breastfed for the first two years of life, either by their own mother or by a wet-nurse. Using a wet-nurse could be highly desirable for a number of reasons, including allowing the mother to deal with domestic chores with minimal interruption. Based on the discovery of baby bottles with nipples in some Greek communities (see Figure 3.5 in Chapter 3), it would seem that in some instances, infants could be bottle-fed. A recipe from the much later medical author Soranus (second century CE) contains water, flour, honey, milk, and wine, suggesting that the Greeks understood the concept of baby formula, which was probably what went into the bottles. A fragmentary treatise in the Hippokratic corpus entitled *Peri Odontophyies* ("On Growing Teeth" = teething) indicates that the teething process was just as painful and annoying in ancient times as it is now.

The milk that went in, by whatever means, had to come out again, and potty training was another constant in the lives of infants. Potties were ceramic and were something like a combination of potty and highchair (see Figures 1.1 and 1.2).

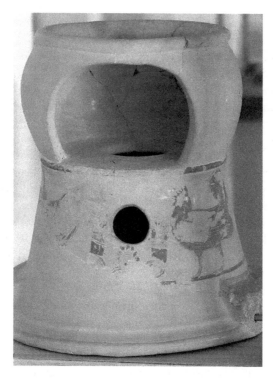

Figure 1.1
Child's high-chair/potty, ceramic, from Athens.
(Agora Museum, Athens, Greece/The Bridgeman
Art Library)

The overall messiness of babies and their various orifices was a subject appropriate even to the finest works of literature. In Homer's *Iliad*, Akhilleus' foster father Phoinix lays claim to the affections of the greatest of the Akhaians by reminding him (Bk. 9. 485–491):

And I made you this way, god-like Akhilleus,
Loving you from my heart. When you did not wish
To go to dinner with any other, or to eat in the halls,
Until indeed I sat you upon my knees
And gave you your fill of meat, having cut it up for you, and pouring wine.
Often you wet the robes on my chest
Spitting up wine in irksome childishness.

Likewise, the playwright Aeschylus has Orestes's nurse recount the trials of her duties to the future king of Mycenae (*Libation Bearers* ll. 749–762):

Dear Orestes, the care of my heart,
Whom I cared for, receiving him from his mother.

Figure 1.2
Attic red-figure chous with potty, ca. 440–430 BCE. British Museum GR1910.6-15.4. (Drawing by Paul C. Butler)

Woken at night by his shrill cries,
And so many pointless troubles I suffered,
For it was necessary to care for him as for a dumb beasty—
How couldn't you? A mind like that—
For a child cannot yet verbalize, being in his nappies,
If he's hungry, or thirsty, or needs to tinkle.
The young belly of children is autonomous!
Of these things I was prophetess, but I often got it wrong, I think,
And was laundress to the child's nappies,
Laundress and feeder with the same goal,
I was mistress of both tasks,
Having Orestes, receiving him from his father.

And, okay, sometimes spewing infants were just plain funny, especially in the hands of an awkward daddy, as in Aristophanes' *Clouds* (ll. 1380–1385):

Who the heck raised you, shameless one,
Taking note of all your lispings, whatever you were thinking.
If you said "drink," I knew and gave you something to drink;
And having asked for "mamma" I came bringing you bread;
And hardly had you said "kakka" but I seized you and doorwards
Carried you and held you WAY forward!

Toys were prevalent in the lives of children, and one can imagine that
even the poorest children had carved animals and rag dollies. Vase paintings
(as in Figure 1.2) show that popular toys for infants were rattles, push-carts
with handles, model animals, dolls (often with movable limbs, see Figure
1.3), and spinning tops. Toys for slightly older children included hoops, balls,
rocking horses, and knucklebones—an early form of dice. Children also had
pets, typically birds of different types, puppies, farm animals, possibly rabbits,

Figure 1.3
Terracotta jointed doll, Corinthian, h. 12 cm, fifth
century BCE. Rogers Fund, 1944 (44.11.8).
(Image copyright The Metropolitan Museum of
Art/Image source: Art Resource, NY)

and even monkeys. The poet Anytê captured an especially endearing moment of child-animal play:

> The children put purple reins on you, Mr. Billy-Goat
> and a bridle on your bearded throat,
> and teach you horse-racing round the god's temple
> so he may watch them having fun as children do. (trans. Plant 2004, 58)

Small children shown on grave reliefs usually hold such animals, little girls with small birds and boys often with dogs. While this may have emphasized the tender age of the child, showing him/her with a cherished pet, it also symbolically represented the child as only halfway between being a wild thing and a civilized citizen adult. In a way, children were animals.

How the child was presented to the rest of the community depended on the polis and the child's sex. As one may imagine, there was more effort to publicize a new son than a daughter. In Athens and the Ionic regions, new sons were presented to their phratriai (extended clans) on the third day of the Apatouria festival, called the Koureôtis. The Apatouria was an annual religious festival that, among other things, solidified the phratry's group identity. The Koureôtis was the first occasion when fathers could introduce their sons to the phratry, where they had to swear that the child was their own, born in legitimate wedlock. There was no comparable ritual for girls (Garland 1990, 121). A second opportunity to present one's children (definitely sons, possibly daughters) to the Athenian community took place at the Choes festival during the Anthesteria (the festival of new wine). All boys (and girls?) aged around three to four received a mini wine juglet and got their first taste of wine among the citizenry. Archaeologists have uncovered many such miniature vessels, usually with pictures of small children on them. Toddlers in Attika who died before their Choes ritual were often buried with such items.

Childhood

The true socialization of children began around age six or seven, when education was expected to begin. Henceforth it was typical for both sexes to associate primarily with members of their own sex and age group. Our clearest evidence for this comes from Sparta, where boys entered the *agogê*—long-term military boarding school—at this age. The boys were assigned to *agela*, literally "herds," where they were raised with other boys of their own age (*bouai*) led by a *bouagos*. The focus of their education was on being good soldiers: literacy was minimal, but endurance was highly valued. Around age 11, things got pretty bad for Spartan boys. According to Plutarch (*Life of Lykourgos*, 16.6):

> And when they were twelve years old they went without a khiton, receiving one cloak once a year, being unwashed in body and having no baths or lotions,

except for some few days of the year when they enjoyed some such amenities. They used to sleep together by troop and band upon rushes, which they used to gather for themselves from the reed beds growing along the Eurotas [River], breaking off the tips with their hands—no iron! In winter they tossed down so-called Lukophon and mixed that with the rushes, that plant being thought to give some warmth.

Likewise, around this age their food rations were severely curtailed, forcing them to steal food whenever possible.

According to the fourth-century historian Ephoros, a similar system was in place on Doric Crete as well. Here, boys were taken to the men's cafeterias where they sat on the ground and ate together, wearing the same shabby clothes winter and summer, waiting on the men. Later, they were required to "learn letters and the songs dictated by law, and some types of music" (Strabo 10.4.19; see also Chapter 4).

Things were better for Spartan girls, due once again to lawgiver Lykourgos's interest in eugenics. As the fourth-century Athenian historian Xenophon wrote in his *Constitution of the Lakedaimonians* (1.3–4):

> The other [states], for their part, raise the girls who are to give birth and be educated "in fine fashion" on the most moderate amount of grain and the fewest delicacies possible; they refrain from wine either altogether or they have it diluted with water. The other Greeks think it best that their girls do their wool-working in silence, just like the many craftsmen who are sedentary. Those girls raised thus —how is it to be expected that they should give birth to anything exceptional? But for his part, Lykourgos believed that slave-women were sufficient to provide clothing, and thinking that the best occupation for free women was childbearing, he first arranged for the women to care for their bodies no less than the men. And then, just as for the men so too for the females, he established competitions of speed and strength against each other, believing that the most robust offspring resulted when both parents were strong.

Because girls had to grow up to be good mothers, rather than good soldiers, they could spend more time at home with their female family. Their group/ public education seems mainly to have consisted of participation in choruses, where the girls learned to dance (the equivalent of gym class) and to sing songs that educated them in the ways of history, philosophy, and ethics. Boys also took part in choruses, but this was only a small subsection of their overall education. Plutarch dedicated an entire book to the sayings of Spartan women, thus highlighting their own, admittedly unique but meaningful, forms of philosophy.

As the preceding quotation makes clear, girls in the rest of Greece were far, far less well educated (and fed) than their Spartan sisters. According to some of our evidence, Athenian girls especially were kept as ignorant as possible, apparently on the grounds that this would make them both docile and tamable. Thus Xenophon writes in his dialogue *Oikonomikos* ("Household Management") of his contemporary Iskhomakhos (7.5–6):

> "And what, Sokrates," he said, "would she have known when I received her— she was not yet 15 years old when she came to me, and the time before that she sat under great care that she might see and hear and say as little as possible. For does it not seem to you to be sufficient if, when she came to me, she only knew how to produce a cloak having received wool and having seen how the wool-working supplies were given to the servants? Then, about the appetite," he said, "all is well, Sokrates; she came to me having been well educated. Such training seems to me to be the best for both men and women."

As discussed in Chapter 2, Iskhomakhos's wife winds up leaving him for their own son-in-law, which is as good an indication as any than the keeping-the-women-folk-dumb-and-in-the-dark technique still had a number of bugs in the system. Nevertheless, as Iskhomakhos/Xenophon relates, even "ignorant" girls received education in the form of household maintenance, learning such feminine tasks as spinning and weaving, cooking and managing slaves, and even rudimentary medicine (*Oik*, 7.35–37):

> It will be necessary for you . . . to remain indoors and to send out those whose work is outside the house, and for those whose work must be done inside, you must supervise them; and you must receive what comes into the house, and you must apportion what is spent, and you must provide and take care for necessities, so that that which has to last a year does not get spent in a month. And you must attend to as much wool as is brought to you, so that there is clothing for all who need it. And indeed you must busy yourself with the flour so that it stays edible. In truth, one of your duties . . . perhaps will seem rather annoying: you must nurse anyone of the household servants who may be sick.

Quite simply, girls learned to be housewives, often working alongside their mothers and helping with tasks about the house such as cooking and the fiber arts. The fourth-century poet Erinna recalled in her poem *The Distaff*:

> Young girls, we held our dolls in our bedrooms
> Like new wives, hearts unbroken. Near dawn your mother,
> Who handed out wool to her workers in attendance,
> Came in and called you to help with the salted meat. (trans. Plant 2004, 50)

Such an image is physically preserved in a Boiotian terracotta showing an older woman (mother?) cooking alongside a little girl, now in the Museum of Fine Arts in Boston (see Figure 1.4). The weaving skill of younger girls is graphically preserved in a famous vase painting now in the Metropolitan Museum in New York, showing females of varying ages working beside a pair of looms (see Figure 1.5).

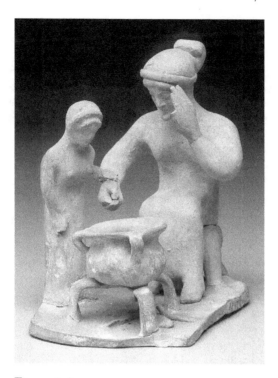

Figure 1.4
Boiotian Terracotta: Woman cooking, watched
by a girl, 500–475 BCE. Museum of Fine Arts,
Boston 01.7788. (Photograph copyright 2013
Museum of Fine Arts, Boston. All rights
reserved/The Bridgeman Art Library)

Many Greek females did receive more formal education. Female poets such
as Sappho and Korinna testify to the literacy and talent exhibited by at least
upper-class Greeks. About seven vases from Classical Athens depicting scenes
of daily life (including a mother whacking her son with a sandal) show women
either reading or, more specifically, holding written texts in front of them
while listening to recitation. It seems likely that some women learned to read
at least for the purpose of helping to educate their own children. One such
vase painting shows a woman looking at a book roll while a young boy faces
her—an early quizzing scenario from ancient Athens. A similar sentiment is
expressed by the Macedonian princess Euridikê, who wrote:

> Eurydikê daughter of Sirras presented this
> to the Muses when she filled the longing for knowledge in her soul.
> For the delighted mother of thriving sons labored
> to learn letters, the record of speech. (trans. Plant 2004, 44)

Figure 1.5
Attic black-figure lekythos with women spinning and weaving, ca. 550–530 BCE.
Metropolitan Museum of Art, 31.11.10. (Drawing by Paul C. Butler)

Education was very much a private affair outside of Sparta, and individual parents were responsible for the education of their offspring. Professional-grade education was restricted, as one might imagine, to the upper classes, the folks who could afford the time and resources necessary to hire the appropriate teachers. Sons were placed in the charge of a *paidagogos*, literally "child-leader" who served as both chaperone and teacher. Many paidagogoi were certainly slaves, and thus, technically, cost-free after the initial purchase. Others could be rather pricey; both Demosthenes (*Against Aphobus* 1.36) and Lysias (32.28) mention that a paidagogos could cost about 2 *drakhmai* (12 obols) a day. A skilled worker probably earned only about 1 to 1.5 drakhmai a day, meaning that good teachers were costlier than artisans, and only the wealthy could have their children so educated. Boys who received such formal education usually had three main courses of study. First there were their letters—*grammata*. Basically, they learned to read and write. Second, they learned music, both to dance and to play musical instruments. Finally, there was athletic training. These were the necessities of life for an eventual man who might one day defend his homeland from invaders or possibly reign victorious at the Olympic games, but who had little concern with running a farm or pottery factory. There were slaves for those sorts of things, after all.

Evidence suggests that there may have been a touch of hostility between boys and their teachers. In a quite famous example, Herakles once beat his lyre teacher to death with his own musical instrument. This was almost certainly an extreme example (like everything involving Herakles), but it probably did represent some wish fulfillment on the part of Greek boys. Once when describing the harsh, unbearable character of a military leader,

Xenophon noted that "many would desert him; for there was no attractiveness about him, but he was always severe and rough, so that the soldiers had the same feeling toward him that boys have toward a schoolmaster" (*Anabasis* 2.6.12). On the flip side, of course, students, especially of the upper classes, could be utterly unruly, such that even Aristotle commented on how the "fortunate" (read: wealthy) "are not willing to be governed and do not know how to be, and they have acquired this quality even in their boyhood from their home life, which was so luxurious that they have not gotten used to submitting to authority, even in school" (*Politics* 4.1295b15).

The nature of education began to change in the Hellenistic period, when the Greek world expanded rapidly east and south, democracies were replaced by monarchies, and leaving home to seek one's fortune became far more common. The epigraphic evidence suggests that public education was given to free young boys and girls. In third-century Teos (see below, in the section on *Boys*), boys and girls were taught together for three years, learning reading and writing. By "fourth grade," though, only boys continued at school, learning music in addition to their letters. In Pergamon on the coast of Turkey, both received considerable literary education, and inscriptions record prizes for girls specifically for recitation of epic, elegiac, and lyric poetry, as well as general reading and penmanship (*kalligraphia*) (Cole 1981, 231).

Adolescence

In ancient Greece, as now, adolescence was that awkward time between childhood and adulthood, when one was expected to take up certain adult-like responsibilities without quite getting all adult privileges. In their wisdom, the ancient Greeks never tried insisting that these were the best years of anyone's life. For the most part, this time of life was marked by physical maturation, that period when girls and boys physically develop into women and men, the former preparing to become child-bearers, the latter to be responsible soldier-citizens. This was the time when the secondary sexual characteristics manifested, along with the eternally famous teenage libido. Then as now, adolescents found ways of personally dealing with said libido, perhaps a touch to the dismay of their elders to judge from a passage in Aristotle (HA 7.581b12–21):

> Girls of this age have much need of surveillance. For then in particular they feel a natural impulse to make usage of the sexual facilities that are developing in them; so that unless they guard against any further impulse beyond that inevitable one which their bodily development of itself supplies, even in the case of those who abstain altogether from passionate indulgence, they contract habits which are apt to continue into later life. For girls who give way to wantonness grow more and more wanton; and the same is true of boys, unless they be safeguarded from one temptation and another; for the passages become

dilated and set up a local flux or running, and besides this the recollection of pleasure associated with former indulgence creates a longing for its repetition. (trans. Wentworth Thompson 1952, 107)

Girls

For girls, adolescence was all about sexuality and the state of their "passages." Unlike boys, the transition from child to adult could be terribly short for females, consisting of the brief time between menarche and motherhood. Menarche, probably occurring around ages 12 to 14, marked a girl as ready for marriage and reproduction. Medical writers even claimed that it was imperative to marry off a girl as soon as her menses began, as the vagina had to be opened for the blood to escape. If the girl were left "constricted" for too long, she could suffer a number of nasty physical consequences, ranging from what in modern times we would call severe depression to suicidal insanity. The Hippokratic medical corpus had an essay on the "Illnesses Affecting Maidens," wherein the author claimed that virgins who have not been "opened" cannot readily expel menstrual blood from their bodies. The blood then settles around the heart (the ancient Greek center of thought), causing madness. The girls become delirious, afraid of the dark, have hallucinations, and eventually try to commit suicide either by throwing themselves down wells or by hanging. As a cure, the doctor recommends marriage and penile intercourse (Hanson 1990, 324). And so in many poleis, girls were married in their early teens. Sparta was, of course, the outlier, where girls were not wed until age 18.

As marriage was the most momentous moment in a maiden's life, considerable attention was placed on getting a good catch. In the lower classes, girls generally had to make do with the guy next door. Amongst royalty, dynastic marriages were arranged. In the upper classes, however, parents could go through considerable efforts to get a good match for their daughters and thus make profitable family allies. Although many aspects of matchmaking rested solely on the shoulders of the parents, society provided some opportunities for girls to flaunt their stuff and catch the attention of possible partners.

In Sparta, for example, Plutarch records that Lykourgos made a point of allowing girls to be visibly naked frequently, in part to attract the eyes of the city's youth (*Lyc.* 14:2):

He worked out the bodies of maidens with races and wrestling and discus throwing and javelin hurling, so that foetuses would be strong in strong bodies and would develop better having had good beginnings, and so that the maidens themselves might endure childbirth well and easily deal with parturition. And freeing them from all softness and effeminacy and a sedentary nature he accustomed the girls no less than the boys to march in parade and dance in religious rites and to sing in the nude, being seen by the young men present.

The technique seems to have worked, although the other Greeks were not too sure how they felt about this, as Euripides complained in his play *Andromakhê* (ll. 595–600):

> . . . not even if she wanted to could some
> Girl of the temperate Spartans be so;
> They leave their houses along with the boys—
> Thighs naked and peploi undone.
> They have races and wrestling bouts together
> And things just insufferable to me!

In Athens, where girls were probably the most sheltered of all Greeks, aristocratic girls took part in highly publicized religious rites that placed them before the eyes of the entire city. For example, every year, the city came together to honor their patron goddess Athena in a festival called the Panatheneia. The ritual featured a parade consisting of priests, priestesses, cult functionaries, and citizens taking part in various aspects of the day's activities. One such cult functionary was the *kanephoros*, the young teenaged girl who carried the basket containing tools for the sacrifice. The kanephoros came from one of the most aristocratic families of Athens and had to be a girl of pristine virtue. Although Greek girls seldom wore much jewelry, vase paintings of kanephoroi, in Athens and throughout the Greek world, show them done up to the nines, dressed in elaborate (expensive) dresses and decked out with the finest of the family jewels (see Figure 1.6). Such *kosmesis* (dressing up) is consistently associated with seduction in Greek literature (Aphrodite's seduction of Ankhises, Hera's seduction of Zeus, Pandora's seduction of men in general) and gives evidence that our young aristocratic girl was making the most of the occasion to catch as many eligible male eyes as possible.

Although such grand spectacles were reserved for the aristocracy, there were many, many other religious processions in Athens and other cities in which families of all classes took part. The role of kanephoros always fell to a maiden, as did other ritual roles, and thus all girls had opportunities to let themselves be seen by their fellow citizens. This, of course, is in addition to the inevitably visible tasks of daily living such as getting water from the city fountain and doing laundry, tasks that, according to Homer himself, were even appropriate for princesses, such as Nausikaä here with her handmaids (*Od.* 6.85–98):

> But when they came to the fair flow of the river—
> Where the laundry pools were abundant, and very much
> Fair water flowed forth to clean soiled things—
> There they unhitched the wagon from the mules
> And they shooed them along the whirling river
> To munch the honey-sweet grass. But from the wagon they

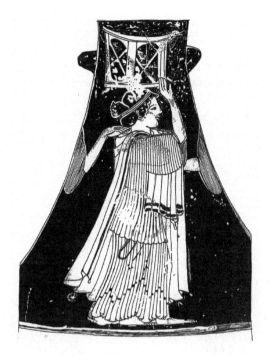

Figure 1.6
Attic red-figure oinochoe from Chiusi, Italy,
showing a kanephoros. Triptolemos Painter, ca.
500–450 BCE. Antikensammlung, Staatliche
Museen Berlin, 2189. (Drawing by Paul C.
Butler)

Took the clothes with their hands and brought them to the dark water,
Quickly they tread upon it in the pools, making a game of it.
And when all the laundry was washed and clean and
They had laid it in a row along the bank, where
The sea most washed away the pebbles on the land,
Then they bathed and rubbed themselves with olive oil
And ate lunch lounging by the bank of the river,
Waiting for the sun's gleam to dry the clothes.

Although the Greek ideal may have been to keep virgins out of public
sight, this was seldom practical, and most girls had opportunities to socialize
with the greater community. This especially comes across in Plutarch's
accounts of the girls of the island of Keos, where (*The Virtues of Women* XII):

It was a custom for the maidens of the Keians to proceed together to the public
shrines and to spend the day with each other. And their suitors watched them
playing and dancing. In the evening each one in turn went and served each

others' parents and siblings, even to the point of washing their feet. Frequently they have more than one lover, [but] so orderly was their love and customs that when a girl became engaged to one, the others stopped forthwith. And the end result of this good order of the women was that neither adultery nor seduction of unwed women was recalled as happening among them for 700 years.

Such prenuptial rituals served two purposes. One the one hand, of course, they allowed nubile girls to attract male attention. On the other hand, in their own ways they prepared girls for married life. In addition to their attention-getting qualities, Spartan athletics existed to aid Spartan females in their eventual roles as mothers. In Keos, the local rituals accustomed girls to the types of services they would be called upon to provide when they had households and children of their own.

Some events took girls out of their neighborhoods altogether and into the greater Greek world. Opposite the Olympic games held by men in honor of Zeus were the Heraia, the games held by girls and women in honor of Hera. Girls who won received a portion of the sacrifice to Hera and the right to leave portraits of themselves at the goddess's temple (notches in the columns show where these once hung). Spartan girls took part in such races, and bronze figurines depict them in mid-stride with one breast bared (see Figure 1.7). As an extreme example, every year two girls from Italian Lokris had to travel to Troy to serve as virtual slaves in the temple of Athena, atoning for the sin of Lokrian Ajax, who raped a girl in that temple. Such potential for travel was, inevitably, reserved for the wealthy, and girls never did get to travel as much as their male compatriots under any circumstances.

Menstruation and concomitant marriage were the first steps on the road to adulthood for females, but the final necessary step was parturition. Women were not really women until they were mothers. The stages of adolescence for a female, then, consisted of her days as a *parthenos*, a nubile virgin technically capable of but not socially recognized as being a mother. For a brief period, she was a *nymphê*, or bride (we get the word "nymphomaniac" from it), and finally a *gynê*, or woman, once she had her first child. It is interesting to note that the ancient Greeks used the same word for both "woman" and "wife" (gynê), showing that it was pretty much unthinkable for a female to be one without also being the other. (For more detail on the female experience of marriage, see Chapter 2.)

Of course, for much of Greek history, the idea of "adult female" was somewhat relative anyway. Women were perpetually seen as legal minors who had to be under the authority of a male guardian at all times, usually her father and then her husband. Adolescence for females, then, was that period when girls came to terms with the fact that they were soon to be handed over to a strange man twice their age who would have legal control over them and for whom they would bear children and tend the house. It seems possible that the *Illness of Maidens* may have had less to do with menstrual flow and perhaps a lot more

Figure 1.7
Late Archaic bronze figurine of a running girl,
probably Spartan. British Museum GR 1876.5
.10.1. (The Trustees of the British Museum/Art
Resource, NY)

to do with premarital despair. Anyway, once a girl was married and produced
an heir, she was officially "grown up." No further changes in her status
occurred until she hit menopause.

Boys

Up until around age 16 to 17, well-off boys would continue their baseline
education, still focusing on letters, music, and athletics. The third-century
inscription from Teos mentioned earlier in this chapter spells out quite clearly
the progression of education from child to young adult and what boys
especially experienced (SIG^3 578):

> At the annual election of the magistrates and after the election of the
> secretaries there are to be appointed three grammar teachers who are to teach
> the *paides* and the girls . . . There are to be appointed two athletic trainers
> (*paidotribai*) . . . There is to be appointed a kithera- or a psaltry-teacher [types of
> lyre], who is to teach those *paides* who might have been passed on to the next

year, and of these whom he is to teach each year, the younger ones are to be taught music in general and either to be a kithera or psaltry player, but the ephebes are to be taught only music in general. The headmaster (*paidonomos*) is to decide about the ages of these *paides* . . .

After notification to the demos the *paidonomos* and the *gymnasiarkhos* (gym-teacher) are to hire an infantry drill master and a teacher of archery and the javelin. These are to teach the ephebes and those *paides* who have been enrolled in the music lessons . . .

The *paidonomos* and the *gymnasiarkhos* are to see to it that the *paides* and the ephebes are carefully exercised in their lessons just as is prescribed for each of them in the laws. If the grammar teachers argue about the size of their classes, the paidonomos is to settle the dispute and they are to abide by his decision. The grammar teachers are to produce the customary exhibitions in the gymnasium and the music teachers in the bouleuterion and the *paidotribai* in the stadium. (Miller 1991, 132–133)

Certain aspects of education apparently never change. Teachers quibbled about class size, and parents were still obligated to watch and listen to their children in amateur music recitals. At least we have no recorded complaints about having to "teach to the test" or fretting over Intelligent Design. (If you have no idea what I'm talking about, be grateful).

The comic playwright Aristophanes, writing in late fifth- early fourth-century Athens, gave a more personal description of what education consisted of "back in the good old days" in his play *The Clouds* (ll. 961ff.):

I shall speak now about how education was in the old days
That flourished when I spoke, and temperance was customary.
First then it was required that the voice of a grumbling child was never heard;
Likewise for the neighboring children to march together in orderly fashion, naked
To the kithara-teacher's place, even if it were snowing oatmeal!
Furthermore, it taught them to memorize songs—legs uncrossed!—
Either "Pallas, Dread Destroyer of Cities" or "Some Far Distant Shriek,"
Pitching high the harmony which our fathers passed down.
And if someone of them joked around or went around the bend
Like these fancy-dancy artists now in the manner of Phrynis,
He was beaten down with many lashes for having tarnished the Muses.
And sitting in the wresting teacher's place it was
Incumbent for the kiddies to cover their thighs
So that they might not reveal anything untoward to those outside.
In addition, on standing they were to sweep up, and thus not to provide
An image "of youth" for their lovers.
And no boy then would anoint himself with oil below the navel, so that they were
Fresh and dewy in their naughty bits and their cheeks bloomed like apples.
Nor would they speak in a high voice striding before a lover,

Declaring himself with his eyes.
Nor was it permitted when dining to take up the head of a radish,
Nor to snatch either dill or celery from one's elders,
Nor to be a picky eater, nor to giggle, nor to cross one's feet.

Although Aristophanes thought rather highly of this form of education, he realized that there was a *lot* more to the lives of youths than becoming virtuous, and in the same comedy he noted that a proper education tended to be balanced by the pleasures of youth (ll. 1072–1082):

For consider, Lad, everything involved in temperance,
Of how many sweet things you are about to lose—
Boys, women, kottabos ["beer pong"], food, drink, giggling—
And what is life worth to you, if you are deprived of these?
Well then, I proceed to the necessities of nature.
So you've screwed up, been in love, had an affair and then got caught—
You are destroyed, for you are unable to articulate.
But by consorting with me—
Going with nature—leap up, laugh, think it nothing shameful
For if you, the adulterer, should happen to be caught, reply to him thus,
How you have done nothing wrong, and then throw it back on Zeus
How even he is weaker than love and women
And you, a mortal—How can you be more powerful than a god?

As noted both by Aristophanes and the Teos inscription, athletics were a very important aspect of a boy's education, and those boys either especially gifted or especially wealthy competed in games beyond the schoolyard (see Chapter 4). Already by age 10 or 11, boys might compete publically in local games in honor of local divinities. By ages 12 and 13, the more talented young athletes might travel abroad and compete in the Panhellenic games, such as those at Nemea and Olympia (as in The Olympics, both in honor of Zeus). To judge from the victory odes of the fifth-century Boiotian poet Pindar, teenaged boys seemed to like the more aggressive sports, especially the pentathlon, wrestling, and the *pankration* (a no-holds-barred fighting bout probably a bit similar to modern MMA fighting) (Burnett 2005, 45–47). Thus Pindar began the ode for Kleandros of Aigina who was victorious in the pankration at both Nemea and Isthmia (*Isth.* 8, ll. 1–7):

For Kleandros and for his youth, young friends,
Someone must go to the grand
Outer gate of his sire, Telesarchos, there to
Rouse up the revel that brings
Glorious ransom from toil—repayment for
Victory taken at Isthmia
And for his Nemean dominance! (trans. Burnett 2005, 180–181)

Any high school football star who has come back from the Big Game victorious can imagine the kind of welcome an athlete like Kleandros received when he got home.

During the final years of a boy's education, around ages 17 or 18, he was called an *ephebe* (*epi* = "around," *hebe* = "youth"), the term seen earlier in this chapter in the inscription from Teos for the oldest of the schoolboys. As inscribed there, these years were heavily invested in military training, when many boys got their first taste of military life. Aristotle gives us an excellent summary of what such life was like for Athenian boys, at least (although the experience of other Greek boys was probably similar) (*Ath.Pol.* 42):

> When the ephebes have passed their citizenship review, the fathers, having gathered them together by tribes and having taken an oath, choose three from their tribes of those over 40 years of age, whom they deem to be the best and best prepared to care for the ephebes. And from these the people elect one from each tribe as a supervisor; and from the other Athenians a marshall over all of them. These men gather the ephebes and first give them tours of the sanctuaries. Then they proceed to the Piraeus, and some guard Mynikhia, and some guard Aktê. And the people also elect two coaches for them, and teachers, who teach them to fight in armor, and shoot a bow, and fight with spear, and to fling the sling. And they give for rations one drakhma each to the supervisors; four obols each to the ephebes. Each supervisor receives the monies for his own unit and buys the supplies for everyone in common (for they eat together by unit), and he tends to everything else. And the first year passes thus. In the following year, when the Assembly has gathered in the theater, they (the ephebes) display to the people their manoeuvres, and receiving a shield and spear on behalf of the city they patrol the countryside and spend time in the garrisons. So they guard for two years, wearing capes, and they are free from all taxes—and they may neither sue nor be sued, so that there may be no pretext for absence, except concerning inheritance or an epikleros, or if there is an ancestral priesthood for someone. When the two years are up, they go live with everyone else.

When their period of ephebe-ship was complete, they received their arms and swore an oath in the sanctuary of Aglauros (misinscribed as Agraulos in the inscription) on the Acropolis to protect Attika (Tod 1985, 204):

> Gods. Priest of Ares and Athena Areia Dion son of Dion, Akharneus dedicated. Ancestral oath of the ephebes, which it is necessary for the ephebes to swear. I shall not disgrace the sacred weapons nor shall I abandon my comrade wherever I am stationed. I shall defend the sacred and holy things, and I shall not hand down a lesser fatherland, but one better and stronger by my power and that of everyone. And I shall heed always those governing well and the established holy laws and those established sensibly in the future. And if someone should destroy (these), I shall not turn away by my power and that of everyone, and I shall honor the sacred and ancestral things. Witness Deities:

Agraulos, Hestia, Enyo, Enyalios, Ares and Athena Areia, Zeus, Thallo, Auxo, Hegemonê, Herakles, ancestral boundary stones, wheat, barley, grape vines, olive and fig trees.

In addition to such public displays of maturity and patriotism, boys-now-turned-men also made personal dedications of thanks to the deities who allowed them to arrive unscathed to the edge of maturity. Thus the *Greek Anthology* preserves the words of one Kalliteles ("fair-ending") when offering a dedication to Hermes, the god of boundaries (GA 6.282):

> To you, Hermes, the felt hat of well-carded lamb's wool
> Kalliteles hung,
> And a double pin, and a strigil, and
> An unstrung bow, and a worn, greasy cloak,
> And arrows, and an ever tossed ball.
> But you receive, Friend of Boys,
> The gifts of well-ordered adolescence.

Upon completion of the ephebate, until they reached about age 59, citizen males were liable for military service.

Spartan males had their own, somewhat more extreme, rite of passage to undergo before they might enter into adulthood, and this was the *krypteia*. The krypteia was like a secret, state-sponsored terrorist organization, composed of boys between the ages of 17 and 19. It was their duty to live on the frontiers between Spartan society and the territory of the helots, their slaves, where they terrorized and slaughtered the serf population. This kept the helots in a state of constant panic and reduced their numbers, while training Spartans to live off the land and to function in "enemy territory." Once the krypteia was complete, Spartan males were ready for normal active service, which lasted until age 60, assuming you could even keep an older Spartan away from battle at that age (Garland 1990, 179).

For all those folks who actually worked for a living (and there were very many), education was often of a more practical bent, something like the girls helping their moms as seen earlier in this chapter. The Athenian lawgiver Solon legislated that fathers had to teach their sons trades or else forfeit all rights to care in old age. Solon made no such stipulations about education in general. Such father-to-son transmission of practical skills formed the basis of most "informal" education in ancient Greece.

It would appear that in some circumstances, boys could be sent out to learn a profession, and not always under the happiest of circumstances. In the fourth century, a resident alien of Athens sent the following letter home to his mother:

> Lesis sends a letter to Xenokles and to his mother. By no means overlook that
> he is perishing in the foundry, but come to his masters and find something

better for him. For I have been handed over to a thoroughly wicked man; I am perishing from being whipped; I am tied up; I am treated like dirt—more and more!

Unfortunately for Lesis, this lead epistle was discovered in a well in the Athenian Agora—it is unlikely his mother ever received it (Jordan 2000). Nevertheless, for less affluent boys like Lesis, childhood frivolity ended around age 13, when it was time to acquire a trade and support oneself and one's family. They did not compete in the Olympics.

Adulthood

For males, becoming a man was a gradual process. In most poleis, males were understood to have achieved legal majority by around age 18. At this point, the state stopped supporting them if they were orphans, and they could legally engage in professions independently. Nevertheless, men aged 20 to 30 were still thought of as quite young, *neoi* in Athens (literally "new ones") and *hebontes* in Sparta (literally "young ones") (Garland 1990, 200–201). Spartan males married at this point, but they were not free to live with their families until age 30. Most other Greek males married between the ages of 30 to 36, usually to girls only half their age (see Chapter 2). Since most men began having children only around age 30, by the time a man turned 30 himself, his father was probably dead, meaning that one acquired a wife and one's inheritance at roughly the same time. And so, in the eyes of the law and state, one was officially a man.

Women, as discussed previously, were seen as adult as they were going to get once they had given birth to their first child. This was only marginally relevant.

The lives that began around age 30 for males and 16 for females continued until menopause for females and around age 60 for men. During this period, both had families and worked to support them. Males took part in the political and military life of the city, and both men and women were actively engaged in religious life. For the most part, males and females lived separate lives, the women indoors caring for house and household, the males outdoors either working or, for the elite, exercising and philosophizing with other elite males. In short, adulthood was the time when every other aspect of this book was most relevant.

Then, one day, all those ancient Greeks lucky enough to survive so long woke up and discovered that they were old.

Old Age

Adulthood lasted until around age 60 for a man and until menopause for a woman (once again, women's lives were determined by their biology, while men's were determined by their functions in society). After 60, a man became a *gerôn* (old man); around 45 (the usual age of menopause), a woman became a *graia*. For women, this meant, socially, an end to their "usefulness" and the beginning of a new age of freedom. Now that no one was overly paranoid about issues of illegitimacy, older women had the freedom, even in highly restrictive Athens, to go about their affairs outdoors and with no chaperon.

Older women still had numerous functions to perform in society. Apart from being mothers and grandmothers and, by age 48, possibly even great-grandmothers (in many poleis, women would have their first child by age 16, as would her daughter, as would her daughter), women had both religious and social functions in their communities. Certain priesthoods belonged exclusively to women past childbearing years. In Sikyon, one of the priestesses of Aphrodite was the Neokoros ("New Child"), a woman for whom it was no longer permissible to cohabitate with a man. Since marriage and childrearing were common to all Greeks, this was a cult functionary who had passed her childbearing years and now served as a celibate minister to the goddess of sex (Paus. 2.10.4). Other positions were held for life, such as the priestess of Athena Polias in Athens. Lysimakhê, who fulfilled this role in the fifth–fourth centuries, was famous for holding her position for 65 years.

Women past childbearing years also served as midwives. Plato explained this by saying that Artemis, the goddess of childbirth (often syncretized with Eileithyia) did not give birth herself and so neither should her functionaries (*Theaitetos* 149c).

Additionally, older women, presumably past their erotic peak, were welcomed as household servants, both to care for children (they probably had considerable experience) and to tend to the household chores without unduly attracting the eyes of the menfolk. So much is spelled out by the goddess Demeter when she visited Eleusis disguised as an old woman (*Hymn to Demeter*, ll. 137–144):

> "Tell me clearly so that I might understand,
> truly, dear children, to whose house might I go,
> of a man or a woman, so that I might find work
> in good faith? Such work as might be done by an old woman?
> Maybe even cuddling a new-born baby in my arms
> I could nurse him well, and I could care for a house,
> and in the innermost of the lovely rooms I could fluff up the lord's bed
> and teach the women their tasks."

For men, old age meant an end to their period of active military duty, but the beginning of a new phase of political relevance. Age 60 was the base minimum in Sparta for belonging to the *Gerousia*, literally the "Council of Elders." These men served as advisors to the king and had the function of choosing which Spartan babies were allowed to live. In Hellenistic Kyrenê in Libya, a Doric community like Sparta, a charter granted by King Ptolemy I in 310 stated that all 500 members of the council, the 100 members of the *gerousia*, as well as the generals and ephors all had to be at least 49 years old (Garland 1990, 283).

Nevertheless, the new freedoms and opportunities did little to assuage the fact that it really sucked to be old, and the Greeks seldom got tired of complaining about this fact. It was commonly recognized that old age was the time of physical decay, a loss of libido, and possible dementia. A recently discovered poetic fragment from Sappho addresses the physical thusly:

[You for] the fragrant-blossomed Muses' lovely gifts
[be zealous,] girls, [and the] clear melodious lyre:
[but my once tender] body old age now
[has seized;] my hair's turned [white] instead of dark;
my heart's grown heavy, my knees will not support me,
that once on a time were fleet for the dance as fawns.
This state I oft bemoan; but what's to do?
Not to grow old, being human, there's no way.
Tithonus once, the tale was, rose-armed Dawn,
love-smitten, carried off to the world's end,
handsome and young then, yet in time grey age
overtook him, husband of an immortal wife. (trans. West 1993)

The seventh-century poet Mimnermos took on both brain muddle (fr. 5):

Suddenly unspeakable sweat flows down my skin,
I am dismayed seeing the flower of youth,
Joyful and fair, since it would be better to be longer.
But it is of short duration—like a dream—
Honored Youth. Grievous and ugly
Old Age quickly draped over my head
Like a despised enemy, who nullifies a man,
Destroys his eyes and wraps round his mind.

And not so much the loss of libido as the inability to do anything with it (fr. 1):

What life, what joy, without golden Aphrodite?
I should die when these things don't concern me:
Secret love and honey-sweet gifts and the bed;
Such are the alluring flowers of youth
For men and women. But grievous old age
Has come, which makes a man shameful and weak,
Ever evil anxieties plague his mind,
Nor does his face rejoice at the sun's gleam,
But he is hateful to boys, contemptible to women . . .
Such a troublesome thing god has made—Old Age.

Arkhilokhos, the seventh-century lyric poet and curmudgeon, took his usual bitter approach:

A life of doing nothing is good for old men,
Especially if they are simple in their ways,
Or stupid, or inane in their endless blabber
As old men tend to be. (trans. Barnstone 1988, 33)

The Greek medical writers were far less poetic in their treatments of decrepitude, which is probably why they were invited to fewer parties. The Hippocratic author of the *Aphorisms* claimed that the elderly were subject to (3.31):

Difficulty in breathing; catarrh accompanied by coughing; diseases of the urinary tract; difficult micturition; arthritis; nephritis; dizzy spells; apoplexy; cachexia; itchiness; insomnia; watery discharge from the bowels, eyes, and nose; dullness of vision; glaucopia; and hardness of hearing. (trans. Garland 1990, 249)

Obviously he forgot memory loss.

Perhaps in direct opposition to or denial of such sentiments, old Greek men, in time-honored tradition, had mid-life crises. Plutarch, in his philosophical work "Should Old Men Take Part in Public Life?" talks of men who, "having lived blamelessly for many years under the same roof as his wife, kicks her out when he gets old and either lives alone or takes a mistress instead of his wedded wife" (Garland 1990, 207). They probably also bought little red sports chariots for themselves.

Considering their lack of good judgment at this age, the idea of dementia worked its way into at least the Athenian law courts. Thus the orator Isaios, in his "On the Estate of Nikostratos," argued "For the law allows no one to dispose of his own property if his reason is impaired by old age or disease or the other causes with which you are familiar" (4.16).

This state of being out of one's mind was called *paranoia*, and it marked the stage at which an old person entered a second childhood, once again needing physical care and being seen as a minor in the eyes of the law. At such times, old parents came under the protection of the *graphê goneôn kakôsis*, or "action concerning the mistreatment of elders." This law forced sons specifically to care for their old parents, not to beat them, but to provide them with the necessities of life. A man who did not adhere to this action was legally deemed unqualified for government and military positions in Athens. Thus, there were laws in place to see to the care of the citizen elderly at least.

Old age was that period when, regardless of "greater life experience" and "accumulated wisdom," the body was dying and friends had already died, and it was simply time to face up to life's final curtain. Perhaps the most sorrowful expression of this state came from the public funeral oration by Lysias, wherein he asked (2.73):

> For what could be more painful than this, to bear and bury one's own child, then in old age to be disabled in body, having lost all hope, having become unloved and impotent, those same people who once envied them now pity them; death is more desirable to them than life.

Aristotle noted that just because the elderly had less life to look forward to did not mean that they were willing to give up a second of it. In his *Rhetoric*, he writes that the old "are fond of life, especially in their last days, because desire is directed towards that which is absent and men especially desire what they lack" (2.1389b36). The fifth-century Athenian playwright Sophokles lived well into his 90s, and at the end of his life, he penned the words spoken by his chorus in *Oedipus at Kolonos* (ll. 1210–1236):

> Whoever wants a greater portion than the norm
> To live, he's a fool—
> It is quite evident to me—
> Since many long days indeed set down
> Close-set griefs, with joyfulness nowhere near them,
> Whenever someone falls beyond what it fitting.
> The ally who comes to all alike—
> Hades—when fate, unwedded,
> Unaccompanied by the lyre or dance, appears;
> Death at the end.
> Not to be born beats all, really. Second best is, upon appearing,
> To go back whence one came
> As quickly as possible.
> Thus when youth-bearing, light-hearted folly passes,
> What harsh affliction is outside, what labor within?
> Jealousy, strife, contention, battle,
> And murder—and in the end add abhorrent,
> Utterly impotent, unsociable, unloved old age, so that
> Evil of every evil dwells with one.

It is interesting to note that this was the same drama that the novogenarian quoted when his own son brought him to court to claim that he had become too decrepit to manage his estate. Upon asking if his verses sounded like the work of an idiot, the jury pronounced him sane and more than competent (*Life of Sophokles* 13).

Perhaps the most amusing détente with death was achieved by Zeno, the founder of the Stoic school of philosophy. According to both Diogenes Laertius (7.28) and Lucian (*Makr.* 19), when the 98-year-old philosopher was walking into the Assembly he tripped, fell, and consequently called out to Hades, "I'm coming already; why are you shouting?!?"

BODY

Body and Soul

Much like in modern times, the ancient Greeks believed that, on a most basic level, their identities were divided into two components. One component was the body, either *demas* or *sôma*. Originally, the demas was the living body, while the sôma was what remained after death—a corpse. Eventually, the word sôma could be used to speak of a living body as well. The other part of the individual was the soul, or *psykhê*. Although in modern times we think of the psyche as the mind and thus have words like "psychology," our earliest evidence from the Greeks suggests that the psykhê was originally a bit more like a soul, or even a ghost, than a mind. Specifically, it was the element of the persona that left the body upon death. Unlike the body, it was completely insubstantial, sometimes capable of communicating with the living (mainly in dreams), but completely incapable of touching the living or anything else. Thus, in book 23 of Homer's *Iliad*, while Akhilleus was sleeping (ll. 65–69):

> Then came the spirit (*psykhê*) of poor Patrokles
> To him, in size and fair eyes his likeness,
> And in voice, and such were the clothes about his skin—
> He stood above Akhilleus' head and addressed a word to him.

But when Akhilleus tried to touch his old friend (ll. 99–104):

> So speaking he held out his hands to his friend,
> But he held nothing—the spirit, like smoke, went under the earth
> Muttering. Akhilleus was stunned and leapt up,
> And he beat his hands, and said in lament,
> "Alas! Even in the halls of Hades there is
> Some soul and image, but there is no mind in it at all!"

A similar event occurred to Odysseus when he met his mother in the underworld (*Odyssey*, Bk 11, ll. 204–222):

> So she spoke, but I went thinking in my mind
> To grasp the spirit of my dead mother.
> Three times then I rushed forward, and my heart pressed me to take her;
> Three times she flew out of my hands like a shadow or a dream,
> And a sharp pain grew great in my heart,
> And I spoke winged words to her:

"My mother, why don't you stay when I want to hold you,
Although in Hades, can't we even throw our arms
Around each other and have our fill of cold lament?
Is august Persephonê stirring up a phantom
That I might grieve even more wretchedly?"
So I spoke, but my revered mother answered me:
"O my dear child, most ill-fated of men,
It is nothing Persephonê, daughter of Zeus, does to beguile you,
But this is the custom of mortals once someone has died.
For sinews no longer hold the skin and bones,
But these things are tamed by the fierce force of the blazing fire
When first the heart leaves the white bones,
But the spirit flutters off like a dream."

Technically, then, the psykhê was that element of the personality that continued into the afterlife after the death of the body. However, the psykhê did
not really exist until death. In life, you had a demas; after death, you had a
sôma and a psykhê that looked just like your demas, except that it had no
physical manifestation.

Over time, these notions changed a bit. As stated previously, the sôma
came to be understood as the living body, not just the corpse. Additionally,
ideas about the psykhê and its relationship to the sôma changed. For philosophers such as Plato and religious sects such as the Orphics, the psykhê became
eternal, that part of the individual that endured both during and after life.
Furthermore, heralding in later ideas regarding the body and soul, the psykhê,
rather than being a "flittering ghost with no real heart in it," became the
nobler aspect of the person. For the Orphics, this was explained through their
very notion of how humanity came into being. Once upon a time, Dionysos
was the son of Zeus, and Zeus adored him. Hera, Zeus's wife (but *not* Dionysos's mother), got jealous and convinced the Titans to kidnap the child and
eat him. So they did, although Dionysos's half-sister Athena managed to save
his heart. When Zeus found out about it, he killed the Titans with a lightning
bolt, resurrected Dionysos with the original heart, and created human beings
from the ashes of the now utterly smitten Titans. The human body, then, is
composed of the dead ashes of evil Titans. *However*, because they had just
eaten Dionysos, there was still some of the god in the remains, and that bit
is in humanity as well, existing as the psykhê, that divine spark in the human
body. (More on this in Chapter 7.)

With Plato, we see the beginnings of the idea that not only is the psykhê/
soul superior to the body, but also that it gets judged based on the actions of
the person while alive (a *very* familiar concept in modern times). Thus in
the *Laws*, the philosopher claimed (12. 959a):

It is necessary to trust in the law-giver both in other matters and when he
says that the soul is in all ways better than the body, and in life itself each

manifestation of ourselves is nothing except the soul. The body follows each of us in appearance, and having died one might say that the bodies of the deceased are images, but the actual being of each one of us is the so-called immortal soul, which then goes off to other deities to render an account—just as the ancestral law says—which is an inspiring hope for the good, but a great evil for the bad.

As the classicist Jean-Pierre Vernant put it, "We have thus passed from the soul, ghostly double of the body, to the body as ghostly reflection of the soul" (Vernant 1991, 190).

Liquids, Solids, Spaces

Psykhê notwithstanding, the actual sôma itself was very physically composed of various liquids, solids, and spaces, not to mention the energies that give it all "life." The liquids were what are known as the Four Humors, which seem like they should be sardonic, sarcastic, raunchy, and punning, but are actually water (*hydôr*), blood (*haima*), phlegm (*phlegmos*), and bile (*kholos*). It is not difficult to determine where the idea of these humors came from. We sweat and urinate out water; we very obviously bleed. Phlegm pours out especially during cold and flu season, and bile is the dark stuff that comes out when wounds are deep enough. These latter two humors were considered especially relevant for the emotions, with excesses of phlegm or bile having negative consequences on the moods. Emotive states notwithstanding, the appropriate balance of these humors was necessary for the proper functioning of the body. Too little water obviously resulted in dehydration and thirst. Too little blood led to death quite directly. Too much bile led to insanity, while too much phlegm caused lethargy. The author of the medical treatise *On Diseases* (IV 39) argued that each of the four humors was stored in reservoirs in the body, which released the necessary liquids when needed. If a person were deficient in one or the other, the body would crave foods or liquids that would restore the deficit (once again, like being thirsty causes you to replace water).

Imbalances in the humors were seen in the ancient medical texts as a major cause of illness. According to the Hippokratic author of *Diseases of Women*, written in the fourth century BCE (1.1):

I say that a woman's flesh is more sponge-like and softer than a man's; since this is so, the woman's body draws moisture both with more speed and in greater quantity from the belly than does the body of a man . . . And when the body of a woman—whose flesh is soft—happens to be full of blood, and if that blood does not go off from her body, pain occurs whenever her flesh is full and becomes heated. A woman has warmer blood and therefore she is warmer than a man. If the existing surplus of blood should go off, no pain results from the blood. Because a man has more solid flesh than a woman, he is never so totally overfilled with blood that pain results if some of his blood does not exist each month. He draws whatever quantity of blood is needed for his body's nourishment; since his body is not soft, it does not become overstrained nor is it heated up by fullness, as in the case of a woman. The fact that a man works harder than a woman contributes greatly to this; for hard work draws off some of the fluid. (trans. Lefkowitz and Fant 1992, 234)

The author of this treatise goes on to note that a superabundance of blood is most likely to build up in a woman who has never given birth, since neither her womb nor vagina are necessarily open enough to permit the egress of blood.

Which brings us to solids. As one might expect, the Greeks had a much better understanding of the outside of the body than the inside. Eyes saw, ears heard, tongues spoke and tasted, hopefully not at the same time. Hard work built up shapely muscles and burnt off liquids. Genitals led to sex and repro-duction. All these things were covered with a layer of flesh, which, be it female and spongy or male and hard, contained what we would call the inter-nal organs.

What went on inside of the body was inevitably more confusing to the Greeks, and quite a bit ickier. As Aristotle himself noted (*PA* 645a28–30): "It is not possible to look at parts that constitute the human race, such as blood, flesh, bones, vessels, and other such parts, without considerable distaste" (trans. Holmes 2010, 85). The first internal part of the body that the Greeks came to understand (sort of) was the diaphragm, containing the *phrenes, thumos, kardiê, êtor,* and *nêdus.* One might take the phrenes as lungs (sort of) and the thumos, kardiê and êtor as the heart (more on the nêdus later in this discussion). Origi-nally, the understanding was that this is where thought took place. You could tell because during moments of stress or fear, you could actually feel yourself thinking extra hard. So much comes across in the very beginning of the *Iliad,* when Agamemnon insults Akhilleus (Bk. 1. 188–195):

So he spoke, and the son of Peleus became distressed, and in his heart (*êtor*)
In his shaggy chest he contrived in two directions,
Whether taking the sharp sword from his thigh
To kill Atreides, moving aside the others,
Or to still his anger (*kholos*) and restrain his heart (*thumon*).
While he pondered these things in his mind (*phrenes*) and heart (*thumon*),
He took the great sword from its scabbard.
Then Athena came from the sky . . .

The nêdus can be translated as either "belly" or "womb" and basically refers to the hollow space right under the diaphragm. As Hesiod tells us in his *Theogony* (ll. 886–891, 899–900):

Zeus, King of the gods, made Metis his first wife;
Wisest she was of gods and mortal humans.

> But when indeed she was about to bear the goddess owl-eyes Athena,
> Then, having fooled her mind with a trick,
> Wily words, he put her into his belly (*nêdus*),
> By the cunning words of Earth and starry Ouranos.
> . . .
> But Zeus put her into his belly,
> So that the goddess might speak to him of good and evil.

So Metis, whose name means "cunning wisdom," lived in Zeus's nêdus/belly where she was able to advise his own phrenes in matters of wisdom. Eventually, of course, she gave birth to Athena, who emerged from Zeus's head. People tend to assume that this means that Athena, Goddess of Wisdom, was born from the center of Zeus's thought—a wise goddess born from the brain. However, as we have seen, for the Greeks of this time, the center of thought was actually the diaphragm. If Athena were to have been born from the "center of Zeus's thought," she would have had to have burst forth from his chest like one of those monsters in *Aliens*. Instead, if we might apply some later Greek medical theories, the brain was believed to be where sperm was produced, which flowed thence down the spinal column to the penis. Athena, then, was not born from Zeus's mind, but from his upper testes, just as the other child born from Zeus, Dionysos, was born from the Sky God's inner thigh. (In my mythology classes, this inevitably leads to the joke that in modern times, we say that men have two "heads" and always think with the wrong one, whereas in ancient Greece, they said that men had two heads and thought with neither.)

The other main cavity in the body was the *gastêr*—the stomach. The gastêr was the part of the body that demanded food, and it was a source of great irritation for humans. As far as the immortals were concerns, humans were "nothing but bellies," as the Muses insulted Hesiod on Mount Helikon (*Theogony*, l. 26). Odysseus, having starved for days, was led to complain (*Od.* 7. 216–221):

> "For nothing else is more shameless than the hateful belly,
> Which bids one by necessity to remember it
> And distresses more and brings suffering to one's mind.
> And so I have pain in my mind, which always
> Commands me to eat and drink, and makes me
> Forget everything I suffer, and orders me to fill it."

Problems

The greatest divide between the common folks and the medical writers was in understanding how the body worked, and most especially what happened when it didn't. Most people thought illnesses were brought on by the deities, and regardless of the cause, the deities were also the best chance of getting rid of medical problems. Physicians, on the other hand, believed that medical problems were mainly brought on by imbalances in the body, such as the surplus of blood in women, as seen earlier in this chapter. The contrast between these two approaches comes across quite well in the Hippokratic treatise *On the Sacred Disease* (Epilepsy), §§1–2 (excerpted):

> Perhaps it isn't like this, but people needing a livelihood devise and elaborate all sorts of things about this disease as well as all other matters, attributing to each deity the cause of the suffering. For it is not a single engulfing issue, but often such things as these come to mind: If [the patients] imitate a goat, if they bellow, if they convulse on the right side, they say that the cause is the Mother of the Gods. But if he cries more sharply and vigorously, like a horse, then they say Poseidon is the cause. If some faeces come out, which often happens to those suffering from the disease, the name of Enodia is put forth. If [the cry] is more delicate and piercing, like a bird, it's Apollo Nomios. And if foam flows from the mouth and he kicks with his feet—Ares is the cause. When night terrors and fears and paranoia emerge, and they [the patients] leap from their beds and flee outside in terror—then they say it's the stroke of Hekatê and the assault of the Heroes.
>
> So they use purifications and incantations, and it seems to me that they make the divine most profane and unholy. For they purify those having the disease with sick blood and other such things just as if they had some miasma [ritual impurity]—be it an avenging deity, or having been drugged by humans, or having done something impious—when it is necessary for them to do the opposite of these things—to sacrifice and pray and to go to the sanctuaries supplicating the deities. But they do none of these things, merely purify.
>
> But this illness does not seem to me to be more divine that the others. It has a nature which is like the other diseases, and a cause from which each originates. And I believe that this nature and cause originate from the same thing as divinity and all other things; and its cure nothing less than the others . . .

So the more popular idea was that certain deities were responsible for causing certain health problems, while a minority view existed (and grew over time) that argued that the body was perfectly capable of getting messed up on its own without help from the divine.

For most Greeks, certain specific medical crises were the purview of particular deities. For example, Apollo and Artemis were bringers both of plague and, quite the opposite, painless, inexplicable deaths. Apollo appears as the god of plague at the beginning of the *Iliad* (1. 47–53):

> . . . He [Apollo] came resembling night.
> Then he sat apart from the ships; he released an arrow—
> Terrible was the clamor of the silver bow!
> Mules first he struck, and the swift dogs,

But then he sent a piercing arrow flying at the men themselves.
Ever the close-set fires burned with corpses.
For nine days the god's arrows struck along the army . . .

Artemis was also a sender of plaques. At Kondylea, she sent a plague to the people until they set up a hero cult to the children who first called Artemis Strangled (an indication of her virginity). At Kalydon, where they forgot to offer her appropriate sacrifices, she sent the famous Kalydonian Boar, which devastated the land until brought down by the virgin huntress Atalanta and the hero Meleager.

More commonly, though, Artemis was understood to be a killer of women, especially those in childbirth. At her sanctuary in Brauron (not far from Athens), women who survived childbirth sent offerings of clothing to the goddess in thanksgiving. Although the clothes themselves do not survive, we do have inscriptions from the site giving inventories of the goddess's "acquired wardrobe" (*IG* II^2.1388; 1400; 1514G). For those women who did not survive, clothing votives were sent on their behalf to Iphigeneia at Brauron, one of the earliest of Artemis's "victims."

On a more personal level, Aphrodite could cause love sickness, while the goddess Lyssa and the god Dionysos could both provoke insanity. Several tales relate how Dionysos, being denied his proper worship, descended on a town and caused all the women to go stark raving mad, leaving home and heading to the hills to dance and occasionally rip apart a living creature with their bare hands and eat it raw.

Basically, illness, both physical and what we in modern times call psychological, was sent by the deities. The human body was very literally subject to the gods.

One way to cure an illness, then, was to find out why the responsible deity was annoyed and to make reparations. By the fifth century, however, a new god became extremely popular in the embodied community, and that was Asklepios, God of Healing. He had major sanctuaries in Epidauros and Corinth, and a significant piece of real estate on the Athenian Acropolis. Looking at the votives and inscriptions left in his temples gives interesting insight into how the Greeks dealt with their bodies, what their medical complaints were, and how they understood those problems to be resolved.

One way to thank a deity such as Asklepios for healing some part of you was to offer a votive dedication of the healed body part. Travelers to Greece can see something similar in many churches, where previously ill parishioners have left small, metallic votives of eyes, ears, and other body parts hanging in the church. The votive body parts that were discovered reinforce the idea that the ancient Greeks had a much better sense of what was going on with their external body parts than with anything on the inside. Excavations carried on at the Corinthian Asklepeion (sanctuary of Asklepios) revealed: 10 legs with thighs, nine feet to knees, 25 feet, nine entire arms, three hands to elbows, one upper arm, about 20 complete hands and fragments of another 125, 65 breasts (singly or in pairs), 35 male genitals, six heads (two female, four male), three eyes, and several ears (appearing, like the breasts, both singly and in pairs) (Lang 1977, 15–19). External body parts monopolized the votive deposit.

A roughly similar spread was recorded in the ancient inventories of the Athenian Asklepeion (like the inventories at Brauron, the cultic officials had to keep track of donations before they were put away during major cleaning events). Here F. T. van Straten reckoned (*IG* II^2 1532–1537, 1539):

Body	65
Half Body	1
Back of Body	2
Head	4
Face	17
Face without Ears	1
Lower Face	1
Half Face	1
Eyes	154
Nose	1
Jaw	2
Mouth	8
Teeth	1
Ears	25
Neck	1
Chest	2
Breasts	13
Abdomen	1
Pubis	3
Genitals	15
Heart	5
Bladder	1
Arm/Hand	24
Fingers/Toes	3
Leg	41
Hips	2
Knee	3
Lower Leg	1
Feet	2 pairs

(van Straten 1981, 109)

Of particular interest here is the fact that internal organs are recognized, at lest the heart and what is probably the bladder. This list records dedications dating from the middle of the fourth century to the end of the third, and this inclusion of internal organs serves as an indication that internal anatomical knowledge was on the rise during this period, even among the "lay folk."

Nevertheless, the votives remain heavily skewed to the external body parts. For an understanding of what was going on on the inside, we can take a look at the "case histories" recorded at the god's sanctuaries. In these instances, the priests recorded what had happened after the patients had come to the god's sanctuary, purified themselves with ritual, and then slept in the temple's inner sanctum—the *abaton*. It was during their sleep that the patients received the cures for their ailments. The inscriptions, like the votive body parts, provide fascinating insight into how the common man and woman on the street understood the mechanisms of their own bodies.

(#1) Kleo was pregnant for five years. Having been pregnant for five years she came as a suppliant to the god and slept in the abaton. As soon as she left the abaton and was outside the sanctuary, she bore a boy, who immediately upon being born washed himself in the fountain and walked around along with his mother. Experiencing these things she inscribed on the votive: "The size of the pinax [plaque] is not all that amazing, but the divinity is. For five years was Kleo pregnant in her belly, until she fell asleep and he made her healthy."

(#6) Pandaros the Thessalian had marks on his forehead. He, while sleeping saw his face. It seemed that the god bound his marks with a ribbon and told him that when he got outside of the abaton to take off the ribbon and to dedicate it in the temple. When day came he went out and removed the ribbon, and he saw that his face was devoid of marks, and he dedicated the ribbon bearing the marks from his brow in the temple.

(#8) Euphanes, a child from Epidauros. He, suffering from stone, fell asleep and it seemed to him that the god stood above him and said, "What will you give me if I make you healthy?" And he said "Ten dice!" The god laughed and said that he would cure the problem. When day came he left healthy.

(#12) Euhippos had a spear tip in his jaw for six years. While he was sleeping the god took out the spear tip and gave it to him, right into his hands. When day came he left healthy, holding the spear tip in his hands.

(#14) A man with a stone in his penis. He saw this when asleep: It seemed that he was "with" a handsome boy. Upon ejaculating he cast out the stone and having picked it up he left holding it in his hands.

(#18) Alketas of Halieis. He being blind saw this when sleeping: It seemed to him that the god approached him and opened his (the man's) eyes with his (the god's) fingers, and that the first thing he saw was the trees in the sanctuary. When day came he left healthy.

(#19) Heraieus of Mytilenê. He had no hair on his head, and too much on his chin. He was ashamed and mocked by others, so he slept [in the abaton]. The god anointed him with a drug and made his head grow hair.

(#25) Sostrata, a woman of Pherai, was pregnant with worms. She being entirely ill was carried into the sanctuary in a litter and fell asleep. There she saw nothing apparent while asleep, so she went back home. After this, it seems that someone by the area of Kornoi met up with her and her companions, a handsome man who, learning from them about their lack of luck, asked them to set down the couch upon which they were carrying Sostrata. Then, opening her abdomen he excised a quantity of all sorts of living things—two footbaths full! Having sewn up her stomach again and having made the woman well, Asklepios revealed to her his presence and told her to send back to Epidauros a thank offering for the treatment.

(#26) Lyson of Hermionê, a blind child. He, while awake, had his eyes cured by one of the dogs in the sanctuary. He went away healthy.

(#28) Kleinatas the Theban had lice. He, having some great quantity of lice on his body arrived and fell asleep and saw a vision. It seemed that the god stripped him naked and stood him upright and swept away the lice from his body with a broom. When day came he left the abaton healthy.

(#29) Hagestratos with a headache. He had insomnia because of the pain in his head. When he was in the abaton he fell asleep and while sleeping saw this: It seemed that the god cured his headache and, standing him up straight and naked, taught him a throwing technique for the pankration. When day came he left healthy and not long after he won the pankration competition at the Nemean Games.

(#42) Nikasibula the Messanian, sleeping for children saw a dream. It seemed that the god came to her bringing a snake slithering with him. She had sex with it. And from this two male children were born to her that year.

On the flip side of these miraculous recoveries were the medical histories. One of the ways that early physicians learned the science of medicine was through observation, which they recorded, much as we do today in medical journals. The descriptions are usually a bit more graphic than the inscriptions above, and the outcomes more depressingly realistic. The following few case studies come from the Hippokratic treatise *On the Epidemics*.

(1.4.9) For Kriton the Thessalian foot pain grew severe from the big toe while he was going about upright. He took to bed the same day; shuddering, nauseated, light fever, was delirious at night. One the second day there was swelling of the whole foot, and around the ankle was reddish with rigidity, black blisters, sharp burning, delirium. Unmixed fluid from the bowels, bilious and frequent. He died on the second day from the onset.

(3.1.9) The woman lodging with Teisamenes: for her an onset of grievous intestinal obstruction. Much vomiting, unable to drink, pains about the diaphragm and in the region beneath the entrails. Twisting of the bowels set in. Not thirsty. She became feverish, cold in the extremities, nauseated, sleepless, minimal urine (thin), faeces undigested (thin). Nothing could help her; she died.

(3.1.10) On the first day fever seized a woman of those who lodge with Pantimides—after a miscarriage. Tongue dry, thirsty, nauseated, sleepless. Bowels turbulent with thin stools, copious and raw. On the second day she had stiffness, severe fever, much coming from the bowels; she did not sleep. On the third day the pains were worse. On the fourth day she was delirious. She died on the seventh day. Throughout the bowels were loose with many thin, undigested faeces; minimal, thin urine.

(3.3.6) In Abdera an acute fever seized Perikles; at the same time there was pain, great thirst, nausea, and he was unable to drink. There was swelling of the spleen and heavy-headedness. On the first day he hemorrhaged from the left. The fever greatly increased; he urinated much cloudy, white liquid which did not clarify with standing. On the second day everything was worse—the urine was thick, but with more sediment. The nausea decreased; he slept. On the third day the fever softened—plenty of urine, concocted, having much sediment. A quiet night. Fourth day—midday he had much warm sweat all over, no fever, no cries, no relapse.

Perfection

And so the body could be weak and subject to both gods and nature. But the Greeks did not get overly worked up about such issues, and their interest in the body (excluding the medical writers) tended more toward the aesthetic rather than the symptomatic. As with perhaps all peoples, the ancient Greek physical ideal, the one(s) rendered countless times in sculpture and painting, did not necessarily reflect the body of the average ancient Greek. As the physical anthropologist M. Grmek once put it:

> The inhabitants of Greece in the Mycenaean, archaic, and classical periods were thickset and sturdy, with relatively short lower limbs. The image of their general appearance that one obtains from osteoarchaeological evidence does not coincide with the idealized representation of the human body in Greek sculpture. (quoted in Stewart 1997, 12)

Basically, the Greeks tended to portray themselves in art in idealized form, rather than what the average man or woman on the street actually looked like. One might compare the images of people one sees on the modern fashion magazine cover, which seldom coincide with what one sees in the office on any given day (unless, of course, one happens to work for a fashion magazine).

Nevertheless, the art does allow us to understand what the ancient Greeks preferred for the human body, that is, what their aesthetic proclivities were. Two sculptures of the Classical period are generally regarded as embodying, literally, the Greek conceptions of male and female physical perfection: the Doryphoros by Polykleitos and Praxiteles' Knidian Aphrodite (see Figures 1.8 and 1.9).

The Doryphoros ("Spear-Bearer") was made by Polykleitos in the mid-fifth century. He stands approximately 6.5 feet tall and as such was probably a good foot or so taller than the average Greek male. The war spear he carries

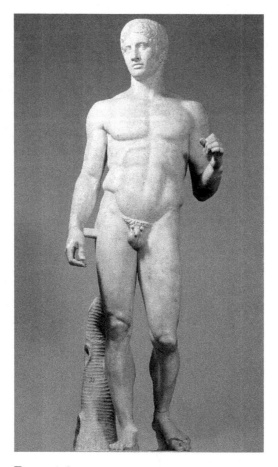

Figure 1.8
Doryphoros (Spearbearer), Roman copy of
Greek original by Polykleitos of Argos, ca. 440
BCE. (Museo Archeologico Nazionale, Naples,
Italy/Art Resource, NY)

indicates that he represents a warrior more so than an athlete, although these
two categories overlapped in all but circumstance. Greek warriors did not go
into battle naked, of course, so the nudity of our sculpture is not realistic but
rather symbolic of the subject's heroism while expressing his physical perfection. Males in Greek sculpture are often, although not universally, portrayed
naked so as to embody a number of ideas, ranging from heroism and athleti-
cism to democratic equality to defeat and death. In real life, men wore clothes
most of the time, except in the bath and athletic competition and training;
they certainly geared up for war.

The Doryphoros's idealism mainly rests in his perfect moderation between
opposing states of being. He is a young man, not having yet grown his beard,

Figure 1.9
Roman copy of Aphrodite of Knidos by Praxit-
eles, ca. 340 BCE. From the Villa dei Quintilii,
Rome. (Vanni/Art Resource, NY)

thus placing him at the acme of youth when men are at their most desirable
(at least to other men). His stance is balanced between rest and movement,
placing him at the ready without wasting effort. He is neither too thin nor
too muscular, giving him a body that is accessible but only with considerable
effort. Finally, as noted by art historian Andrew Stewart, "Its pose was rigor-
ously worked out so that each weight-bearing limb of muscle was placed in
diagonal opposition to a relaxed one; its body was perfectly proportioned
according to a formula that related all its parts mathematically to one another
and to the whole, and it was finished with meticulous accuracy of detail"
(1997, 88).

Some such details are consistent with elements deemed aesthetically pleasing in other male statues. The shoulders and chest are broad and the abdomi-
nals muscular. The buttocks, thighs, and calves are exceptionally well
developed, and the penis is small and uncircumcised (not a Greek practice).
In short, the Doryphoros is the idealized rendering of the warrior-athlete,
what every Greek male should aspire to be.

Things are always harder for women, and aesthetics are no exception. While men who trained most of their lives to be warriors struggled to look like a warrior, the ideal female was Aphrodite, Goddess of Love; mortal women didn't have a chance. Praxiteles wrought his Aphrodite Euploios ("Fair Voyage") in approximately 350 for the people of the island Knidos, who mounted it in a circular sanctuary on a promontory of their island.

The statue was revolutionary for being the first to portray a female, and a goddess at that, completely in the nude. Up to this point, it was traditional that only males be portrayed naked, as discussed previously. The female body was almost always kept under wraps, "contained by clothes, constricted by a belt, capped by a veil, and controlled by a man—and it's still dangerous even then" (Stewart 1997, 41, adapted). Although the notion of the irresistible female body may have been one reason for this consistent clothing, another is that the naked female seemed vulnerable. With the exception of some Near Eastern–inspired nude female terracottas and the Lakonian mirror handles they inspired, most naked females in the archaic and early classical Greek repertoire were either prostitutes or rape victims. Only later in the classical period did nudity manifest to reveal women's erotic aspects, as with our Knidia or red-figure vases showing young brides at the nuptial bath.

The Knidia is six feet tall, and thus, like the Doryphoros, towered above normal people. She is completely nude save for a headband and jeweled armband, although she does reach for her nearby clothing. The ideal female, she is not muscular but has sloping shoulders, rounded limbs, a convex stomach (but no potbelly!), small breasts, and exceptionally well-rounded buttocks. For a statue made of Parian marble, she looks amazingly soft. Her eyes are slightly downcast, and her lips are parted. Remarkable to the modern viewer (although not necessarily the ancient), she has neither pubic hair nor vulva. The slightly downcast eyes and the hand reaching for her clothing give a vague sense of modesty, as does the hand completely inadequately covering her pubis. None of these things detract from the blatant eroticism of the work (technically, they enhance it by drawing attention to the nudity and pubis), appropriate for a goddess who embodied sexual desire. Centuries after the sculpture was finished and displayed, an author named Lucian wrote a semicomical passage about it in a work called "Loves." Here he claimed that a man named Kharikles was so enamored of the statue that he kissed it passionately upon first seeing it from the front. A more homoerotically inclined friend of his named Kallikrates madly embraced the statue when he first saw it from the rear, and the sanctuary's priestess told them about a man so driven mad with passion by the statue that he literally molested it. Where he ejaculated there remained a stain on the statue's thigh to that day (insert your own "statutory rape" joke here). Clearly, Praxiteles got it right.

Two things must be kept in mind when considering these aesthetic ideals. The first is that neither statue still exists. Both were destroyed in antiquity and survive now only in Roman copies. As such, we do not know the *exact* rendering of either. This is especially so with the Knidia, as there are variations in the many Roman copies that still exist. (The most famous is in the Vatican collection, which begs the question what a pope wanted with a statue of a naked sex goddess.) Second is the fact that these sculptures portray masculine aesthetics. They are statues made by men for a paying male clientele, even though they were ultimately to be viewed by both men and women. We have no way of knowing what women would have preferred as an ideal female or male body, although I have the suspicion that the ideal penis size would have grown a bit.

Imperfection

As one might imagine, perfection was a rarity in the ancient world, at least outside the realms of the high arts. As the osteological evidence indicates, the ancient Greeks could be a shortish, squattish group, and there are references in the ancient medical records to obesity and pimples.

Of greater concern were those individuals who suffered deformities, ranging from "invisible" disabilities such as blindness or deafness to full-scale problems such as loss of limbs. The osteological data provide evidence for clubfoot, congenital spinal malformation, congenital hip dislocation, and spina bifida (Garland 1995, 12). A single cemetery of 233 skeletons in Pantello in southern Italy yielded 131 cases of bone pathologies due to fractures, metabolic disorders, and infection (Garland 1995, 19). Disabilities could range from birth defects to battle traumas—thus there were different vulnerabilities at different points in life.

Babies born with obvious malformations were unlikely to reach their first birthday. In Sparta all (or at least all male) infants were inspected at birth. It is highly unlikely that any infant not of one of the royal families would not have been condemned immediately (as noted earlier in this chapter). Elsewhere, malformed infants probably had no ability to survive their ailments, and Greek families generally had the option of exposing unwanted infants within the first few days after birth. That some parents accepted the challenge of rearing a "defective" baby is intimated in a statement of Pseudo-Aristotle (*Ath.Pol.* 7.1335b 19–21) that there should be a law to prevent the rearing of deformed children.

Nevertheless, certain malformations were deemed treatable, such as clubfoot and hunchback. According to the Hippokratic treatise on joints (62) clubfoot could be cured in young children by a combination of physiotherapy, bandages, and wearing corrective shoes. The same treatise was far less optimistic about the cure for hunchbacks (43), which involved "violent shakings" and attachment to a ladder, sometimes upside down (Garland 1995, 128). The potential for cures no doubt helped to lessen the number of postpartum abortions due to deformity.

Some congenital disabilities, of course, show up only later in life, such as mental retardation and blindness. Individuals with mental retardation were very much dependent on the kindness of their families and communities, although it must be remembered that in the overwhelmingly agricultural economies of ancient Greece, there was still quite a bit of work high-functioning people with mental disabilities could accomplish. Blindness could perhaps be less of an issue than one might expect in the age before Braille. Keeping in mind that the majority of any ancient Greek population was illiterate, the lack of Braille (or any comparable reading system) was not as strongly felt as it would be today. As in all preliterate societies, memory was highly valued, and as is commonly suggested, the blind compensate for their loss with extraordinary mental skills, including memory. As Aristotle once claimed, "The blind have a better memory in that, being free from the contemplation of visible phenomena, their power of memory is more powerful" (*EE* 1248b 1–3). Blindness is also commonly coupled with high bardic skills in the Greek literary repertoire, including Homer himself and the epic bard Demodokos in the *Odyssey*. At its fullest extent, blindness might be coupled with prophetic abilities, as in the case of the renowned "seer" Tiresias, guide to Kadmos, Oedipus and, a bit more successfully, Odysseus.

Nevertheless, most people were neither a Homer nor a Tiresias, and the difficulties of blindness in an age before the Disabilities Act should not be overly diminished. At least there was little shame in such a disability. So much cannot be said for other physical problems. Lameness of the limbs could be such a deficiency that even a god complained of the problem. Hephaistos, god of smiths and artisans, was either born lame in the legs or became that way after Zeus threw him out of Olympos. In Book 8 of the *Odyssey*, the god complains (ll. 308–312):

"Aphrodite, daughter of Zeus, always dishonors me,
Being lame, but she loves destructive Ares,
Because he is handsome and swift-footed, while I
Am infirm. But nothing else is to blame
But my two parents, who ought not to have had me!"

A similar problem beset Labda of the Bakkhiadai clan of Corinth (Herodotos, 5:91–92). Although a member of the ruling, and intermarrying, aristocracy, Labda could not get a proper husband because of a bodily malformation. If, as is often suggested, her name is related to the letter lambda (λ), it could be that she had one leg shorter than the other. Her parents were forced to find her a husband from amongst the common folk, leading to Labda giving birth to Kypselos, tyrant of Corinth and defeater of the Bakkhiadai (see later in this chapter). Labda must have loved it.

It was more likely that a member of the aristocracy could survive a disabled childhood, like Corinthian Labda or the Spartan king Agesilaos. Otherwise, most children so born would have died very young. However, disabilities acquired later in life due to illness or accident were also extremely common, and there was no potential for throwing out the deformed baby with the bath-water at that point. According to the studies of Gmerk mentioned earlier, about 10 percent of all known Greek skeletons have at lest one fracture, and four-fifths of these occur in men. It turns out that warfare is pretty dangerous, as is hard labor, and few men made it through life without damage. Life was not necessarily any better for the city-dwellers, where density and insufficient circulation of water and air resulted in increased bacterial infections, including the notorious plague that wiped out at least one-third of the Attik population during the Peloponnesian War in 430 BCE.

For those truly damaged by life, whether from birth or later, some suggested that the best thing to do was simply to let them die. Plato/Sokrates, in his creation of the ideal society in his work the *Republic*, claimed (3.407c–d):

> Therefore, these things being known, we say that even Asklepios heals those having bodies healthy by nature and daily regimen, but at some point some distinct illness gets hold of them. These shown to be of good constitution he heals by drugs and surgery, casting out their illnesses, and he orders them to go on living normally, so that the state should not suffer. But those bodies ill throughout he does not help with regimens to lessen it a bit and to extend a bad life for a person, and so they might have offspring that will be born like them, as seems likely. One not able to live by a steady course, do you think that he should require healing, as he is not useful either to himself or to the state?

Nevertheless, perhaps because warfare had such a high potential for damaging, but not necessarily killing, the warrior population, Athens at least took on the responsibility of caring for its invalids. As early as the days of Peisistratos (sixth century), there was a law stipulating that those maimed in war would be maintained at public expense (Plutarch, *Solon* 31.2). By the fourth century, as the *Constitution of the Athenians* relates (49.4):

> The Council inspects the disabled. For there is a law that bids the Council to inspect those possessing inside of three minai and who are disabled in body such that they are incapacitated and cannot work. To each of these they give a daily stipend of two obols for necessities.

The law does not specifically state that those on the dole are war veterans, but this probably constituted a large percentage of those involved. Two obols per day was not very much money, less than a laborer would earn at this point in time, so those receiving state aid still needed the support of family to survive (Garland 1995, 36). Life was tough.

Emotions

The ancient Greeks believed that the seat of the emotions, as with thought, was either in the diaphragm or the liver. In this they were in line with the rest of the ancient world, such as Mesopotamia, where the expression "He had a ferocious liver" means that he was angry, and convinces new Akkadian students that they simply must have done their translation wrong. Nevertheless, emotions were internal, one of the physical reactions of the body to external stimuli (Konstan 2006, 23, 31).

The fullest study of the emotions was done, of course, by Aristotle in his work on *Rhetoric*. His purpose was to figure out how to manipulate the emotions to bring people over to the speaker's cause, much as in the case of modern public relations (PR) specialists. Motivation aside, his study defined and provided a list of what the ancient Greeks thought of the basic range of emotions. For him, emotions are "all those things causing people to change and differ in regard to their judgments, and which attend upon pain and pleasure" (1378a20–23). His list of basic emotions as given in his work the *Nicomachean Ethics* comprises appetite, anger, fear, confidence, envy, joy, kindness, hatred, longing, emulation, and pity (1105b). For the most part, he recognizes a short series of basic feelings and their opposites, thus fear is the opposite of confidence, and kindness is the opposite of hatred.

A bit like in modern times, there was a basic ambiguity about the emotions and their ability to derail reason. On the one hand, the Greeks recognized that emotions were natural and healthy, and the Greeks were an emotive people with the exception of certain philosophical groups such as the Stoics. On the other hand, the Greeks understood that acting impulsively could lead to disaster, and nothing sparked impulse like passion.

The general ambiguity of emotion comes across especially well in the Greeks' rapport with anger (*orgê*). On the positive side, Aristotle noted that this passion was necessary to be a good citizen (*Nic.Eth.* 1126a):

> For those not angered by such things as they ought to be seem to be foolish; likewise those not angry as they ought to be, nor when. For it seems that they neither perceive nor suffer, and thus they do not get angry nor defensive, and to endure being treated contemptuously and seeing one's household so treated is slavish.

In this he was supported by the orator (functionally a lawyer) Lysias, who reminded the jury of their duty to use anger in defense of the city, once again emphasizing the need for anger in good citizenship (15.9):

> And indeed, O men of the jury, if this seems here to be a great penalty and the law extremely harsh, remember that you did not come here to make laws about these things, but to vote according to the current laws, not pitying the wrong-doers, but being very angry with them and helping the whole city.

So much for the good. But the Greeks recognized that they could also be very stupid when under the influence of anger, and everyone from poets to lawyers to generals warned against it. Although Lysias might try to use the jury's anger to his favor, Antiphon, speaking in a murder case, countered that (*Herodes*, 5.72):

> For it is not possible for an angry person to think well on anything—for that by which he thinks, his judgment, is destroyed. It is a great day amongst days, O gentlemen, that separates judgment from anger and can find the truth of what happened.

Anger's ability to counter rational thinking was especially problematic in warfare, as was learned by the Spartan ruler Teleutias when attacking the city of Olynthos. According to the report preserved by Xenophon (*Hellenika* 5.3.5-6), Teleutias became livid when the Olynthian cavalry attacked and slaughtered one of his squads. In angry vengeance, he ordered a full-out assault on the enemy, drawing so close that he and a good portion of his men were slaughtered. And so Xenophon reflected (5.3.7):

> I say that one ought not to punish even a slave in anger—for often even masters, being angry, suffer more evils than they make. And to set out against the enemy in anger but without judgment is a total mistake. For anger is thoughtless, but judgment seeks out how not to suffer anything while doing some harm to the enemy.

And besides, there's no glory in fighting for emotion, at least according to Aristotle: "Humans, then, suffer when angry, and enjoy taking vengeance. But those soldiers fighting for these things are not courageous, for they [fight] not for the good or as logic [demands], but out of emotion" (*Nic. Eth.* 1117a5). I cannot imagine, however, that Aristotle ever would have said this directly to Akhilleus's face, whose entire motivation in the *Iliad* was his anger, originally against Agamemnon and then against Hektor. No one in ancient Greece would have contended that he did not fight honorably, angry or not. Although it was pretty stupid of him, under the influence of anger, to get Patrokles killed.

Another emotion that had its good and bad sides was fear (*phobos*). According to Aristotle (*Rh.* 1382a21):

> Let fear be some pain or confusion deriving from fantasies of harsh destruction or suffering. For not all bad things are feared, such as wrong-doing or slowness, but only those that produce great pains or destruction, and these only if they are not distant but appear to be about to happen nearby. For things at a great distance do not frighten, only those things nearby that can kill. But things that aren't close, people don't think about them.

A similar sentiment was expressed by the Archaic, Parian lyric poet Arkhilokhos:

> Look, Glaukos, how heavy sea waves leap skyward!
> Over the Gyrai rocks hangs a black cloud
> A signal of winter storm.
> From the unforeseen comes fear. (trans. Barnstone 1988, 6)

Aristotle and Arkhilokhos probably would have been terribly amused by some of the things people fear today, such as death by shark attack after seeing *Jaws*, even when one lives in Kansas. Nevertheless, fear could be a useful emotion in daunting circumstances, especially in its ability to temper anger and over-confidence. Thus Xenophon once argued in the persona of Sokrates that (*Mem.* 3.5.5):

> Confidence instills carelessness and indifference and disobedience, while fear makes people more attentive and obedient and better disciplined. Take as an example those on ships. Whenever they fear nothing imminent they are full of unruliness. But if they fear a storm or attack, not only do they do everything they are told, but they also carry out their orders in silence, just like a chorus.

Nevertheless, fear certainly had its bad side, especially in its ability to induce total brain-freeze in speakers and cowardice in soldiers. In a fragment of a lost play entitled *Alkmaion*, Euripides noted that (fr. 67) "When someone gets up to speak at a trial on a matter of life and death, fear impels a human's mouth to terrified babble and prevents the mind from saying what it wishes" (Konstan 2006, 152). Or, put more simply by Thucydides (8.87.4), "Fear wipes out presence of mind."

The best cure for fear, especially in a military context, was not alcohol but shame. Actually, the Greeks had two separate but related concepts of shame—*aidos* and *aiskhynê*. Aidos might be understood as a kind of reverence and self-respect; it keeps you from doing something bad. Aiskhynê is shame and humiliation, what you feel after you did something bad. Combined they lead to a sense of horror at doing the wrong thing, out of fear or otherwise, such that one will lose all status in society. Thus Aristotle mused (*Rhet.* 1383b):

> If indeed shame is so defined, it is necessary to feel shame about those same things which of all bad acts seem to be shameful either to oneself or to those one thinks about. These actions come from bad character: Throwing away one's shield or fleeing, for example, for these come from cowardice. And stealing a deposit or acting unjustly, for these come from injustice. And having sex with those one shouldn't, or belonging to those one shouldn't, or when one shouldn't, for these come from lack of self-control.

David Konstan, who is a specialist on ancient Greek emotions, continued with Aristotle's ideology:

> Other examples of vices are wrongful gain, illiberality or servility, effeminacy, small-mindedness, meekness, and conceitedness, each manifested in visible outward behaviour, such as making a profit off the poor, lack of generosity, flattery, lack of endurance, and blowing one's own horn. All these actions are evidence of personal defects, and it is these in turn that, when recognized, lead to a loss of esteem and status. There are thus three elements that together prompt the emotions of shame: a particular act (throwing away one's shield in battle); the fault of character that is reveled by the act (cowardice); and the disgrace or loss of esteem before the community at large. (2006, 101)

It was this sense of shame that Hektor recalled when explaining why he kept on fighting against the Greeks. When his wife Andromakhê begs him to rest from fighting in Book Six of the *Iliad* he replies (ll. 441–446):

> And indeed these things are all of concern to me, wife. But great shame
> Would I feel before the Trojan men and women with trailing robes,
> If I were weak and shirked away from battle.
> Nor does my heart lead me that way, since I have learned to be brave
> Always, and to fight in the front ranks with the Trojans,
> Defending the fatherland and great honor for myself.

Later, in Book 22, Hektor comes face-to-face with an extremely angry Akhilleus. Although his parents beg him to come within the citadel walls, Hektor refuses, musing (ll.99–110):

> Ah, me! If I dive into the gates and walls,
> Polydamas will be the first to reproach me,
> He who bade me to lead the Trojans into the city
> On that night when divine Akhilleus roused up destruction.
> But I didn't listen—it would have been better to.
> Now when he destroys the people through my presumption
> I am ashamed before the Trojan men and women with their trailing robes,
> Lest someone worse than I say:
> "Hektor destroyed the people, he who trusted in his strength."
> Thus will they speak; but for me it will be much better
> To go against Akhilleus there, killing him,
> Or to be destroyed by him in glory before the city.

The seventh-century poet Tyrtaios sang of this relationship between battle prowess, shame, and courage in his song on the Spartan Soldier, which begins (frag. 10):

For it is a fair thing when a good man dies
Standing in the front ranks defending his fatherland.
But leaving his city and fleeing the rich fields
Is the most horrid thing of all,
Wandering with dear mother and old father
And with small children and wedded wife.
For he is hateful to those around him; he will come upon them
Resembling want and hateful poverty.
He shames his clan and disgraces his shining face;
All dishonor and cowardice follow him.

However, not everyone had similar sentiments when it came to dying with
honor rather than shirking with shame, as expressed by the poet Arkhilokhos:

Well, what if some barbaric Thracian glories
In the perfect shield I left under a bush?
I was sorry to leave it—but I saved my skin.
Does it matter? O hell, I'll buy a better one. (trans. Barnstone 1988, 32)

He might have been better off with the alcohol.

Shame existed outside the realms of warfare, too, of course. In conversa-
tions between the sexes, for example, the naughty thoughts of one party could
manifest as a kind of aidos which, if found out, could lead to aiskhynê. In a
lyric conversation between the poets Sappho and Alkaios, the latter must
admit:

Violet-haired, pure, honey-smiling Sappho,
I want to speak to you, but shame disarms me.

To which Sappho replies:

If you cared for what is upright and good,
And your tongue were not concocting trouble,
Shame would not be hiding in your eyes
And you would speak out your real desires. (trans. Barnstone 1988, 84)

In a society as competitive as that of the ancient Greeks, it is inevitable
that the emotions of envy and jealousy would be prevalent. Technically, envy
occurs when you resent another person his/her looks/good fortune/love life/
whatever, whereas jealousy is when you specifically begrudge another person
having some specific quality or object (such as your own desired lover). Both
of these concepts ran together in ancient Greece and can be treated together.
Envy/jealousy could be a simple *phthonos* or a severe *nemesis*, an emotion that
was personified and divinized into the avenging goddess Nemesis in the
Classical period and who had a famous cult site at Rhamnous in Attika, near
Athens. For Aristotle, phthonos was the pain at seeing another person do

better than you, especially when you did not believe that that person deserved it. More generally, phthonos was to begrudge somebody something for what-ever reason, and in the Homeric texts the verb "phthonein" could simply be translated as "to begrudge." Nemesis was somewhat different and consisted of the pain felt when seeing someone fare well or badly contrary to just deserts. Phthonos, then, was a bit more like what we might consider envy today, whereas nemesis is more of an indignation against the injustices of the uni-verse. The goddess Nemesis righted those wrongs and thus was a goddess of justice.

Simple rivalries could, of course, provoke simple jealousies in day-to-day living. When speaking of the material life of farmers in his *Works and Days*, the eighth-century poet Hesiod insisted that (311–313):

Work is no shame; unemployment is shame.
If you work, quickly will the unemployed envy you
Growing rich—Excellence and renown accompany wealth.

But the two main arenas of the more spiteful emotions were popular success and love. While neighbors might mutter under their breath about someone's new hedge clippers, no one had to *worry* about envy and jealousy as much as the elite. Those members of the upper classes who were successful in athletics or politics (and, really, these were the same privileged families) could be sub-jected to a kind of emotional payback from their shabbier fellow citizens. It is no wonder that Pindar, the fifth-century poet who wrote for athletic victors, felt the need to include in his praise poems comments such as, "If someone is devoted entirely to excellence with both expenses and hard work, one must give those who achieve it a lordly vaunt with no begrudging thoughts" (*First Isthmian* 41–46). Pindar's rough contemporary Bakkhilides had similar issues with his clients and audiences, forcing him to demand (13.199–209):

If audacious envy does not
Overpower someone,
Praise the wise man
Justly. There is blame for all
Mortals when it comes to deeds.
But truth loves
To win, and the all-tamer—Time—
Always fosters well-done deeds;
The idle tongue of ill-wishers diminishes out of sight.

The problem of envy also infected politics, affecting tyrants and com-moners alike. Many of the praise poems sung advising against envy specifically were those sung in honor of high aristocrats who held power in their respec-tive poleis, be they individual tyrants such as Hieron of Syracuse (in Sicily), or the democratic yet noble-born Megakles of Athens. Tyrants were seen as being especially susceptible to envy and jealousy, as they had a lot to lose and there was nothing to restrain either their power or their emotions. Plus, they were in a better position to act on their less virtuous drives. In a dialogue appearing in the *Histories* of Herodotos, the Persian advisor Otanes notes (3.80):

> For hubris appears in one from the good things present; and envy from the beginning emerges in man. Having both, then, he [the tyrant] has all the worst. For being sated with hubris he enacts many arrogant deeds, and likewise through envy. And yet it seems a tyrant should be without envy, having all good things. But the opposite of this happens to his citizens. For he envies the best who live near him, and he welcomes the worst of his citizens, and he is too good at accepting slander!

To quote an expert on Herodotean politics, Thomas Harrison:

> Envy, it appears, can be indiscriminate. It need not be felt only for those . . . who have more material blessings, but also for others, those who you fear may usurp or pretend to your material blessings, or those you fear might deserve them more. Like the appetite of the Lydian king Cambles, such a glutton that he woke to discover that he had eaten his wife, envy cannot be satisfied. (2003, 152)

In Athens, the jealousies of the common people (the *demos*) could especially manifest in the law courts, as jurors voted with their spite rather than any sense of justice (be this deliberately or not). Technically, it was to harness just this aspect of popular psychology that Aristotle wrote his *Rhetoric* in the first place. Orators certainly tried to use the spite of the people to their advantage, except that as (usually) members of the upper classes themselves, the orators found that they had a formidable task in allaying the jealousies of the demos both against their clients (who could afford to pay for lawyers) and themselves. As one famous fourth-century orator—Isokrates—put it (15.142–143):

> "For," he said, "some men through envy and poverty are so aroused and ill-wrought that they fight not against evils but successes, and they hate not only the most reasonable of people, but also the best of occupations. And concerning other evils: on the one hand they side with evil-doers and are of like mind with them; on the other hand they destroy those of whom they are jealous, if they can. They do these things not in ignorance about what they vote on, but rather to help commit injustice, and not expected to be found out. Saving those like themselves they think that they are helping themselves."

It's hard not to get the impression that these same jealous jurors got reincarnated as the audiences for the *Maury Povich Show* and *Judge Joe Brown*, at least to read the way Isokrates describes them. Nevertheless, petty jealousies could ultimately be detrimental to the state, causing people to convict or even banish others based solely on matters of envy and spite. One rather humorous anecdote bears this out nicely. In the early fifth century, a man called Aristides the Just lived in Athens; he was one of the men who ultimately helped win the war against the Persians. Before the invasions, though, the city held an ostracism—a vote to decide if the people wanted to banish anyone from the city for 10 years. On his way to the vote, Aristides met up with an illiterate farmer who asked him if he (Aristides) would write the name "Aristides" on his ballot. Aristides was a bit taken aback and asked the farmer what Aristides had ever done to him. "Nothing," the man replied, "I'm just sick of hearing him called 'The Just' all the time." Aristides wrote out his name as asked and went on. It's hard not to get the impression that the illiterate farmer got reincarnated as a Florida voter in the 2000 elections.

So basically, envy and jealousy were the ways commoners got to throw their weight around in politics. The other major arena for envy and especially the modern understanding of jealously was love. Some things never change, and love triangles were, to judge from the literature, just as prevalent in ancient Greece as they are now. Really severe cases could involve running off with the queen of Sparta and having her husband and brother-in-law and all of Greece come and claim her back while destroying your city and killing all of your men and enslaving your women. But this was pretty atypical. More common were the petty rivalries for one or another beloved. One famous example was the powerful jealousy the Athenian aristocrat Alkibiades felt for the philosopher Sokrates. As recounted in a dialogue about love—the *Symposion*—Sokrates evinces terror when the young man enters the room and sees him sitting next to a handsome man. Sokrates begs the host (213d):

> Agathon, see if you might protect me, as the love of this man for me is no trivial matter! For since that time when I fell in love with him, it hasn't been possible for me to look at or chat with any handsome fellow, as he being jealous has fits of envy and abuse, and he hardly keeps his hands off me! . . . His mania and violent sexuality have me scared off my ass!

Envy and jealousy in the context of romance were more likely to be the subjects of comedy rather than tragedy. Certainly such emotions had their tragic sides—Deaneira accidentally murdered her husband Herakles when trying to give him a love potion upon discovery of his new young mistress in Euripides's *Trakhiniai*, and Medea very actively murdered her children, her rival, and her rival's father when her husband Jason tried to leave her in Euripides's *Medea*. The ancient Greeks, being ancient Greeks, took such stories as lessons on the passionate, uncontrollable, and ultimately dangerous nature of women, rather than lessons on why it's a bad idea to piss women off. Nevertheless, romantic jealousy was very much the stuff of comedy, especially in Athenian

New Comedy, the closest cognate to modern sit coms. In one not atypical example—"The Shorn Girl" by the fourth-century playwright Menander— our hero Polemo ("war-like") goes nuts when he sees his concubine Glykera ("Sweet") kissing an unknown man. In a fit of jealous rage, he cuts her hair and goes wailing off to his best friend Pataikos. By the time Polemo has worked himself into a semisuicidal fit, we find out (you saw this coming) that the strange man was Glykera's brother, and Polemo realizes that he went liter- ally mad with jealousy. (In the twenty-first century, we would probably have Glykera having an actual romantic relationship with her brother as a final twist.) Jealousy could certainly be painful but was generally recognized as dangerous only in political contexts and Euripides.

The ancient Greek understanding (not irrational, really) was that if you were angry, jealous, or envious of someone long enough, you grew to hate that person or type of person. For the Stoic philosophers, "Hatred is a desire for something bad to happen to another, progressively and continually" (Diogenes Laertius *Lives of the Philosophers,* 7.113). Like any other emotion, it had its good and bad sides. Ideally, one should hate bad people; hating good people was a sign of bad character (Isokrates 15.142). The Athenian orator Aiskhines claimed that individual/personal enmities could be seen as socially useful insofar as they prompted men to prosecute fellow citizens for violations against the law and thus protect the community.

Such personal enmities (*ekhthrai*) did occasionally manifest in the law courts, and for precisely the reason Aiskhines described. When the Athenian orator Lysias brought a lawsuit against one Alkibiades for military desertion, he opened his plea by saying, "There was in the past, O men of the jury, a longstanding enmity between our fathers, and since I have long considered this man a criminal, and have now been badly treated by him, for all these reasons I shall attempt with your help to punish him for all his actions" (Lys. 14.2).

The role of longstanding hatred, bordering on family feuds, was even more manifest in a suit between Diodotos and Euktemon and a man named Andro- tion (Demosthenes 22). In addressing the jury, Diotodos explained very clearly exactly why he bore such a grudge against the defendant (1–2):

> Whatever Euktemon, O men of the jury, suffered at the hands of Androtion, he believed that it was necessary to help the city and get justice for himself, and I too shall endeavor to do this, if I can. What had happened—many and terrible things, all against the law when Euktemon was so brutalized—these are less than the things that happened to me because of Androtion. This man [Euktemon] was set up to be unjustly deprived of property by you; but for my part, no one of humanity would ever receive me if the confabulations made by him were believed by you. For he accused me of things anyone would shrink ever to say, unless he happened to be like *him,* saying that I killed my own father, *and* he had a charge of impiety set not against me, but against my uncle,

charging him with impiety for associating with me . . . If it happened that my uncle was convicted, who would suffer more wretchedly than I because of this? For who, either friend or *xenos*, would ever want to be near me? What city would ever permit me to be in it, believing me to have done such impious things? Not one!

Aristotle was rather adamant that there were clear distinctions between hatred and anger. Anger was directed at specific people and could be mollified over time, whereas hatred was more generalized, more entrenched, and lacked the pain that accompanied anger. In short, Aristotle did not see hatred as passionate. Nevertheless, the boundaries between hatred and anger were certainly blurred in real life, and both had their full complement of passion, especially as one sees in the mad invective of Arkhilokhos against a former friend:

> . . . being driven aside by a wave,
> And in Salmudessos, bereft of well-minded companions,
> May Thrakians with mohawks
> Seize him, may he suffer countless evils,
> Eating slavish bread,
> Shivering, freezing, from the tumult
> May he be tangled in seaweed,
> May his teeth rattle, like a dog lying on his belly
> Through illness,
> On the edge of the sea, vomiting waves.
> O how I wish to see these things,
> He who wronged me and trod an oath underfoot,
> He who once was my companion!

Hell hath no Fury . . .

The ancient Greeks also had a number of positive emotions, stuff to counter the anger and fear and shame and envy and jealousy and hatred. Love, desire, fondness, and gratitude will be the subject matter of the next two chapters, so I shall not be presenting much on them here. However, the Greeks also recognized the milder emotion of pity, the opposite of envy, and were fully cognizant of its benefits. For Aristotle, pity was "a kind of pain in the case of an apparent destructive or painful harm of one not deserving to encounter it, which one might expect oneself, or one of one's own to suffer" (*Rhet.* 1385b13). For Aristotle, there was an intellectual aspect of pity, whereby the pitier had to determine if the one suffering were functionally "guilty" or not, and thus "deserving" or not. The idea of merit does not show up as much in other references to pity—compassion, really—in other Greek texts, probably because in reality, pity/compassion negates the ability to see the sufferer in a bad light. Furthermore, the most common objects of pity in ancient Greece were hard to think of as meriting suffering—the dead, the injured, the sick, the poor, the old, women, and children, and especially these last three categories when combined with "war victim" (Sternberg 2005, 20).

Victims of warfare, which was endemic in ancient Greece, were some of the most common objects of pity. As early as Homer's *Iliad*, we read of the Trojan princess Andromakhê begging her husband not to fight out of pity for her (6.429–432):

> Hektor, but you are to me father and revered mother,
> And also brother—you are my young spouse.
> But come now and pity me and stay upon the tower,
> Lest you make your child an orphan, and your wife a widow.

Such notions were especially prevalent in the fourth century, when memories of the Peloponnesian War were still fresh, interpolis squabbles common, and a possible war with Macedon loomed menacingly. Thus the Athenian orator Demosthenes called to mind an embassy to the north (19.65):

> For when then we were heading to Delphi, by necessity we had to see all these things—houses razed to the ground, walls stripped, the countryside empty of those in youth, a few women and children and elders—all piteous! No one could express fully in words the evils that are there now.

The orator (and frequent opponent of Demosthenes) Aiskhines recalled of the city of Thebes (3.157):

> In your minds imagine these misfortunes, and imagine seeing the city taken, the walls razed, burning houses, women and children led off into slavery, old men and women late in life unlearning freedom, weeping, supplicating you, not angry at those taking vengeance, but at those at fault for these things, enjoining you by no means to crown the curse of Greece, but rather to guard against the divinity and ill-luck that pursue humanity.

Pity for the plight of children of all ages for many reasons appears in the historical accounts. Already mentioned was Andromakhê's plea for her own child Astyanax, who, nevertheless, wound up being tossed from the walls of Troy upon the conquest of the citadel. A tale with a happier outcome appears in Herodotos's *Histories*, when he explains the origins of the tyranny in Corinth. It all began when an oracle prophesied that the child of one Eëtion would overthrow the ruling Bakkhiadai clan (5.92c–d):

> Getting together in secret, they decided to destroy the child of Eëtion as soon as it was born. Just as soon as his wife gave birth, they sent ten of their own to the deme in which Eëtion lived to kill the child. Arriving in Petras and approaching Eëtion's courtyard, they asked for the child. Labda, knowing nothing of why they came and thinking that they were there for love of his

father, handed the child over to one of them. Their plan had been that the first of them to get hold of the child would dash it onto the street. But when Labda carrying the child handed him over, by good chance the child smiled at the man who took him, and seeing this, pity kept him from killing anyone, and having compassion he handed him over to the second man, who gave him to the third, and so on until, having been passed about, the child went around to all 10 of them, none of them wanting to do the deed. Having handed the child back to its mother and heading outside, they stood around by the gates upbraiding each other, especially accusing the first guy who took the child, in that he didn't act according to the plan. Then, after a time, they decided to go back and all take part in the murder.

But it was fated that an evil for Corinth would sprout from the family of Eëtion. For Labda heard everything they said standing by the gates. Fearing lest they change their minds and, getting hold of the child a second time, kill him, she carried him and hid him in the most unlikely place she could think of—a storage bin (*kypselos*)—believing that if they returned they would conduct a thorough search, looking everywhere they could think of. And this in fact did happen. They returned, and when they looked everywhere and could not find the child, it seemed best to them to leave and to tell those who sent them that they did everything that they were supposed to. And this is what they did. And after this the son of Eëtion grew up, and because he escaped danger in a storage bin, they named him Kypselos.

The sight of the baby smiling moved his assassins to pity, and thus the boy grew up to overthrow the Bakkhiadai and establish a tyranny over the city.

As stated earlier, Aristotle's purpose in writing the *Rhetoric* was to teach orators how to persuade juries, and thus pity and its manipulation featured prominently in the Athenian court system at least. Defendants would weep openly in the courts in the hopes of eliciting pity on the part of the jurors. If that did not seem sufficient, they could pull out the big guns and bring in their children to cry before the jury, invoking pity at least for the families of the defendants if not for the defendants themselves. Not everyone was thrilled with this, of course. Xenophon, in the character of Hermogenes, remarks in his *Apology* that jurors often acquit the guilty "either pitying them because of their speech or because they spoke winningly" (4). In Plato's work of the same name, Sokrates, on trial for impiety and corrupting the youth, point blank refuses to bring his small children up onto the stand, even though others had been content to do so. As he argues it (34b–d):

Well then, gentlemen. These things I might tender in self-defense, and perhaps there are other such things as well. And perhaps someone of you might get angry, remembering himself, when he was bound to contend in even a lesser struggle, supplicating the jurors with many tears, bringing up his children so that, as much as possible, he might be pitied, as well as other members of his household and many friends. But I shall do none of that, even though I might seem to be in the greatest danger of all. Perhaps then someone thinking of these things might be more unfeeling to me, and getting angry because of these things vote against me in anger. If someone of you should act thus—I don't expect as much, but if—I think it would be fitting for me to say this to him, "O best of men, I have relatives and family, for, as Homer once put it, I am not born 'from oak and stone,' but from humans, so that I have relatives and sons, O men of Athens: three teen-agers and two children. But nevertheless I shall not bid any of them to come up here begging for you to acquit me." And why shall I not do these things? I am not being presumptuous, O men of Athens, nor am I disrespecting you; but whether I keep heart before death or not is another matter, but concerning the reputation of me, you, and the whole city, it does not seem to me to be better to do these things, being at my age and having my reputation.

Ultimately, one might argue that Aristotle was right about the emotions, that they can short-circuit rational thinking. The Stoic philosophers certainly believed so, which is why they tried to remain stoic. But the idea that passions, violent passions, could evoke grief was not merely a mantra of the philosophically inclined; many Greeks understood that the passions could be dangerous, or at least lead to pain. And thus Arkhilokhos proclaimed:

O my soul, my soul—you are mutilated helplessly
By this blade of sorrow. Yet rise and bare your chest,
Face those who would attack you, be strong, give no ground.
And if you defeat them, do not brag like a loud-mouth,
Nor, if they beat you, run home and lie down to cry.
Keep some measure in your joy—or in your sadness during
Crisis—that you may understand man's ups and downs. (trans. Barnstone
    1988, 35)

2

Peri Oikias kai Aphroditês: On Family and Sexual Relationships

ON FAMILY AND ITS RELATIONSHIPS

Marriage: Some Basics

For the ancient Greeks of all periods, the single life was never a feasible option. Men and women were expected to marry and have children, to whom they would pass on the family possessions and traditions. There were certain political reasons for this, of course: The state needed citizens, workers, warriors, and the ability to produce more of the same. But there were more personal reasons for this universal need to marry. The ancient Greeks very much believed that the pairing of men and women was a necessary and desirable partnership based on the complementary natures of the two sexes. As Aristotle put it as unromantically as possible in his *Nicomachean Ethics* (1162a):

> Affection for husband and wife seems to originate according to nature, for humanity by nature is inclined to live in pairs, even more so than in cities, to such an extent that the household is older and more indispensable than the polis, and procreation more common for living beings. For other creatures cohabitation is for this purpose; but humans live together not only for the sake of reproduction, but also for the necessities of life—for forthwith tasks are divided up, some for the man and some for the woman, and thus they help each other, putting their individual assets together for the common good. Because of these things friendship seems to be both sweet and useful. And as well it might be because of virtue, if this is reasonable—for there is virtue in each one of them, and they might cherish that in each other. And it seems that children are a bond . . .

For others, it was the begetting of children that was the primary cause for marriage. According to the Athenian comedic poet Menander, marriage existed "for the ploughing of legitimate children." In Xenophon's work *Oikonomikos* ("Household Organization"), the Athenian gentleman Iskhomakhos explains to his young wife (7.18–19):

> For it seems to me, wife, that the gods themselves quite prudently set up this yoke, which is female and male, so that they might be most to one another in their partnership. For, firstly, this yoke of child-bearing is laid upon us so that the generation of living beings not fail. Then, the care of the elderly is provided for by this yoke.

Iskhomakhos goes on to explain the gender-based division of labor that allows families to thrive. Males, being stronger and hardier, work out-of-doors, tending farms, business travel, and military duties. Women, being the weaker sex, are best fitted for indoor tasks, such as spinning and weaving, storage of goods, and childcare. The full range of tasks accomplished by both partners allowed for the continuation of the family and household, which itself formed the backbone of society.

Marriages were arranged by the parents of the bride and either the groom himself or members of his family. Only in extreme cases, it would seem, did Greek girls have any influence about whom they would wed. Greek marriages were patrilocal, and families were patrilineal. This means that the bride left her family to live with her husband's upon marriage, and children were considered to be first and foremost their father's offspring. Thus names were given as Name Patronymic, something like John son of George or Hans Anderson, and children inherited from their father's household. This is not to say that there was no relationship with the maternal family. Women bequeathed their dowries to their children, so children inherited from the maternal clan as well as the paternal.

Husbands were older than their wives. As early as the poetry of Hesiod, composed in the late eighth century BCE, Greek men were advised (*Works & Days* ll. 695–700):

> It is the right time to lead your wife home
> When you are not much less than 30 years old
> Or much more. A timely marriage is thus:
> The wife four years from youth should marry in the fifth.
> Marry a virgin, so that you might teach her good habits.
> Most of all, marry someone who lives near you . . .

"The fifth year" was about four years after menarche, suggesting that Greek girls married at about age 16 to men about age 30. This age distinction, especially for first marriages, was typical in most of Greece throughout the Archaic and Classical periods. There were, of course, some exceptions. At places such as Sparta, the age difference might be only a few years—a 24-year-old male marrying an 18-year-old woman (who, being more physically mature, would bear healthier children). In fourth-century Athens, by contrast, the difference could be much greater, typically 15 to 17 years, especially when it was believed that girls, for the sake of their virtue and health, could be married off as young as 13 years of age. In one rather extreme case, the Athenian philosopher Sokrates announced at a trial that he was 70 years old and had young children at home. In the aftermath of the highly destructive Peloponnesian War, parents were literally scrambling to find husbands for their daughters in a city recently depleted of most of its manpower. A 50-year age difference was, under the circumstances, acceptable (for the parents, that is; Sokrates was less than thrilled about his young wife Xanthippê, and we do not know her thoughts at all). The typical age differences, plus the practice of patrilocal marriage, created very different takes on marriage as experienced by males and by females.

The Male Experience of Marriage

There is something paradoxical about the range of reactions to marriage expressed by ancient Greek men. Technically speaking, males had far more authority, rights, and what we might term support networks in their familial relationships than women. They stayed in their natal homes on their own property with their own families, and in many *poleis* (cities), they had full legal authority over their wives for life. However, this does not mean that they could actually control their wives. Furthermore, since men were very much expected to spend their time out-of-doors while the women remained inside, the house was, in spite of male ownership, feminine space. Basically, whenever the husband went home, he entered alien territory controlled by someone he was technically, but not really, supposed to be in control of.

Considering the contrast between the ideal and the reality of married life, it is little wonder that some of the earliest reactions to the institution were less than enthusiastic. The complaints tended to involve the fact that, Zeus being a heartless bastard, marriage inevitably involved at least one female. And so some men had the "ball and chain" opinion of marriage, somewhat reminiscent of Archie Bunker. (If you are British, replace Archie Bunker with Alf Garnett.) As Hesiod griped in his poem *Theogony* (ll. 603–612):

Whoever flees marriage and the baneful works of women,
Not wishing to marry, he comes to a destructive old age
Through want of a caretaker; not lacking a livelihood
In life, on dying his relatives divvy up his possessions.
But for him whose fate is to marry,
Who has a trusty spouse suited to his mind,
For him forever the evil is equal to the good:

But for him who has a bad wife,
He lives having incessant grief in his chest
And heart and mind; it is an incurable evil!

To use a modern colloquialism, Hesiod had issues. He was not alone in this. The sixth-century poet Semonides from Amorgos went farther in his railing against marriage in his long poem *On Women*, which ends:

But these other tribes [of women], through the machinations of Zeus,
Are a bane, and remain with men.
For Zeus wrought this greatest evil—
Women! And if they appear to help in some way,
In this it especially becomes an evil,
For never does one get through a whole day
In peace, whoever lives with a woman,
Nor quickly does Famine leave his house—
Wretched housemate, bitchy goddess!
But whenever a man most seems to enjoy himself
At home, either by divine dispensation or human kindness,
Then she complains and crests for battle.
For wherever there is a wife, no guest coming
To the house may he receive readily.
And whoever seems to be the most temperate,
She happens to be the most egregious;
For while her husband gapes . . . the neighbors
Rejoice, seeing him as he errs.
And if each one praises his own wife remembering,
And he blames another's—
Well, we don't understand that we all have the same fate.
For Zeus made this greatest evil
And set a fetter unbreakable around the feet,
From which Hades received those who
Contended because of a woman.

For all men's authority in marriage, then, some clearly felt very much put upon by their female significant others, and to judge from Semonides, nagging was an issue. Furthermore, because of the male-female division of space, men were seldom able to supervise their young wives, young wives who, as we remember, did not necessarily have any say in whom they married. Since the Greeks believed that women did have sex drives but did not have much by way of willpower, concerns about adultery could dominate a man's thoughts about marriage. This concern could become full-fledged paranoia if combined with the thoughts that: (1) women had managerial control over her husband's house and property and (2) there was no way to determine the paternity of the son(s) who would inherit the husband's stuff.

And so one of the greatest concerns for husbands was the issue of trust. The texts reveal that new husbands were often concerned about their wives' loyalties and continued affections. A wife might prefer the attentions of another, possibly younger, man, and thus not only cuckold the husband but put his household and the reputation, if not the actual citizenship, of his children at risk.

One of the most famous examples of the cheating wife and disgraced husband appears in an Athenian court case known as "On the Murder of Eratosthenes" written by the defendant's speechwriter Lysias. As the defendant Euphiletos tells it, he brought home his new wife at the typically young age, and at first he was careful to keep an eye on her in her comings and goings. However, once their first child was born, he assumed that she was now secure in her affections, and he granted her greater liberty of movement. Alas, at the funeral of Euphiletos's mother, a man named Eratosthenes caught sight of the young wife and within a short period of time proceeded to seduce her. The two carried on their affair in secret until the servant of Eratosthenes's previous mistress told Euphiletos what was going on. One night, Euphiletos caught the couple together and killed Eratosthenes. As he explained it to the jurors at his subsequent trial, he should be found innocent of homicide, for the laws of Athens proclaimed that "no person shall be found guilty of murder who catches an adulterer with his wife and inflicts this punishment" (trans. Lefkowitz and Fant 1992, 70). This speech provides one of the best looks into the daily lives of average Athenian citizens and is thus given in greater detail in the sidebar, On the Murder of Eratosthenes (5–14).

It is hardly to be wondered at that death was seen as a reasonable punishment for adultery, considering the role of cheating wives in Greek literature. Certainly the most famous example is Helen of Sparta (aka Helen of Troy), who instigated the entire Trojan War by leaving her husband Menelaos to run off with the handsome young Trojan buck Paris. Adultery not only started the war, it ended it. For when Menelaos's brother Agamemnon finally returned to Mycenae after a decade of fighting, he was murdered in his own house by his own wife who had been sleeping with his own first cousin Aigisthos. What both of these tales emphasize, besides just the disastrous wages of infidelity, is that husbands simply had no control over their wives, be they home or not.

What could be especially problematic in marriages was the age difference between husband and wife. On the one hand, of course, this intensified the perceived power differential between the spouses, such that one would almost naturally expect the husband to take both a fatherly and patronizing approach to his teenaged bride. However, doing the math, we see that if a man who is 30 marries a girl who is 15 and they have children right away, the wife is about 30 years old when her own 15-year-old daughter is about to marry a 30-year-old man. In short, mothers were the same age as their sons-in-law, meaning potential liaisons could emerge within the family. In one historical case reported in Athens, a woman named Khrysilla, wife of Iskhomakhos (possibly the same Iskhomakhos mentioned above in Xenophon's *Oikonomikos*), seduced and eventually ran away with her daughter's husband Kallias, bearing him a son (Andokides *Myst.* 124–127).

Similar scenarios appear in drama. One famous example was the love triangle between the Athenian hero Theseus, his young Cretan bride Phaidra, and Theseus's son from a previous relationship, Hippolytos. Although the ages of neither Theseus nor Phaidra are given, the fact that Theseus already has a son who is in his late teens would suggest that he is at least in his late thirties to forties. Phaidra, as a young wife being portrayed on a classical Athenian stage, would probably be understood to be in her late teens or early twenties. It is easy to understand, then, when Phaidra falls in love with her stepson, although Euripides the playwright is careful to put the blame for this squarely on Aphrodite's shoulders. Eventually, of course, tragedies being what they are, Phaidra kills herself, falsely accusing Hippolytos of attacking her. Theseus seeks revenge on his supposedly duplicitous son and brings about his death. The perceived lack of female fidelity thus destroys the paternal household.

The ancient Greek male certainly had many causes for concern regarding his wife and the trials of marriage. In spite of this, though, it appears that then, as now, many husbands did truly love their wives, and a happy marriage was considered to be one of the greatest joys on earth. So much was first recounted by Homer. In Book Six of the *Odyssey*, the hero Odysseus, who himself struggles for close to a decade to return to his beloved wife Penelopê, offers a heartfelt blessing to the princess Nausikaä (ll. 180–185):

> For you may the gods grant what you desire in your mind—
> A husband and home, and may they also give good
> Companionship. For nothing is better or finer than this—
> When a man and woman have a home, living in companionship.
> It is a great sorrow to ill-wishers,
> A joy to their well-wishers. They are best spoken of.

Some of the most important testaments to this are the grave markers that husbands erected for the wives who predeceased them. For his wife Aspasia in fifth-century Khios, her husband recorded:

> This is the tomb of a worthy wife, here by the road that throngs with people, of Aspasia, who is dead. For her noble disposition Euopides set up this monument for her; she was his consort. (trans. Lefkowitz and Fant 1992, 16)

Likewise for the fourth-century Athenian woman Dionysia:

> It was not clothing, nor gold that this woman admired during her life—it was her husband and the good sense that she showed in her behavior. And in

return for the youth you shared with him, Dionysia, your tomb is adorned by your husband Antiphilos. (trans. Lefkowitz and Fant 1992, 16)

Certainly some of the most amusing portrayals of marriage come from the pen of the fifth-century Athenian comedian Aristophanes. Granted, he wrote fiction that was specifically intended to be funny, so to what extent it reflected reality is certainly debatable. However, one might also argue that the best comedy is that which humorously reveals the absurdities of daily life, warts and all. If so, then we might perhaps consider some of the scenes in Aristophanes's plays as well-cast portrayals of at least some Athenian familial relationships.

Here then we see what might be understood as the ultimate paradox of the husband's role in marriage. In spite of his possession of the house, the land, the furniture, the children, and, technically, the wife, he is utterly dependent on the wife for all the daily necessities and comforts of life. And so we find the old husband Blepyros from Aristophanes's *Ekklesiazouzai* when he wakes to find that his wife Praxagora has left the house. There he is, unable to find his wife, find his clothes, or even manage his bodily needs (*Ekklesiazouzai*, ll. 311–325):

Blepyros: What's the matter? Where has my wife gone?
It's now close to dawn and she's not to be seen!
And I was lying down before taking a shit,
Looking to get my slippers in the dark,
And my cloak; but when I was groping about there
I couldn't find them, while at the door
Pounds this turd! So I take
This half-double-cloak of my wife's
And I draw on her Persian bootsies.
But where's someplace clean, where someone can take a dump?
Anyplace at night is fine, right?
For no one's around to see me shit.
I think I'm pixie-led, bringing home a wife at my age—
I deserve to get these hard knocks.

Perhaps no passage in ancient Greek literature expresses the male approaches to marriage better than the complaints of the young husband Kinesias after his wife has left him and their home to take part in a sex strike to end the Peloponnesian War (*Lysistrata*, ll. 887–891):

Kinesias: Make it quick, now! I've had no joy or pleasure in my life since the day Myrrhinê left the house. I go into the house and feel agony: everything looks empty to me; I get no pleasure from the food I eat. Because I'm horny! (trans. Henderson 1996, 71)

The Female Experience of Marriage

The literature from ancient Greece paints a fairly consistent picture of the female experience of marriage. In the beginning is a young maiden playing or dancing with her girlfriends in a flowery grove or field. Suddenly, without warning, she is snatched away by a male agent, taken from her former life and brought, shrieking and wailing, to an unknown man to be his bride. If the story progresses long enough, however, this original image of heartless abduction is palliated as the bride acquires new privileges and prerogatives in her new status as wife and mother.

The quintessential manifestation of this process is in the abduction of Persephonê as related in the *Homeric Hymn to Demeter* (see the appendix to Chapter 7). When the hymn begins, Persephonê, called Korê—"Maiden"—is out playing with her girlfriends in a flowery field. Just as Korê reaches out to pluck an especially beautiful blossom, the earth beneath her feet opens up, and the girl is grasped by her uncle Hades, who whisks her down to the underworld on his chariot to be his bride (ll. 19–30):

Having seized the unwilling, wailing girl, he
drove off in the golden chariot. She cried out at the top of her lungs,
beseeching her father, highest and best son of Kronos.
No one of the immortals nor of mortal humans
heard her voice, nor the olive trees with their shining fruit,
save only the daughter of Perses, ever of youthful spirit,
outside of her cave—shining-veiled Hekatê,
and King Helios, shining son of Hyperion.
They heard the girl crying for her father Kronides. But he was
sitting all alone far from the gods, in his much-besought temple
receiving fine sacrifices from mortal humans.
At the suggestion of his brother Zeus, he led away the unwilling girl . . .

The story leaves Persephonê until the end, when her mother Demeter, holding all of humanity hostage, negotiated to get her daughter out of the underworld and, functionally, out of her marriage. But before letting Persephonê leave, Hades made a last effort to hold onto his bride by informing her of the benefits of marriage (ll. 360–370):

"Go, Persephonê, to your blue-robed mother,
having a gentle mood in your heart and breast for me,
nor feeling exceedingly dejected on other matters.
I'm not a bad husband among the immortals,
being a brother of Father Zeus. Being here
you shall rule over all, as many as live and crawl,
and you'll possess fantastic honors among the immortals.
There will be payment for all days for the wrong-doers,
to those who do not supplicate your mood with sacrifices,

offering guiltlessly, making proper gifts."
So he spoke, and wise Persephonê rejoiced, swiftly jumping up with joy.

Although the *Hymn to Demeter* reveals a happy outcome for the bride, the majority of the texts emphasize instead the more harrowing early phases of girls' initiation into married adulthood, especially the girls' severance from their childhood companions. This is perhaps best expressed in the works of the Lesbian poet Sappho, who wrote her lyrics in the early sixth century BCE. Two poetic fragments in particular seem to capture both sides of a relationship broken when a girl is taken away into marriage. In the first, we see the young bride lamenting as she is taken away from her younger life (fr. 83):

I truly wish to die.
She left me crying
very much, and she said to me,
"We know what awful things we suffer,
Sappho, as unwillingly I leave you behind."
And I replied to her,
"Go in joy and remember me,
for you know how we are fettered
who cannot go with you.
But I want you to remember, if you forget,
how many sweet and lovely things we shared,
how many garlands of violets
and roses you wove sitting by me;
how many necklaces
twined about you soft neck
were made of lovely flowers,
and you anointed your fair-tressed head
with copious, regal myrrh oil;
and lying on soft beds girls
with all they most wished for beside them."

Once the bride has gone to her new life, the poet must then offer comfort to the girlfriend left behind, here emphasizing not only the loss of the young friend now so far away, but the new and glamorous status that she has acquired, like Persephonê, as a result of her married status:

Yes, Atthis, you may be sure,
Even in Sardis Anaktoria will think often of us,
Of the life we shared here, when you seemed the goddess incarnate
To her and your singing pleased her best.
Now among Lydian women she in her turn stands first,
as the red-fingered moon rising at sunset takes
precedence over stars around her;

her light spreads equally
on the salt sea and fields thick with bloom . . . (trans. Barnard 1958, #40)

Sappho also provided an exceptionally rare insight into girl's inauguration into adult sexuality. In one of her epithalamia ("wedding songs"), she described defloration as:

Like a hyacinth in the mountains
Trampled by shepherds until only
A purple stain remains on the ground (trans. Barnard 1958, #34)

Apparently, husbands and wives needed time to develop a mutually sexually pleasing relationship.

Thoughts on marriage varied in ancient Greece as much as they do today. Some marriages were no doubt happy and fulfilling, while others were at best endured. The one constant, though, was that marriage must take place, and few things were quite so lamented as the fate of those who never fulfilled their lives through wedlock and parenting. In some instances, this could be punishment inflicted by the state on those who contravened its demands. Such was the case in militaristic Sparta, where cowards were punished not only by not being allowed to marry and have children, but also by having to watch as their siblings were made to endure the same fate. So recounts Xenophon in his *Constitution of the Lakedaimonians* (9.5):

In Lakedaimon everyone would be ashamed to take a coward with him to the mess hall, as would they all to be matched with him in wrestling . . . he must support the maidens of his household and explain to them why they are manless. He must suffer a hearth devoid of a wife, and he must pay a penalty for it. He must not wander about cheerfully nor imitate the innocent, or he must suffer blows from his superiors.

On a practical level, of course, this resulted in the predicaments envisioned by Hesiod earlier: the man without heirs has no one to care for him in old age, no one to inherit his property, and no one through whom to continue the family lineage. But even besides that, for both male and female, being deprived of married life was seen as a harsh punishment, seriously detracting from one's ability to live life to the fullest.

More commonly, it was death that kept young men and women from fulfilling their familial roles. Girls especially were mourned as having married Hades, god of death, rather than a mortal husband, and references to lost nuptials were recorded on their gravestones and in poetry. "Hymenaios, attendant of marriages, did not bless you in the house, Plangon, but wept for your perishing outside. Your mother dissolves at your misfortune, nor do the sad groans of lament ever leave her" (CEG[2], # 587).

On a scarier level, girls especially who died before marriage or successful motherhood could reemerge as maleficent ghosts who preyed upon both infants and young brides. Such ghosts/demons were called *Aorai*, literally those who died before their time. In a sense, by killing children and other not-yet-mothers, they reproduced in a way that they could not in life, creating other Aorai who would then continue the killings. Three such demons were especially known in ancient Greece—Lamia, Gello, and Mormo—who in many ways served as the bogeywomen used to frighten children into good behavior. As the fourth-century poetess Erinna recalled in her poem *The Distaff*:

> What terror the monster Mormo brought when we were both little girls:
> On her head were massive ears and she walked
> On four legs and kept changing her face. (trans. Plant 2004, 50)

INTERFAMILIAL RELATIONS

Parents and Children

Considering the extent to which parent-child relationships form the core of most psychiatric dialogues in modern times, it is understandable that these relationships in ancient Greece could be complicated. A few details must be kept in mind.

- As discussed earlier, Greek men did not marry and thus become heads of their own households until they were in their 30s, generally at that point when their own fathers, then in their 60s, would die and leave the family property to the sons, who would then be financially independent. To put this another way: In most Greek poleis, men did not truly come of age until their fathers died. No matter how good the father-son relationship might be, this fact was bound to create some conflicts of interests between the generations.
- As also discussed earlier, Greek girls left their natal families upon marriage to join their husbands' households. As such, close relationships between parents and daughters were inevitably finite. Daughters left their homes in the mid-teens to become wives and mothers in their own right, changing allegiance from their own fathers' household to that of their husbands'. Furthermore, since it was the father who married off the daughter, the loss of a daughter to marriage could instigate feeling of animosity against him on the part of either the daughter herself and/or the girl's mother.
- In many poleis, such as Athens, women, being legal minors, were perpetually under the authority of a male guardian called a *kyrios*. Her first

kyrios was, of course, her father, then her husband. If a woman did not die in childbirth (and this was common) there was a good chance that she would outlive her husband. If she was young, of course she might remarry. But if she was older, guardianship could easily devolve onto her oldest son. In an interesting reversal of familial dynamics, then, a mother became the legal dependent of her child.

The borderline obsession the ancient Greeks had with the generational replacement of fathers with sons formed the core of some the earliest literature in the western canon. One of the dominant themes running though Hesiod's *Theogony*, the *Birth of the Deities*, is what is known as the Succession Myth. This narrative follows three generations of fathers being overthrown by their sons in order to seize control of the universe. First there was the sky-god Ouranos, the son and first consort of the goddess Earth. Ouranos figured out pretty early that if he could have sex with his mother, there was no good reason why their resulting children could not do so as well. And so, in an effort to keep Mother Earth for himself, he refused to let his children be born.

This did not go over well with Earth, who happened to have all her children within her body as allies. Creating a sickle of adamant, she convinced her youngest son Kronos to castrate Ouranos and thus liberate their progeny. This Kronos did, and thus he replaced his father as king of the deities.

Of course, if one son can overthrow and replace a father, there's no reason another cannot do so as well. To secure his dominance, then, Kronos had to be sure that his own children would not be a threat. And so he ate them. Once again, it was time for Mom to step in. Kronos's wife Rhea hid their last son and fed Kronos a rock instead. When the son, Zeus, was old enough to take on Dad, he led a full-scale rebellion against the older generation of deities. Zeus was victorious and became master of the universe in his defeated father's stead. Furthermore, by means of what might be called selective birth control, Zeus was able to keep a limit on which sons were born to him. The series of generational conflicts came to an end.

It is unlikely that such maneuverings were commonplace in the daily lives of Greek mortals, but the dynamics expressed in the Succession Myth do reflect certain realties of life in the ancient Greek family. The father was head of the household (a miniature king of the universe) until he died. His sons could not acquire the land, house, and possessions to become fully fledged, independent citizens until their father died and they received their inheritance. No matter how much sons may have loved their fathers, and vice versa, that fact inevitably entailed that sons were waiting for their fathers to die, and fathers knew that their sons were there to replace them.

This very mortal dynamic informed much ancient literature, especially the Athenian tragedies, which took their heart and soul from familial trauma. The story of Oedipus, who killed his father and married his mother, can easily

be understood in this light. On a psychological level, the father Laios is horri-
fied to discover that his own son will kill him (it is the sign of his own mortality) and marry his wife, Oedipus's mother (thus replacing the father very
literally as head of household in the paternal bed). Rather than seeing the
Oedipus tale as an example of Freud's Oedipus Complex whereby the son
wants to replace the father and possess the mother, we might say that it shows
the anxiety of the father as he is replaced by the next generation. A similar
conclusion might be drawn from story of Phaidra, Hippolytos, and Theseus
as discussed previously.

Nevertheless, since generational replacement was and is a commonplace of
the mortal condition, it is to be expected that most men accepted the fact that
their sons were there to replace them, and they dealt with it rather graciously.
In Book Six of Homer's *Iliad*, we see Hektor expressing the seemingly modern
hope that his son will lead a better life than he did (Il. 466–481):

> So speaking glorious Hektor reached out to his child.
> But the child turned back crying to the bosom
> Of his well-girt nurse, fearing his dear father's appearance,
> Afraid of the bronze and seeing the horse-hair crest,
> Seeing it bobbing at the top of his frightening helm.
> At this his dear father and reverend mother laughed.
> Immediately shining Hektor took the great helm from his head
> And set it gleaming upon the ground.
> Then he kissed his dear son and took him in his hands
> And said a prayer to Zeus and the other deities:
> "Zeus and other gods, grant indeed that this my child,
> Just as I am, may become splendid amongst the Trojans.
> Strong and brave, and may he rule Ilion in strength.
> And then may someone say, 'He is better than his father by far.'
> Coming from war, may he bear bloody booty
> From the enemy he killed and gladden his mother's heart."

Bringing such sentiments into the realms of the historical, the Roman-age
biographer and moralist Plutarch recorded of the Spartan king Agesilaos
(25.5):

> And Agesilaos was especially fond of his children, and about him they say this
> concerning his playtime: That he mounted a reed like a horse, playing with his
> little children in the house. On being seen by one of his friends, he asked him
> to tell no one before he himself became the father of children.

Such expressions of affection in the literature are seldom paralleled in the
art, where depictions of common fathers and sons (as opposed to, say, Zeus
and Hermes) are relatively rare and derive exclusively from Athens. Votive
reliefs portray larger fathers presenting typically young sons to deities such as

Figure 2.1
Attic red-figure hydria with boy at brothel. Attributed to the Harrow Painter, ca.
460 BCE. Tampa Museum of Art. J. V. Noble Collection. (Drawing by Paul C.
Butler)

Athena (goddess of the city) Theseus (the Athenian national hero) and
Herakles (Greek hero *par excellence*). These votives may commemorate
coming-of-age rituals, reflecting another important function of the father,
which was to present his legitimate sons to his phratry and thus establish his
sons as full Athenian citizens. We might say that dads took political care of
their sons. They also seem to have helped them come of age in other ways:
One Athenian vase depicts what appears to be a father taking his young son
to the brothel for the first time (see Figure 2.1).

In spite of the potential for dominance inversion between mothers and
sons (see earlier discussion), such relationships were also understood to be
generally loving and intimate (although *not* as intimate as between Oedipus
and Jokausta!). One snippet from the dialogues of Sokrates as recorded by
his companion Xenophon sounds almost humorously modern (*Memorabilia*
2.2.5–10, slightly excerpted and set into dialogue format):

Sokrates: The woman conceives and bears the foetus, being oppressed and risking
her life, and sharing her nourishment with which she feeds it, and with

much labor she labors and gives birth and rears and cares for it, neither having received anything good nor really knowing the nursling; she does not get to enjoy his ability to recognize her, what he needs, but she guesses what is fitting and pleasing and tries to provide and care for him a long time, both day and night enduring hard work, not knowing if she will receive something good in return for all this . . .

Leokrates: But really, if she did all these things and even so much more, no one could endure her phenomenal bad temper!

Sokrates: Which do you think is harder to bear, the savagery of a wild animal or your mother's?

Leokrates: I think that of a mother like mine!

Sokrates: Has she ever yet hurt you by biting you or having kicked you, such as many people have suffered from wild animals?

Leokrates: But by Zeus! She says things no one throughout his whole life could want to hear!

Sokrates: But you, how many trials do you think you caused her with your voice and deeds, being difficult from childhood, and causing problems day and night, and how much did she suffer when you were sick?

Leokrates: But I never, ever said or did anything that she might be ashamed of!

Sokrates: What then? Do you think it's more difficult for you to hear the things she says than for actors, whenever in the tragedies they say the most extreme things to each other?

Leokrates: But, I think that at that point they don't think either that the inquisitor questions them so as to punish them, or that the adversary threatens in order to hurt them—it's easier to bear.

Sokrates: And you know well that what your mother says not only does no harm but that she wishes good things for you as for no one else, and you get angry? Or do you think your mother is ill-minded to you?

Leokrates: Oh no! I don't think that at all!

Sokrates: Well then, you know that she is well-minded to you and cares for you to the best of her ability when you are sick so that you might get healthy and want for no necessities, and in addition to this she sends many good prayers to the gods on your behalf and offers vows for you—and you say she's a pain? I think that if you cannot bear such a mother, then you cannot endure good things at all . . .

If smother-mothering and childhood rebellion are nothing new, the relations between Spartan mothers and sons could easily chill modern blood. Quite the opposite of the overprotective paradigm, Spartan women were famous even in antiquity for their desire for family honor, which frequently involved the death of sons in war. The Spartan queen Gorgo, for example, was famous for two sayings that reveal much about the rapport between Spartan mothers and their sons. As Plutarch recorded it (*Moralia* 240e):

One being asked by some Athenian woman, "Why do you Spartan women alone rule your men?" She said, "Because only we give birth to men."

It was also possibly she who went on record for sending off her son to battle with a shield and these words: "Son, with this, or on this" (i.e., come back victorious or dead). These were not the words of a singular, somewhat sociopathic mother, either. According to the pro-Spartan Athenian historian Xenophon, when the Spartans finally lost to the Thebans at the Battle of Leuktra in 371 BCE, the Spartan women acted thus (*Hellenika* 6.4.16):

> And they [the Ephors] gave the names to the respective households of those who had died; but they ordered the women not to make an uproar, but to bear their suffering in silence. On the next day it was to be seen how the relatives of those who had died were out and about shining and radiant in appearance, while those of those reported living—they were few to be seen, and they went about looking gloomy and abject.

This is not to suggest that Spartan mothers did not love their sons. Gorgo's previously presented quotation shows that they took considerable pride in their ability to produce such fine men. But Spartan women were as concerned about the welfare of the state as were the men, and they placed this value above simple familial affection. As Plutarch recorded in his *Life of Lykourgos*, just as defending the state was the primary duty of Spartan males, creating warriors was the main duty of Spartan females.

Relationships between daughters and parents were different than those between sons and parents, insofar as they were viewed as somewhat temporary. Daughters were, of course, blood relatives, and the legal codes of several poleis gave them certain rights and duties regarding members of their natal family, especially as concerns death rituals. Nevertheless, rather than hanging out waiting for Dad to die, girls left their natal families in their teens, and for especially high-ranking girls there could be little chance for seeing close relatives again (see Sappho earlier in this chapter). This could put a strain on familial relationships, especially depending on how closely bound daughters were with their parents. The most extreme example, once again, is expressed in the *Homeric Hymn to Demeter*, where the goddess of grain nearly starves humanity to extinction to retrieve her daughter Persephonê from what was, in reality, a very good match. In modern times, we would probably call this codependency.

In reality, though, not all girls went into oblivion upon marriage, and there is evidence, especially from Athens, that the mother-daughter relationship remained strong even after the latter's marriage. From a legal perspective, such relationships appear in the fourth-century orations of Demosthenes and Isaios. The former (Oration 41) mentions a mother who throughout her life made loans to her sons-in-law for the benefit of her daughters, and both generations of females stood witness to the families' economic transactions. Mother, then, continued to be a forceful presence in her daughters', and sons-in-law's, lives.

In Isaios Oration 6, a divorced woman schemes with her two daughters from the failed marriage to acquire some of her former husband's property upon his death. In the case of Khrysilla, mentioned previously, mothers might also run away with their sons-in-law, creating havoc for the family generally. A similar scenario occurred at the royal level in Hellenistic times, when the Ptolemaic Egyptian queen Berenikê II engaged her daughter to Prince Demetrius of Greece but then wound up having an affair with him herself. According to the Greek historian Pompaios Trogus, the daughter retaliated by having her mother assassinated (Justinus 26.3.2–8). In spite of these titillating tales, such scenarios were probably quite rare.

The real relationships between mothers and daughters, like far too many aspects of women's lives in ancient Greece, are mostly lost to us due to the general absence of the female voice in our extant records. Athenian tragedy gives many examples of the mother-daughter relationship, but all of these were penned by men, just as our vase paintings were rendered by male hands. Some paintings do show scenes of everyday life, such as mothers assisting their daughters at their weddings, but such scenes give us the facts, rather than the emotions, of the events they portray. One of the few places a female voice carries through is, of course, the poetry of authors such as Sappho and Anytê, who did compose songs about familial relationships. Thus Sappho tells us how:

I have a small daughter called Kleis, who is like a golden flower.
I wouldn't take all Croesus's kingdom with love thrown in for her. (trans. Barnard 1958, #17)

On a more sorrowful note the Hellenistic epigrammatists Anytê lamented:

Again and again Kleina weeps upon the tomb of her girl,
A mother crying out for her dear, short-lived child,
Calling to the soul of Philainas, who before her wedding
Made her way across the pale stream of the river Acheron. (trans. Plant 2004, 57)

Another closely related place where the female voice comes through is grave markers. The gravestone of Plangon and the epigram to Philainas mentioned earlier are two such examples of the grief experienced by a mother at the loss of her daughter. Some gravestones recorded verbally the sorrow of the mother for her child—"I lie here, a marble statue, instead of a woman, a memorial to Bittê, and of her mother's sad grief" (CEG 153.G, from Amorgos). Others merely showed portrayals of women and children saying their last farewells (see Figure 2.2). Although fathers were more likely to erect grave monuments for their sons, mothers verbalized their sorrow more frequently on daughters' gravestones, a testament to the strength of their bonds.

Figure 2.2
Grave stele of Archestrate, marble, ca. 370 BCE.
Found in Markopoulo (ancient Hagnous), Attica.
National Archaeological Museum, Athens,
Greece, Inv. 722. (Vanni/Art Resource, NY)

In the end, in spite of a full plethora of neuroses and intergenerational havoc, Greek parents did love their children. As Euripides expressed it through his character Herakles in *Herakles* (ll. 633–636):

> Here all mankind is equal:
> rich and poor alike, they love their children.
> With wealth distinctions come: some possess it,
> some do not. All mankind loves its children.

About 200 lines later, Herakles kills his children, and his wife, because he goes insane and, let's face it, Greek tragedy is like that. Nevertheless, the final word on parent-child relationships is that they were generally loving.

Siblings

Relationships between brothers had a number of problems similar to those between fathers and sons. Although brothers did not have to wait for each other to die before real living began, they were in competition with each other for the resources of the paternal estate, and this could certainly create friction. One of the most famous examples of this was between the Archaic poet Hesiod and his brother Perses. According to Hesiod's *Works and Days*, the poet had to bring his own brother to court over the inequitable distribution of their inheritance (ll. 35–40):

> But forthwith let us settle out dispute
> By straight judgments which are best from Zeus.
> For already we divided the estate, but having
> Snatched up many things you carried them off, much gratifying
> Bribe-swallowing kings, who wish to judge such a case—
> Fools!

In contrast, the ties between brothers and sisters were seen to be especially tight and dear. One might suppose that this had much to do with the lack of competition between them and the fact that in many cases the sister was marrying into the brother's circle of comrades.

One of the best anecdotes in this regard comes from the *Histories* of Herodotos. Although the family presented is Persian rather than Greek, it is clear that the Greeks were expected to value the story, and, as discussed below, they replicated it in their own literature. When Intaphernes, a comrade of King Dareios, was imprisoned along with several members of his family for treason, his wife came to the prison to wail for them every day. Eventually, this got to Dareios, who, according to Herodotos (3.119):

> Sending a messenger he spoke thus, "O woman, King Dareios grants one of your imprisoned relatives to be delivered, the one you wish from them all." And she considered and replied thus, "If indeed the king grants the soul of one, I choose of them all my brother." Hearing of this Dareios was amazed and sent the following reply, "O woman, the king asks what you are thinking, abandoning your husband and children to come to select your brother, who is more distant than your children and is less dear than your husband." And she replied, "O King, there may be another husband for me, if the gods will it, and other children, should I lose these. But my father and mother are no longer alive, so there could be no other brother for me in any way." She said that this was her logic. And it seemed to Dareios that the woman spoke well. And he sent out her brother and added the oldest of her children as well, so as to gratify her . . .

A major audience of Herodotos's work was Athens, where not long after, the playwright Sophokles put almost identical sentiments into the mouth of his young heroine Antigonê in the tragedy bearing her name (ll. 904–915):

> And indeed I honored you well, according to the wise.
> For never if I were the mother of children,

Or if my husband, having died, were wasting away,
Would I take up this labor in violation of the citizens.
By grace of what law do I say these things?
If my husband should die, there's another one,
And a child from another man, if I should lose the first.
But since mother and father are covered in Hades
It cannot be that any other brother might bloom ever.
For such truly I honored you, by that law;
But these things seemed to Kreon to err and
to enact horrid things, O dear brother!

Certainly one of the most (in)famous brother-sister relationships from ancient Greek history was that between the fifth-century Athenian statesman Kimon and his sister Elpinikê. Plutarch, writing about Kimon and his contemporary Perikles, had this to say about the siblings' devotion (and possibly more!) to each other:

There are those who say that Elpinikê did not secretly live with Kimon, but openly as one married. She was unable to get a proper bridegroom of the noble class because of her poverty. But when Kallias, one of the wealthy amongst the Athenians, fell in love [with her], he approached her ready to pay in full her father's fine to the demos. They say that she was persuaded and that Kimon gave Elpinikê to Kallias in marriage. (Plutarch: *Kimon* 4.7)

And it seemed that even previously Elpinikê had provided a benefaction for Kimon from Perikles, when Kimon was on trial for his life. For Perikles was one of the prosecutors put forth by the demos, and when Elpinikê went to him and begged him, he smiled and said, "O Elpinikê, you are an old woman, an old woman, to do such things at your age." But truly he only rose once to speak [in the trial], acquitting himself of the case, and of the accusers he hurt Kimon the least when he left. (Plutarch: *Perikles* 10.5)

Ancient Greek families, like all families, had their complexities. Basically, they were loving units of parents and children, and the *oikos*, or household, was always recognized as the most fundamental unit of society. Tensions existed, of course, as well as competition and the simple hullabaloo of daily human interaction. Usually this was minor and not too different from what we experience today (to judge from daytime television).

ON LOVE AND SEX

Like people pretty much anywhere, the ancient Greeks experienced both love and sexuality outside of marriage as well as in a familial context. It probably also goes without saying that the previous statement, to the best we can tell, applied far more to men than to women. As is inevitably the case, we have more data about men, and most of those data were produced by men as well.

One point is of critical importance when discussing the intimate sex lives of the ancient Greeks: The Greeks did not have our concepts of homo- and heterosexuality. In modern times, we tend to assume that people are either one or the other, with a small group self-identifying as bisexual. For the ancient Greeks, all people were essentially bisexual, being attracted to members of their own and the opposite sex depending on circumstances such as age and occasionally even class. Nevertheless, the technicalities of sexuality and love differed substantially depending on the sexes of participants, so it is handy here to divide a study of Greek sexuality into "heterosexual" and "homosexual" components, otherwise known as "relationships that can cause pregnancy and/or cost a lot and thus must be treated with phenomenal care" and "relationships that modern scholars are still trying to wrap their heads around."

"Heterosexuality"

The ideal scenario in ancient Greece was that heterosexual love should be reserved for one's spouse. Women's sex lives were very much constrained because of concern for their reproductive functions. The patriarchal moeurs of ancient Greece demanded father-son transmission of property, so clear-cut paternity was always of major concern. For a woman to be sexually attracted to a man other than her husband had the potential of bringing a bastard into the paternal estate, not to mention a rival male into a husband's house and property. Such were the concerns presented in Lysias's *On the Murder of Eratosthenes* as presented the sidebar. Ideally, then, women should love only their husbands.

Technically, the reverse was also true: in a heterosexual context, men should really love only their wives. This certainly does *not* mean that men were sexually restricted to their wives. Quite to the contrary. Access to slaves and/or prostitutes of both sexes was always available to Greek men and in some instances was actually seen as right, if not a full-blown necessity. According to the comic poet Philemon, the Athenian statesman and reformer Solon established tax-funded brothels in the city so that all men would have equal, and thus democratic, access to sex (fr. 4).

Nevertheless, men were restricted in their potential for forming extramarital, heterosexual, romantic relationships. One source of restriction was, of course, the wife, who could not, technically, stop her husband from fooling around with slaves, prostitutes, and the like but who could complain incessantly and make hubby's life hell as a consequence. Once again, consider the scenario in *Eratosthenes*, when the wife "playfully" locks her husband in the

On the Murder of Eratosthenes (5–14)

For I, O Athenians, when it seemed good to me to marry and take a wife into the household, I was so disposed at that time neither to annoy her nor to let her be too much to herself, to do whatever she pleased; I guarded her as best I could, and I paid attention to her as was reasonable. But when a child was born to me, then I trusted her and handed over to her all my affairs, believing her to be the best house-mate. And in this early period, O Athenians, she was the best of all, for she was excellent at running the household and quite thrifty and ran all things with precision. But when my mother died, her death was the cause of all my ills! For attending her funeral my wife was seen by this man, and in time corrupted. For looking out for her maid-servant wandering in the agora, he spoke to her and ruined her.

First, though, O Men (for it is necessary that I describe these things to you completely): my house is a split-level; it has equal space upstairs and downstairs for the women and men respectively. But when our child was born, his mother nursed him, and so that she not, whenever she had to bathe him, endanger herself going down the stairs, I lived upstairs, the women-folk downstairs. And this became so commonplace that often my wife went downstairs to sleep with the baby, so as to breast-feed him and keep him from crying. And things continued this way for a long time, and I never suspected anything, but I was so foolishly disposed that I thought my wife to be the most temperate in the city. Time went on, O Men. I came home unexpectedly from the fields one day, and after dinner the baby started to cry. The maid-servant did this to provoke him, to make him cry. For it turns out that the man was in the house, as I later learned. So I told my wife to go on and breast-feed the baby, so that he would stop making that racket. But at first she didn't want to go, as she was glad to see me, having returned for a while. But then I got angry and ordered her to go. "Oh yeah," she said, "so that you can try your luck with the serving-girl, just like you attacked her earlier when you were drunk!" I laughed, and she got up and closed and bolted the door, pretending that she was joking. And I took none of this to heart or really thought much about it, happily going back to sleep, having come from the fields. When day came, she came and opened the door. When I asked her why the front door made a noise in the night, she said that the lamp went out by the baby, and that she went to relight it at the neighbor's. And I shut up and figured that that was that. But it seemed to me, O Men, that she had leaded her face, even though her brother had died only thirty days before. Nevertheless, I said nothing about this, leaving the house and going out in silence.

bedroom to keep him from visiting the household slaves while she supposedly nurses. For the sake of domestic bliss, men did have to show some restraint.

There was also a limitation on which females were available for romantic dalliances. Adultery could be punishable by death, so other men's wives were not available. Since unmarried daughters were eventually going to be other men's wives, most girls were also barred from sexual access. Per the scenario discussed earlier, the household slaves were only partially accessible. Furthermore, there is no reason to assume they particularly liked their masters, which itself might put a crimp in the pleasure derived from sex with them. So in the end, most Greek men, if they wanted some nookie on the outside, were stuck with prostitutes.

There was certainly no dearth of prostitutes in ancient Greece, ranging from an-obol-a-bang brothel slaves through well-trained and well-paid flute girls and dancers up to the comparatively elite *hetairai*, the "companions" who were apparently desired as much for their company as they were for sex. They were expensive. Quite simply, a man's finances did not allow him excessive access to too many prostitutes, thus once again limiting his access to extramartial sex. As ever, upper-class males had greater access to sex for pay, and wild orgies were a popular motif on the elite bowls and cups used for the all-male drinking parties called *symposia* (see later in this chapter).

In the end, though, the family was the core of any Greek society, and it was desirable for that core to be stable. Such stability came from genuine affection between husband and wife, an affection that over-road all other sexual imbalances. The ideal example of this is that greatest of ancient Greek love stories, the *Odyssey*. In spite of her husband's 20-year absence, Penelopê remained faithful to Odysseus not only out of a desperate love of her husband, but as well to preserve the kingship for their only son Telemakhos. For his part, Odysseus did have sexual relations with other females, including two goddesses, during his absence from Ithaka. The ancient Greek notion seems to be that "if you can't be with the one you love, love the one you're with, provided you are male." But it is clear that Odysseus very much loved Penelopê, even giving up eternal life with the goddess Kalypso to be with her. Not only did this increase Odysseus's fame, it also stabilized the royal household and thus the island of Ithaka itself. A stable household leads to a stable society.

Heterosexual sex had its limitations in ancient Greece, and heterosexual love was not too far behind. Of course, people are people, and the ancient Greeks seldom tired of complaining that Aphrodite, the goddess of love and sex, conquered anyone and anything she felt like. Unrequited love ran rampant through ancient Greece just like it does everyplace else, and was a common subject for lyric poetry especially. In one of her poems, Sappho complains:

It's no use, Mother dear,
I can't finish my weaving.
You may blame Aphrodite, soft as she is;
She has almost killed me with love for that boy! (trans. Barnard 1958, #12)

(I have the strong impression the speaker was told to get her butt back into gear and finish her weaving in spite of her debilitating heartbreak.)

The schoolgirl crush was balanced at the other end of the spectrum by the heartache felt by the older gentleman who discovers that youth goes to youth and that the young ladies seem to prefer the other young ladies to him. So griped the archaic poet Anakreon of Teos (fr. 358):

Eros, the blond god of lovers,
Strikes me with a purple ball
And asks me to play with a girl
Wearing colorful sandals;
But the girl is from beautiful
Lesbos, and scorns my white hair,
And turning her back runs gaping
After another (girl). (trans. Barnstone 1988, #123)

A couple points are worthy of note here. Just because the girl was from the island of Lesbos did not mean that she was a lesbian in the modern sense of the word. If she's going after another girl, it's because the other girl was the best option around, especially in comparison to the white-haired old guy.

Second, as Claude Calame, a well-known classicist, once pointed out, certain types of love are appropriate to certain genres of literature. Epic literature is notable for its reciprocating love stories, such as between Odysseus and Penelopê, or even Akhilleus and Briseis. By contrast, lyric poetry is famous for its lovelorn pathos, and thus the longings expressed here are at least in part dictated by the nature of the song itself. To give a modern parallel: You are far more likely to lose your wife, your dog, and your truck in country-western music than you are in rap (although this may change in the future).

Sex Apart from Love: The Symposion

The artistic evidence from the symposia mentioned above provides an interesting insight into the sexual fantasies of Greek, and especially Athenian, men. The symposion, literally "drinking together," was a gathering of males in the designated men's room of the house to drink and entertain each other. Entertainment ranged from philosophical discussions through singing and playing musical instruments to all-out sexual orgies with the slave boy wine pourers and prostitutes provided by the symposion's host. These orgies typically decorated the pottery associated with the party, and thus we get a glimpse of what Greek men thought it was really like to cut loose. Archaic

Figure 2.3
Attic black-figure orgy scene. Antikensammlung, Staatliche Museen Berlin, 3521.
(Drawing by Paul C. Butler)

and Classical vases from Athens show scenes of a room full of males having group sex with several naked females. In some cases, the men patiently wait their turn; in others, the females have sex with two men at once (see Figure 2.3). This sex could be vaginal, anal, and/or oral. Fellatio appears frequently in such scenes; to date, there is only one known portrayal of cunnilingus (see Figure 2.4). Apparently in such scenarios, female pleasure was not a concern.

It is not entirely clear, based on the data at hand, that men would know what that would consist of anyway. Another common motif on the symposion ware was women with dildos, inserting them both vaginally and orally. The only known representation of clitoral stimulation apart from the unique cunnilingus representation comes from a homoerotic scene between women (see later discussion). This plus the verse from Sappho about defloration mentioned previously give the impression that ancient Greek male sexuality was exclusively phallic and occasionally rather brutal. This is not to suggest that men could not be tender with loved ones. It merely emphasizes the extent to which males had the opportunity to indulge in purely physical, nonreproductive, nonemotional, wholly one-sided sex, and the extent to which this was accepted and even lauded in contemporary society. There is no female equivalent.

In contrast to the, shall we say, rugged quality of heterosexual orgy scenes, homosexual liaisons were never depicted so violently. Males did have sex with other males in these contexts, typically with an age difference manifest by facial hair. No male ever appears to be getting raped by one or more other

Figure 2.4
Attic red-figure kylix with scene of orgy and cunnilingus. Attributed to the Thalia
Painter, ca. 510 BCE. Antikensammlung, Staatliche Museen zu Berlin, 3521.
(Drawing by Paul C. Butler)

males, nor are males cast in a variety of apparently degrading poses. The only
known exception to this is a vase painting showing a Persian soldier about to
be raped by a Greek; clearly there were still some bitter feeling about the Persian
invasions (see Chapter 5). Otherwise, when really wild sex between males was
depicted, mythical satyrs (oversexed devotes of Dionysos) were used instead of
mortal males. In addition to the scenes of copulation, courting scenes between
males appeared, showing an older male offering a rooster or hare to a boy, often
while pointing to the boy's genitals to make his intentions perfectly clear (see
later in this chapter). The kind of violent sexual abandon that could be shown
of males penetrating females did not extend to males penetrating other males,
even in the context of mythical heroes and deities. Ancient Greek men were
evidently quite uncomfortable with even the notion of male sexual subjugation.

"Homosexuality"

For all intents and purposes, heterosexual love was very much a family
affair, with predictable and small-scale exceptions here and there. Homosexual love and sex was a completely different matter.

The ancient Greeks are famous for their homosexuality. The terms "lesbian," "Sapphic," and even "homoerotic" derive from Greek, as do, with greater cultural baggage, the words "paedophile" and "pederast." Years ago when I was in graduate school, there was some turmoil about gay bashing in the local fraternities, which sparked a chalk-writing campaign of the phrase "Homosexuality: a Greek institution!"

Unfortunately, some 2,000+ years of cultural filters make it difficult in modern times to understand how the ancient Greeks experienced their homoerotic relationships, especially because they are so different from our own. The ancient Greeks could no more fathom marrying a person of the same sex than we could of being required to marry. Some of the ongoing questions are: Did their homosexual relationships express a kind of dom.-sub. relationship, where the penetrator achieved some kind of dominance over the penetratee? Were they a rite of passage, whereby an older generation brought the younger generation into political maturity? Were the relationships between differently aged or classed partners, or were they between peers? Did homosexuality change over time through history? Did the artistic expression of desire reflect an actual union, or even an actual desire, or were these merely social conventions? That is to say, were there traditions in a social group that made the expression of homosexual desire expected, even necessary, like in modern times adolescent males (and probably a lot of females) are expected to express lustful feelings for Angelina Jolie, even if they are gay or simply not interested in busty, maternal women?

Considering the kinds of questions that exist, we can at best take a surface survey of the evidence for homosexual relationships and see what can be gleaned from the data.

Females

There is annoyingly little evidence for erotic relationships between females, as, once again, so much of our evidence derives from males, and this was a topic that they seldom broached. Also remember the evidence from the symposion ware that showed single females engaged with one or more dildos, suggesting that the male understanding of female sexuality was primarily concerned with penetration. There are three main categories of evidence about ancient lesbianism. The first are the occasional scraps of information presented by male writers, typically philosophers. Thus in his *Laws*, Plato observes that (636c):

> And whether one consider these things playfully or seriously, it must be noted that for females and males to come together for procreation is according to nature, but men with men, or women with women is contrary to nature, and this audacity of the first was through their utter weakness to pleasure.

By contrast, in the *Symposium*, his dialogue about sexuality, Plato places a fascinating "hypothesis" about the origins of human love into the mouth of Aristophanes, the comic playwright (and thus the whole hypothesis might be taken as just a tad tongue-in-cheek). According to the comic (§191), all humans were once double, with two heads, two pairs of arms and legs, and two sets of genitals. Having become too mighty, the gods punished humanity by splitting us in two, and now we all singly seek out our literal other half. Some of these doubled pairs were wholly male, and thus men seek their male other halves. Likewise for paired females, who seek out their *hetairistriai*, their female companions. Nothing good, of course, came from those freaks who were part male–part female, always seeking heterosexual unions.

An alternate approach was taken by the Roman-period moralist and biographer Plutarch in his biography of the Spartan reformer Lykourgos (18.4). Here Plutarch discusses the Spartan practice of pairing younger boys with older lovers so as to teach them manliness. The tradition was so well incorporated into the society that, like the males, Spartan girls took noble women as lovers. Opinions clearly varied considerably among men on the topic of female homosexuality.

The modicum of evidence we have on the subject that comes from the female voice is more consistent: female-female eroticism was a good thing. So much appears primarily in the lyrics of Sappho, the Archaic poetess who inadvertently gave rise to the term "Lesbian." (It's worth noting that in ancient Greece, Lesbian women, that is, women from the Island of Lesbos, were famous for two things: being exceptionally beautiful and being particularly adept at fellatio. Amusingly, Lesbians were not known to be lesbians.) We have already seen some of Sappho's lyrics concerning female homoeroticism, especially in contrast to the anguish involved in leaving said relationships to marry. This is certainly not to say that homoerotic relationships were without their grievances even in the absence of men, especially in lyric! The one complete poem we have from Sappho is about the grief the poetess as named feels when her love is rejected by (yet another) young female:

Ornate-throned, immortal Aphrodite
child of Zeus, wile-weaving, I beseech you,
do not with ache and anguish overwhelm,
Mistress, my heart.
But come here, if ever before
hearing my prayers from afar,
listening, leaving your father's house
of gold, you came.
On a yoked chariot, beautiful swift sparrows brought you
on fluttering wings to the dark earth from heaven
through the middle air.
Quickly you came. And you, O blessed one,

smiling on your immortal face,
asked on what account I am suffering again, and
on what account was I summoning again,
and what did I want most in my raving heart to happen.
"Whom do I persuade now,
to lead you back to her dearest love?
Who, O Sappho, wrongs you?
For if she flees, soon will she follow;
and if she does not receive gifts, then she will give.
And if she does not love, soon she will love even if she does not wish it."
Come to me now, release me from this grievous care!
What my heart desires to come to pass, make happen.
and you yourself be my ally.

Although some scholars have suggested that Aphrodite plans to seize emotional control of the young lady and compel her to return Sappho's love, this is not actually the case. As classicists Anne Carson and Ellen Greene have observed, there is no reason to assume that Sappho will be the object of the girl's affections. Instead, we might simply understand that just as Sappho suffers from unrequited love now, so too will the girl, in her own time, with some other unresponsive female. That's simply how love works. Nevertheless, the homoerotic relationships described by Sappho appear to be sensual and both emotionally and physically fulfilling.

The final source of information about female homoerotic relationships comes from the vase paintings, thus placing certain limitations on the evidence. First, they come almost exclusively from Athens. Second, to the best we can tell the vast majority, if not all of them, were painted by males. Finally, we do not always know what, exactly, we are looking at. For example, is a hug a sign of affection or a sign of eroticism? When a bride appears surrounded by *erotes* (little love gods) and her wedding party, are we to understand this as a homoerotic scene, or are brides simply understood to be inherently erotic? Are naked women shown together sexually involved, or are they prostitutes, there to titillate a male audience? Do the same poses and scenarios that we understand to express male homosexuality apply to females?

There are many pottery forms that we know were mainly used by women, such as the jewelry box (*pyxis*) and the wedding-bath jar (*lebes gamikos*). Such items, made for a female viewership, often show young women in all-female groups, occasionally accompanied by Aphrodite and/or Eros and/or erotes. As Nancy Sorkin Rabinowitz has argued, it is possible that such scenes might have meant different things to different viewers. (Rabinowitz 2002, *passim*) Men may have assumed a natural, low-key sexuality in such scenes—the bride and her female attendants preparing for a girl's wedding and first night of reproductive sex. By contrast, female viewers may have seen a scene of female homoeroticism, the erotic desire that played through a room of nubile girls on the threshold of adulthood who had not quite yet exchanged their homoso-cial/erotic tendencies for the world of heterosexuality. In other words, the men may not have realized that they were pointedly excluded from the sexual-ity of the scene.

More common are those scenes of female homoeroticism presented on objects primarily used by men, especially drinking cups (used in the sympo-sia). Even in these scenes, though, the possible eroticism expressed between the females is far, far less overt than the heterosexual orgies mentioned earlier and again later in this chapter. That an erotic encounter is taking place at all may only be hinted at by a female grabbing another by the wrist in the same manner as bridegrooms grasp their new brides (see Figures 2.5 and 2.6)—or, possibly, by the way one female gestures at another female's clothed and covered genitalia, in somewhat similar fashion to the same gesture made by older men to boys in the pederasty scenes (as discussed later). In similar fash-ion, in some paintings coming from places other than Athens, we see

Figure 2.5
Attic red-figure pyxis with wedding scene. Attributed to the Wedding Painter, ca. 470–460 BCE. Louvre L 55. (Drawing by Paul C. Butler)

Figure 2.6
Attic red-figure kylix with a pair of adolescent girls. Attributed to the Painter of Bologna, ca. 460 BCE. Metropolitan Museum of Art Rogers Fund, 1906, 06.1021.167. (Drawing by Paul C. Butler)

depictions of two women sharing a mantle, taken as an erotic encounter when shown with two males. Even the comparatively blatantly sexual scenes are tame: nude females (prostitutes?) drink and/or play the flute in scenes identical to the males' symposia. No overt sex is happening, merely a strong sense of female eroticism. The closest we ever come to what sort of looks like a lesbian encounter is on a red-figure cup from Tarquinia (see Figure 2.7). Here we see two nude females, one standing and holding a vase, the other sitting at the feet of the first and touching her genitals. Interpretations range from digital stimulation to delousing . . .

What all the data have in common is that female homosexuality is subtle and nonviolent, be it in poetry or in that bastion of typically violent orgy

Figure 2.7
Red-figure cup with two women, from Tarquinia,
Italy. (Drawing by Paul C. Butler)

imagery, symposion ware. Furthermore, with few exceptions (Plutarch, possibly Sappho), lesbian encounters occurred between peers—females of the
same age and apparent social class. What is at issue is mutuality and, presumably, intimacy.

Males

Male homoerotic relations have been under intense scrutiny for the past
few decades, so it is no wonder there is considerable debate regarding the
nature of male-male sexual relations. Perhaps the most popular understanding
of ancient Greek male homosexuality is that Greek men liked to have sex
with boys, literally pederasty (*pais/paidos* = "boy" and *erastes* = "lover") (keeping in mind that a "boy" here is actually a teenager; see later discussion). As
we shall see, there is sufficient evidence to suggest that this was the case in
many parts of ancient Greece. However, the debate hovers around whether
such relationships existed throughout the various Greek communities or if
they pertained exclusively to upper-class society. In other words, did all Greek
males experience homosexual relationships at some point in their lives, or did
such relationships exist only among the rich? A secondary issue pertains to
age. Although we have considerable evidence for pederastic relationships
(between males of different ages), to what extent did Greek men engage in
homosexual relationships with men of their own age? For the following

discussion, then, it may be best to understand that our evidence pertains to the upper echelons of Greek society, those peoples who had enough money to record their lives for posterity. We shall consider matters of class and age after.

There can be no doubt that what we would term male homosexuality was practiced openly in ancient Greece. The standard form of such relationships, the form for which we have the most copious evidence, was a (semi)erotic relationship between an older man (over about 25 years of age) and an adolescent, ideally around 16 years old, just before he gets hairy on cheeks and testicles. The ideal milieu for such relationships was typically the gymnasium, where men and boys would strip naked to flaunt their athletic prowess. The gymnasium of Athens had an altar to Eros located at its entrance, and the laws of the city forbade slaves to use the facilities and thus to connect with freeborn boys. In Thebes, Aristotle records that lovers swore their oaths of loyalty to each other at a gymnasium named after Iolaus, the helpful young *eromenos* of the hero Herakles (Calame 1999, 102–103).

In its ideal form, the pederastic relationship was understood to be educational, as the older male (the *erastes*, or lover) coached the younger male (*eromenos*, or beloved) in virtue and the qualities of a good citizen. Or as it was designated in Sparta, the *eispnelas* ("inspirer") educated the *aïtas* ("listener"). This is *not* to say, however, that the relationship lacked a physical element. While the *erastes* was teaching the *eromenos* to be a good person, he was also lusting after his physical attributes, and the relationship would eventually be consummated either anally or intercrurally (between the thighs).

The full gambit of the pederastic relationship is expressed succinctly by a fourth-century historian named Ephoros who wrote about the customs of the Dorians (Greeks living in the Peloponnese and Crete, see Chapter 5). According to him, in Crete it was customary for an older erastes/eispnelas to take a fancy to a younger eromenos/aïtas. The erastes would inform the eromenos' family of his intentions; if they approved, he would "kidnap" the object of his affections. The erastes then took the boy out to the country for two months along with other male companions, where they camped and slept together, while the older man educated the younger. At the end of the two months, the lover returned the beloved with many fine gifts, including clothing and weapons. Such a coming-of-age ritual was deemed most prestigious for the boy.

Such relationships always occurred openly with the knowledge of the potential eromenos' father (and possibly mother). Relationships were won by persuasion, never compulsion. Thus Theognis, a sixth-century poet from Megara wrote (Bk II: 1235–1238):

> O boy, you who have mastered my mind, listen!
> I'll tell a story neither unpersuasive nor unpleasing to your heart.
> But dare to consider the tale with your mind; it is not necessary
> To do what goes contrary to your heart.

Rape was never an aspect of ancient Greek pederasty, and the well-being of the younger partner was always of very much concern.

Almost by contrast, pederastic desire was seen to be particularly grievous to the potential erastes, who might experience great, even painful longing for the object of his affections. The emotional state of the erastes was often likened to a kind of semi-voluntary slavery, one of the few instances when free Greek citizens were willing to admit that they were totally whipped. Plato's character Kritoboulos claims it would be "sweeter" to be a slave than free, if only Kleinias would be his master (*Symp.* 4.14). Poetry is filled with testaments to such dominating anguish of the heart. Quoting Theognis again we read (Bk II: 1319–1322):

> O boy, since to you the goddess Kypris has given desirable grace,
> Your face is a concern for all the young men.
> Listen to my words and set grace in my heart,
> Knowing that love is so hard for a man to bear.

Likewise Anakreon of Teos, the same fellow who kvetched that young girls preferred each other to him with his white hair, complained:

> O sweet boy like a girl,
> I see you though you will not look my way.
> You are unaware that you handle the reins of my soul (trans. Barnstone
>   1988, #125)

And the fifth-century Boeotian poet Pindar once praised the object of his affections thusly (fr. 123):

> It is necessary at the right moment to cull loves, my heart, in the flower of
>   youth.
> But once seeing the sparkling splendor of Theoxenos' eyes,
> One who does not swell with desire, from adamant
> Iron was his black heart wrought,
> With a cold flame! Being dishonored before quick-glancing Aphrodite,
> Either he suffers violently for money, or by feminine courage
> He follows a wholly chill path—slavishly.
> But I, for her sake, like the wax of holy bees burned by the sun
> Melt when I see
> The young limbs of young lads in youth.
> And in Tenedos Persuasion and Grace
> Dwell in the son of Hagesilaos.

Of course, it is unlikely that all such relationships were so painful, remembering that lyric poetry tends to focus on the trials of love to begin with.

In spite of the potential anguish on the part of would-be lovers, the upper classes at least believed such relationships to be a good thing, ideally instilling virtue in lover and beloved if carried out appropriately. In Sparta, as recorded in Plutarch's *Life of Lykourgos* (17.1), 12-year-old boys were put into the company of potential eispnelai from the company of well-favored young men, just as older men scrutinized them at their exercises so as to serve as surrogate fathers and tutors for the future Spartiates. The idea seems to be that older male members of society engage with the boys to inculcate and improve them. Likewise, in his treatise on love, the *Symposion*, Plato argues through the character of Pausanias that (178c–d):

> I cannot say that anything is really better for one being young than a helpful lover, and for a lover a boyfriend. For love is necessary for people, to lead them throughout life so that they care to live well; neither family implants this well, nor honors, nor wealth, nor anything so much as love.

In addition to the moral-building qualities of same-sex love, there was also sex itself. Although the ideal was for the potential eromenos to play "hard to get," eventually he gave in and put out. Another character of Plato's *Symposion* put this most eloquently (184c–e):

> It is necessary to compare these two standards—one dealing with the love of boys, the other philosophy and other such virtue, if we might agree that it is a good thing for the boyfriend to gratify the lover. For whenever the lover and boyfriend aim for the same goal, each maintaining propriety—the lover aiding the pleasing boyfriend in whatever way proper; the boyfriend justly aiding him who makes him good and wise—then the lover having been able to contribute some of his store of knowledge to the boyfriend's erudition, and the boyfriend needing to acquire wisdom for his education, then, indeed, when these two come together it is proper and customary. ONLY then is the boyfriend right to gratify the lover, never otherwise.

Sometimes lovers put it far less eloquently. A sixth-century man named Krimon from the island of Santorini (ancient Thera) left two rock inscriptions for posterity (IG XII^3: 537–538):

> "In this place Krimon humped the boy whose brother is Bathykleos."
> "In this place Krimon humped Amotion"

The word I translate here as "humped" (*oiphô*) refers to mounting when used of animals, anal intercourse when applied to two men. Virtue was apparently not so much on Krimon's mind here, or, for that matter, being indoors.

Subtlety was seldom a matter of concern in these paederastic relationships, notable especially in some of the means of courting one's hopeful beloved. A bit like Krimon above, potential (or possibly successful) erastai could advertise their love, as opposed to their conquests, by inscriptions, be they on rock or on pottery. Thus once again on Thera we find many fourth-century rock-cut inscriptions claiming that, "Aetes is handsome, fair-faced, sweet, and graceful"; "Aetes is starry-faced"; "Herophon is sweet"; "Herophon is golden"; "Muiskos is graceful and handsome." (Garlan and Masson 1982, 6–12) In Nemea we read that both Epikrates and Akrotatos are "*kalos*" (handsome), with similar inscriptions coming from Athens.

Exclusive to Athens are similar attestations painted on pottery, called, logically enough, kalos-inscriptions. For about 50 years in the mid-fifth century, Athenian vase painters included on some of their wares graffiti claiming that some such individual is handsome. Leagros was kalos, as was Glaukytes and Agasikrates. In some instances, the graffito merely reads "the handsome boy" (*ho pais kalos*), apparently allowing whoever was making use of the item to supply ideologically his own potential beloved. Although in some instances the inscription may refer to one of the boys painted on the object, this was not always the case; attestations of admiration could appear almost randomly.

The Athenian vase paintings, along with our inscriptions from Krimon the Stud earlier, give us some of our best evidence concerning the consummation of a pederastic relationship, when, as Pausanias argued earlier, it was right for the boy to "give in." As we learn though the paintings, there were regular aspects of courtship on the path to sexual fulfillment. Most important was the offering of gifts such as hares or roosters to the eromenos. In some

Figure 2.8
Attic red-figure kylix (tondo) with pederastic
courtship scene. Ashmolean Museum, Oxford.
(Drawing by Paul C. Butler)

examples, the offering of the gift might be accompanied by a very blatant gesture, such as the erastes pointing to the eromenos's crotch (see Figure 2.8).
Later the eromenos might reach out to touch his lover's chin, and the two
may even share a cloak in a gesture of intimacy (as we saw above for women
as well). Some paintings show the boy reaching up to kiss his lover. A few
paintings go so far as to show intercrural sex, with a bearded man placing his
erect penis between the thighs of a young man. The eromenos in these scenes
seldom appears to be enjoying the encounter himself (showing neither smile
nor erection), suggesting that it was perhaps deemed inappropriate for males
to enjoy being "bottom." Anal sex, if it did occur in pederastic relationships,
was not shown in the paintings.

This is not to say that it did not appear at all. A very few Athenian vase
paintings show males having anal intercourse. However, in these few instances,
there is no apparent age difference between the males involved. As such, it
appears that what we have here is not a pederastic relationship, but either a simple homosexual relationship between two similarly aged men or an initially pederastic relationship that continued into the adult lives of the participants.

This iconography provides some of the slight evidence we have for long-
term homosexual relationships in ancient Greece. Once again, as stated in
the beginning of this chapter, heterosexual reproduction was required of all
Greeks, and thus it was not really feasible to be exclusively homosexual. However, evidence shows that some men did maintain very long-term sexual relationships. Two protagonists from the previously mentioned *Symposion*—
Pausanias and Agathon—were long-term lovers, eventually, according to
Aelian's *Varia Historia*, moving to Macedon when they felt that their home
town of Athens was less than supportive of their relationship.

This fact in itself suggests that male homosexuality may not have been as
widely accepted in Athenian society as much of the previous data would lead
one to believe. Evidence from other media, such as comic plays and speeches
from legal disputes, suggest quite strongly that the nonelite members of
Athenian society may have scorned either homosexuality generally or pederasty specifically in the Classical period.

What is significant in these sources is that, unlike the lyric poems or expensive vase paintings, the texts pertaining to drama and court cases were
directed at the common man, not members of the upper classes. As such, it
is possible to get a glimpse at what happened when an author was trying to
get on the good side of ancient Athens' equivalent of Joe the Plumber. For
example, in his comedy called the *Wasps*, Aristophanes reminds the audience
that after winning a prize in drama (*Wasps* 1023–1028):

> Finding great favor and being honored as no one ever amongst you,
> They do not say that he ended up vain or with a swollen head,
> Nor attempting to carouse around the palaistra, nor if some lover
> Urged him to lampoon his hated boyfriend;

Never does he claim to have been persuaded by anyone.
He stayed respectable, keeping proper thoughts.

Several of Aristophanes's characters accuse each other of homosexual relations, typically using terminology related to being a "wide-ass" (*euryproktos*) or
a bugger (*lakatapugon*). Perhaps most significantly, his more sympathetic characters have difficulty in distinguishing between pederastic relationships and
prostitution, both, essentially, being sex in exchange for "gifts." (Although
I doubt many prostitutes were paid in chickens. Or virtue.) The common
masses, it would appear, did not appreciate the subtleties of erotic inculcation
and may have been actively hostile to a practice that distinguished the upper
classes from the low-born. In some ways, this may be compared to modern
times, when the educated and artistic are more likely to be "openly gay" than
blue-collar workers who evince active hostility to "faggots."

Nevertheless, at least some "commoners" were willing to participate in the
cult of youth exemplified by the pederastic relationship, even if they were
commoners very much involved with the city's elite. Here I am thinking specifically of Sokrates, who discusses pederastic relationships with no hint of dis-
approval in several of his philosophical dialogues as preserved by his student
Plato. The sidebar about *Kharmides* offers a snippet of a dialogue showing
the philosopher utterly smitten by one of the most eligible *eromenoi* in town.
(See also the sidebar in Chapter 4, *Lysis*.)

Kharmides (153d–155e)

*When we had enough of these, then again I was questioning those there about phi-
losophy—how was it now, and about the young men, if any among them stood
out in terms of wisdom or beauty or both. And Kritias, casting his eyes at the door,
saw some young men entering and playing around with each other and following
behind the throng:*

Kritias:	Concerning the pretty boys, Sokrates, I think you'll soon see for yourself. For those who happen to be entering now are the entourage and lovers of the most handsome fellow around these days, and it seems that even he is coming and will soon be here.
Sokrates:	Who is he, and who is his father?
Kritias:	You know him, I think, but he was not yet a young man before you left—Kharmides, son of Glaukos my uncle, so he is my cousin.
Sokrates:	By Zeus, I do know him! For he was not so paltry nor yet still a child, and now I think he must be indeed quite a young man.
Kritias:	Soon you will see what kind of young man he has become.

And while he was saying these things Kharmides entered.

Sokrates: I can't judge one way or another, my friend, for I am as unskilled as a white line when it comes to handsome males—for pretty much all men in youth seem handsome to me. But really then this one appears amazing to me in shape and beauty, and all the others really seem to love him too, as I see it—they are so awestruck and discombobulated when he enters. And surely many other lovers follow behind. And what's amazing is that it's not just the men; as I look at the boys not one of them is looking at anything else, no matter how small, but everyone is gazing on him as on some sculpted work of art.

Then Khairephon called to me:

Khairephon: How does this young man strike you, Sokrates? Isn't he a looker?
Sokrates: Marvelous!
Khairephon: Really, if he wants to strip, you'll forget all about his face—he is that good looking.

Everyone agreed.

Sokrates: By Herakles, how you all say the fellow is irresistible! If yet there should happen to be in him one other small detail . . .
Kritias: What's that?
Sokrates: If he happens to have well cultivated his soul. I think it likely, Kritias, this one being a member of your family.
Kritias: He is utterly beautiful and good in this regard.
Sokrates: Why then shall we not undress this part of him and examine it before checking out his body? For he should be as happy to chat as any of those his age.
Kritias: Indeed, as he is both a philosopher and a poet, both as it seems to himself and to others as well.
Sokrates: My dear Kritias, this fine attribute started in your family with Solon. But why don't you introduce the young man to me, calling him here? For I think if he were even younger it would not be shameful for us to converse with him in front of you, you being his cousin and chaperone.
Kritias: You have a point. I'll call him

And he said to the attendant, "Child, call Kharmides, saying that I want him to meet a doctor about those weaknesses he was telling me that he was suffering."

Kritias: Just lately he's been suffering from headaches when he gets up in the morning, so why not pretend that you know something about what stops headaches, some cure for him?

Sokrates: I don't, but bring him here anyway.
Kritias: He'll come.

And indeed it was so. For he came, and occasioned much laughter—for each one of us sitting near him quickly yielded to his neighbor, so that he might sit next to him, until we stood up those sitting at the end and we cast down the flanks. But he came and sat down between me and Kritias. Then indeed I was at a loss, and my former confidence vanished—the idea that I could easily converse with him! And then, when Kritias was telling him that I was knowledgeable about cures, he looked at me with those eyes in such an innocent manner and was about to ask, and all those in the palaistra gathered around us in a tight circle, and then, O Noble Being, I saw inside his robe, and boy did I get hot! And I was no longer able to control myself, and I thought that Kydias was the wisest of men when it came to matters of sexuality, he who said, when counseling another about a handsome boy, to take care not to bring the fawn to the lion's house, having a portion of his flesh seized. For I seemed to myself to have been seized by some such savage passion. Nevertheless, when he asked if I knew a cure for his head, with great effort I replied that I did.

Self-Love: Masturbation

As mentioned briefly in Chapter 1, masturbation was a hallmark of the adolescent, one that should be curbed, according to Aristotle. Nevertheless, the ancient Greeks were humans, too, and autoerotic gratification was a hallmark of the adult as well. The two main words used for the act were *dephomai* (literally "to soften oneself") and, less commonly, *anaphlaô* ("to pound up"). As an ancient commentator on Aristophanes's *Frogs* once put it, "They said 'to *anaphlan*', to soften the privates—and to drag down the covering skin of the acorn; the 'acorn' is the tip of the penis" (Stafford 2011, 341). Both terms seem to be associated with males, and we have no textual references to the practice amongst females (but see later in this chapter). A rather explicit how-to is given in Aristophanes' *Knights* (ll. 24–29):

Nicias: Now shake as if you were masturbating, say first "way," then "runner," and then go on doing it faster and faster.
Demosthenes: Way, runner, way, run—away!
Nicias: There, isn't that sweet?
Demosthenes: By Zeus, yes! Except that I'm afraid for my skin that this is a bad omen.
Nicias: What do you mean?
Demosthenes: Masturbators lose their skin! (trans. Henderson, 1966; cited in Stafford 2011, 339)

Figure 2.9
Attic red-figure kylix (tondo) with masturbation scene, in the manner of the Euergides Painter, ca. 500 BCE. Brussels Cinquantenaire Museum R260. (Drawing by Paul C. Butler)

A few late sixth-century Athenian vases depict masturbation, pretty much inevitably on symposion ware. The most explicit depiction appears on the tondo of a red-figure cup dating to around 500 and inscribed with the word *prosagoreuô* ("I speak forth") (see Figure 2.9). Here is a young man (no beard) wearing a garland indicating that he is coming (no pun intended) from a symposion. He grips his erect penis, and white dots emanating from the tip make it clear what point exactly he has reached in his endeavor. The wine krater is nearby, so let's hope he aimed carefully.

A more interesting depiction appears on the tondo of the kylix mentioned earlier showing the only known portrayal of cunnilingus from ancient Greece. Here we see four individuals (see Figure 2.10). The young male to the left is masturbating while watching the other three. The other three consist of a

Figure 2.10
Red-figure kylix with scene of drinkers and
hetairai, Attic, d. 37.5 cm, sixth century BCE.
Thalia Painter (sixth-fifth century BCE). Antiken-
sammlung, Staatliche Museen, Berlin, Germany,
Inv. V.I. 3251. (Antikensammlung, Staatliche
Museen, Berlin, Germany/Art Resource, NY)

bearded man (in the middle of a horizontal threesome) being spanked by the
nude woman stretched out on top of him. Beneath these two is a reclining
woman who appears to be masturbating, to judge from the placement of her
fingers between her legs and her closed eyes.

CONCLUSIONS

The ancient Greeks were ultimately a bit ambivalent about love,
frequently expressed in an ambivalence about its goddess—Aphrodite.
On the one hand, we have the declaration from the seventh-century poet
Mimnermos who asked,

> What life, what joy, without golden Aphrodite?
> I should die when these things don't concern me:
> Secret love and honey-sweet gifts and the bed;
> Such are the alluring flowers of youth
> For men and women.

On Family and Sexual Relationships   *99*

By contrast, Sappho expresses the physical pain caused merely by the sight of one's beloved:

> He seems to me equal to the gods,
> whoever sits beside you and listens
> to you talking sweetly
> and laughing desirably,
>
> which makes the heart in my chest fly;
> for whenever I look upon you for an instant
> I can no longer find a single word,
>
> but my tongue is broken, and instantly
> delicate fire runs beneath my skin,
> and I see nothing with my eyes, my
> hearing pounds,
>
> a cold sweat covers me, trembling
> grabs all of me, I am paler than dry grass,
> and I think that I am little short
> of dying.

The ancient Greeks both enjoyed and suffered from love, much as in modern times. The primary difference between then and now was the range of potential love objects available amongst the Greeks.

3

Peri Philias: On Friendship

HUMANS AND HUMANS

Like most people everywhere, the ancient Greeks spent a lot of time dealing with people who were not family members. There is a tendency in some older scholarship to suggest that this was really true only for men—that men had numerous relationships outside of the home, whereas women, ideally, spent all of their time in the house surrounded by family members exclusively (keeping in mind that the household slaves were considered to be a part of this extended family—the *oikia*). In reality both males and females had friends and enemies outside the confines of the home, and there were important social rules for dealing with "outsiders," be that defined as people not part of the *oikia* or people not part of the polis. Two of the most important ideologies in this regard were the notion of *xenia* and the policy of helping one's friends and harming one's enemies.

Xenia

The closest definition we have to this all-pervasive ancient Greek concept is guest-friendship. Xenia was a bond formed between two strangers, one of whom was originally in the position of guest, the other in the position of host. The guest, generally understood as a traveler, would seek out the hospitality of the host. The host, by the unwritten laws of xenia, was obliged to shelter, feed, clothe, and protect the guest. When possible, an exchange of gifts sealed the friendship. Once the xenia bond was formed, the two partners were friends for life, being able to call upon each other for help and forever refraining from harming each other in any way. Furthermore, the bonds of xenia were so strong that the relationship was passed down through generations. The great-grandson of the guest was still an ally, if you will, of the great-grandson of the host, and vice versa.

The earliest description we have of the formation and endurance of the xenia bond appears in Book Six of the *Iliad*. Here, the Greek hero Diomedes confronted the Trojan ally Glaukos, each going into extreme detail about their identities and families (guns really have changed warfare). As soon as Diomedes heard of Glaukos's lineage, he replied (215–232):

> "See now, you are my xenos from the days of our fathers.
> For godly Oineus once received noble Bellerophontes
> In our halls, keeping him for 20 days.
> They offered each other fine friendship gifts:
> Oineus gave a shining purple belt,
> And Bellerophontes a two-handled golden cup
> Which I left in my house, coming here.
> . . . . .
> So now I am your dear friend in the midst of Argos,
> And you in Lykia, when I should come to that land.
> Let us avoid each other's spears even in the throng.
> There are plenty of Trojans and allies in battle for me to kill,
> Whomever the god sends me, or I run down with my fleet feet,
> And many Akhaians for you to slaughter, if you can.
> Let us exchange armor with each other, so that others
> Might know that we swear to be friends from the days of our fathers."

So in the midst of battle, two warriors on opposing sides would not fight each other because of the xenia bond formed by their grandparents. Such a practice was not reserved merely for epic; even in the fifth century, xenia relationships were deemed stronger than political ties. At the outbreak of the Peloponnesian War in 431 BCE, the Athenian statesman Perikles advised the entire population of Attika (the region for which Athens was the "capitol city") to abandon their homes and farms to move into the secure space of the walled city of Athens. Their property, would be destroyed, but not their lives. There was only one glitch with this plan (at least until the plague broke out): Perikles's land was safe, as Perikles was the xenos (guest-friend) of the Spartan king and war leader Arkhidamas. This led to a complication, since it made Perikles look like a hypocrite, asking others to sacrifice their homes while secure in the knowledge that his own was safe (Thucydides 2.13.1):

> While the Peloponnesians were still gathering both at the isthmus and on the road before entering into Attika, Perikles, son of Xanthippos, being the tenth general of the Athenians, knew the invasion was coming and suspected that Arkhidamas—who happened to be a xenos of his—might perhaps spare his personal lands and not ravage them, either personally wishing to do him a favor, or having been ordered by the Lakedaimonians to bring slander upon him, just as he had publically demanded the expulsion of the cursed ones because of him. Speaking to the Athenians in the Assembly, he told them that Arkhidamas was a xenos of his, but that this should not be a problem for the city. Furthermore, should the enemy not ravage his lands and household properties just as they did to the others, Perikles would give them over to be public property so that no one should suspect him on their account.

Xenia relationships were not reserved exclusively for the upper classes. When Odysseus returned to Ithaka disguised as an itinerant beggar, his own swineherd Eumaios (who did not recognize him), gave him a warm welcome (*Odyssey* 14, 50ff,):

> "But follow me; let's go to the hut, old man, so that you,
> having sated yourself with bread and wine to your heart's content,
> might say where you come from and how much you have suffered."
> Thus spoke the godly swineherd heading to the hut. . .
> . . . .
> . . . And Odysseus was glad
> That he was thus received, and he spoke a word and called him by name,
> "May Zeus and the other immortal gods grant you, xenos,
> What you most desire, because you received me so graciously."
> And you, Eumaios Swineherd, answered him saying,
> "Xenos, it is not right, even if someone worse than you came,
> To dishonor a xenos—for all xenoi come from Zeus,
> And beggars too. And our gifts, though small, are dear."

Disregarding such relationships was very much frowned upon throughout ancient Greek history. As noted by Eumaios, all strangers and beggars (potential xenoi) come from Zeus, and abusing them in any way would be punished. The entire city of Troy was demolished when its prince Paris eloped with the wife of his xenos Menelaos. In fifth-century Athens, mistreatment of xenoi could be used against one during lawsuits, as the orator (the ancient Greek equivalent of a lawyer) Aiskhines did of his contending orator Demosthenes. In his speech *Against Ktesiphon*, wherein Aiskhines accused Ktesiphon of proposing a law contrary to the laws of Athens, Aiskhines attacked Ktesiphon's lawyer by reminding him in front of the Athenian jury (Aiskh. 3.224):

> And this same man you *twice* tortured with your own hand—whom you wrote up to punish *with death*; with this same man you lodged in Oreus, and you ate from the same table, and drank, and poured libations, and you gave your right hand to him as friend and xenos. Him you killed. And concerning these things you were called out, by me, amongst all the Athenians, and you were called a xenos-killer. You did not deny the impiety, but gave such an answer that the demos and as many xenoi standing about the Assembly cried out—for you said that the salts of the city were worth more than the table of a xenos!

Yes, in an Athenian court of law, in front of hundreds of Athenian citizens there to protect the interests of Athens, a man was condemned for valuing the city above a xenia relationship. This was simply not acceptable.

Xenia relationships were certainly more prevalent amongst the upper classes, simply because they had more opportunities to travel and thus come across strangers. Nevertheless, all classes in ancient Greece, even slaves, had opportunities to travel, especially for religious reasons such as festivals, games, and initiations (see Chapter 7). It was socially mandatory that all such strangers be well received and aided in their travels.

Friends and Enemies

If the importance of xenia was a constant in ancient Greece, so too was the value of friendship. There is some debate in the modern scholarship about how the Greeks understood friendship. For some scholars, friends were people you liked and with whom you maintained some sort of relationship. For others, friends were those people who could help you in times of need and who could, of course, count on you in their own duress. This latter view seems to suggest that there was no actual affection involved in ancient Greek friendships, merely a kind of self-serving practicality. In truth, the former view is more likely, without utterly discounting the latter practical aspect. As the philosopher-historian Xenophon described it (*Hiero.* 3,2):

> For he who is really loved by friends, joyfully do they see him, and joyfully help him, and they miss him if he goes away somewhere, and most joyfully do they receive him back on his return, and they rejoice together in his good times, and suffer with him if they should see him failing.

The same author also noted that "For humans have friendly aspects by nature; for they need each other and pity each other and working together help each other and, knowing this, are grateful to each other" (*Mem,* 2.6.21). An especially detailed description of the selfless, aesthetic pleasures of friendship comes later in Xenophon's narration, wherein he relates how the philosopher Sokrates would serve as an "intermediary" in helping a young man named Kritoboulos make friends (*Mem,* 2.6.35):

> If you might grant me even further to say about you, that you are concerned for your friends and that you enjoy nothing at all as much as good friends, and you exalt in the successes of friends not less than your own, and you enjoy the good things of your friends not less than your own. And, in such a way, these things be known, you do not stop contriving for your friends, and that you know the virtue of a man to be at its zenith in helping friends and harming enemies. I totally believe myself to be useful for you in the quest for good friends.

The idea that friendship had a practical (even exploitative) aspect derives from the fact that the Greeks saw reciprocity as an important component of friendship. This certainly does not mean that affection was not involved, but rather that the process of making friends entailed much of the "Do Unto Others" philosophy. As early as the eighth century, the practical poet Hesiod, in his poem *Works and Days*, which gives instructions for daily living, advised his brother Perses (*W&D*, 342–360):

Call your friend to a feast—leave your enemy.
It is best to call him who lives close to you,
For if something untoward happens in the area
Neighbors go ungirt; kinsmen girt.
A bad neighbor is hell, as much as a good one is a great blessing.
He has gotten a good share who has gotten a good neighbor.
An ox would not die, except for a bad neighbor.
It is good to receive from a neighbor, and good to give back
To him fairly, and then some, if you are able,
So that later, being in need, you might find him flush.
Don't make bad profit! Bad gains equal ruin.
Love the friend, and visit him who visits,
And give to him who gives, and don't give to him who doesn't.
One gives to the giver; no one gives to the non-giver.
Give is good; Take is bad—a giver of death.
For the man who willingly gives, even something big,
Rejoices at the gift, and cheers in his heart.
But he who, drawn to shamelessness, takes something himself,
Even a small thing, his own heart freezes solid.

A similar notion is spelled out in a friendly chat between Sokrates and a young man named Khairekrates, as recorded by Xenophon in his *Memorabilia* (2.3.11–13):

Sokrates:	Tell me, if you should want to prevail upon one of your associates to invite you to dinner when he is sacrificing, what would you do?
Khairekrates:	It is obvious that I myself should begin, when I sacrifice, by inviting him.
Sokrates:	And if you should want to persuade some one of your friends, whenever you leave home, to care for your things—what would you do?
Khairekrates:	Clearly, first I would put my hand to caring for his things when he is away.
Sokrates:	And if you should wish to have a xenos receive you, when you came to his city—What would you do?
Khairekrates:	Clearly I should first receive him when he came to Athens. And if I should wish him to be eager to accomplish for me the things that brought me—obviously it would be necessary for me first to do the same for him.

Even the deities held the reciprocity of kindnesses between fellow deities in high regard. One of the most touching scenes in ancient Greek literature (in my opinion, anyway) is the reception of Thetis in the forge of Hephaistos, when the goddess came to ask the god for new armor for her son Akhilleus. Hephaistos cannot do enough for the goddess, recalling (*Iliad* 18.394ff):

Well truly now a goddess awesome and revered to me is here,
Who saved me, when pain took me, one falling far
By the wish of my dog-faced mother, who wanted
To hide me, being angry. Then I would have suffered pains at heart
Had not Eurynomê and Thetis received me to their bosom,
Eurynomê daughter of back-flowing Ocean.
With them for nine years I wrought cunning metal crafts—
Bent and round brooches, and earring and necklaces
In the hollow cave. And around flowed the current of Ocean,
Vast, murmering with foam. No one else
Knew, neither of gods nor of mortal men.
But Thetis and Eurynomê knew, who saved me.
And now she has come to my house. And I must pay
To fair-tressed Thetis in full the life-debt I owe her.
But you now set before her a fine entertainment
While I put aside the bellows and all my tools.

Historians and orators both Greek and Roman preserved tales of selfless, loving friendship, partially as a record of what was admirable in humanity and also as lessons to be followed (called *exempla*, literally *examples* of good and bad behavior). One of the most famous friendships known from ancient Greece was that between Damon and Phintias, as preserved in the *Memorable Deeds and Sayings* of the Roman author Valerius Maximus. According to this narrative, Damon and Phintias were close friends who resided in Sicily (part of the greater Greek world) in the fourth century. The Syracusan tyrant Dionysios intended to put Phintias to death but allowed him a reprieve to return home briefly to put his affairs in order provided that Damon stay in his place. If Phintias did not return to face his execution by the appointed day, Damon would die instead. As the date grew nearer, everyone worried about Damon's safety except for Damon himself, who in no way doubted his friend's loyalty. Phinitas, of course, arrived on the day for the execution and stood ready to lose his head, and thus save that of his friend. Dionysios was so astounded by the friends' loyalty that he freed Phintias and asked if he, too, might join in their friendship (*Memorable Deeds and Sayings* 4.7.1). (They refused him, by the way; Dionysios of Syracuse was a bit of a jerk.)

Valerius Maximus tells another story, this one about Alexander the Great and his best friend Hephaistion (yes, they were probably lovers, but this does not change the fact that they were also best friends). After having conquered Persia, Alexander, with Hephaistion in tow, went to visit the wife of the former Persian king. When the two approached, the former queen bowed down and greeted Hephaistion as king, thinking that he was Alexander. When her gaff was brought to her attention, she was terrified, but Alexander merely replied, "There's no need to get upset just because of a name: he is Alexander too" (4.7.2). In this Alexander (or Valerius Maximus) surely upheld Aristotle's notion that "A friend is a second self." (*Nic. Eth.* 1171b)

Another story pertains to Alexander's father. Once, after the Macedonian Olympic games (which were different from the Greek Olympic Games), Philip of Macedon was partying with several guests, and, being in very good humor (and probably very drunk), he was granting wishes left and right to his guests. Only one man refrained from asking for anything, a man named Satyros. Finally (Demosthenes 19.194–195):

> [Philip], being full of youthful enthusiasm, bade him speak, as there was nothing he wouldn't do for him. And [Satyros] said that Apollophanes of Pydna was his xenos and friend, and when he died, having been slain by treachery, his relatives were afraid and sent his daughters, who were children, to Olynthos. "Those daughters are now of an age to marry; but since you seized that city, they are now your captives. I ask and beg you, then, to give them to me. And I wish for you to know what kind of gift you would be giving me, if you should grant them. I shall profit nothing from it, should I receive them, but I shall establish and pay their dowries, and I shall not allow them to suffer anything unworthy of us or of their father." Those present at the symposion, having heard this, made such a banging and uproar all around that it persuaded Philip to grant the gift. And this even though that same Apollophanes was one of the men who assassinated Alexander, Philip's brother.

Satyros risked the king's extreme displeasure to request the custody of his friend's daughters so that he might marry them off at his own expense, according to his dead friend's presumable wishes. He was a very good friend.

There is, of course, less information on the friendships of women. Nevertheless, we do know that girls and women had friends outside of the family, just as males did. One of the most detailed descriptions of female childhood friendship is given by the poet Erinna in her work *The Distaff*, wherein she reminisced on her now-departed friend Baukis:

> . . . into the deep wave
> You jumped from the white horses with a crazy step.
> "I've got you," I cried, "my friend." And when you were the tortoise
> Jumping out you ran through the great hall's court.
> Unhappy Baukis, there are my laments as I cry for you deeply,
> These are your footprints resting in my heart, dear girl,
> Still warm; but what we once loved is now already ashes.
> Young girls, we held our dolls in our bedrooms
> Like new wives, hearts unbroken. Near dawn your mother,
> Who handed our wool to her workers in attendance,
> Came in and called you to help with salted meat.
> . . . . . .
> But when you went to the bed of a man
> You forgot all you heard from your mother while still a child,
> My dear Baukis. Aphrodite filled your thoughts with forgetting.
> As I weep for you now I desert your last rites,

For my feet may not leave the house and become unclean,
Nor is it right for me to look upon your corpse,
Nor cry with my hair uncovered, but a red shame
Divides me . . . (trans. Plant 2004, 50)

A somewhat similar sentiment appears on a late fifth-century inscription from Athens (CEG 97):

Because of your true and sweet friendship, your companion (*hetaira*) Euthylla placed this tablet on your grave, Biotê, for she keeps your memory with her tears, and weeps for your lost youth. (trans. Lefkowitz and Fant, 1992, 170)

An interesting detail about Greek vocabulary: Euthylla calls herself the *hetaira* of Biotê. The word *hetaira* is Greek for female companion, just as the masculine form *hetairos* means "male companion." However, whereas *hetairos* always means companion/friend, the word *hetaira*, especially when used by male authors (that is, a good 99 percent of our Greek authors), came to have the meaning of upper-class prostitute. One might compare it in English to the words *master* and *mistress*. While these started out as merely masculine and feminine versions of the same concept, the feminine version came to have sexual overtones, such that it now means a woman having an affair with a married man, not any kind of female ruler. The use of the term *hetaira* here is one of the few examples that show that the word referred to (non-meretricious) friendships amongst women.

Another source of information about female friendships comes from inscriptions on votive dedications. An article of clothing dedicated by a pair of friends in Thessaly had the accompanying inscription (FH 152 G):

Praxidikê made this garment, Dyseris designed it; the skill of both is united. (trans. Lefkowitz and Fant 2004, 170)

And so good friends helped each other out. Ideally, the benefactor should not flaunt his (or her) kindnesses, as the orator Demosthenes once suggested (18.269):

I believe that the benefactee ought to remember forever, but the benefactor ought to forget immediately, as it behooves the one to be useful, and the other not to be petty. To remind someone of one's good deeds and to speak of them is little short of reproach.

Besides, considering the reciprocal nature of friendship, the benefactor would eventually become the benefactee, and everything would balance out in the long run. If they did not, then there were problems because there were few things more despicable than a false friend. As such, care was needed when forming (hopefully) lasting bonds. As the Athenian orator Isokrates advised (1.24):

> Make no one a friend before you have inquired how he has made use of previous friends, for you may expect him to be the same to you as he was to them. Become a friend slowly and deliberately, but having become one, try to hold the course; for it is equally shameful to have no friends as to abandon many companions. Neither test friends to your detriment, nor wish to be untried by them.

Hesiod, in his *Works and Days*, was even more detailed in his advice on friendship and the need for reciprocity, even to the point of demanding that slights be repaid two-fold (707–716):

> Don't make a companion equal to a brother;
> But if you do so, you should not do wrong by him.
> Don't speak a false if pleasing lie; and if your companion should start
> And say or do something unpleasant
> Pay him back twice over, remember that! But if
> Later he returns to you in friendship, be willing to do right by him—
> Accept him. A worthless man makes friends here and there;
> But don't let some mind belie your face.
> Don't get a reputation as one with many xenoi, or as one with none at all.
> Be neither a friend of bad men, nor a slanderer of good ones.

Even Sappho recognized that friendships could have their limits, once writing, "Before they were mothers, Leto and Niobê were the best of friends." (Later Niobê bragged that she had 14 children, in contrast to Leto's two—Apollo and Artemis. The offended deities retaliated by killing all 14 of Niobê's children. No friendship is going to survive that.)

Certainly the best description of bad friendship and the problems it entails was described by Plutarch. Sparing no imagery, the philosopher wrote (*On Having Many Friends*, 94d–e):

> It is a difficult thing, and not very easy to flee or to put aside a displeasing friendship. But just as harmful and annoying food is neither able to remain inside one without causing pain and harm, nor can one eject it as it entered, but digested and with a disgusting appearance, in such a way a bad friend either causes pain and suffering being present, or by force and with enmity and hostility is cast out like some bile. [Yes, it's Roman era, but I couldn't resist.]

The corollary to the "helping friends" mentality was "hurting enemies." As Odysseus related to Princess Nausikaä in Book 6 of the *Odyssey* (182–185), "For nothing is better or greater than this, when a man and a woman have a home, sharing one mind in harmony—a great pain to their ill-wishers, and pleasure to their well-wishers." There was seen to be nothing wrong with this ideology. Quite to the contrary, the desire to harm one's enemies, or the enemies of one's friends, was seen as moral and beneficial, a kind of self-defense that was understood in the end to be pleasurable. The poet Pindar could pray, "May I be a friend to a friend; but to an enemy an enemy. I shall attack in the manner of a wolf, treading the crooked streets" (*Pyth* 2, 84–85). The Athenian historian Thucydides was most emphatic of all, claiming: "And we shall consider it to be perfectly customary concerning adversaries to strike down with full vengeance the aggressor; and to defeat an enemy is the sweetest thing for us, as the saying goes" (7.68.1).

Now, this is not to say that the Greeks spent any considerable amount of time going through the streets of their villages and cities attacking each other on a regular basis. "Hurting" one's enemies was generally far more subtle, flaring up in courtrooms, providing "boos" at athletic events, and rejoicing in an enemy's hard times. Although Hatfield and McCoy–style family vendettas may have typified the Dark Ages and early Archaic periods (1100–700 BCE), arbitrators and laws were established very early on, to judge from Hesiod, to avoid such messiness and to minimize violence. So although the Greeks might have taken every opportunity to help their friends, the harming of enemies was a bit more of an ideal than a practice *per se*.

Besides, for some Greeks, any antagonism against another could be seen as a want of virtue. At the end of his dialogue *Gorgias*, Sokrates, as written by his student Plato, said (527c–d):

> Truly be persuaded by me and follow me there where, having arrived, you will be happy both living and in death, as the story goes. And let someone disdain you as a fool, and abuse you if he wishes, and by Zeus, be of good cheer if he strikes you with an insulting blow. For you will suffer nothing terrible, if in reality you are good and noble, practicing virtue.

In other words, turn the other cheek. But such a sentiment was very much in the minority. And the Athenians executed Sokrates for corrupting the youth with such sentiments, which should tell you something.

HUMANS AND ANIMALS

The ancient Greeks did not just share their lives with other humans. In addition to foreigners, about whom they had varying opinions (see Chapter 6), most Greeks interacted on a daily basis with animals, which provided food, power, entertainment, and companionship. In reality, animals were far more present in the daily lives of the ancient Greeks than they are today in the developed West. Contrary to the image one might get from the literary sources, the ancient Greeks actually did not eat as many animals as we do in modern times (assuming you are not a vegetarian or tree-hugging vegan, like the author). However, animals were vital for transportation and as beasts of burden. Instead of the family car, you had the family mule. Instead of the family tractor, you had the family ox. And, since most clothes were made at home beginning with raw ingredients, sheep were vital for keeping the family warm, with their processed wool while living and cushioning fleeces once dead. Furthermore, the most important ritual in ancient Greek religion was animal sacrifice, which gave the Greeks the opportunity to sit down to a meal with the deities. As such, animals played a vital role in ancient Greek religion (see Chapter 7). All this stands in addition to the prevalent imagery of animals in ancient Greek literature, ranging from the similes of Homer to the fables of Aesop.

Food (and Sacrifice)

The ancient Greeks were not big meat eaters. Animals were too valuable for their other contributions to society to slaughter too freely, and, for the most part, the Greeks were too good at agriculture to need much supplementing with meat products. At any given time, at least 80 percent of the population was engaged in agriculture, and (agricultural) self-sufficiency, called *autarkeia,* was the ideal. The average farmer probably worked about five acres or so of land with the help of his family and one or two oxen to pull the plough. Wealthy farmers owned quite a bit more land, as well as the slaves (and animals) to work it, and the highest level of Athenian society at least was reserved for those whose properties produced the equivalent of 500 *medimnoi* (1 *medimnos* = about 52 liters) of grain per annum. The daily diet consisted mainly of these grains—either as bread or porridge—along with legumes; vegetables such as turnips, radishes, lettuce, cucumbers, artichokes, leeks, celery, cabbage, and onions; fruits such as apples, pears, pomegranates, grapes, and figs; cheeses mainly made from goat's milk; and herbs, especially mint, dill, and garlic (which, counterintuitively, was thought to be an aphrodisiac). This diet was complemented by seafood. Sweets were restricted to fruits, honey, and occasionally dates. Wine was abundant and normally drunk in a watered down state so that even children over three years old could partake of it. The ancient Greeks did not drink milk and thought that such a practice was utterly barbaric.

And yet anyone who has ever read the works of Homer no doubt came away from the experience with the general notion that the Greeks ate a lot of meat, as meat is the focus of every description of feasting, ranging from royals feasts to casual dinners to the meals of slaves.

> The corridors and courtyards and homes were full of gathered men;
> There were many, both young and old.
> For them Alkinoös sacrificed twelve sheep,

Eight white-tusked boars, and two ambling oxen,
And he flayed their skins, and they prepared a lovely feast. (*Odyssey* 8.57–61)

But he [Akhilleus] set down a great meat tray in the fire's gleam,
And on it he set the back of a sheep and a fat goat,
And the backbone of a hog rich in fat.
And Automedon held them down for him, and godlike Akhilleus cut them.
And he cut up the meat well, and stuck it onto spits.
The son of Menoitios [Patrokles], peer of the gods, kindled a great fire.
But when the fire burned out and the light died off,
Spreading the embers he stretched out the spits above them
And sprinkling divine salt he set them on the fire dogs.
And when indeed it was roasted and was heaped on the cutting board
Patrokles took bread and distributed it to the table
In lovely baskets, and Akhilleus distributed the meat.
And he sat opposite godly Odysseus
By the other wall, and he bade Patrokles, his companion,
To sacrifice to the deities.
And he tossed offerings into the fire.
And they stretched out their hands to the good things lying ready before them.
  (*Iliad* 9.210–221)

So speaking he quickly fastened his robe with a belt,
And he went to go to the pig sties, where the group of pigs were kept.
There, picking out two he sacrificed both
And he singed them and cut them up and stuck them onto spits.
Having roasted everything he brought Odysseus
Everything hot on the spits. He sprinkled white barley,
And in the cup he mixed honey-sweet wine. (*Odyssey* 14.72–78)

There are a few reasons for this discrepancy between the literature and the reality. First of all, everything in Homer is a bit larger than life, and the exaggeration in diet is no exception. Plus, Homer focused on the entertaining and exciting, not necessarily the accurate; many a scholar has noted the fact that no Homeric heroes in our texts ever go to the bathroom ("Then, like a mighty racehorse, godlike, swift-footed Akhilleus took a leak on the walls of Troy").

Additionally, especially for Akhilleus and Eumaios, lifestyle was a major determinant in choice of meal. Akhilleus was a soldier on campaign, not someone with ready access to the literal fruits of his farm. Animals are well known to be handy food-storage devices: they store grains and foods inedible to humans (like hay), and provide sustenance when agricultural provender is not readily available. And if Eumaios offered a meal of pork to his guest, this probably has a lot to do with the fact that he was a swineherd—pork was inevitably what was for dinner.

Most important, though, is the matter of sacrifice. As stated previously, animals were, in general, too valuable to be killed for a daily meal. However, they also served as a bridge between mortals and immortals when humans slaughtered animals in sacrifice to the deities. In contrast to Near Eastern deities, Greek gods did not actually eat meat—or human food at all. It was repugnant for them to fill their immortal bodies with dead things (which, face it, is what food is), and the gods ate food called *ambrosia*, literally "immortal." Apparently the gods just liked the smell of barbeque, leaving the actual meat of the sacrificed animals for the humans to enjoy. The most common context for eating meat in ancient Greece, then, was in the religious context of sacrifice, when the humans helped themselves to the parts of the dead animals not desired by the gods. Thus, when Homer claims that Alkinoös "sacrificed twelve sheep," it is a literal sacrifice.

The most common flocks in ancient Greece were goats and sheep. Sheep were mainly valuable for their wool and, eventually, meat, while goats provided hair, milk (used for cheese), meat, and even occasional entertainment. Not unlike modern times, sheep were understood to be rather dull, intellectually speaking, although the fighting spirit and determination of rams was recognized and respected. Goats, especially male goats, had a far worse reputation. They were considered to be lust-crazed and to stink to high heaven (a problematic combination remarkably reminiscent of Peppy le Pew). Nevertheless, as Aristotle did once comment (*Hist. An.* 9.3), "You will have a warmer bed amongst the goats than among the sheep, because the goats will be quieter and will creep up towards you; for the goat is less tolerant of the cold than the sheep." One really must assume that the quality of life among shepherds was less than phenomenal, especially if it was preferable to sleep with smelly, horny goats rather than docile living pillows.

Hunting

So basically, the Greeks derived pretty much all the food they needed from farming, along with some fishing and pasturing of small flocks of sheep and goats for things like cheese and wool. Occasionally they would sacrifice an animal (or, at really big events, hundreds of animals) to the deities and enjoy a truly massive picnic celebration. All things considered, it would not seem that hunting would be a major concern in ancient Greece, just like in modern times hunting is not necessary for food. Nevertheless, like now, hunting in ancient Greece became a sport, a pastime of the aristocracy mainly so that they could flaunt their hunting horses and hunting hounds while pretending they were taking part in a kind of militaristic training rather than admitting they got off on killing creatures that never bothered them in the first place (see above: tree-hugging vegan). Hunting, although restricted to a small portion of the population, was another major context for human-animal interactions in ancient Greece, both concerning the animals hunted and the animals used in the hunting process.

To judge from the hunting manuals and vase paintings, the main animals hunted were deer, rabbits, foxes, and boars (see Figure 3.1). If you were really insane (a.k.a.: stupid), you might also go after bears. Individual men (women did not hunt outside of myth) might hunt alone or in groups (especially if going after larger prey), but the preferred means of hunting generally involved at least one dog. Thus a hunting manual written in the fifth century by Xenophon described a rabbit hunt, including details on how best to treat your dogs (Xenophon, *On Hunting* 6.12−17):

> Having bound the dogs, each separately, outside of the forest, in such a way that they are easy to release, set up the nets as related. After this place the net-watcher on guard; he then takes the dogs and sets out to the game's retreat. Promising to split the game with Apollo and Artemis Agrotera, release one dog, whichever one is best at tracking. In winter, do this at daybreak; if summer, during the day, and between these times for the other seasons. As soon as the dog gets the scent let loose another dog. That one goes on the other side of the track, but don't let her get too far out. Then release the others one at a time, and follow without overly pressing them on. Call each one by name, but not too much, so as not to overexcite them at the critical moment. And the dogs, in joy and exhilaration, will bound forth to disentangle the paths, two or three times running back and forth across them amongst themselves, criss-crossing the tracks, circling, going straight, bending, pulling together, loosening up, finding and losing it again. The dogs themselves chase along, quickly wagging their tails and tilting back their ears, with eyes flashing! Whenever they circle the hare, they indicate this to the hunter with their tails, quivering their whole bodies, attacking violently, rapturously giving chase, vigorously running together, quickly reconnoitering, dividing up, assailing once again. They end up at the hare's den, and charging it. Suddenly the hare leaps up and flees, causing the dogs to bark. Then call out, "Go, dogs! Beautiful! Well done, indeed, dogs!"

Fortunately, the Greeks had some sense of sustainability, and realized that certain animals had to be left alone if they wanted to continue hunting through the years. Likewise, not all animals gave the same level of sport. Thus the same text also advises (Xenophon, *On Hunting* 5. 14):

> Hunters, however, release the very young to the Goddess. Those already one year-old run fast at the first stretch, but not after; for they are nimble, but not very strong.

To judge from the literature, the Greeks were *very* attached to their hunting dogs, and some of the most touching passages of ancient literature—both epic and the more personal lyric and epigrams—testify to the love held between men and their dogs. One of the only passages in Homer that has the potential to move even modern readers to tears is when Odysseus, finally

Figure 3.1
Attic red-figure kylix depicting a deer hunt. Attributed to the Epeleios Painter, ca. 510–500 BCE. Louvre G 22. (Drawing by Paul C. Butler)

home in Ithaka but still in disguise, sees his pathetic old hunting dog lying neglected in his house, the first creature to recognize that Odysseus had returned (*Odyssey*, 17, 291–327):

A dog lying there held up his head and ears—
Argos, belonging to stout-hearted Odysseus, whom he himself once
Reared, not badly, before he went off to holy Ilion.
Previously young men used to bring him
[hunting] after wild goats and deer and rabbits.
But now, with the king far away, he lay despised
In a large heap of manure of mules and oxen, spread out
Before the doors until the servants of Odysseus should come
To fertilize the broad field.
There lay the dog Argos, full of ticks.
Then indeed, as he knew Odysseus was near,
He wagged his tail and cast back both ears,
But was no longer strong enough to approach closer to his master.
And Odysseus, looking aside wiped away a tear,
Unseen by Eumaios. He immediately questioned him:
"Eumaios, what strange thing is this, a dog there lying in the manure.
It has a fine body, although I don't know for sure
Whether he has speed to run equal to his appearance,
Or if he is no better than men's table dogs,
Which masters care for for their pleasure."
And you replied to him, Swineherd Eumaios, saying:
"That dog is of a man who died very far away.

If he were in form and action
Such as he was when Odysseus left him behind going off to Troy
Quickly would you be amazed seeing his speed and prowess.
For then, roaming the depths of the woods, no prey he pursued
Escaped him, whoever he chased. And he was very good at tracking.
But now he's had the worst of it; his king died far from his homeland.
The careless women don't tend to him,
And the servants, whom kings no longer rule over,
They don't bother to work properly.
For broad-browed Zeus takes away half their virtue,
The day they come into slavery."
Thus he spoke entering into the well-inhabited halls.
He went straight to the main room along with the noble suitors.
But black death took Argos according to his fate,
As soon as he saw Odysseus in the 20th year.

Apparently, even in the absence of Chihuahuas, the ancient Greeks had little useless dogs that received fawning love and no respect. The lyric poet Simonides offered this epitaph to one of his favorite dogs, now departed:

On Lykas, a Thessalian Hound:
Bitch-hound, hunter, even your dead white bones
Terrify the beasts of the field,
For your bravery is common knowledge
From Pelion to far Ossa
And on the dizzying sheep-paths of Kithairon. (trans. Barnstone 1988, 138)

And the Athenian law-giver Solon one remarked (Solon fr. 23):

Fortunate is he who has dear children, and whole-hoofed horses
And hunting hounds and a friend in foreign parts. (trans. Dillon and Garland
    2000, 90)

Dogs could appear on funeral stelai, especially of young males, testifying to the boys' upper-class status and the military prowess they certainly would have shown had they lived to adulthood (see Figure 3.2).

Pets and Companions

Dogs were not just used for hunting; they, as well as other animals, were kept as pets and companions by the ancient Greeks, not too far off from what we do today. As noted previously, the Greeks had neither Chihuahuas nor pugs, but this does not mean that they were wholly bereft of silly little dogs. Instead, they had the Melitaian lapdog, described as being the size of a weasel, with up-swept curly tails (see Figure 3.3). These were the status-display dogs of ancient Greece, useless for hunting anything much larger than a mouse.

Figure 3.2
Fourth-century BCE grave stele of boy with dog
and family members, Attic, marble. Attributed
to Skopas of Paros. National Archaeological
Museum, Athens, Greece. Inv. 86g. (Album/Art
Resource, NY)

But they were loving, dedicated little creatures. The Roman Era historian
Aelian records that when the Theban war hero Epaminondas was condemned
to death by his fellow countrymen, his beloved Melitaian puppy greeted him
cheerfully upon his return from court, prompting Epaminondas to note, "This
guy returns all the good he received from me, graciously, while the Thebans,
having frequently fared well because of me, sentence me to death" (*Varia
Historia* 13.42). (Epaminondas, by the bye, is the fellow who defeated the
Spartans—The SPARTANS!—at the Battle of Leuktra in 371 BCE.) This
same author also relates how the Greek musician Theodoros was so bonded
with his Melitaian that when Theodoros died, the dog threw himself into
the coffin to be buried with his companion, sticking by him in death as in life
(*De Natura Animalium* 7.40). So there is definitely something to be said for
"useless" little rat-dogs.

Figure 3.3
Attic red-figure chous with woman, child, and Melitaian dog, ca. 420 BCE. Universität Erlangen-Nürnberg. I321. (Drawing by Paul C. Butler)

The love that Greeks felt for their canine companions is evident in the art, literature, and archaeology. In addition to texts such as the *Odyssey* and Aelian, we even have epigrams to dogs, such as that penned by the third-century Arkadian poet Anytê:

> You too once perished by a many-rooted bush,
> Lokrian, swiftest of the puppies who love to bark;
> Into your nimble paw such a cruel poison
> Sank the speckle-throated viper. (trans. Plant 2004, 58)

Archaeologically, one might note the dog burial discovered behind the Stoa of Attalos in Athens. It contained a single dog, with a great big beef bone lying by its head (Calder 2011, 82).

Generally speaking, the Greeks preferred short, spirited names for the dogs. Those especially recommended by Xenophon are: Psykhê (Spirit), Thymos

(Passion), Porpax (Shield Grip), Styrax (Spike), Lonkhê (Lance), Lokhos (Ambush), Phroura (Guard), Phylax (Guard), Taxis (Brigade), Xiphon (Sword), Phonax (Blood-Thirsty), Phlegon (Blaze), Alkê (Prowess), Teukhon (Crafter), Hyleus (Woody), Medas (Crafty), Porthon (Destroyer), Sperkhon (Speedy), Orgê (Passion), Bremon (Growler), Hybris (Pride), Thallon (Sprouter), Rhomê (Strength), Antheus (Blooming), Hebê (Youth), Getheus (Joyful), Khara (Joy), Leuson (Stoner), Augo (Keen-Sighted), Poleus (Rover), Bia (Violence), Stikhon (Rank-and-File), Spoudê (Speedy), Bryas (Owl), Oinas (Vine), Sterrus (Strong), Kraugê (Uproar), Kainon (Killer), Tyrbas (Tumult), Sthenon (Strong), Aither (Aether), Aktis (Splendor), Aikhmê (Spear-Point), Noes (Councellor), Gnômê (Intelligence), Stibon (Tracker), and Hormê (Dasher) (*On Hunting* 7.5).

The Greeks also had pet cats but only rarely so. They seldom appear in either the literature or the artwork, and no cat names have come down to us. Apparently the Greeks felt that cats were aloof and self-serving. They did function as mouse control, but for this task the Greeks tended to prefer weasels and martens.

Mice were a problem in ancient Greece, insofar as they ate everything. A gold ring in the British Museum shows a mouse with two grains of wheat in its mouth; the mouse is shackled to a pillar, literally in handcuffs, clearly guilty of theft. Even the gods complained about the little thieves. In the Homeric *War of Frogs and Mice*, Athena clearly establishes whose side she is on (178–184):

> O father, never would I come as helper to
> Mice in distress, since they have done me many evils,
> Destroying garlands and lamps for the oil.
> And this very much stung my mind, what they did:
> They gnawed up my peplos, which I wove working
> From a fine warp, spinning a fine weft,
> And they finished it with holes!

(On a similar note, I once completed the warping to stick weave an oud strap for my husband and looked down to find my bunny eating it at the other end. So it's not just mice.)

It is clear that many Greeks just plain liked animals. The epigrams of Anytê offer heart-felt testimonies to many animals, some familiar farmyard denizens and others wild creatures from the sea:

Rooster: You will no longer get me up out of bed as before
Rising at dawn and rowing with your compact wings.
For Sinis sneaked up on you while you slept
And killed you, swiftly digging his claw into your throat. (trans. Plant 2004, 58)

Goat: Look upon the horny goat of Bromios, how haughtily
He looks down his flowing beard

Exulting because often in the mountains
A Naiad took the rough hair around his cheeks in her rosy hand. (trans.
Plant 2004, 58)

Dolphin: No longer exalting in the swimming seas
Will I toss my neck, rising from the depths,
Nor will I blow around the fine prow of a ship
Leaping and enjoying the figure-head.
But the sea's blue wetness threw me up on dry land
And I lie on this narrow strip of beach. (trans. Plant 2004, 58)

Horse: Damis set up this memorial for his horse, steadfast
In battle, when Ares struck its blood-red
Chest, and black blood bubbled up through the leather shield
Of its skin, and soaked the soil with grievous slaughter. (trans. Plant 2004, 58)

As the last poem expresses, the ancient Greeks really loved their horses. In an age without Bentleys and BMWs, the horse was a primary object of status display. As early as the Geometric period of Greek (pre-)history, horses adorned small trinket boxed, serving as a symbol for overall prosperity (see Figure 3.4).

Figure 3.4
Horse pyxis, ca. 760–750 BCE, Attic, Late Geometric, ceramic. h. 17 cm., diam. 24.7 cm. h. without lid 7.7 cm. Museum purchase, y1928–16. (Princeton University Art Museum/Art Resource, NY)

Horses were seldom used in farm work in ancient times. Instead, they were reserved for warfare and chariot racing, and they required gobs of money (just as the most expensive modern sport is polo). If the highest levels of Athenian society were reserved for the *Pentakosiomedimnoi*, the second highest level was reserved for the *Hippeis*, the Knights, those who could afford to bring a horse into battle. Losing a horse in combat was a true tragedy, as commemorated by Damis above. The mere image of the horse could serve as iconographic shorthand for warrior. On the Athenian Parthenon, the ephebes (young men around 18 years of age; see Chapter 1) appear with horses, intimating their role as the future defenders of the city, not to mention their upper-class status.

The most prestigious sport in the ancient games was the chariot races, where two, three, or four horses drew a chariot around an arena (see Chapter 4). The chariot races receive the most detail of all the competitions in the funeral games of Patrokles in Book 23 of the *Iliad*. Herodotos records that the Athenian gentleman Kimon won three Olympic victories with the same set of mares, who were buried right next to him upon their death (6.103). In Byzantine times, one's political affiliations were directly tied to the chariot team one supported. In lieu of Republicans and Democrats, there were the Greens and the Blues, something like having Manchester United as one's political party.

One must remember, though, that chariot racing was exceptionally danger-ous, as the horses could collide, injuring each other and potentially dragging the charioteer to his death. In the 1925 version of the movie *Ben Hur*, several horses and riders died during the filming of the chariot race scene. In Greek myth, the young hero Hippolytos (whose name means "Looser of Horses") was killed when his chariot horses panicked and dragged him to his death. The danger, however, was apparently worth the risk because the rewards to be gained were exceptional. Also, and perhaps more relevantly, the person who gained said rewards was the horse breeder, not the person risking his life on the chariot. This is how Kyniska, a princess of Sparta, once won at the Olympic Games. In spite of the fact that women were barred from the Olympics on pain of death, her horses won the four-horse chariot competi-tion. Thus she left this commemoration of her victory (AP XIII.16.G):

My father and brothers were kings of Sparta. I, Kyniska, won a victory with my swift-running horses and set up this statue. I claim that I am the only woman from all of Greece to have won this crown. (trans. Lefkowitz and Fant 1992, 161)

If Kyniska was the first woman to win at the chariots races (in absentia) in the early fourth century, she was not the last. In the third century, Bilistiche, the mistress of Ptolemy Philadelphus, won at the four-colt chariot race, while Aristoklea from Larisa won the two-horse chariot race in the second century. The victor lists from the Athenian Panathenaic festivals of the second century list Zeuxo, Enkratia, and Hermionê as chariot victors (Lefkowitz and Fant 1992, 161–162). Chariot racing was a good way for wealthy women to break into men's sports.

Certainly the most famous tale of human-horse bonding is the story of Alexander the Great (before he was great) and Boukephalas as recorded in his biography by Plutarch (6, 1–5):

> Once when Philoneikos the Thessalian led Boukephalas for sale to Philip for thirteen talents, they went down to the plain to check out the horse. And the horse seemed to be difficult and altogether intractable, neither being approachable for mounting nor submitting to the voice of any one of Philip's men, but he was utterly rebellious. But when Philip got annoyed and bade him be lead away as completely savage and undisciplined. Alexander appeared and said, "What a horse they are letting go because of inexperience and softness, as they cannot manage him." At first Philip kept quiet, but as Alexander frequently interrupted and Philip got irritated, he said, "Do you rebuke your elders as though you know more or are better able to handle a horse?" And Alexander replied, "I should be able to handle this one better than another." "And if you can't, what penalty will you pay for your rashness?" "By Zeus," he said, "I shall pay the price of the horse." There was laughter at this. So fixing the price between them, Alexander ran directly to the horse and seized the reins, turning the horse towards the sun, as it seemed that he knew that seeing his shadow fall and tremor before him bothered him. And so running beside Boukephalas and petting him a bit, Alexander saw that he was full of heart and spirit. Quietly removing his mantle and rising up he carefully mounted. Taking the bit by the reins, without striking or tearing him, he saw that the horse was no longer afraid and was actually ready to run. And so he released him and drove him on with a daring voice and a kick. At first those with Philip were in anxiety and silence. But when Alexander turned about and rushed forward rejoicing, they whopped and hollered all around. But his father, it is said, cried tears of joy. And when Alexander dismounted, Philip, kissing his head, said, "O child, seek for yourself an empire equal to you, for Macedon won't contain you."

Some other names for horses, other than Ox-Head (Boukephalas), that have been recorded are Xanthos (Blond), Kalliphoras (Beautiful Mane), Phalios (White Brow), Semos (Distinguished), Kallikomê (Fair Mane), and Pyrrhikomê (Fiery Mane).

Animals and Children

Animals were understood to be sentient beings with a modicum of intelligence but not much in the way of acquired wisdom. In this they were not much different from children. The Greeks noted a close correspondence between children and animals, a fact that was especially commemorated on children's grave reliefs. As noted earlier in this chapter, dogs could appear on boys' funerary stelai both as a memorial of the bonds forged with the family dog and as a symbol of the boy's potential as a hunter/warrior (see Figure 3.2). Little girls, when shown with a dog, appeared with puppies—less brutal, more cuddly. Young girls might also be shown with birds, often doves or geese, symbols of unachieved sexuality (both animals were sacred to Aphrodite). In addition to their symbolic value, these grave reliefs also portrayed aspects of reality. As noted in Chapter 1, children often had pets in ancient Greece, and portrayals of children with their pets added to the pathos of their premature loss.

For children who were *not* dead (and there were many), animals filled their world with companions and comfy imagery. This is especially apparent on the red-figure vases from fifth- and fourth-century Athens, where both boys and girls appear with dogs and puppies (accounting for about a third of the depictions), birds, goats, sheep, rabbits, tortoises, and even deer. Remarkably, even insects could serve as children's pets, as Markos Argentarios recorded in the *Greek Anthology* (7.364):

For her grasshopper and cicada Myro set up this tomb,
Casting a prayer and dust about them with her hands,
Crying longingly by their pyre. For Hades
Seized the one songster, and Persephonê the other.

In addition to pets, animal-shaped toys and infant paraphernalia generally were as popular in ancient Greece as they are now (minus the Disney copyright). For reasons on which we shall not speculate, piggies were especially popular in this regard, serving as models for both baby bottles (see Figure 3.5) and rattles.

Work Animals

As noted earlier in this chapter, the Greeks used animals for work, especially around the farm. The most common agricultural assistants were the ox and the mule, both of which could be used for ploughing and as beasts of burden. As Hesiod recommended in this *Works and Days* (436—440):

. . . Get two male oxen—nine-years-old—
For they are strong, not exhausted,
Being in mid-youth; they are best for working;
They don't fight in the furrow and break the plough
And leave the work undone.

Mules were not quite as strong as oxen and thus were more likely to be used as beasts of burden. Being known as especially intelligent animals, several fables refer to their wily attempts to avoid work. One author records how a mule tasked with drawing a cart filled with salt started to drag his charge

Figure 3.5
Baby bottle in the form of a piggy, ca. 450 BCE. Cleveland Museum of Art,
1975.91. (Drawing by Paul C. Butler)

through water to lighten the load. He was rewarded with a cart filled with
sponges. Another mule tried to imitate his owner's beloved Melitaian puppy,
frisking and fawning to predictably disastrous results.

In some cases, even horses could be used as work animals, especially in
their later years. Epigrams in the *Greek Anthology* commemorate former race
horses who, living past their peak, found themselves demoted to beasts of
considerable burden (9.20):

> I was once a crown-bearer on the Alpheios, Sir, twice
> Heralded by the water of the Kastalia,
> I was once cried out at Nemea, and at Isthmia,
> As a colt, I ran equal to the winged winds.
> But now that I'm old, see here how
> I am driven to circle the rocky circuit, an outrage to my crowns.

Such treatment might at least be seen as preferable to the death dealt out to
comparable creatures in modern society. The Greeks were practical in this
respect—waste not, want not—but they could show their gratitude to animals
who were dedicated workers, even in old age. Addaios of Macedon records
how (*Greek Anthology* 6.228):

> By furrow and old age worn out, nevertheless Alkon
> Did not lead his work ox to the killing axe,
> Respecting his labors. He now, somewhere in the deep meadow,
> Lowing enjoys freedom from the plough.

Likewise, Aristotle records how mules might live into their eighties (*Hist. An.* 6.24):

> Mules live for many years. There was once one who had lived for even 80 years, when the Athenians were building their temple. He was discharged then due to his old age, but he continued accompanying and urging on the yoke-team to their work, such that they voted that the grain-merchants might not drive him away from the bread-boards.

Ethics and Cruelty

The ancient Greeks were quite certain that there was a definitive distinction between humans and animals, and that animals existed for the benefit (exploitation) of humans. This is presented most clearly by Aristotle, the fourth-century philosopher who also explained why some people are just innately slaves and that women must be subjected to men because they never achieve intellectual maturity (not that I am bitter). Thus he wrote in his *Politics* 1256b22 15–23:

> So equally it is clear that even for those grown-up one must suppose that plants exist for the sake of animals, and the other animals for the sake of humans' benefit, the domesticated ones both for use and food, and the wild ones, if not all of them at least the majority, for food and other helpful things, so that both clothing and tools might come from them. If then nature does nothing in vain and fruitlessly, it is necessary that nature has done all these things for humans' sake.

Aristotle and, even more so the Stoic philosophers, believed that animals were without reason, and thus humans were under no ethical compulsion to treat them morally. This idea that animals were somehow ethically outside the boundaries of (human) justice existed since the days of Hesiod, who wrote in his *Works and Days* (276–280):

> For humans Kronides ordained this law;
> For fish and wild beasts and winged birds
> To eat each other, as there is no justice amongst them.
> He gave justice to humans, which is best by far.

The Stoic position was pithily summarized by Diogenes Laertius in his *Life of Zeno*, writing (*Lives of the Philosophers* VII, 129):

> Moreover, it is their teaching that no justice exists between humans and other animals because of their dissimilarity. So Khrysippus says in the first book of his *On Justice* and Posidonius in the first book if his *On Duty*. (trans. Newmyer 2010, 74–75)

The average Greek was probably not overly influenced by the cogitations of the philosophers, and one could certainly debate the extent to which animals were held to a different level of ethical treatment than humans. This is not necessarily to suggest that animals were treated better in antiquity (although the absence of suburbs and factory farms certainly improved their lots generally). Rather, humans were often treated worse, especially slaves. Slaves working in the mines were much worse off than a beloved dog or horse.

Such ambiguity in treatment comes across in a practice nowadays seen as morally reprehensible—cockfighting (see Figure 3.6). For us, it is an illegal bloodsport. For the Greeks, it was, at least in theory, a lesson in courage. Believing that roosters preferred death to loss in combat and that a defeated rooster never recovered from such a disgrace (he certainly never crowed again), the ancients attributed to various culture heroes the institution of annual cockfights in the city of Athens, intended to teach battle virtue to young men. For Aelian it was Themistokles, the hero of the Battle of Salamis, who instituted annual cockfights in the Theater of Dionysos to make better soldiers of the Athenian youth (*Varia Historia* 2.28):

> After the victory over the Persians the Athenians established a law that cocks fight at public expense in the theater during one day of the year. I shall relate how this law came into being. When Themistokles led out the city forces against the Barbarians, he observed cocks battling. Nor did he see them to no effect—he halted the army and said to them, "These ones suffer neither for fatherland nor for ancestral tombs, nor for ideology, nor for freedom, nor for children; but rather each suffers not to lose, not to yield one to the other." Saying these things, then, he inspired the Athenians. Accordingly, the event became a symbol of excellence for them, and it was desired that they watch it as a reminder of like deeds.

This perceived battle ferocity and refusal to yield on the part of roosters explains why vase painters often portrayed this creature on the shields of soldiers. Although in modern times we read this symbolism quite differently ("Chicken!"), in ancient times the rooster was a symbol of battle prowess and almost suicidal determination.

Ethics and Kindness

The problem with maintaining that animals are morally exempt because of their lack of reason/wisdom/language is that anyone who has ever observed an animal for any extent of time figures out that animals are not stupid, illogical, or morally bankrupt. Even Akhilleus used the image of the mother bird as the ultimate symbol of altruism and self-sacrifice (*Iliad* 9, 314–327):

> Just as a bird brings food to her flightless young,
> Although it fares badly for her,
> So I have spent many sleepless nights . . .

Figure 3.6
Attic red-figure krater with cock fight. Attributed to the Menelaos Painter, ca. 440 BCE. National Museum, Warsaw, Poland. (Drawing by Paul C. Butler)

Aristotle and the Stoics were ultimately ambivalent in their treatments of animal intelligence. True, they claimed that animals lacked the higher reason of humans and the human ability to contemplate divinity. However, they also noted that animals cared well for their young, acted intelligently in times of crisis, were capable of "arts" such as architecture (birds building nests), and avoided danger (which is more than some people would say of the average teenage male human). The fifth- and fourth-century philosopher Demokritos, most famous for his work on atomic theory, staunchly maintained that animals were ethical and that humans had the moral obligation to arbitrate their ethical behavior just as they did other humans. Thus humans had the right to kill animals that did or intended to act unjustly and that caused injury contrary to justice (fr. 257−258 DK). Perhaps the most amusing take on the rational, even human-like, behavior of animals was recorded by Aelian in his *On the Nature of Animals* concerning the Stoic philosopher Kleanthes of Assos (331−232 BCE) (VI, 50):

They say this story compelled Kleanthes of Assos, against his will, to consider and reject his strongly held belief that they were utterly without reason. Kleanthes happened to be sitting and relaxing a while. There were a bunch of ants by his feet. And he saw a line of one group of ants carrying an ant corpse to the nest of another group of ants who were unrelated to them. And they stood by the edge of the anthill with the corpse, while the other group came up to meet the first group as if for some purpose. They went up and down several times, and in the end the second group carried out a worm as if it were a ransom. The first group took it, and they deposited the corpse that they had brought. The second group received it joyfully, as though it were a son or a brother. What was it Hesiod said about these creatures, that Zeus separated them, and indeed even that fish and wild beasts and winged birds he gave to each other to eat, since there is no justice among them, but he gave justice to humans? But Priam would not say these things, as he released Hektor for much treasure and many wondrous things from a human and hero and descendant of Zeus, and he himself being human and a descendant of Zeus.

If animal intelligence (or even sentience) were not enough to compel kindness to animals, one philosophy called for it unambiguously. The sixth-century philosopher Pythagoras (of Pythagorean Theorem fame) taught belief in metempsychosis, the idea that souls travelled amongst different bodies throughout different lifetimes, much as the notion of *Samsara* in Hinduism and Buddhism. Even if one were not concerned with kindness to animals per se, one should at least be reticent about injuring potential dead relatives and loved ones, and thus refrain from harming animals for fear that they might actually contain the souls of one's forefathers and departed companions. This philosophy, and its practical applications, was immortalized by the sixth-century poet Xenophanes of Kolophon when he wrote:

> One day a dog was being thrashed in the street,
> And behold, Pythagoras, philosopher of spirits,
> Was walking by.
> His heart was in his mouth for the poor pup.
> "Stop! Stop!" he cried.
> "Don't beat him anymore.
> This is my dear friend's soul.
> I recognize the voice when I hear him bark." (trans. Barnstone 1988, 130)

It is likely that Xenophanes himself found the anecdote rather amusing, and considering the anonymous man's treatment of the dog, it is evident that not many people shared Pythagoras's religious or ethical views.

Animals and Medicine

As discussed in Chapter 1, there was an extensive religious component to much ancient Greek medicine, whereby people sought cures from the temples of the healing deity Asklepios. According to several of the inscriptions, which recorded the miraculous cures of the faithful, animals played a role in the divine healing process when the god used different creatures to tend to his patients. One such healing animal was the dog, which was thought to be able to cure illnesses with its tongue (an opinion shared by most dogs to the best I can tell). Thus among the votive inscriptions from the Asklepeion in Epidauros (see Chapter 1) we read:

(#20) Lyson of Hermione, a blind child. He, while awake, had his eyes cured by one of the dogs in the sanctuary. He went away healthy.

(#26) A dog cured an Aiginitan child. He (the child) had a tumor in his neck. When he came before the god, one of the dogs of the sanctuary cured him with his tongue while the boy was awake and made him well.

These inscriptions give evidence that the sanctuary of Asklepios at Epidauros kept dogs as part of the religious personnel and that the cures were effected not in dream (as was more common at the sanctuary), but in normal, waking life. The god's dogs, then, were truly understood to have healing powers.

Another animal that could affect cures was the goose. According to an inscription, a man from Khios was suffering from gout. While taking a walk at the sanctuary, a goose bit his feet and, by causing him to bleed, cured him (Edelstein and Edelstein 1998, 237). It is interesting to note that both the dog and the goose were specifically associated with the Mesopotamian (modern-day Iraq) healing goddess Gula. For whatever reason, both animals had close associations with healing and medicine in the ancient world.

More unique to the Greeks was the snake as healing animal. This creature was sacred to Asklepios, and this is why a pair of snakes wrapped around a stick is the modern symbol of medicine. The links between snakes and healing probably derive from the snake's practice of shedding its skin, seen in antiquity, logically, as a form of rejuvenation. For the Greeks, it appears that a snake could actually embody the god and thus be an incarnation of the god's presence. Once again from the Asklepeion:

(#17) A man had his toe cured by a snake. He (the man) was afflicted with a vicious wound on the toe of his foot. During daytime he was carried out by the [temple] servants to sit somewhere. When he fell asleep in that place, a large snake came out of the abaton and cured the toe with its tongue. Having done this, he went back into the abaton again. Upon waking healed, [the man] said that he saw a vision. It seemed to him that a handsome young man poured a drug onto his toe.

There are some slightly different accounts for the ladies:

(#39) Agameda of Keos. She, sleeping [in the temple] for children saw a dream. It seemed to her in her sleep that a snake lay on her belly. And from this she had five children. [The inscription does not mention if she had all five at once, although this is unlikely.]

(#42) Nikasibula the Messanian, sleeping [in the temple] for children saw a dream. It seemed to her the god came to her bringing a snake slithering with him. She had sex with it. And from this two male children were born to her that year.

Freud would have had a field day . . .

Names

The importance of animals, especially horses, in Greek culture can be seen in ancient Greek naming practices. The following are just a few names one might come across in the historical and literary texts.

Philippos (Loves Horses)
Hipparchos (Horse Leader)
Khrysippos (Gold Horse)
Ktesippos (Horse Owner)
Hippolytos (Horse Looser)
Xanthippê (Blond Horse)
Hippodameia (Horse Tamer)
Hippodamas (Horse Tamer)
Hippomakhos (Horse Battle)
Hippothoös (Swift Horse)
Hipponoös (Horse-Minded)
Melanippos (Black Horse)

Areilykos (Ares' Wolf)
Autolykos (Wolf)
Loukos (Wolf)
Lykophontes (Wolf-Killer)
Lykophron (Wolf-Wise)
Lykourgos (Wolf Worker)
Lykomedes (Wolf Ruler)

Kyniska (Puppy)

Leonidas (Lion's Son)
Leokritos (Lion Judge)

Boukolos (Docked Bull)
Boukephalas (Ox-headed)

Eëtion (Eagle)

Drakon (Dragon) (or Really Big Snake, which is also kind of cool)

4

Peri Synousias: On (Public) Relationships

As we saw in the previous chapters, the ancient Greeks were a predominantly household/family-based society. Property belonged to the family far more so than to the individual, trades were typically handed down from parent to child, care went up and down the generations depending on age. The important life rites took place in the context of the family—weddings, funerals, births, and induction ceremonies such as the Apatouria in Athens.

Nevertheless, the Greeks also had their long-term, extrafamilial relationships, as discussed in Chapter 3. These ranged from the friendship with the girl next door (the distance of which being predicated on the city, village, or farmstead where one lived) to the more distant but just as binding ties of *xenia*, which prevailed across seas and across generations.

Then, of course, there were those less binding, less intimate, but more pervasive relationships—the acquaintances formed from living a daily life in a primarily urban- or village-based society (see Chapter 5). Two (often hopelessly intertwined) utterly prevalent aspects of ancient Greek society brought people together more than any other: religion and competition. Religion, with its public celebrations and communal organizations, is the subject of Chapter 7. Nevertheless, it must be noted here in brief that many of the aspects of daily and less-than-daily life in ancient Greece pertained to religion in some way, from the meals shared at home to the great Panhellenic sports contests like the Olympics.

The competitive spirit was also an all-pervasive, relentlessly dominant aspect of the ancient Greek mentality, and far more social events had a competitive aspect than we might assume in modern times. Some things had a rather obvious competitive vibe, such as sports or the military (victory was paramount in both). But, as we shall see, the Greeks could make *anything* competitive, and it is important to recognize that much social interaction was based on this competitive mentality—officially and unofficially. As such, it is worth taking a moment to explore the Greek notion of why you can never be too competitive.

A FEW WORDS ON WHY YOU CAN NEVER BE TOO COMPETITIVE

The ancient Greeks thrived on competition, and, as one might expect, over the years they came to make many facets of their lives competitive. Reasonably, an early aspect of competition was little more than keeping up with the Joneses, doing well almost to spite your next-door neighbor, and to keep from floundering so badly that your neighbor could buy your farm (ideally, you wanted to do so well that you could buy his). In his *Works and Days*, the eighth-century poet Hesiod personified this drive as the positive aspect of the goddess Eris, whose name technically means "strife" or "contention." (She was the goddess who was not invited to the wedding of Peleus and Thetis, got insulted, and tossed in the golden apple with the inscription "To the Fairest," causing one heck of a fight between Hera, Athena, and Aphrodite, which resulted in the Judgment of Paris, the Trojan War, and, ultimately, the downfall of Mycenaean civilization.) Strife was generally seen to be a bad thing, but she was capable of instilling that need to be better that drove on archaic farmers literally to be all that they could be, and ideally better than everyone else. Thus Hesiod's didactic poem on how to survive in business begins with a hymn to the goddess (*Works and Days* 11–26):

> And so there is not one kind of Strife, but on the earth
> There are two—the one the thinking man would praise;
> The other is blameworthy. They have distinct hearts entirely.
> For the one incites evil war and battle—
> Bitch! No mortal loves her, but of necessity,
> By the will of the immortals they honor grievous Strife.
> The other dark Night bore first,
> High-throned Kronides set her, dwelling in the aither,
> In the roots of the earth, and she is much better for men;
> And she stirs up even the hapless to work.
> For one craves work seeing another
> Wealthy, who rushes to plough and plant
> And well order his home. And neighbor vies with neighbor
> Rushing to wealth. This Strife is good for mortals.
> And potter begrudges potter, and artisan artisan,
> And beggar envies beggar, and singer singer.

So basically, competition makes us better. The Greeks really took this to heart, and over time more and more facets of their civilization came to take on competitive aspects. For example, it would appear that the Greeks invented the beauty contest. For men. Oh, sure, there were beauty contests for women, of course. In the sanctuary of Hera on the island of Lesbos the Archaic lyric poet Alkaios mentioned how (fr. 130b):

> . . . I dwell, keeping my feet out of trouble, where Lesbian women with trailing robes go to and fro being judged for beauty, and around rings the marvelous sound of the sacred yearly shout of women . . . (trans. Campbell 1982, 303)

And Athenaios provides even further data, in more places (*Deipnosophistai* 13.609e–f):

> I also know about a beauty contest for women that took place once—Nikias in his *Inquiries into the Arkadians* says about it that Kypselos himself established it, having founded a city in the plain by the Alpheios River. In it he settled some Parrasians and dedicated a temenos and altar to Demeter Eleusina, in whose festival the beauty contest is held. And the first one to win was his own wife Herodikê. This same contest still takes place even now, and the women competitors are called Gold-Bearers.

But then Athenaios goes on to note (609f–610a):

> Theophrastos says a beauty contest [of men] takes place in Elis, and the judging is accomplished with zeal, and those who have won the competition receive weapons, which they dedicate, according to Dionysios the Leukrian, to Athena. And the winner is beribboned by his friends and leads the parade up to the sanctuary. The crown given to them is of myrtle, as records Myrsilos in his *Historical Paradoxes*.

Even earlier in his eternally meandering narrative, he attests (13.565f):

> For in the Euandria ("good manliness") contests they judge the most handsome, and these they entrust to be the van guard. And in Elis there is a beauty contest, and to the first (-place winner) it is granted to carry the goddess' panoply; and to the second to lead the ox; the third sets up the burnt offering. Herakleides the Lembian recounts that in Sparta the handsomest man and the most beautiful woman are admired more than anything, and that the most beautiful women are of Spartan origin.

(Actually, there is debate as the locale of the most beautiful women in ancient Greece. Sparta produced Helen, of course, so that gave them a considerable advantage on the beauty scale. But the women of the isle of Lesbos were also deemed to be the most attractive. It's a bit like the competition between the Swedes and Brazilians now.)

The need to single out the most handsome male for the sake of a religious ritual also took place in the Boiotian town of Tanagra in central Greece.

Here, according to Pausanias (9.22.2) at the festival of Hermes Kriophoros ("Ram-Carrying"), the most attractive young man was chosen to walk around the circuit of the city wall holding a lamb on his shoulders, in imitation of the deity who once so banished a plague from the town.

There was even a male beauty contest amongst the competitions of the Panathenaiac festival in Athens. According to an early fourth-century inscription (*IG* II² 2311.75–76; see sidebar), the winner of the *euandria* competition and his tribe received an ox; according to Aristotle (*Ath. Pol.* 60.3), he received a shield. It would seem that the tribe in general received the ox for the sacrifice, and the man personally received the shield as his own prize. Once again, the matters of religion and competition merge in what in modern times would be a wholly secular (and generally female) event.

IG II² 2311 (Attika, circa 400–350 BCE)

For the Child Kithera-Players
First Place—a crown
Second Place . . .
Third Place . . .

Kithera-Singers
First Place—a crown
    Of gold leaves = 1,000 drakhmai
    Silver = five drakhmai
Second Place—1200 drakhmai
Third Place—500 drakhmai
Fourth Place—400 drakhmai
Fifth Place—300 drakhmai

Men's Aulos-Singers
First Place—a crown and 300 drakhmai
Second Place—100 drakhmai

Men's Kithera-Players
First Place—a crown and 300 drakhmai
Second Place—200 drakhmai
Third Place—100 drakhmai

Aulos-Players
First Place—the crown . . .
Second Place— . . .

To the Boy Winning the Stadion Race—50 amphoras of olive oil
Second Place—10 amphoras of olive oil

To the Boy Winning the Pentathlon—30 amphoras of olive oil
Second Place—6 amphoras of olive oil

To the Boy Winning at Wrestling—30 amphoras of olive oil
Second Place—6 amphoras of olive oil

To the Boy Winning at Boxing—30 amphoras of olive oil
Second Place—6 amphoras of olive oil

To the Boy Winning at the Pankration—40 amphoras of olive oil
Second Place—8 amphoras of olive oil

To the Youth ("beardless") Winning the Stadion Race—60 amphoras of
olive oil
Second Place—12 amphoras of olive oil

To the Youth Winning the Pentathlon—40 amphoras of olive oil
Second Place—12 amphoras of olive oil

To the Youth Winning at Wrestling—40 amphoras of olive oil
Second Place—8 amphoras of olive oil

To the Youth Winning at Boxing—40 amphoras of olive oil
Second Place—8 amphoras of olive oil

To the Youth Winning at the Pankration— . . . .
. . . .
. . . .
. . . .
. . . . . amphoras of olive oil
Second Place. . . . .

. . . . . . Two-Colt Chariot Race—40 amphoras of olive oil
Second Place—8 amphoras of olive oil

Two-Horse Chariot Race—140 amphoras of olive oil
Second Place—40 amphoras of olive oil

For the Warriors

For the Winner in Horseback Racing—16 amphoras of olive oil
Second Place—4 amphoras of olive oil

For the Winner in the Two-Horse Chariot Race—30 amphoras of olive oil
Second Place—6 amphoras of olive oil

For the Winner in the Yoked Processional—4 amphoras of olive oil
Second Place—1 amphora of olive oil

To the Javelin-Toss from Horseback Winner—5 amphoras of olive oil
Second Place—1 amphora of olive oil

Victory Prizes

Boys' Fire Dance—1 bull, 100 drakhmai
Youths' Fire Dance—1 bull, 100 drakhmai
Men's Fire Dance—1 bull, 100 drakhmai
Men's Beauty Contest (by tribe)—the winner wins a bull and 100 drakhmai
    To the tribe—1 bull, 100 drakhmai

To the Winner of the Torch Race—1 water jug, 30 drakhmai

Victory Prizes for the Boat Races

To the Winning Tribe—3 bulls, 300 drakhmai, 200 free meals
Second Place—2 bulls, 200 drakhmai

While the beauty contest might not strike the modern reader as that strange in the range of competitive possibilities (after all, we have them now, for women, men, and even children), the ancient Greeks did not stop there in their ongoing trend to make so many aspects of life competitive. Most musical and theatrical events were understood to be competitive (as well as religious) in nature. Even the humblest facets of domestic life could take on a competitive edge. After discussing the euandreia, Athenaios goes on to record (13.610):

> In some places this same Theophrastos says there are women's contests for sobriety and house-keeping, just like among the barbarians. In other places there are beauty contests, as though it's necessary to esteem this, just like in Tenedos and Lesbos. But this comes from nature and luck, while it is necessary to set honor upon sobriety. For beauty is in this way beautiful; otherwise it might lead to wantonness.

Yes, contests of sobriety and housekeeping. Unfortunately, there are no descriptions or explanations of rules for these anywhere. But perhaps the most amusing testimony to the competitive nature of the Greeks comes from the inscription on a fifth-century black figure vase from Athens, which reads, "I am Melosa's prize. She won a victory in the girls' carding contest" (Lefkowitz and Fant 1992, 162).

(For those of you living primarily in the twenty-first century who have no idea what a "record" is much less "carding," carding is part of the process of preparing fibers for spinning and weaving. Carding consists of combing or brushing the fibers—wool, flax, *et cetera*—so that they all line up in one direction and can thus be spun into yarn. In ancient Greece, young girls would be tasked with the rather simple job of carding, leaving the far more difficult processes of drop-spinning and weaving to older females.)

(For those of you who still live in the twenty-first century, "drop-spinning" is the process of literally turning loose fibers into yarn by spinning them together, using a weight to keep the spinning constant while carefully using the fingers to maintain an even amount of fiber going into the thread. Years ago when I was teaching a group of mythology students about how Herakles, as part of one of his punishments, had to dress as a woman and drop-spin at the feet of Queen Omphalê of Lydia, one of my student asked if drop-spinning was like break-dancing. It isn't. Or at least shouldn't be.)

The interesting thing is that, ultimately, this sense of competition brought the Greeks together more so than it tore them apart. This is mainly because the Greeks tended to compete in groups in sizes ranging, of course, from the individual (think of Melosa here) to peer groups of about a dozen people to entire military regiments. Even those athletes who competed singly represented their *poleis* and thus brought glory (or not) to their hometowns. The competition that set "us" against "them" inevitably created strong bonds amongst "us." As the ancient Greek social historian Nick Fisher considered the centripetal and centrifugal aspects of wide-scale competition:

> As the Greeks recognized from Hesiod's *Works and Days* onwards, *eris, philonikia* ["loving victory"] and *philotimia* ["loving honor"] were seen as inherently double-sided and ambivalent, constructive and destructive, both in the unlimited and in the restricted forms of contests. Those striving to excel in political arenas may be seen as gaining prestige by benefiting their communities, or by pursuing their conflicts to excessive and socially damaging levels; they may promote either social and economic mobility, or conflict and war . . . [T]he desire to win and be competitive and successful should not be seen as a specifically aristocratic or upper-class disposition of value, but as a motive which operated powerfully on everyone, elites, and non-elites alike . . .
>
> Training and competing for these events . . . involved intense and often pleasurable collaboration between the rich and the less rich, all driven by the competitive desire for collective victory. The language of *leitourgia* ["paying for large-scale events"] *euergesia* ["doing good works"], *charis* ["grace"], and *philotimia*, of individual ambition, involving reciprocal pleasures and mutual community benefits, linking together liturgists, participants, and general citizen

audiences, is routinely deployed in the law court speeches (from the beginning of the fourth century), and in inscriptions (from the mid fourth century) as central elements in the beneficial effects of these festivals. (Fisher 2011, 178, 200)

CONTEXTS FOR SOCIAL INTERACTION AMONG THE ANCIENT GREEKS

Choruses

A section on the ancient Greek chorus could technically go just about anywhere in this book. It was an element of adolescence and education, and thus Chapter 1; it formed bonds of friendship and even erotic attachments, and thus Chapters 3 and 2. Choruses were seen as indispensable elements in civic religion, thus Chapters 5 and 7. So I chose to put them here, in the middle of the book.

A chorus was a group of anywhere from two to 50 people of the same age who sang and/or danced together to musical accompaniment (lyre or flute) as part of some sort of official occasion, be that a religious ritual or a personal celebration such as a wedding (*especially* a wedding). Perhaps the most consistent aspect of the ancient Greek chorus was its communion of like-aged peoples, *helikes* or *halikes* in Greek (see Figure 4.1). Thus in his third *Pythian Ode* Pindar tells the tale of Philyra, who bore a child to Apollo before marriage (ll. 17–19):

> She did not wait for the bridal table to come,
> Nor the shouts of the full-toned hymnals, such as
> Maiden age-mates love to sing to their
> Companions in the evening-songs.

Likewise in his drama *Iphigeneia at Tauris*, the Athenian playwright Euripides put into the mouths of his female chorus (ll. 1143–1148):

> May I stand, a maiden, in choruses
> Of glorious weddings,
> Whirling with age-mates, friends,
> The thiasoi, away from my mother,
> To contests of grace,
> Luxurious strife of tresses . . .

Choruses of older age-mates also existed, consisting of bands of mature men and women. And so Herodotos records the establishment of a women's chorus on the island of Aigina (5.83):

> Because they were enemies the Aiginitans injured the Epidaurans . . . and most especially they seized their statues of Damia and Auxesia and brought them

Figure 4.1
White ground libation bowl (phiale) with girls' chorus, Attic, ca. 450 BCE.
Museum of Fine Arts, Boston, 65.908. (Photograph copyright 2013 Museum of
Fine Arts, Boston. All rights reserved./The Bridgeman Art Library)

home and dedicated them in the midst of their land—Oia is the name of the
place—at most some twenty stadia from the city. Having been dedicated in this
land they supplicated them with sacrifices and ribald women's choruses;
choregoi of ten men were appointed for each of the divinities. The choruses
insulted none of the men, but only the local women.

While choruses of age-mates were the norm in ancient Greece, there was
no perceived need to keep them strictly sex-segregated. Both same-sex and
mixed-sex choruses existed, although the same-sex variety was far more
common, especially in the later Classical period in the more public venues.
Nevertheless, already from the time of Homer, mixed choruses appeared as
common aspects of daily life, as the poet described as part of the decor on
the shield Hephaistos wrought for Akhilleus. Here, as part of the happy life
of peaceful villagers (*Iliad* 18.593–605):

There darling youths and worthy maidens
Danced, holding each other by the wrist.
The maidens had fine linens; the youths wore well-woven
Khitons, lightly glistening with oil.

And the maidens had lovely garlands; the youths had
Golden knives on belts of silver.
And sometimes they ran on deft feet
Quite easily, like someone fitting the potter's wheel and
Setting clay in his palms—he will test to see if it will run.
Other times they ran in lines towards each other.
The large throng stood about the lovely chorus,
Enjoying it. And the godly singer sang along with them,
Playing the lyre. And two tumblers amongst them
Led the song, whirling in their midst.

Likewise in the *Odyssey*, when the house of the recently returned Odysseus created the mirage of a wedding party in the royal house (23.143ff):

First they bathed and tossed on khitons.
The women arrayed themselves. The god-like singer took up
The hollow lyre; in them he aroused desire
For sweet song and faultless dance.
The great house echoed round with the feet
Of dancing men and fair-belted women.
Thus someone from outside, hearing those inside, would say,
"Truly then someone has married the much-wooed queen . . ."

The historical foundation of one such ritual with a mixed chorus on the island of Samos was preserved in Herodotos, recording the time that (3.48):

Periandros son of Kypselos [of Corinth] sent off three hundred sons of the most eminent men of the Korkyrians to Sardis, to Alyattes, for castration. When the Corinthians bringing the boys docked at Samos, the Samians learned of the story—how they were taking them to Sardis. First they instructed the boys to take refuge in the sanctuary of Artemis, and then they did not allow them to drag the suppliants from the sanctuary. Then when the Corinthians denied them food, the Samians had a festival, which is still held even now in the same way. For at night, so long as the boys were suppliants, they set up choruses of maidens and youths, and they officially established that the choruses should carry cakes of sesame and honey, so that the Korkyrian boys, snatching them, might have food. And this took place until such time as the Corinthian guards left for home. Then the Samians returned the boys to Korkyra.

Choruses, then, were opportunities for young people to meet members of the same and opposite sex, and to become socialized to dealing with people outside of the familial context. Most importantly for the ancient Greeks, choruses were modes of education. The arts of song and dance promoted discipline and grace, while the ability of chorus-mates to dance together and sing together was important for the harmonious interaction of fellow citizens of both sexes, as noted by the fifth-century Athenian philosopher Plato in his work *Laws* (664b–665a):

> We spoke, if we recall, at the start of our talk about how the nature of all the young is fiery, not the sort to keep quiet either in the body or voice, but they always blather randomly and leap about; and the perception of order for both of these [body and voice] does not pertain to other living beings, but only to humans alone. Indeed, to the ordering of movement the name "rhythm" is given, and that of voice—when the sharp is mixed with the deep—the name offered is "harmony." The two together is called "chorustry."

The Roman-era historian Polybios was quite detailed in his discussion of the role of the choruses in the education and enculturation of the people of Arkadia (4.20–21):

> For music, real music, is a benefit for all peoples to practice, and is mandatory for the Arkadians. For music must not be thought—as Ephoros says in the introduction to his universal study, which is not at all in accord with his uttered statement—to have been introduced to humanity for trickery or enchantment, but that the old Cretans and Lakedaimonians brought flute and rhythm to war instead of trumpets, as seems probable, or the first Arkadians took up music for the whole state to such an extent that not only boys, but also young men until age thirty are perforce brought up with it, though in other matters they are most austere in their lifestyle. For these things are commonly known to all: First of all, that pretty much only amongst the Arkadians are the children from infancy accustomed to sing the customary hymns and paians, which each sings according to the ancestral tradition of the local heroes and deities. Then later, learning the traditional tunes of Philoxenos and Timotheos, with great zeal they dance every year in the Dionysia, to flutes, in the theaters—the boys in the children's competitions, the young men in the so-called men's contests. And likewise throughout life, in their gatherings, they do not bring in foreign elements among them, but they set up groups to sing to each other. And of other educational matters they deny that it is a shame not to know something; but it isn't possible to deny knowing the art of song, because everyone has to learn it, nor can they decline singing, because that is the real disgrace amongst them. And really, in marching to the flute and making formations, they do so like dancing with choreographed moves and extravagance, annually displaying their form in the theaters to the citizens . . . Wishing to soften and temper their stubborn and harsh nature, they both introduced all these things mentioned above, and have common gatherings and great sacrificial rites, in which both men and women equally take part, and also choruses of maidens as well as of boys, and in sum they devised everything attempting to tame and soften their harshness of the soul through the regulation of their customs.

And our old friend Atheniaos, recalling the choruses of the days of old, recounts (14.628e–f):

For the type of dance in the choruses then was elegant and magnificent, as though they imitated the movements of men at arms. Thus even Sokrates in his poems says that the best dancers are also best in warfare, speaking thus:

"Those in choruses best honor the deities, and are best in war."

For some choruses were practically just like armed manoeuvres, and they displayed not only the good order of the rest, but also the care taken of the bodies.

So, how did a chorus "work"? As noted previously, a chorus consisted of anywhere from two to a dozen to 50 age-mates who trained together to learn a song and/or dance to perform for a specific function such as a religious ritual or a special event such as a wedding. These *choreutes/choirtes* were led by an individual called the *choregos*, the leader of the chorus. In same-sex choruses, the leader was typically the same sex as the rest of the group; in mixed-sex choruses the leader was always male. The choregos stood out in some way, almost inevitably being the most attractive member of the group. She or he might also be just a tad older, or taller, or at least more mature, than the rest of the chorus. So much is evident as early as Homer's *Odyssey*, when Nausikaä goes to do laundry with her girlfriends (6.99–109):

> But when they had enjoyed lunch, she and her servant girls
> Played with the ball, having tossed off their hair-bands.
> White-armed Nausikaä began the song for them.
> Like arrow-pouring Artemis darts about the mountains,
> Of lofty Taygetos, or Erymanthos,
> Enjoying boars and fleet deer,
> While with her nymphs, daughters of aigis-bearing Zeus,
> Nature-dwellers, play, delighting the mind of Leto.
> Artemis holds her head and brows above them all,
> Easily recognized she is—they all are beautiful!
> Thus the untamed maiden stood out amongst her hand-maids.

The devotion that chorus mates are supposed to feel for their choregos comes across most strongly in one of the very few choral poems for girls that has come down to modern times. This is the so-called *Parthenaion* ("Maidens' Song") by the lyric poet Alkman (see sidebar *Parthenaion*). Here, in what appears to be a split chorus of girls, each side sings about the beauty and perfection of their individual choregoi—Hagesikhora and Agido. These super-peers (if you will) were responsible for starting the dance or song for the rest of the chorus, and for leading either the choral procession or centering the dancing circle. Those of you who have seen modern Greek or Bulgarian dances are familiar with the position at the head of the circle and have seen how the modern choregos adds fancier steps to the baseline choreography of the dance. Somewhat by contrast, in ancient Greece, the choregos at least began in the center of the circle, rather than being part of it. In some instances, the choregos could actually be the musician playing the music to which the rest of the chorus sang or danced. So much was true of the paradigmatic, heavenly chorus in Greek tradition: Apollo with his lyre serving as choregos to the chorus of Muses.

Alkman's *Partheneion*

There is some vengeance of the deities;
He is blessed, whoever gladly
Lives out the day
Without tears. I sing
The light of Agido—I see
Her as the sun, which for us—
Agido bears witness—
Shines. The illustrious choregos
Does not allow me to praise
Or to blame her. For it seems she is
Preeminent, as if someone
Should set in the herds a horse
Strong, victorious, sounding-hoofed,
Of winged dreams.

Or do you not see? The Enetian
Racing horse. The flowing hair
Of my kinswoman.
Hagesikhora shines
Like unmixed gold,
And her silver face;
Why do I tell you openly?
Hagesikhora herself,
The second after Agido in beauty,
Will race like a Kolaxian horse against Ibenian.
For the Pleiades fight us
As we bring a cloak to Orthria
Through ambrosial night, like Sirius
Star rising.

For neither something of violet
Is enough to defend one,
Nor a colorful snake
All of gold, nor a Lydian
Headband, of young girls,
Soft-eyed, the delight.
Nor Nanno's hair,
Nor even divine-faced Areta,
Nor Sylakis and Kleësisera,

Nor going to Ainesimbrota and saying
"Astraphis—were that she were mine!"
And Philylla to glance here
And lovely Damareta and Ianthemis—
But Hagesikhora guards me.

For is fair-ankled
Hagesikhora not near here?
Doesn't she stay close to Agido
And together praise the festival?
But, deities, please receive
Our prayers. For fulfillment and
Perfection are of the deities. Chorus-leader,
If I might speak. I myself
Am a maiden; in vain from the perch I screech,
An owl. But I most of all want to delight
Aotis—of our sufferings
She was the healer.
But young girls were treading the
Lovely path from Hagesikhora.

For the trace-horse
Likewise . . .
The helmsman, one must
On a ship obey him most of all.
She is not more songstress
Than the Sirens,
For they are goddesses. But against eleven
This one of ten children sings.
It cries out like a swan on
The streams of Xenthos River.
Her lovely blond hair . . .

Finally, in addition to the chorus and the choregos was the poet, the individual who wrote whatever it was that the chorus sang. More likely than not, this poet was then present to direct the chorus in the performance of the piece, probably playing the musical accompaniment while the choregos served as subdirector, especially for the dance. A poem from the *Greek Anthology* says as much about the famous Lesbian poet Sappho (9.189):

Come to the shining temenos of bull-faced Hera,
Lesbians, circling with delicate strides of your feet.
There set up the fair chorus for the goddess; for you will Sappho,
Holding her golden lyre in her hands, be leader.
Blessed in the delightful dance—the sweet song
Of Kalliopê herself you will think you hear.

It was through the poetry that much of the educational aspect of choral performance was manifest. The poems (what remains of them) contain stories of mythology, history, and lessons in right conduct, all of which functioned to instill factual data and moral lessons in the chorus members who performed the songs in question. This, of course, was in addition to the physical aspect of learning choreographies, which instilled bodily discipline and the ability to coordinate movements, leading to better military formations for boys and general grace for girls. In short, for much of early Greek history, the chorus was the equivalent of grade school.

As noted earlier, choruses were organized for specific reasons, typically religious festivals where they hymned and entertained the deities. Another common function of the chorus was to celebrate weddings, such as is expressed at the beginning of Theokritos's *Thirteenth Idyll*, theoretically performed at the wedding of Helen of Sparta herself (ll. 1–8):

> Once upon a time by blond, Spartan Menelaos
> Village maidens wearing blooming hyacinth
> Stood in a chorus before the newly painted bedroom,
> Twelve, foremost in the city, great wealth of the Lakonians,
> Because Tyndareos' daughter received the love
> Of her suitor—Helen, and the young son of Atreus.
> And they all sing one song, stomping
> Their intertwining feet; under the roof rang with the wedding song!

In classical Athens, numerous religious festivals occurred year round that required male choruses. These choruses were gathered and organized according to tribe (of which there were 10 in Athens from the end of the sixth century), and appear to have contained males of all classes within those tribes. As such, the various civic choruses were opportunities for boys and men of different classes to mingle and get to know their fellow citizens. According to the statistics mustered by Nick Fisher:

> The City Dionysia demanded . . . 500 boys and 500 men for the cyclic dances, and 36 adults for tragic choruses, increased to 45 after the 460s; the cyclic dances at the Thargelia came to demand half as many as the City Dionysia, as tribes doubled up, 250 boys and 250 men, certainly by the mid fifth century, and perhaps immediately following 508/7. By the later fifth century there were liturgically-funded cyclic choruses as well as the Greater and the Lesser Panathenaia . . . [B]y c. 440 there may well have been a further 1,000, or perhaps 500, choral performers. . . . Comedies at the City Dionysia, requiring 120 chouretai, began in 487/6; the addition of tragedies and comedies at the Lenaia seems to date c. 440s . . . This brought in a need for a further 24 tragic and 120 comic choretai (though metics were eligible as well as citizen here). In addition to the city festivals, we should assume widespread citizen participation, possibly at lower levels of expertise, in the choral competitions in the Rural Dionysia of the demes. (Fisher 2011, 187–188)

In short, Athens needed approximately 5,000 chorus performers per year, equaling some 10 to 20 percent of the population. This was indeed a good way to get to know one's neighbors.

Unfortunately, some of the same problems that plague modern coaches and high-school theater directors plagued the ancients as well. The biggest problem was that one suddenly found oneself responsible for teenagers, who are internationally notorious for being idiots and doing stupid things like drinking themselves to death. A court case from classical Athens suggests that something similar occurred to one choregos/director when a member of his chorus died from drinking poison. (Please note that at this point, the definition of "choregos" had changed slightly to refer to the adult who paid to organize and train the chorus, rather than the peer who led them.) Brought up on charges of homicide, the choregos described the process by which he gathered and trained his chorus, and how his personal oversight may have lapsed (Antiphon 6.11–14):

> When I was appointed choregos for the Thargelia and got Pantakles as instructor and the Kekropid tribe in addition to my own (the Erekhtheids), I managed the chorus as best as I was able and most justly. So first I set up a most serviceable training room in my house, the very one in which I taught for the Dionysia when choregos. Then I collected the chorus as best I could, neither fining anyone nor bringing in a pledge by violence nor making any enemies, but just as it was the sweetest and most suitable on both sides; I urged and asked, and they willingly and agreeably provided. And when the boys came, at first I had no time to be there and to care for them myself, for it happened that I was then involved in that legal suit with Ariston and Philinos, which I had worked on for a long time, right up until the impeachment, which I rightly and justly displayed to the Council and the Athenian people. For the boys I devised this: I appointed Phanostratos to look after them, if it might be necessary for the chorus. He is a fellow citizen of these accusers, and my own son-in-law; I gave him my daughter, and deemed him best to care for them. And in addition to him were two men; the first was Ameirian of the Erekhtheids, whom his tribesmen themselves elected to assemble [a chorus] and to tend to the tribe on many occasions, finding him useful. The other . . . from the Kekropid tribe, likewise was accustomed to assemble for that tribe. Then there was a fourth man—Philippos—to whom it had been assigned to purchase and spend on whatever the teacher or those other men might have asked for, so that they might coach the boys to the best of their ability and no one should want for anything because I was busy. This was the management of the chorus . . .

Finding the "best" chorus, "without making any enemies"(!) was of great importance to the choregos because, as you may have guessed, the choruses were competitive. For the triumphant choregos, there was much status to be had, many commemorative stelai to be erected, and many leafy chaplets to

wear. It is thus hardly surprising to note just how much money the more affluent choregoi might spend on these endeavors. One defendant in a lawsuit
from fourth-century Athens bragged to the jury (Lysias 21.1–2):

> I was certified of age in the arkhonship of Theopompos, and being appointed
> choregos for the tragedies I spent 30 minas, and in the third month after that,
> having won the men's chorus in the Thargelia, two thousand drakhmai, and in
> the arkhonship of Glaukippos, for the fire-dances for the Greater Panathenaia,
> eight hundred drakhmai. And being choregos for the men at the Dionysia
> during that same arkhonship, I won and spent on it, including the tripod
> I dedicated, 5,000 drakhmai, and in the arkhonship of Diokles at the Lesser
> Panathenaia, three hundred on a cyclic chorus.

Interestingly, the man was brought up on charges of taking bribes.

The Palaistra and the Gymnasion

The *palaistra* is literally the "wrestling room," while the *gymnasion* is the
"place to get naked." (Really.) Together they functioned as the centers of
learning in the ancient poleis, where boys (and occasionally young girls) went
to receive both physical and intellectual education. As such, they were a complement to the more free-form choruses. The latter, as we saw previously, were
ad hoc groups of peers who trained together for specific performances, learning
history, morality, and group motion via dance in unison. The sports complexes comprised of the palaistrai and gymnasia were where (usually) males
of different ages came together to train in athletics, learn music and how to
play musical instruments, learn their letters, and engage in discussions
between the generations. In modern times, we have schools with gyms
attached; in ancient Greece, they had gyms that were schools.

The physical realia of both palaistrai and gymnasia (usually appearing
together as a unit, and called by either name almost randomly) have come
down to us from both literature and archaeology. Both sets of data somewhat
postdate the periods of concern in this book, but they appear to reflect older
traditions and thus will be of use here. The best verbal description we have
of the layout of the palaistra comes from the Roman-era author Vitruvius Pol-
lio, who wrote a monumental treatise on architecture (no pun intended).
Chapter 11 of Vitruvius's work concerns the palaistra, which Vitruvius notes
is not a Roman structure, but which he covers for the sake of tradition (5.11):

> The oblong peristyle in a palaistra should be so formed that the circuit of it
> makes a walk of two stadia, a distance which the Greeks call the *diaulos*. Let
> three of its colonnades be single, but let the fourth, which is on the south side,
> be double, so that when there is bad weather accompanied by wind, the drops
> of rain may not be able to reach the interior. In the three colonnades construct

roomy recesses with seats in them, where philosophers, rhetoricians, and others who delight in learning may sit and converse. In the double colonnade let the rooms be arranged thus: The young men's hall in the middle; this is a very spacious recess (*exedra*) with seats in it, and it should be one third longer than it is broad. At the right, the bag room; then next, the dust room; beyond the dust room, at the corner of the colonnade, the cold washing room, which the Greeks call *loutron*. At the left of the young men's hall is the anointing room; then, next to the anointing room, the cold bath room, and beyond that a passage into the furnace room at the corner of the colonnade. Next, but inside and on a line with the cold bath room, put the vaulted sweating bath, its length twice its breadth, and having at the ends on one side a Laconicum, proportioned in the same manner as above described, and opposite the Laconicum the warm washing room. Inside a palaistra, the peristyle ought to be laid out as described above. But on the outside, let three colonnades be arranged, one as you leave the peristyle and two at the right and left, with running-tracks in them. That one of them which faces the north should be a double colonnade of very ample breadth, while the other should be single, and so constructed that on the sides next to the walls and the side along the columns it may have edges, serving as paths, of not less than ten feet, with the space between them sunken, so that steps are necessary in going down from the edges a foot and a half to the plane, which plane should be not less than twelve feet wide. Thus people walking round on the edges will not be interfered with by the anointed who are exercising. This kind of colonnade is called among the Greeks *xystos*, because athletes during the winter season exercise in covered running tracks. Next to this xystos and to the double colonnade should be laid out the uncovered walks which the Greeks term *paradromides* and our people xysta, into which in fair weather during the winter, the athletes come out from the xystos for exercise. The xysta ought to be so constructed that there may be plantations between the two colonnades or groves of plane trees, with walks laid out in them among the trees and resting places there, made of *opus signinum*. Behind the xystos a stadium, so designed that great numbers of people may have plenty of room to look on at the contests between the athletes. (trans. Morgan 1914)

Different activities took place in the palaistrai and gymnasia. There was more of a lecture component to the palaistra, of course, but in terms of sports the palaistra was the place for things like wrestling (obviously), boxing (think of the punching bag room), and the pankration (ancient Greek MMA). Track and field took place in the gym. Apparently the Greeks figured out that it's really bad to put your wrestlers in the same building as your javelin throwers.

The various sports complexes employed various men to educate their charges. One of the best sources for information on this is the third-century inscription from Teos presented in Chapter 1. Here we read about the *gymnasiarkhos*, who was the equivalent of a modern school principal, being in charge of the building, its staff, and the program of education delivered. He was

Figure 4.2
Attic red-figure kylix with boys' school scene, signed by Douris, ca. 490–480 BCE.
From Cerveteri, Italy. Staatliche Museen Berlin, Antinkensammlung F 2285b.
(Drawing by Paul C. Butler)

assisted by the ancient vice principal—the *paidonomos*. Both of these men were required by law to be over 40 years old. They hired the instructors, settled disputes, and were in charge of the testing that determined if the various age grades were fit to move on in their studies, which they were required to do once a year. Beneath these administrators were the teachers themselves—the *didaskaloi*. Some taught letters, some taught music (see Figure 4.2), some taught archery and/or javelin throwing, and some specially hired teachers taught military drills. Then there was the *paidotribes*, the physical trainers-*cum*-coaches.

These older men were responsible for educating the future male citizens of the polis. Their students appear to have ranged in age from childhood—young boys who needed to be escorted to class by their *paidagogoi*, literally "boy-leaders" or, more accurately, caretakers (the word only *sounds* like a kiddie strip club)—all the way to the ephebes, who were around 18 years of age. Men between the ages of 20 and 40 do not appear to have been allowed in the palaistra complexes for fear that they would "corrupt" (seduce) the young students. Great care was taken to avoid that, including limiting who could enter the palaistra and when. So much is recorded in the laws of Classical Athens, as was recited during a fourth-century court case involving male prostitution. Here, in his *Against Timarkhos*, Aiskhenes had read out in court the law (*Against Timarkhos* 12):

> The boys' teachers will open the school not before sun-rise, and will close it before sun-set. And it is not permitted for those over the age of the boys to

enter when the boys are within, unless he be the teacher's son or brother or daughter's husband. If someone should enter contrary to these stipulations, let him pay the penalty with his death. And the gymnasiarkhs for the Hermaia may not permit anyone of adult age to enter the games. If he should permit this and not expel him from the gymnasium, let the gymnasiarkh be liable to the law of corruption of the free-born. The choregoi appointed by the demos must be at least forty years old.

Ultimately, the Greeks didn't really need older men for matters of love and seduction; this took place between boys of various ages, anyway. We see this in one of the Platonic dialogues, wherein Sokrates (a bit more of a rogue than most people seem to realize) grilled the older adolescent Hippothales rather mercilessly about his affections for a young fellow palaistra-mate named Lysis, after whom the dialogue is named. The opening of the dialogue gives a good introduction of the role of the palaistra and its frequenters in ancient Greece (see the sidebar about Lysis; see also the side bar in Chapter 2 about Kharmides). Here we see that various age groups interacted in the palaistra, the older Hippothales being totally crushed out on the younger Lysis. This older boy went to school not in the company of any paidagogos, but with his friends. He was clearly welcomed to invite Old Man Sokrates into the edifice, who was welcomed there to provide discussion and instruction to the younger students. These students did not only study edifying topics such as philosophy and wrestling, but they played games with the ancient equivalent of dice. And it is interesting to note that two of our modern terms for places of education, the academy and the French lycée, both come from these two Athenian sports-complexes—the Akademy and the Lykeion—frequented by Plato and Aristotle.

Plato *Lysis* 203a–205a and 206c–207b

I was making my way from the Akademy straight to the Lykeion on the road outside the city wall under the wall itself. When I was near the little gate by which is the spring of Panops, there I happened across Hippothales son of Hieronymos and Ktesippos the Paianian and some other young men with them, all standing together. And Hippothales seeing me approached.

"O Sokrates," he said, "where are you heading, and from where?"
"From the Akademy," I said, "straight to the Lykeion."
"Well come here," he said, "straight to us. Won't you turn aside? It's worth it."
"Where," I said, "do you mean, and who is with you?"
"Here," he said, showing me a walled enclosure in the area right opposite the wall, and an opened door. "We're passing time," he said, "here, both ourselves and several other fine fellows."

"And what indeed is this place, and what your pastime?"
"A palaistra," he said, "newly built. The pastime is much discussion, in which we would gladly share with you."
"Fine, then," I said, "and well done. Who's the teacher here?"
"Your comrade," he said, "and admirer—Mikkos."
"By Zeus!" I said, "He's not a measly man, but a worthy professor."
"Would you then follow," he said, "so that you might see the fellows here?"
"Firstly I would gladly hear on what stipulation I enter, and who is the handsome fellow among you?"
"Each of us to one or another, O Sokrates."
"And who to you, O Hippothales? Tell me this."

And on being asked he blushed. And I said, "O child of Hieronymos, Hippothales, you don't even have to say whether you're in love or not. For I know that not only are you in love, but also that you are already so far gone in your passion. I may be paltry and useless in other matters, but this was given to me by god—right quickly can I recognize the lover and beloved."

And hearing this he got even redder. So then Ktesippos said, "It's so pretty when you blush, O Hippothales, and shrink from telling Sokrates the name! If he even spent a minute with you, he would be beside himself from hearing you eternally talking. Really, O Sokrates, he has made us all deaf and has stuffed our ears with 'Lysis!' And if he should get a bit tipsy, then it's all too easy for us even waking from sleep to think that we hear the name of Lysis. And the things he describes minutely in prose—they're awful, but not completely awful. But whenever he attempts to gush poetry and treatises at us. . .? And it's worse than that, because he sings to the kid in this amazing voice, which we have to endure hearing. And now being asked by you, he blushes."

"Is then," I said, "this Lysis someone young, as it seems? I would think so since I don't recognize the name on hearing it."
"Not entirely," he said, "these guys call him by his own name, but he is still called for his father because his father is exceptionally well-know. And I know well that you are hardly ignorant of the boy's appearance, for from that alone it is enough to recognize him."
"Tell me," I said, "whose boy is he?"
"Demokratos'," he said, "of Aixonê, his eldest son."
"So!" I said, "O Hippothales, how noble and dashing this love you have discovered all over! And show me some of the things you showed them, so that I might know if you know the things it's necessary for a lover to say about boys, either to him or to others."
"Do you really value anything he says, O Sokrates?" asked Hippothales.
"I wonder whether you are in denial of the love of which he spoke," I said.
"Not at all," he said, "but I *don't* write poems or stuff about the boy!"

"He's not sane," said Ktesippos, "but he acts like a loon and raves like a maniac."

. . . .

"For should you enter with Ktesippos here and sit down and have a chat, I think he'll come to you himself, for he loves to hear you debate, O Sokrates, and likewise, as they are conducting the Hermaia, the young men and the boys have been mingled together in the same place—so they'll come to you. And if not, he is a close friend of Ktesippos through his first cousin Menexenos. For of everyone Lysis happens to be best friends with Menexenos. So have him summon Lysis if he doesn't come otherwise."

"Make it so," I said. And taking Ktesippos with me I entered the palaistra; the others came in after us.

Having entered we there came upon the boys having just made a sacrifice, and the religious matters having recently been accomplished they were all playing knucklebones [dice] and were especially well dressed. Many in the courtyard were playing outside, but some were playing odds-and-evens in a corner of the changing room with several knucklebones, taking them from some little baskets. Meanwhile others were standing about watching. And Lysis was certainly there, and he stood amongst the boys and young men, wreathed and with a distinguished appearance. He was not only worthy of the "handsome" but also of "fine and noble" [*kalos kagathos* in Greek, a hendyades equivalent to "Best and Brightest" in English]. And we headed over to the opposite corner and sat down, as it was quiet there, and we discussed something with the others. And so Lysis turning about frequently watched us, and clearly he was anxious to come over. For a while, though, he was at a loss and was standing by himself, shrinking from coming over. But when Menexenos came in from the courtyard after playing, and he saw me and Ktesippos, he came over to sit with us; and seeing him Lysis then followed and joined our group, sitting by Menexenos. And then the other fellows came over, and especially Hippothales, when he saw so many standing there. But he stood hiding amongst them where he thought that Lysis wouldn't see him, fearing lest he irritate him. And so he stood by and listened . . .

There can be no doubt that strong friendships between males were forged in the palaistrai between people of different ages and even different classes. But even without the formation of such strong bonds, it was here that males came to know and train with their fellow citizens, to have their earliest love affairs, and to be inculcated with the ideals of the polis. They also learned how to punch, both physically and verbally. As Stephen Miller, an expert in ancient Greek sports put it:

> [T]hese were training grounds for every young man and for every aspect of the man. Successful athletes emerged from the playing fields of the Akademy and Lykeion, and successful poets, playwrights, politicians, and philosophers emerged as well. Here young legs and young minds were stretched and prepared for all life's competitions. (Miller 2004, 185)

It is extremely difficult to determine to what extent females used the palais-trai and gymnasia. Based on the works of Xenophon and Plutarch, it appears evident that Spartan girls and women, at least, used the sports centers as much as the men did. It was the Spartan lawgiver Lykourgos who insisted that girls and women train alongside the men-folk, just as scantily clad, so that they would be healthy and thus bear healthy children for the state (see Chapter 1). The evidence from other poleis is far more meager. As we shall see later in this chapter, girls did compete in athletic events, which might suggest that there was some place for them to train back home, although certainly not in the same facilities as did the males. The sanctuary of Artemis at Brauron, close to Athens, had a palaistra as one of its facilities, and pottery fragments from the site depict girls racing. This sanctuary was predominantly used by females for initiation ceremonies, which would suggest that there was some palaistra-use by girls, even in staunchly patriarchal Attika.

As stated at the beginning of this chapter, religion was all-pervasive in ancient Greek life, and these ancient Greek health clubs were no exception. The gods of the gym were typically Herakles—the god of strength and striving generally, Hermes—the god of racing and wrestling, and Eros—the god of erotic attachment (figure it out for yourself). Other deities who could be present were Apollo—god of music, and the goddess Athena—the patroness of letters and learning. But this masculine gender tendency should not blind one to the fact that apparently all the deities like sports, and sports facilities could be dedicated to goddesses just as readily as to gods. Thus in 565 BCE in Athens (*IG* I^3 507):

> The sacred ministers made the race track—Krates, Thrasykles, Aristodikos, Bryson, Antenor . . .
>   They first established the games for the grey-eyed Maiden [Athena]

Sports

What the kids (and adults) learned in the gyms was put into effect in the sports competitions, and it was here that they entered an even larger world. Many sporting events were, of course, local affairs, competitions established to delight the deities who were their chief audience. But the larger events, such as the Olympics, were Panhellenic in scope, even to the point of being a defining criterion for what it meant to be Greek at all (see Chapter 5). Participating in such events brought individual Greeks out into the greater Greek world and allowed them to interact with a fuller range of individuals than could be expected in the home polis (with the possible exception of Athens, which was about as cosmopolitan then as New York City is now).

Games and Play

Not all athletic events were necessarily grand in scope, however. In ancient Greece, as now, sometimes folks just played, and some of their athletic pastimes look remarkably similar to what you might see on a suburban street or a park today. For example, it might not be all that surprising to discover that the Greeks could swim (no city was ever that far from a body of water). Spandex had not yet been invented, so swimming, as many other sports, was done in the nude (see earlier discussion about gymnasions). (This is probably less likely to be seen in the park, but you never know.) Thus on a red figure amphora from about 520 BCE we see a group of girls getting undressed to go swimming (see Figure 4.3). One girl is already stroking freestyle with some fish while she waits for her girlfriends to join her.

Figure 4.3
Attic red-figure amphora with girls swimming. Andokides Painter, sixth century BCE. Louvre F 203. (Drawing by Paul C. Butler)

The Greeks also had various ball games. As early as Homer's *Odyssey*, we hear about the juggling-like dances of the Phaiakians (8.399–411):

Alkinoös bade Alios and Laodamas
Alone to dance, since no one rivaled them.
And then they took in their hands the lovely ball
Of purple which skillful Polybos made for them,
And the one would toss it to the shadowy clouds,
Doubling backwards; then the other, rising up from the earth
Easily caught it, before his feet touched down.
But when indeed they had tested throwing the ball straight,
Then they danced upon the much-nourishing earth,
Tossing the ball. And the other youths beat time,
Standing by the contest, and a great din arose.

About a thousand years later, we get additional information about ball games from a second-century CE rhetorician named Pollux, who wrote (9.103–107):

The names of children's ball games were *episkyros*, *phaininda*, *aporraxis*, and *ourania*. Episkyros is also called *ephebikê* and *epikoinon*; it is played in teams divided equally. Then in the middle they trace a line with chalk, which they call "skyron," upon which they set the ball. Having drawn two other lines, one behind each of the teams, the first ones to take the ball cast it over the other team, whose task it was to run and cast back the moving ball until one team got it behind their opponents' line.

Phaininda is so-called either from Phainindos—who first invented it—or from "phenakizein" ("to trick"), because one feints to one while throwing to another, totally tricking his expectations. One might conjecture that it is like the game with the small ball, the one named for snatching, and probably it ought to be called the soft-ball game.

In aporraxis, it was necessary to bounce the ball on the ground vigorously, trying to dribble the ball with the hand, and then counting the number of bounces.

For ourania one bending backwards casts the ball to the sky ["*ouranos*"]; it was the task of those leaping to catch it before it hit the ground, just like Homer showed among the Phaiakians. When they send the ball against the wall they calculate the number of hits. And the one with the least is called "donkey" and does everything set before him; the winner was "King" and commanded.

One ball game was played with a smallish ball that the players would move on the ground with horns attached to sticks (see Figure 4.4). It looks for all the world like field hockey.

The Big Four

At the far extreme of kids' play, though, were the great Panhellenic festivals, those competitions held in honor of the deities that summoned athletes

Figure 4.4
Plinth of kouros statue depicting players with sticks and ball, known as "Hockey
players." From the Kerameikos necropolis in Athens. National Archaeological
Museum, Athens, Greece, Inv. 347. (De Agostini Picture Library/G. Dagli Orti/
The Bridgeman Art Library)

from all over the Greek world. These games were quite different from what we
experience today, either at their namesake—the Olympics—or even in normal professional sports. For one thing, most of the competitions were enacted
in the nude. The footraces, discus throwing, wrestling, the pankration were all
done by naked athletes and are thus called the gymnastic ("nude") events.
Boxers, however, did wear gloves. Second, there were no team sports; it was
individual athlete against individual athlete. Third, there was only one winner per game, no second or third place. Fourth, there was no standardization
of much of anything. Every stadium excavated has a different length for the
races, ad hoc boxing rings, and so on. Fifth, instead of getting yellow cards,
warnings, or monetary penalties, athletes who screwed up were flogged.
The referees are easy to spot in the ancient depictions because they stand
by the athletes and carry *rhabdoi*—rods used to thwack competitors who jump
the gun in racing or gouge out eyes in the pankration (see Figure 4.5). Sixth,
competitors were divided up by age categories—boys, youths, and men; or
girls and women. Perhaps most surprising is that you didn't technically have
to be alive to win. You had to be alive to *compete*, of course (rules are rules),
but if you died in the process, you could be awarded your victory crown post-
mortem, something like Heath Ledger winning an Oscar several months after
his death. Two stories have come down to us about athletes who simultaneously died and won in the ring. As related by Pausanias (8.40.3–5):

For the Argives gave the crown in the Nemean Games to Kreugas—having died—because when he was fighting against Damoxenos of Syracuse, Damoxenos overstepped the agreement between the two of them. For they were about to come together for a boxing match in the evening, and they agreed in ear-shot [of others] to take turns allowing each one to give the other a punch. For those boxers then, unlike now, there were no sharp straps around the wrists of each; but rather they fought with soft gloves, tied under the hollow part of the hand, so that their fingers were left bare. These soft gloves were made of fine strips of raw ox hide plaited together in the old method. So then Kreugas took a punch at Damoxenos' head. Then Damoxenos asked Kreugas to lift his hand. When he lifted it, Damoxenos struck with his fingers under the ribs, and from the force of the blow the finger nails and hands went into the body and seized the entrails inside and ripped them out. And Kreugas released his soul on the spot, and the Argives cast out Damoxenos because he overstepped the agreement and instead of one punch he responded with many blows. And to Kreugas—now dead—they gave the victory and made a likeness of him in Argos, and in my day it's still there in the sanctuary of Apollo Lykios.

Similarly, Philostratos tells a tale that took place during the pankration competition at the Olympics of 564 (*Pictures* 2.6):

Thus his opponent seizing Arrikhion around the middle then thought to kill him, and he cast his right forearm around him and choked off his breathing. Fixing his legs on Arrikhion's groin and winding the ends of both feet around

Figure 4.5
Attic red-figure kylix with scene of the Pankration, from Vulci, Italy. Foundry Painter, ca. 490–480 BCE. British Museum #E78 (1850.3-2.2). (Drawing by Paul C. Butler)

each knee, by choking him he damaged him while the sleep of death raced over his senses. But because he relaxed the grip he had on his legs he did not derail Arrikhion's strategy, for kicking out the edge of his foot Arrikhion (now risking his own right knee which was left hanging) he got his opponent in a groin hold until he could no longer wrestle against him. Then setting himself on the left he violently closed in his knees on the opponent's foot, and thus he ripped the opponent's ankle out of its socket. So as Arrikhion's soul was leaving the body, the body was powerless to act, but the spirit gave him the strength to support him.

It was written that the one who was choking him resembled a corpse, and he signaled with his hand that he conceded.

Kind of as a corollary, provided you were alive, you didn't technically have to compete to win. Some athletes, especially in the more brutal sports, had such amazing reputations that no one really wanted to fight them. Such was the case with Milo, the champion wrestler from Kroton in southern Italy. At the Olympic Games of 520, no one would come out to fight him, much less try to throw him the three times necessary to win the bout. However, as Milo went up to get his prize (*Greek Anthology* 11.316):

Into the sacred arena Milo the wrestler once arrived alone. Immediately the *athlothetes* called to have him crowned. Heading up he slipped and fell on his hip; and they cried that he should not be crowned, if he fell all by himself. Standing in their midst he cried back:

"That wasn't three times. I fell once; let someone throw me the other two!"

So the big games had some distinctive features. There were four primary Panhellenic competitions: the Olympic Games held every four years in honor of Olympian Zeus, the Pythian games held every four years for Delphic Apollo, the Nemean games that met every two years in honor of Zeus, and the Isthmian games that also met every two years in honor of Poseidon. The really hard-core athletes would do the full circuit, attending six competitions every four-year cycle. Here they would meet up with other athletes, hard-core and otherwise, as well as with their various trainers, attendants, families, and fans.

The festivities started a full 10 months before the games, when the hosting city appointed the officials who would serve as regulators and referees for the competitions. They required considerable time to be instructed in their duties. Then about one lunar month before the actual games began, Greece itself declared a truce so that people could get to the games in relative safety. This sacred truce, the *ekekheiria* ("holding back of hands"), was proclaimed by religious officials who traveled throughout Greece to the various poleis to initiate the start of the sacred month. These ambassadors, as we might think of them—the *spondophoroi* ("truce-bearers") and *theoroi* ("envoys")—were sent to specifically designated cities as far afield as Cyprus and Sicily, where they were received, hosted, and aided by pre-selected *theorodokoi* ("envoy-receivers"). To act as a theorodokos was deemed a great honor, both locally and on a pan-Greek scale, and the function was offered as a mark of distinction to those whom a city wished to celebrate. Thus a stele from Argos dating to the third century records (BCH 77, 389.6–10):

> It seemed good to the people that Agatholes son of Nikostratos of Athens be proxenos and benefactor of the city of the Argives, both himself and his descendants, and a holy ambassador of Nemean Zeus and Argive Hera. They are to be free from taxation and have asylum—even financial—both by land and by sea, both in wartime and in peace. And they will have front-row seats in the games which the city holds. And this statement of proxenia will be inscribed in the sanctuary of Lykian Apollo.
>
> Phaullos son of Phaullos said it.

Immediately following the declaration of the truce, the athletes themselves made their way to the games. The competitors were required to get to the games a month in advance, initially to be vetted (What age category? Are you really from where you say you're from? Are you guilty of any impieties that would tarnish the games?) and then to train under the eyes of the Hellanodikai, the official judges of the games. What becomes quickly obvious is that only people who could afford to travel to the various games *and* take off a month from work could compete. As such, even though the games were technically open to all Greeks of the appropriate gender, they were inevitably restricted to the more affluent members of society.

Affluence, however, is relative, and there was definitely some class snobbery taking place at the games. At the top of the social elite were the equestrian competitors. No, not the horses themselves (that we know of), but the horse raisers and trainers who were considered to be the official competitors in such events as the chariot races, rather than the actual jockeys or charioteers (much like in the modern sport of horse racing). Such snobbery came most clearly to the fore in the case of the fifth-century Athenian nobleman-playboy-traitor Alkibiades, who once sent *seven* chariot teams to the Olympics and wound up winning first, second, and fourth places. As his son Isokrates later recounted in an utterly absurd run-on sentence (Isokrates 16.32–33):

> Around this time seeing the festival in Olympia was loved and admired by all peoples, and that the Greeks there made a display of wealth and bodily strength and training, and that the athletes were admired and the cities of the victors became renowned, and in addition to these things believing that the public services performed here [Athens] on behalf of the commoners benefited the citizens, while those performed at that festival on behalf of the city became known to all of Greece; considering these things, although he was neither

poorly trained nor sickly in body, he snubbed the gymnastic competitions, seeing some of the athletes were low-born and lived in measly cities and were of paltry education; instead he set his hand to horse-breeding, which is the task of the most fortunate—no one base might do it, and not only did he surpass his fellow competitors, but he also surpassed all victors ever!

Yes, everyone was just desperately impressed. For a while, at least. About a century later, the Spartan king Agesilaos made the following quite public statement about the athletic value of horse owners (Plut. *Agesilaos* 20.1):

> But then seeing some of the citizens thinking themselves so utterly fan-tastic because they took up horse-breeding, he convinced his sister Kyniska to compete, entering a chariot in the Olympics, wishing to show the Greeks how victory had nothing to do with excellence, but merely wealth and expenditure.

His sister Kyniska, by the bye, was the first woman to win at the Olympic Games, where married women were otherwise banned on pain of death. As Greek girls married in their teens, there were precious few females attending the Olympics (but see later in this chapter on the Heraia).

Other than practical considerations, though, all male Greeks were wel-come to compete in the Panhellenic games (on what actually constitutes a "Greek," see Chapter 5). The very good athletes, even those not from the wealthy classes, could earn their way to the Big Four by competing in the smaller, more localized games, where cash prizes were the norm (see later in this chapter). Plus, the various poleis offered very attractive benefits for vic-tors in the Panhellenic games. In Athens and several other cities, such victors were granted free meals for life in the city *prytaneion*, the equivalent of City Hall, where local and foreign dignitaries would be wined and dined. Thus a mid-fifth-century inscription from Athens reads (*IG* I³ 131):

> Those citizens who have won or will win at Olympia or Delphi or Isthmia or Nemea shall have a free meal every day for the rest of their lives in the prytaneion, and other honors as well . . . Also those citizens who have won the *tethrippon* (four-horse chariot race) or the *keles* (horseback race) at Olympia or Delphi or Isthmia or Nemea shall have a free meal every day for the rest of their lives in the prytaneion.

Since this created a kind of dining club for the high-end athletes, there naturally emerged a kind of camaraderie amongst the sporting class, regardless of financial class. Athletic talent also, and quite understandably, pooled in athletic families, and thus a kind of athletic aristocracy emerged in Greece. Milo the wrestler was only one of a long line of successful athletes from Kroton, which was itself famous in antiquity for breeding victors. One of the most famous athletic families known from the classical world is that of

Diagoras of Rhodes, who himself, his children, and his grandchildren were all repeat victors in the Big Four. As recorded by both Pausanias and Plutarch:

> Upon arrival you'll see these images of the Rhodian athletes—Diagoras and his family. They were dedicated one after another in this order: Akousilaos taking the crown in men's boxing, then Dorieus, the youngest, winning the Olympic pankration three times in a row. And even before Dorieus Damagetos beat those going to the pankration. These are brothers, and the sons of Diagoras. And by them Diagoras himself is set up, carrying off the victory in men's boxing. The statue of Diagoras was made by the Megarian Kallikles, son of Theokosmos, who made the statue of Zeus in Megara. The children of Diagoras' daughters also practiced boxing and had victories at Olympia—in the men's division Eukles son of Kallianos and Kallipateiras, Diagoras' daughter; and Peisirhodos in the boys' division, where his mother dressed up like a male trainer and brought him to the Olympics herself. This Peisirhodos stands on the Altis next to his mother and father. And likewise they say that Diagoras went to Olympia with his sons Akousilaos and Damagetas. When the young men won they carried their father throughout the festival, and the Greeks cast flowers on him and called him blessed for having those sons. (Paus. 6.7.1–3)
>
> Much better was the Lakonian's greeting of the Olympic victor Diagoras, seeing his sons crowned at Olympia, and also his grandsons from his son and daughters, saying "Die, Diagoras—you can't ascend to Olympos!" [Translation: "It ain't gonna get no bett'r 'n this!"] (Plut. *Pelopidas* 34.4)

That mother of Peisirhodos, by the bye, was responsible for the dress code at Olympia. She snuck into the games disguised as her son's trainer, but when he won, she threw off her costume, revealing her sex. The Hellanodikai graciously agreed not to have her executed out of respect for her family (it's never a good idea to piss off a family full of boxers), but they did declare that henceforth the trainers as well as the athletes had to be naked at the competitions.

So it became rather difficult for women to attend the Olympic Games, and they certainly could not compete. Instead, they had their own games, the Heraia, in honor of Hera the way the Olympics were held for Zeus. They took place a little before the Olympics using the same facilities. Pausanias records (5.16.2–6):

> Every fourth year the sixteen women weave a peplos for Hera; and these same women set up the Heraian Games. The contest is a competitive race for maidens. They are not all of the same age, but first are the youngest; after these the second age-group; and finally those who are oldest run. They run thus: their hair hangs loose, the khiton lies a bit above the knee, and they show the right shoulder as far as the chest. The appointed place for these games is the Olympic stadium, but they decrease the race course a sixth (maximum) for them in the race. To the victors they give olive wreaths and a portion of the ox sacrificed to Hera, and they may dedicate portraits of themselves. And the attendants for

the sixteen are, just like the administrators, married women. The maidens' contests go back into antiquity; they say that Hippodameia showed her thanks to Hera for her marriage to Pelops and gathered together the sixteen women, and with them she first established the Heraia . . . And later they entrusted the running of the games to the same women who weave the peplos for Hera. These sixteen women also set up two choruses—one is for Physkoa, and the other for Hippodameia.

Athletics were never as important for females as they were for males. There were fewer formal games for them, and they received nothing akin to the prizes and honors bestowed upon the men. But they were not completely bereft of their sports.

Playing for Cash

Besides the Big Four, there were many smaller, state-sponsored athletic contests throughout Greece. Typically these were just for the citizens of the hosting polis, but often they could branch out and invite citizens from other poleis. One such festival was the Panathenaia in Athens. The games were technically held every year, but every four years, they celebrated the Greater Panathenaia, when contestants from outside of Athens were invited to compete. The prizes to be won at the Greater Panathenaia were astounding, as recorded on an inscription found in Athens that dates to the early fourth century (see the sidebar about IG II^2 2311). For the most part, the athletes (and musicians) won vast quantities of olive oil, which they could both use and sell for extreme profits. The boys in the races received both meat from the sacrifices and cash prizes of several hundred *drakhmai* apiece. As one or two drakhmai was the equivalent of a day's labor for a skilled craftsman, one might say that these boys received the equivalent of a year's salary for one victory.

There were a number of significant differences between the local games and the Big Four. For one thing, there were team sports, such as the boat races. Such team-based competitions served to promote camaraderie amongst the competitors and thus could be seen as small-scale civic-building exercises. Another difference was that there were runners-up: first place all the way to fifth place, each of whom got some sort of prize. This made the trip more worthwhile, as there was a greater chance of winning something for one's efforts. Most importantly, there was money. Wining at the Panathenaia might not be as prestigious as a victory at Olympia, but it was definitely more lucrative and could provide the funds necessary to get an able-bodied athlete to the big games.

Both categories of games, the Big Four and the money games, brought the Greeks together as a people (although with a certain amount of gender skewing, to be sure). Here they reveled in their common culture, their common deities, and their common traditions, while they did their darndest to stop killing each other for up to six weeks at a time (not always successfully). As Stephen Miller put it:

> The games brought all the Greeks together (to the exclusion of all non-Greeks, to be sure) and, in some sense, promoted international (that is, inter-polis) communication and understanding, albeit on a much more restricted level than today. By bringing together citizens of different city-states at a religious festival focused on athletics, the political rivalries that divided them could be ignored for a few days. At the same time, by their insistence that competitors be certified as legitimate representatives of a particular city-state, and in the proclamation of both each competitor's affiliation at the start of the events and the victor's city-state at the end, the games promoted competition and rivalry between the city-states. (2004, 216)

Military

The ultimate culmination of competition and its physical rigors is, of course, war. As a competitive people, the Greeks engaged in war a *lot*, usually with each other (see Chapter 5) but sometimes also with foreign powers, especially the Persians. The need for competent military service pretty much guaranteed that all the poleis invested at least some effort in training their young men to fight, be this as strictly and vigorously as the Spartans or as casually as the Athenians, who had a two-year period of military service for their 18-year-olds (See Chapter 1). What is interesting to note, though, is that contrary to modern tendencies, military service was originally very much an aristocratic privilege in ancient Greece. Our earliest testimonies—those from Homer—indicate that it was mainly kings and princes who went to war, partially because they were the only ones who could afford it (think of the travel, the time away from home, and the need to furnish both oneself and one's retainers with armor, weapons, food, tents, etc.) and partially because it was seen as the duty of kings to fight to defend and to enrich their people, in exchange for which they got to be kings. This was put most succinctly by Kings Glaukos and Sarpedon in Book 12 of Homer's *Iliad* (ll. 310–321):

> Glaukos, why indeed are we two most honored,
> With a seat of honor and meats and full cups
> In Lykia, all beholding us as gods?
> And we dwell on great land holdings on the banks of the Xanthos,
> Fair in orchards and wheat-bearing fields.
> Now it is necessary for us two to stand among the foremost of the Lykians
> And face the raging battle,
> So that someone of the thorax-clad Lykians might say:
> "Not inglorious are our kings, ruling
> Over Lykia, they eat fat sheep
> And excellent honeyed wine. But their strength
> Is good, when they fight among the first of the Lykians."

To judge from the epics, the style of battle at this time was very face-to-face; warriors on either side would literally introduce themselves before engaging in single combat. Thus the exchange between Diomedes and Glaukos (the same guy as we just talked about) discussed in the previous chapter. As discussed, these two heroes discovered in their preliminaries that their grandfathers had been xenoi, friends, and as such, even though Diomedes and Glaukos were fighting for opposite side in the Trojan War, they would not fight each other due to the bonds of hospitality. This brings up another interesting aspect of this early warfare as we understand it: It was remarkably lacking in feelings of antipathy for the "enemy." Fighting seemed to be a matter of course, a job, not something engaged in out of passion. Akhilleus's homicidal rage against Hektor, his desire to eat the latter's liver, was an extreme beyond the telling in ancient Greek mentalities, to the point that even the deities eventually had to tell him to chill and behave. (How often today do you hear about mothers having to tell their sons, "Honey, I want you to stop desecrating that corpse *right now!*"?) Quite simply, perhaps, you have to know someone to hate him or her. You generally don't know your wartime enemies; they live quite apart from you.

More typical of the attitudes between rival heroes is that shown between Hektor, prince and champion of the Trojans, and Ajax, towering shield of the Akhaians. After a fierce battle between the two, they stop fighting when it gets dark out, part in friendship, and even exchange gifts (*Iliad* 7, 287–309):

Then great Hektor of the glinting helm answered him,
"Ajax, since a god has given you mass and force
And prudence, you are the best amongst the Akhaians with a spear.
Now let us stop the fight and combat
For today; later then we might fight, until a divinity
Might judge us and give victory to one or the other.
Night's come already, and it's good to yield to night.
So you go gladden all the Akhaians by the ships,
And most of all your friends and comrades, who are yours.
But I shall gladden the Trojans throughout the great
City of King Priam, and the Trojan women with trailing robes;
They compete in praying for me.
Come let us give fame-worthy gifts to each other
So that someone would say of the Akhaians and Trojans,
'At first they fought in heart-rending strife,
But then bound in friendship they separated.'"
So speaking he gave a silver-studded sword
With a carrying sheath and a well-cut baldric.
And Ajax gave a shining, purple belt.
The two parted, the one went to the host of the Akhaians,
The other to the din of the Trojans. They rejoiced,
Seeing him alive and coming safe and sound,
Escaping the force and baleful hands of Ajax.

Figure 4.6
Chigi Vase, detail of Corinthian olpe showing early phalanx formation and flautist,
ca. 640 BCE. Villa Giulia, Rome, 22679. (DEA/G. Nimatallah/De Agostini/Getty
Images)

This has always struck me like sending a muffin basket to someone with
whom you are currently engaged in a lawsuit, except that your rival would
have less of an opportunity to kill you with the muffin. Hektor and Ajax never
do continue their battle, and later in the book they claim never to have seen
each other before.

In the early Archaic period, a new style of warfare became prominent in
Greece. Instead of single heroes duking it out in the midst of the mêlée, lines
of warriors fought with opposing lines of warriors (see Figure 4.6). Such formation—several soldiers lined up several lines deep, is called a phalanx, and the
soldiers themselves were called hoplites, named after their all-important
shields, the *hoplos*. This fighting style required far more fighters than just kings
and princes, so a greater percentage of what we might now term the citizenry
became involved in military endeavors. I use the word "citizenry" very deliberately here. Although there has been copious ink spilt over the exact cause-
and-effect relationship, it appears that there is a correlation between the rise
of the polis, the rise of the hoplite, and the notion of citizenship in general.
The basic idea is that the polis must grant certain rights and prerogatives—
citizenship—to those who invest their time and resources, and risk their lives,
to defend that polis. Monarchy starts to give way to aristocracy, and

eventually even democracy, as more and more men (and it's always men) enter the fray of battle.

However, it was still necessary to pay for one's own equipment, and, as such, the privilege of fighting, along with its concomitant benefits, was still very much in the hands of the well-off. The ability to pay for armor and weapons, one's panoply, became a requirement and even criterion for full citizenship in many poleis. Thus a late sixth-century inscription from Athens records (*IG* I³ 1):

> It seemed good to the demos: Those who reside in kleruchies (allotments) in Salamis . . . They must pay taxes and fight for the Athenians. The things in Salamis may not be leased, if not inhabited . . . If one should lease, the renter and the rentee each . . . to the public treasurer. The arkhon will collect it, if not, it will be audited. The man himself will furnish arms [*hopla*] valued at 30 drakhmai. When armed [*hoplismenon*] the arkhon will judge the arms . . .

So the Athenian citizens residing on the island of Salamis were required to furnish their own fighting gear to the tune of 30 drakhmai, which, as noted earlier, would be the equivalent of a month's salary. It was not an impossible sum, really, but it did exclude the poorest members of society from taking part in the city's defense.

When fighting on behalf of one's city, then, one tended to associate mainly with members of one's own class. Those who could afford a full panoply and a horse were the cavalry and would be the more affluent members of society. In Athens, the second highest social class was, quite specifically, the *hippeis*—the Knights—those who had enough money to fund a war horse. Lower down on the social scale were those who could afford bronze helmet, breastplate, greaves, shield, spear, and sword. Although pricey, they were also long enduring, provided they were not taken by a triumphant enemy on the field (stripping one's enemies was a common way to end a battle, provided one was the winner); families could pass down fighting gear, making it perhaps just a tad less expensive than having to buy everything new all the time. Below the hoplites were the light-armed troops, who really came into their own only in the fifth century. These were the soldiers who could not afford either bronze armor or weapons but who could don thick linen tunics and light shields, and wield bows, arrows, slingshots, and rocks. Opinions of such fighters varied in ancient Greece. Technically, they never had the prestige of their more heavily burdened fellow fighters and so they were definitely seen as second-class soldiers. They were, however, amazingly useful in battle. Even the Spartan poet Tyrtaios lauded their efforts (fr. 11):

> But, you, light-armed soldiers, crouching beneath your shields at various points in the line, hurl your great stones and cast your wooden javelins against the enemy, arrayed next to the heavy infantry. (trans. Sage 1996, 42)

The Athenian historian Xenophon noted especially the convenience of long-range weapons in warfare (*Anabasis* 3.3.16):

> But I hear that there are Rhodians in our army. It is said that most of them understand the use of the sling, and that their sling bullet carries twice as far as that of the Persians. The latter only have a short range because they use only stones that fit the hand, while the Rhodians know how to use lead bullets in their slings. (trans. Sage 1996, 44)

Perhaps the most elegant debate about the merits of the hoplite fighting face-to-face versus the lightly clad and conveniently distant archer was written by Euripides in his play *Herakles*. In a verbal confrontation between Lykos (the bad guy) and Amphitryon (stepfather of Herakles), we hear (ll. 157–164, 189–203):

> **Lykos:** He gets no reputation for being courageous
> In battle with beasts; in other things he's not so strong.
> He never held a shield in his left hand,
> Nor come close to a spear, but holding a bow,
> The most paltry weapon, he was always ready for flight.
> A man's reproach; there's no courage with a bow;
> But rather for him who endures, facing and staring down
> The swift spear ploughing through, entering the ranks.

> **Amphytryon:** The hoplite is a slave to his weapons,
> And for those ranged with him—not being good men—
> He dies through the cowardice of those near him.
> Having broken his spear he cannot defend
> His body, having just the single point.
> But those who have well-aimed bows to hand,
> One is better, with thousands of arrows to shoot
> At others he saves his body and does not die.
> Keeping his distance he defends himself from enemies,
> Wounding their bodies with invisible arrows,
> Even though they can see, and they can't return it!
> He is well-guarded, and in battle he is
> Most wise, hurting the enemy,
> Saving his own skin, and not depending on luck.

Although Tyrtaios was praising his skirmishers already in the seventh century, it was really in the fifth that one might say a real democracy emerged in the ancient Greek military. The value of lightly armed troops was especially valued after confrontations with the Persians, and they had as their mascot no less a hero than Herakles himself!

But the real functional mixing of social classes in the ancient militia was in the navy. Nowhere else could one find such a thorough mélange of the wealthy, the average, the poor, the foreign, and even slaves, all serving for the benefit of the polis. This is clearest in that most famous of the ancient Greek navies, that of Classical Athens.

At the top of the Athenian naval social hierarchy were the *trierarkhs*, those wealthiest of men who were obliged by the state to pay for the maintenance and functioning of a trireme (a triple-decker ship) for a full year while serving themselves as ship's captain. This was the most expensive of the liturgies, those high-cost benefices demanded by the city, but which provided so much glory for the man who fulfilled them. Running a ship for a year was far more expensive than training a chorus! And because it was such an excellent opportunity to flaunt one's wealth, the trierarkhs rarely skimped on their duties. So much is recounted by Apollodoros, one of the wealthiest men in Athens who took on just such a liturgy (Demosthenes 50.7):

> I, when the sailors commissioned by the demos didn't come, but just a few and those paltry, I sent them away, pledging my own property and borrowing money. First I fitted out a ship, hiring the best sailors possible, giving each of them great bonuses and advances. I got the ship equipped with all my own equipment, taking nothing from the public. The ship was in a most beautiful state, and the most illustrious of all those of the trierarkhs. And now I hired the best crew possible.

(Interesting fact: Apollodoros's father was originally a slave, named Pasion, who worked for a banking company in Athens. He was so competent that upon the death of his owner, he was granted freedom, a wife, and the banking business. He was so successful that his son was one of the wealthiest men in Athens and wound up maintaining his liturgy for six months past the allotted time. Then he sued the man who was supposed to take over the ship, which is why we have his testimony about being a ship's captain)

Apollodoros was not unusual in his desire for a well-manned, elegantly decorated ship. On the eve of the Sicilian Expedition in 413 BCE (when Athens got its butt kicked and pretty much lost its navy), Thucydides records the citizens' preparations and priorities (Thuc. 6.31.3):

> The fleet was prepared with great expenditures on the part of both the trierarkhs and the city, with the public treasury giving a drakhma a day to each sailor and furnishing empty ships, sixty swift ships, and forty transport vessels, and for these the best crews. The contributions of the trierarkhs were added to the pay from the public treasury for the ships' thranites and for the crews and the other decorative devices and expensive equipments used, and to the fullest extent possible each one of them gave it their all so that his own ship would excel in terms of fine appearance and speed.

So much as with the choruses, the wealthy used their contributions to the navy to compete in the social arena. Beneath these wealthy dilatants on the ship were the *epibatai*, the hoplites who were charged with on-board combat.

These were not unlike the normal land-bound hoplites, with the same armor and equipment, and were thus members of the higher classes themselves (although probably nowhere near the trierarkhs). The epigraphic evidence (*IG* I³ 1032) suggests that there were about 10 on each ship, although it is rather difficult to determine what they actually did. Ancient Greek naval combat consisted of ramming the opponent's ships, hopefully sinking them and watching their crews drown. There was little to no armed combat–style fighting on board, at least since the early fifth century. But the hoplites were there, nevertheless. Beneath these were the *hyperesia*, the professional sailors, the fellows who actually maintained the ship and knew (hopefully!) what they were doing. These were the *kubernetes* (helmsman, from which we get the word "governor"), the *keleutes* (rowing master), the *aleutes* (flute player, to keep the rhythm for the rowers), the *naupagos* (carpenter), the *prorates* (lookout), and the *pentekontarkhos* (person in charge of expenditures). Each ship would have one of each and, because they were selected based on skill, none of them were necessarily free citizens. Demosthenes records one *aleutes* who was a slave, and the inscription mentioned earlier lists a *metic* (resident alien) carpenter.

At the bottom of the social ladder were the rowers, about 170 per ship—*thranites* on the top level, *zygians* in the middle, *thalamians* on the bottom (see Figure 4.7). It was with these men that the full democratization of the military took place. Although not necessarily able to afford the hoplite pano-ply, or even necessarily bows and arrows, they could nevertheless contribute to the defense of the city, serve in the military, and thus, on a psychological level, earn their full citizenship. It was hard work, to be sure, but there were numerous perks. As noted previously, a sailor with a good reputation could earn large bonuses from glory-seeking trierarkhs. Apollodoros mentions this again in his suit, claiming (Dem. 50.12–13):

> For having received no pay from the general for eight months, I sailed back bringing the ambassadors because my ship sailed the best. And once back, I was commissioned by the people to bring the general Menon to the Hellespont to replace the decommissioned Autokles, and I set out to bring him with all speed. And to replace the sailors who left I hired others, giving them excellent bonuses and advances; and to those who had remained of the previous sailors I gave something for the upkeep of their homes, which they were leaving, in addition to what they had previously, not being ignorant of their present need, how necessity weighed on each one . . . And the people hearing of these things praised me, and summoned me to dine at the prytaneion.

There was also an element of play involved when they ships were not actually fighting. Xenophon recalls how the general Iphikrates established daily races for the ships when sailing around the Peloponnese; the loser almost literally had to eat a rotten egg (*Hell.* 6.2.28):

Figure 4.7
**Trireme Relief, Attic, marble, fifth century BCE. Acropolis Museum, Athens,
Greece, Inv. 1339. (Ancient Art and Architecture Collection Ltd./The Bridgeman
Art Library)**

Often when the army was about to have breakfast or dinner, he would
withdraw the wing of the fleet from the land and point it towards the shore.
And when they were turned about and the prows were set in order, the triremes
on cue set off racing to land, and it was truly a great victory for the first to get
water and whatever else was needed, and for the first to get breakfast. For those
coming in last it was a great penalty, both in being worse off in all these things,
and in that they had to set sail with the others, at the signal. As a result, for
those arriving first, they could do everything at leisure; for those coming in last,
in a hurry.

Finally, and rather importantly, the various crew members established
close bonds with each other, spanning all levels of class and country. This
comes across most beautifully in an anecdote related by Apollodoros (Dem.
50.47–50):

Kallipos son of Philon of Aixoneus boards, and he tells the helmsman to
sail the ship to Macedonia. When we arrive at a place somewhat opposite

the mainland—the Thasian emporion—we disembarked and were preparing breakfast, when one of the sailors, Kallikles son of Epitrephos of Thria, approached me, saying that he wished to discuss with me some matter pertaining to me. When I gave him leave, he says that he wanted to repay my kindness to him as he was able for what I gave him back when he was in need. "Do you," he said "know why you are making this trip, and for what?" When I answered that I didn't know, he said, "But I'll tell you, for it's necessary for you to hear to plan properly. For you," he said, "are about to take a fugitive man, whom the Athenians have twice now sentenced to death—Kallistratos— from Methonê to Thasos, to Timarkhos, his in-law, as I learned from Kallippos' slaves. You then, if you are sensible, you won't let any fugitive come aboard this ship, for the laws don't permit it." Hearing these things from Kallikles I approached Kallippos, and I ask him where he's taking the ship and for whom. Then he scoffed at me and threatened things of which you are all aware (for you all have experience with the ways of Kallippos). So I say to him that, "I hear that you are sailing to get Kallistratos. Now I shall carry on board none of the fugitives, nor shall I sail out to get one; for the laws don't allow anyone to receive any of the fugitives, and they command that the one who does receive them gets the same [punishments]. So I am sailing back to the general in Thasos." And when the sailors came on board, I tell the helmsman to sail back to Thasos. And when Kallippos spoke against me and ordered him to sail to Macedonia—the general ordered it!—Poseidippos the helmsman answered him that I'm the trierarkh of the ship and the one liable, and that he gets his pay from me; so he would sail where I command, to Thasos, to the general.

The Athenian navy was, in so many ways, a microcosm of Greek society generally, with its carefully constructed class structures, privilege ultimately based more on wealth than breeding, the need of the poor for the wealth of the rich, the need of the rich for the labor and support of the poor, and every-one competing about everything all of the time. As historian Sam Potts so pithily put it:

> It shows wealthy captains, vying with one another to show their service to the state; competitive crewmen, vying for bonus pay and the best rowing berths; grizzled rowers sneering at the idle and lubberly marines, who lounged on deck while the real men pulled the oars; landed men, equipped as hoplites, proud of their arms and holding the poorer and weaponless seamen in contempt; thranites farting in the face of rowers on the lower benches. (2011, 59).

Nevertheless, for all of their constant competing, it was the arenas in which they competed that brought the Greeks together. Dancing together in the choruses, training and studying together in the palaistrai, racing together at the games, fighting together in the field, even competitive wool carding!— these are what bound the people together. Wars and even civic strife may have been endemic in ancient Greece, but it was still possible to call on shared memories to unite the people (Xen, *Hell*. 2.4.20):

Kleokritos, herald of the mysteries, having a very good voice called for silence and said, "Fellow citizens, why do you drive us out? Why do you wish to kill us? For we have never done you any wrong, but we have shared with you the most holy rites and sacrifices and most beautiful festivals, joined together in choruses and been school-mates and army-mates, and we have risked many dangers with you both by land and by sea on behalf of our safety and freedom, common to us both."

Eating Together

For all their competitive spirit, even the Greeks occasionally had to give it a rest. When not vying for who knows what, the Greeks happily came together to share meals. Sometimes this was in the context of religious rituals, where sacrifice and subsequent picnics were the core of Greek religion (see Chapter 3). But even outside of the religious context, the various Greek poleis had numerous institutions that brought both citizens and noncitizens together in a prandial context. One of these was the *symposion*, which was discussed already in Chapter 2. Perhaps more dignified were the *syssitia*, *sitesis*, *xenia*, and *deipnon*

Syssitia

We are fortunate in that many ancient Greek philosophers were in awe of the Spartans and their Dorian cousins the Cretans (on Dorians, see Chapter 5). Because of this fascination, we have numerous highly detailed descriptions of the so-called public messes that in many ways formed the core of these ancient communities. *Syssition* literally means "grain together," much in the way the French *copain* ("companion") means "with + bread = one with whom you eat bread = friend." To one extent or another, the males in ancient Sparta and parts of Crete were expected to take their meals together in the equivalent of ancient cafeterias, rather than eating at home with their families. Females were pointedly excluded from these *syssitia* (called literally *andreia*, "men's places" in Crete; *phiditia* in Sparta), except for the one female hostess recorded in Crete. By contrast, both boys and men ate together in these mess halls, sometimes with the boys serving the men, always with the understanding that the young were there to learn by example from their elders.

There were differences in how these public mess halls were funded. In parts of Crete, there was a somewhat socialist system in place, whereby the andreia were funded publicly through a general tax on agricultural produce and other such commodities. In this way, the full male community could be cared for equally, although it appears that orphans were deprived of condiments ("No father, no fish sauce" apparently). By contrast, in the Spartan system (as well as Lyttos in Crete), each Spartiate (a full Spartan citizen) had to contribute a certain portion of the agricultural goods generated by his *kleros* (allotment of land) as his "dues" to the phiditia/syssitia, along with meat acquired through hunting. Any Spartiate who was unable to meet this requirement because of poverty lost his phidition membership and, with it, his citizenship. This is considered to be one of the reasons that the citizen population of Sparta fell so dramatically by the end of the fourth century—as wealthier Spartans, often women, were able to inherit or even buy up more and more land, increasingly fewer (male) Spartans could make their syssition payments and thus lost full citizenship. Aristotle blamed the women, of course.

It is difficult to tell when these institutions came into being. There is no extant recorded tradition for how the Cretans came up with the practice. The Spartans, of course, attributed the custom to the semilegendary lawgiver Lykourgos, which might put it in the seventh century (???) and which many ancient authors believe he learned from the Cretans anyway. Although many of our sources for these mess halls are rather late (Plutarch, Strabo, Athenaios), Xenophon and Aristotle are fourth-century authors, thus confirming the practices for the fifth century, at least. The bronze inscription from the Lyttos-Aphrati area in Crete given below pushes the evidence for the Cretan custom back into the sixth century. All in all, it would appear that these Doric communal kitchens go well back in Archaic, and possibly even earlier, Greek history. Let us consider what the ancient had to say about these communal kitchens.

Crete

Strabo 10.4.16 and 20:

Of the constitution about which Ephoros wrote I might simply skim over sufficiently the principle aspects. He says that the law-giver seems to have assumed that the greatest good for the cities was freedom—for only this makes private goods of things acquired; whereas in slavery these things belong to the rulers and not to the ruled. It is necessary that those who have freedom guard it. Now there is commensuality when dissention, which comes from greed and luxury, is removed, since for all those living temperately and simply neither jealously nor outrage nor hatred appears for those who are like-minded. And thus he commanded that the children go about in the so-called "herds" and the adult men eat together in the syssitia—what they call "andreia," so that the poorest being fed at public expense might share in the same goods as the wealthy . . .

The children learn letters and the songs dictated by law, and some types of music. Now, they lead those who are still quite young to the andreia-syssitia, and sitting on the ground they live with each other in measly, thread-bare cloaks—summer and winter—and they wait on each other and on the men. And they come together in "battle," and those from the same syssition fight against each other, and against those from other syssitia. A paidonomos presides over each andreion. The larger boys are brought to the herds. The most distinguished of the boys, and the most powerful, assembles the herds, each one mustering as many as he can. The leader of each herd is most often the father of the one doing the mustering; he is responsible for leading them out hunting and racing, and he punishes the disobedient. They eat at public expense. On some prescribed days herd confronts herd in battle, in rhythmic time with both lyre and flute—just as is customary in real warfare, and they bear blows both from hands and from iron weapons.

Athenaios 4.143:

Concerning the Cretan syssitia Dosiadas, in the fourth book of his *On Cretan Matters*, writes as follows. "The Lyttians bring together the common syssitia thusly: Each man contributes one tenth of his produce to the association, and the citizen functionaries divide the cities' revenues among the households of each. Each of the slaves contributes an Aiginaitan stater *per capita*. All the citizens are divided up into associations—they call these 'andreia.' A woman has the care of the syssition, along with three or four chosen from the populace for this service. For each of them there are two assistants who follow them bearing wood. They are called 'wood-bearers.' Throughout all of Crete there are two houses for the syssitia, the one they call the 'andreion,' and the other in which they lodge foreigners, which they call the 'koimeterion' ("lodging place"). In each syssition house, first are laid out two tables called 'foreign,' where those of the foreigners who are present sit. Those for the others are next. An equal portion for each man present is served; and a half-portion of meat is given to the younger men, and they add nothing of the other goods. Then they serve drink at each table, mixed with water. Everyone at the same table drinks this together, and another drink is served to theose who have finished dining. For everyone there is a common krater [wine-and-water-mixing bowl]. For the older men, if they want to drink more, permission is granted. The woman in charge of the syssition openly removes from the table the best of what was served and serves it to those distinguished in war or in intelligence. After dinner, first they are accustomed to discuss political matters; then after that they remember war-time actions and praise men who were noble, turning the young men towards manly virtue."

Pyrgion in the third book of his *Cretan Customs* says that in the syssitia the Cretans dine together seated. He also says that food without condiments is served to the orphans. And that the youngest of them stand and serve. And that after a silent libation to the deities they distribute to all what has been served, and they distribute to the sons who sit below their fathers' chairs a half-portion of what is served to the men, and they distribute an equal portion to the orphans, but each of the customary foods is served to them without condiments in the mix. There are also "foreign" chairs and a third table on the right entering the andreia, which they call that of "Zeus Xenios," or the "xenia table."

The inscription from the Lyttos-Aphrati area of central Crete was cut into a bronze *mitra*, the semicircular abdominal guard worn as part of the warrior's panoply, and dates to about 500 BCE. The text records the prerogatives and privileges awarded to a scribe named Spensithios. Presumably in exchange for his benefices to the city, both he and his descendants got such honors as free-dom from taxation, job exclusivity, and the role as substitute priest, with all accompanying payments. Toward the end of what remains of the inscription, the text reads:

> As lawful dues to the andreion he shall give ten axes' [weight] of dressed meat. If the others also make offerings, the yearly offering also, and shall collect the portion, but nothing else is to be compulsory if he does not wish to give it. (trans. Jeffrey and Morpurgo-Davies 1970, 125)

This text supports what Dosiadas (in Athenaios) said about the Lyttians from Lyttos. As the historian recorded it, each citizen contributed a tenth of his farm produce to the andreia, a sort of tax, if you will. Spensithios, being immune from taxes, nevertheless must contribute a bit to his andreion—both meat and the occasional annual offering. But otherwise, his contributions are completely optional. This system in Lyttos is similar to what we find in Sparta, to which we now turn.

Sparta

Xenophon. *Const. Lak* 5.2–7:

Moreover, Lykourgos, perceiving that the Spartans, just like the other Greeks, lived at home, and knowing that there they slacked off the most, he brought common dining out into common view, believing that commands would be least side-stepped this way. And he arranged the grain for them such that there was neither too much nor any lack. And there are many unrationed portions contributed by the hunters, and sometimes the wealthy have these side by side with the bread. And so the table is never empty of meat, at least until they depart, nor is it extravagant. And he also stopped the drinking of unnecessary beverages, which undo both the body and the mind; he said to drink whenever one is thirsty, believing this to be the least harmful and the sweetest drink. And so dining together like this, how could anyone, either by excess or by drunkenness, harm either himself or his household? And whereas in the other cities, for the most part, age mates stay with each other, with whom modesty is least present, in Sparta Lykourgos mixed them together, so as to educate the many young-folk through the experiences of their elders. And indeed it is the local custom in the eating halls to talk about what someone did well in the city, so that there might be the least hubris, the least paranoia, the least shameful deeds and words. So this eating outside of the homes accomplishes good things, for they are required to walk on the return home, and thus they must take care not to get tripped up by wine, seeing that having dined they cannot remain there, and the walking must be done in the dark as well as in the day—for it is not permitted for those still in the military to proceed by torchlight.

Plutarch, <u>Life of Lykourgos</u> 12:

The Cretans call their syssitia "andreia," the Lakedaimonians "phiditia." . . .
They assemble some fifteen men (more or less). Each member of the syssitia
brings monthly a medimnon of barley, eight jugs of wine, five minas of cheese,
five half-minas of figs, and in addition to these they furnish a small bit of money
for supplies. Otherwise, someone sacrificing first fruits or hunting will bring a
portion to the syssition. For it was only permitted to dine at home whenever
someone was late from a sacrifice or hound-hunting; but it was required that the
others be present. And for the most part they maintained the syssitia quite well.
When Agis was king, when he returned from the battle waged against
the Athenians, wishing to dine with his wife and sending for his portions, the
polemarkhs didn't send them, and when on the following day he didn't offer the
necessary sacrifice because he was angry, they fined him.

Even children used to visit the syssitia; it was just like being brought to a
school of temperance. And they heard political talks and saw teachers of
freedom, and they became accustomed to play and watch without buffoonery
and to being mocked without getting cross. For this certainly seemed to be very
Lakonian: to endure being mocked. But if one could not deal with it he begged
off, and the mocker stopped. For each of those who entered, the eldest pointed
to the door and said "though those no talk heads out." ["What happens in the
syssition, stays in the syssition."] They say they judge those who wish to join
the syssition like this: Each member of the syssition takes a piece of bread in
hand; then the servant carries a pitcher on his head and they cast their bread
pieces in silence, just like a voting ballot. The one who accepts the applicant
casts the bread unmangled, but the one who rejects him crushes it with his
hand. For the crushed piece has the force of one perforated [a negative vote].
And if they find one of these, he is not accepted for admittance, as they want
everyone voting to be in accord with each other. The man so rejected is called
"kaddished," for the jar into which they cast the bread is called a "kaddikhos."
Of their dishes the one most favored by them is the black broth, such that the
elders don't eat bits of meat, but rather give these to the young men, while they
themselves eat the poured-out broth. It is said that one of the Pontic kings
hired a Lakonian cook for the sake of this broth, but when he tasted it he was
repulsed. And the cook told him, "O King, to enjoy this broth it is necessary to
have bathed in the Eurotas River." Drinking moderately they depart without a
lamp, for it is not permitted to walk with a light, neither there nor along
another road, so that they become accustomed to shadows and dealing bravely
with the night and traveling without fear. This then is the organization of the
syssitia.

(Concerning that black broth, there's a story that a visitor from the rather
effete city of Sybaris in Greek Italy went to Sparta, tasted the soup, and
claimed that he now understood why the Spartans weren't afraid to die. Apparently two of the ingredients were vinegar and blood.)

Both

Aristotle *Politics* 1271a:

> The laws about the syssitia—those called phiditia—were not well established by their creator. For it would have been better to have the assembly come from the shared funds, just as in Crete. But amongst the Lakonians each one must bring his own, and since it is difficult for the poor to contribute they are unable to pay this cost, and thus it results in the opposite of the law-maker's intention. For he wished the organization of the syssitia to be democratic, but it has become the least democratic the way it was established. For it is not easy for the very poor to contribute, but their law of citizenship, which is ancestral, says that the one unable to pay the tax may not share in citizenship.

The public messes were seen to be civic building and educational, and even the substrate for military organization. They were not optional, and they forced a kind of balance between a male's identification as a member of a household and his identification as a citizen. In Crete the system served as a kind of social welfare, guaranteeing that all males, at least, were reasonably well fed and treated equally. The system in Sparta wound up having the opposite effect.

Prytaneion   Group eating throughout the rest of Greece was quite different, as is often the case when discussing anything Spartan. Rather than obligatory mess halls, the rest of the Greeks had what are most commonly called *prytaneia* (sing. *prytaneion*), civic halls that served numerous functions, most significantly (here, at least) the reception of guests of state for state-sponsored meals. They also housed certain religious functions, served as courthouses, and often contained the hearth of Hestia, thus serving as the symbolic core of the polis (see Chapter 7). It would not be inaccurate to call the prytaneion city hall. Historiographic and epigraphic evidence for such prytaneia come from several Greek poleis, although inevitably, the vast majority comes from Athens.

Sitesis   There were three different categories of meals, or rather meal programs, offered at the prytaneia: *sitesis*, *xenia*, and *deipnon*. Sitesis was the long-term meal program whereby certain citizens were awarded free meals in the prytaneion for life. We already saw a bit of this earlier in this chapter: Victors at the Big Four athletic competitions were awarded free meals for life in Athens as part of the city's thank offering (*IG* I³ 131). These and other categories of such recipients were recorded in another inscription dating to around 431–421 (*IG* I² 77, ll. 4–18):

> First there shall be sitesis in the prytaneion for him who is the Hierophantes [high-priest of the Eleusinian Mysteries; See Chapter Seven] according

to custom; then for whomever is the oldest male descendant of Harmodios and Aristogeiton [men who killed the Athenian tyrant Hipparkhos and thus ended the period of tyranny in the city], to them shall be the gift according to the grants of the Athenians; and to all those of the *manteis* [soothsayers] whom Apollo the expounder of customs should choose to have sitesis, to these shall be sitesis in the same way. Also those who have won the gymnastic games at Olympia or Delphi or Isthmia or Nemea shall have sitesis in the prytaneion and other honors in addition to sitesis in the same way; then those shall have sitesis in the prytaneion who have won a four-horse chariot race or a horse race at Olympia or Delphi or Isthmia or Nemea, or shall win in the future. They shall have the honors according to the things written on the stele. (trans. Miller 1978, 139–140)

"In the future" means that the statutes of the stele would continue to apply to future victors, not that the manteis already told people who the victors would be.

Other grants of sitesis were awarded on a more ad hoc basis, typically to those seen to have performed an extraordinary feat for the city, preferably military. As the comic poet Aristophanes complained, the brutish, low-born general Kleon received sitesis after defeating the Spartans at Sphakteria during the Peloponnesian War (*Knights* 281–284). According to Demosthenes in his case *Against Aristokrates* (663b), the previously mentioned Iphikrates, who held the ship races around the Peloponnese, was awarded sitesis as well as the right to erect a bronze statue of himself and other gifts. From early third-century Ilion (site of the Trojan War), an inscription recorded, "that there shall be to him (who kills the leader of an attempted oligarchy) sitesis in the prytaneion as long as he shall live" (Miller 1978, 194).

By far the most famous reference to sitesis (more theoretical than real) in Athens comes from Plato, or more accurately Sokrates, when he was found guilty of impiety and corrupting the youth. As recorded in Plato's *Apology*, when Sokrates was called upon to suggest a counter penalty for himself (the prosecution had already called for death), he replied (36c–e):

I was trying to persuade each one of you not to care for any of your things before caring for yourselves, so that you might be your best and wisest, and not to care for the affairs of the city more so that the city itself, and other things of the same sort. What do I deserve to suffer for being like this? Something good, O Athenians, if it is really necessary to propose something worthy. And additionally, something good that would be appropriate for me.

What is appropriate for a poor man—a benefactor—who needs leisure to go about and exhort you about your affairs? There is nothing, O Athenians, more appropriate for such a man than sitesis in the prytaneion. This is much better than if someone of you has won at the Olympics in horse-racing or dual-horses or chariot-racing. For he makes you *seem* to be happy, but I actually make you so, and he doesn't need food, and I do. If, then, it is necessary for me to propose something worthy, this is what I propose—sitesis in the prytaneion.

For probably the first time in his life, Sokrates was less than convincing, and he was offered hemlock in jail rather than wine in the prytaneion.

Although the Athenians were less than enthusiastic about supporting a crotchety old philosopher in the prytaneion, there is some slight evidence that they were willing to support war orphans there. A late fifth-century extremely fragmentary inscription reads, " . . . to give to the orphans . . . the prytaneion . . . " It's not much to go on, but given the dating and context of the inscription, epigrapher Ronald Stroud has suggested the restoration "to give the children of all those killed by the Thirty [tyrants who led a reign of terror in Athens at the end of the Peloponnesian War] an obol of sustenance every day just as is given to war orphans from the prytaneion" (cited in Miller 1978, 19, note 32). This may suggest that the orphans were fed at state expense from the same fund used to run the prytaneion, whether or not the children were actually fed in the structure itself.

Xenia and Deipnon   To eat for free in the prytaneion was deemed a very high honor, and most people (men) really got such a privilege only a few times in life. The short-term meal plans, if you will, were called xenia and deipnon. Xenia, as you may have guessed if you read Chapter 3 carefully, is that hospitality offered to foreigners being entertained by the city, typically foreign dignitaries, ambassadors, and so on. Deipnon, literally "feast," is the honor awarded to citizens of the city itself. So foreigners get xenia; citizens get deipnon. Otherwise, there does not appear to be any difference between the two; both categories seem to have received the same entertainments, food, and drink. Some inscriptions record joint invitations to groups of combined citizens and visitors for meals in their honor in the prytaneion. Thus an inscription from 368 BCE records the will of the Athenian people (*IG II*^{2} 107, ll. 24–34):

> To honor the ambassadors sent to Mytilene and invite them to deipnon in the prytaneion on the next day; to invite the delegates from Mytilene to xenia in the prytenaion on the next day; to invite the delegates of Methymna and Antissa and Eresos and Pyrrha to xenia in the prytaneion on the next day; . . .
> to honor Timonothos and Autolykos and Aristopeithes, the ambassadors who went to Lesbos, and invite them to deipnon at the prytaneion on the next day. (trans. Miller 1978, 151–152)

A similar decree from 478 BCE records (*IG II*^{2} 40):

> To invite the embassy of the Thebans and . . . to xenia in the prytaneon on the next day.
>   To invite Theopompos and . . . and the trierarkh [see above] Aristomakhos to deipnon in the prytaneion on the next day. To honor Antimakhos the . . . of Mytilene and invite him to deipnon in the prytaneion on the next day. (trans. Miller 1978, 150)

The kinds of citizens who got deipnon varied. Many, as seen in the preceding inscriptions, were state representatives, often receiving deipnon upon completion of a trip abroad or when the city was entertaining representatives from the city to which they had been sent (thus the combined xenia and deipnon). Very successful military commanders could be honored with deipnon, such as the trierarkhs Aristomakhos and Apollodoros mentioned here.

Some city functionaries got a kind of long-term deipnon that nevertheless was considered to be distinct from sitesis. For example, as Aristotle records in his *Constitution of the Athenians*, the men responsible for organizing the Greater Panathenaia every four years were so maintained at public expense: "The *athlothetai* (game-directors) receive deipnon in the prytaneion during the month of Hekatombaion, during which the Panathenaia occur, starting from the fourth of the month" (*Ath. Pol.* 62,2). So this is a roughly month-long period of state-sponsored maintenance, but it is still called deipnon.

So how was the food? We don't exactly have any menus or even necessarily precise recipes from the day, but over the course of his own long dinner conversation, Atheniaos did mention that (4.137e):

> He who wrote *The Beggars* attributed to Khionides says that the Athenians, whenever they set out breakfast for the Dioskouroi, set on the tables "cheese and barley cakes and ripe olives and leeks," memorializing their ancient conflicts. And Solon commanded that they serve to those dining in the prytaneion barley bread, and in addition wheat bread during festivals, in memory of Homer.

It is difficult to determine how accurate any of this is, but the text would seem to suggest that in the sixth century under Solon, the fare was rather sparse: barley bread normally; wheat bread on special occasions. Thus one was eating the rough (literally) equivalent of Scottish oatcakes in city hall. By the early fifth century, however, the date assigned to Khionides, the repast had expanded to include cheeses and vegetables. As sacrifices also took place in the prytaneion, literally at the hearth of Hestia herself, sacrificial meat should also be added to the menu.

And, of course, wine. There was probably a symposion element to the entertainments at the prytaneion (although I doubt anything as graphic as what we saw in Chapter 2), and wine was essential for making libations to the deities, which was an integral part of many public functions. So much is suggested by Pindar in his *Eleventh Nemean Ode*, honoring Aristagoras of Tenedos and, in the process, Hestia (ll. 1–9):

> Child of Rhea, who protects the prytaneion, Hestia,
> Sister of Zeus most high and equally enthroned Hera,
> Receive well Aristagoras in your hall,
> And nearby his comrades, with your shining scepture.
> They honor you rightly, guarding Tenedos,

Figure 4.8
Tholos dining ware inscribed "Demosion" ("public"): a black-glaze kylix (P 5517), a small olpe (P 13469), and an official measure (P 3559), Athenian, ca. 470–460 BCE. Agora Museum, Athens, Greece. (Photo by Craig Mauzy/The American School of Classical Studies at Athens, Athenian Agora Excavations)

> Often with libations they adore you, foremost of goddesses,
> Often with smokey savor.
> Lyre and song ring forth for them—
> And Themis is adorned in the eternal tables
> Of Zeus Xenios.

Other references to wine consumption appear in the epigraphy. From northwestern Sigeion in Anatolia came an inscription dated to circa 550 BCE and claiming "I belong to Phanodikos, son of Hermokrates, of Prokonnesos. He gave a krater [bowl for mixing wine and water] and a krater stand and a wine strainer in the prytaneion as a memorial to the people of Sigeion" (Miller 1978, 210).

Some of the feasting paraphernalia has actually come down to us. Rather simple but well-wrought plates and bowls, sometimes inscribed with the word "Demosios" ("Public-Property" or "DE" for short) came to light in Athens, indicating that these wares came from either the prytaneion or the Tholos, where other Athenian functionaries took their state-sponsored meals (see Figure 4.8).

As evidenced by the preceding inscription from Sigeion, Athens was not the only polis to host a prytaneion (merely the one for which we have the most information). Such structures existed throughout the Greek world, serving, for the most part, many of the same functions. Different poleis could have different names for these buildings. The city of Lindos on Rhodes and the island of Karpathos both had a *hierothyteion*, as did perhaps the city of Kamiros, also located on Rhodes. The isle of Knidos, famous for its statue of Aphrodite, had its *damiorgeion*, while Kassandria in northern Greece had an *arkhegeteion*. Halos in Thessaly, according to Herodotos, had a *leïton*, "The Akhaians call the prytaneion 'Leïton' " (Herodotos 7.197). But the name prytaneion was most common.

There can be little doubt that the prytaneion was an exclusive club. Females were certainly excluded, and there were few opportunities for members of the lower classes to get in, not being members of the traditional priesthoods or having the connections to get ambassadorial status. But as we saw earlier in this chapter, really talented athletes could work their way up the social ladder and right into sitesis for life. Talented military personnel such as Kleon could get in. Tyrannicides could get in. So there was at least an interesting cross-section of society.

CONCLUSIONS

The contexts for social interaction discussed here are only a few of the many, many venues that the Greeks had for public interaction. Every polis worth its salt had an *agora* (Greek for "forum," Latin for "piazza"), the central open portion of the city where people could gather, chat, shop, sell wreaths and ribbons and shoes, debate politics, catch up on the news, worship the deities, and be humiliated by Sokrates or one of his snot-nosed, punk, whippersnapper followers who just last week were nice kids who showed some respect to their elders. Some poleis, especially Athens, had law courts, theaters, and political assemblies where citizens, mainly men, got together to contemplate and decide the fates of their cities. What is presented in this chapter are some of the more pervasive and Panhellenic contexts for social interaction between residents of the same cities and the Greeks at large.

5

Peri Poleôs kai Hellados: On City-State and Greece

An ancient Greek's primary loyalties were first and foremost to his or her family (see Chapter 2). Extending past the purely familial, although not always *entirely* separated from it, were further degrees of self-identification in the greater Greek world. Moving beyond family ties, the Greeks identified most closely with their *poleis*—the cities that gave them their laws and customs (both expressed by the word *nomos* in ancient Greek)—and their ties to the deities. The next larger category of belonging was the *ethnos*, from which we derive our word "ethnicity." Unlike the polis, which was bounded in space and citizenship, the ethnos was more a theoretical group, a collective sharing of real or (more likely) imagined ancestors and notions of a homeland, be that the location where people lived currently or a remote homeland from which they emigrated to wind up where they are now. Finally, both in terms of chronology and historical importance was the identity of being Greek, a member of the whole collective of (mostly) Greek-speaking individuals who inhabited lands either originally Greek or colonized by people from those lands.

The ancient Greeks, when they even bothered to consider these categories, could emphasize different ones at different times, depending on the stimulus that brought the matter to attention in the first place. As Irad Malkin (an expert on ancient ethnicity) cogently put it:

> For example, the collective identity of a citizen of ancient Syracuse [on the east coast of Sicily] could be articulated as "Syracusan," "Corinthian colonist," "Siceliot" (=a Greek living in Sicily, of whatever origin), "Dorian," and "Greek." These identities would find expression according to the circumstances. In his political and civic relationship to other citizens of Syracuse he (women shared ethnicity but not full citizenship) was a Syracusan. In terms of international relations the Syracusan's Corinthian affiliation and Dorian identity were meaningful. In terms of cult practices he or she shared Dorian *nomima* and dress. In relation to the native populations of Sicily and to the

menacing Phoenicians, as well as to Greeks of the mainland, a Syracusan was primarily a Siceliot. In relation to Olympia (where the prominence of western Greek dedications has been noted) or to the Persian Wars . . . Syracusans were Greek. (2001, 3)

Basically, these different forms of self-identification became relevant mainly when dealing with those outside of the family, and the form of identification adopted or emphasized depended more on the identity of the "outsider" than any particular feelings of belonging on the part of the Greek in question.

POLIS

"Man is by nature a political animal."

So wrote Aristotle in his treatise on *Politics* (1253^a1–2). This did not mean, as one might take it in modern times, that men (and Aristotle generally wrote about men as opposed to women) were innately involved in the give-and-take behind closed doors that we now associate with the concept of politics. Rather, the word "politics" comes from the ancient Greek word for "city"— *polis*—and Aristotle meant that man (and technically woman) was a creature who naturally lived in a city—Man the City-Dweller. Nonurbanites were barbaric.

In all circumstances, identity with the polis was the most important form of self-identity outside of the family context for any Greek. For one thing, it was probably the oldest form of non-familial identity, as the *poleis* had begun to emerge already in the Greek Dark Ages. Although it would seem that ethnic identities should be older, with ethnological family trees going back literally to the Flood (the Greeks had one, too), these "family" lines are mainly mytho-logical and appear to have far more to do with later Archaic and Classical political situations than anything truly historical (see later in this chapter). Furthermore, at any given time, the Greeks had the most contact with those living next to them, and such relationships would be heavily tempered by issues such as who was or was not a citizen, who could marry whom, who could be tortured, and who could be taxed (usually everyone, much like now). So on a daily basis, it was the polis that gave the Greeks their primary form of what we might call civic identity.

Over the course of ancient Greece's history, there were some 1,500 poleis in existence, although not all of them existed at the same time. Of these, about 600 were located in what might be called Greece proper—the Greek mainland and the west coast of Anatolia. Another 400 or so were the result of colonization and thus existed in southern Italy, Sicily, Western Europe, northern Africa, and all around the Black Sea. After the conquests of Alexander the Great, another 300+ poleis emerged in the Near East as far as the Indus Valley. To put this another way: the Greeks were pretty spread out, and their polis-based society stretched, over time, from Emporion in the Pyrenees mountains to Ai Khanoum in Afghanistan, from Olbia in the Ukraine to Kyrenê in modern-day Libya (Hansen 2006: 31). At the height of their prosperity, there may have been as many as 7.5 million Greeks, or, to put it another way, almost the population of today's Manhattan.

Both physically and conceptually, a polis consisted of an urban core, called *polis*, *polisma*, or *asty*, and a hinterland, called either *khora* or *gê* (literally: "Earth"). Both elements could be referred to individually in city documents, as in this early fourth-century treaty between the poleis of Mantineia and Helisson in Arkadia (*SEG* 37, 340, 1–6):

> Gods. Good Fortune.
> A treaty between the Mantineians and the Helissians. . . .
> Thus seemed good to the Mantineians and the Helissians: the
> Helissians are equal and the same as the Mantineians, having united
> with all of them, both those of Mantineia extending into the khora and those
>   in the city
> of Mantineia, according to the law of the Mantineians . . .

In most cases, the polis itself was walled for defense, the wall either surrounding the entire city or, at minimum, the city acropolis. Not all cities were so enclosed, though; Sparta took pride in having no city walls, preferring instead to be protected by her citizen militia. Nevertheless, such a wall demarcated the boundaries of the city proper—where the polis ended and the khora began. Out in the hinterland were other residential conglomerates, known either as *demoi* ("neighborhoods," especially in Attika), or *komai* (villages). The smallest residential unit was the humble farmstead, which had no name in ancient Greek other than simply *oikos* ("household").

The largest poleis, at least in the fourth century (for which we have the best data), were Syracuse, Sparta, Kyrenê, and Athens. Syracuse during the reign of Dionysios I got as large as 10,000 square kilometers, while Sparta, which had conquered and absorbed the surrounding regions of Lakonia and Messenia, was about 8,400 square kilometers. The city of Athens, with a population of some 200,000 residents, covered some 2,500 square kilometers, and Kyrenê in north Africa, with its 10,000 citizens, was some 4,000 square kilometers. At the other end of the spectrum, the smallest polis we know of was little Belbina, south of Attika, which covered no more than 8 square kilometers and had a population of less than 1,000 people. In this, it was comparable with the *komê* (village) of Askra in Boiotia (hometown of the poet Hesiod) that measured some 10 hectares in area and that had a population of roughly 1,000 people.

The smaller the polis, the more likely any given citizen was to live in it. All citizens of Belbina probably lived within the city walls, going out each day to tend to their farms. There is a good probability that every citizen knew, or at least recognized, every other. By contrast, probably only a quarter to a third of the Lakedaimonians lived in the city of Sparta, and the majority of the Attik population lived in the demoi, not in the asty. As the historian Thucydides put it: "For a long time, then, the Athenians lived in independent communities throughout the land. And since the unification of Attika the old customs continued, most Athenians, those from earlier generations and right down to the war with the Medes, being born and raised in the country" (2.16.5). Nevertheless, as was the case with little Belbina, the residents of various Attik demoi probably all knew, to one extent or another, all of their fellow demes-persons.

In summary, almost all ancient Greeks lived either in or immediately around a city center. The Greeks themselves were certainly more concerned with cities than any other residential category: from the Archaic through Classical periods, our textual sources name no fewer than 447 cities, in contrast to a mere 30 named komai (Hansen 2006, 69). The gross majority of cities, over 80 percent of them, had a population of at least 1,000 people, and about 10 percent, such as Athens and Syracuse, had populations of over 10,000. Most ancient Greeks had the opportunity to know the majority of their co-residents personally, either in the poleis themselves or in the outlying demoi and komai. The ancient polis can, in many respects, truly be called a "face-to-face" society.

It was this personal aspect of the ancient Greek polis that was ultimately of greater importance even than the physical composition of the cities. As M. H. Hansen, an expert on the ancient Greek polis, put it: "a *polis* was a small institutionalized self-governing society, a political community of adult male citizens (*politai* or *astoi*), who along with their families lived in a—usually—fortified city (also called *polis* or sometimes *asty*) or in its hinterland (*chora* or *ge*) along with two other sets of inhabitants, free non-citizens (*xenoi* or often *metoikoi*) and slaves (*douloi*)" (2006, 40–41).

What was important for the sake of civic identity, then, was the concept of a communal body made up of flesh-and-blood citizens, along with a series of institutions that regulated the relations amongst the polis residents. Thus ancient texts rarely refer to the city of "Athens," but rather "the Athenians." The Peloponnesian War was fought not so much between Athens and Sparta as between the Athenians and the Lakedaimonians, the residents of Sparta. The treaty mentioned earlier, between Mantineia and Helisson, you may have noted, actually referred to the Mantineians and the Helissians. Sometimes the citizens of a city could even wind up having a different name from their city altogether. For example, the acropolis of Thebes was, according to tradition (Pausanias 9.5.1), founded by Kadmos, a Phoenician (who was out looking for his sister who had been seduced and abducted by Zeus). The acropolis of Thebes was thus called the Kadmeia, and citizens of Thebes were sometimes known as Kadmeians. However, according to this same myth, when Kadmos was called on to found the city of Thebes, he was obliged to slay a dragon. Having done so successfully, he then (why not?) planted the dragon's teeth in the earth. From these teeth grew soldiers. Once Kadmos convinced them not to kill each other, these "Sown Men" (*Spartoi* in Greek) became the founding fathers of Thebes. Thebans, then, could also be known as Spartoi. So, for clarity, "Spartoi" are Thebans; "Lakedaimonians" are Spartan.

To be a proper polis, though, a city had to have more than just citizens; it also had to have infrastructure and institutions. It is for this reason that the word "polis" is typically translated as "city-state": it is a city with the structures and institutions of statehood. Physically speaking, most poleis had a *prytaneion* ("city hall"), a *bouleuterion* ("council house"), and an *agora* ("civic center"). The prytaneion was where the official hearth of Hestia was located, serving as the symbolic core of the city (see Chapter 7). It was here where ambassadors and Olympic victors were wined and dined (see Chapter 4), and it was from Hestia's hearth that flame was taken from a mother city when founding a colony. The bouleuterion was where the city council met and possibly even lived during their period in office. The agora was originally a "place for speaking" but came to be understood as the civic and spiritual center of the polis. Basically, it was an open space with various markets, temples, and covered halls called *stoas*. In some poleis, this is where the citizens' assembly would meet. It was important to mark the limits and boundaries of the agora, to render it distinct from the rest of the polis, and as such, in Athens at least, there were copious inscribed boundary stones, called *horoi*, that marked the edges of the agora. *Horos eimi tês agoras*; "I am the border of the agora," they state (IG^3 1087).

Part of creating a polis, then, was establishing these various civic structures. To unite a polis from smaller units involved the unification of these institutions, called *synoecism* ("bringing together of households"). So much is recounted by Thucydides in his story of the unification of Attika in the city of Athens by the hero Theseus (of Minotaur-slaying fame) (Thuc. 2.15. 1–2):

> For in the time of Kekrops and the first kings up to the time of Theseus Attika always existed in individual cities, each having their own city halls and magistrates, and if not compelled by some common fear, they did not come together to join in council with the king, but each separately conducted civil affairs and city planning. And some of them even waged war on the kings, like the Eleusinians in the time of Eumolpos with Erekhtheus. But when Theseus was king, having power in addition to intelligence, he marshaled together the land in many respects, and having disbanded the other cities' councils and magistracies, he made them now into one city, creating one city council and city hall. He bound them together, all those who still lived separately as before, and made them use the one city [Athens].

Institutionally, poleis had what might be termed the government itself, the various groups of citizens who functioned according to laws to regulate the city. Generally these consisted of the *ekklesia* ("assembly"), *boulê* ("council"), *gerousia* ("senate" or "council of old men"), *dikasteria* ("law courts"), and *arkhai* ("magistrates"). Depending on where and when the polis in question was, these different functions could have different names and responsibilities. Thus the earliest law we have inscribed on stone from ancient Greece comes from the city of Dreros on Crete, and dates to the mid-seventh century. Here we read:

> May god be kind. The city has thus decided: When a man has been *kosmos*, the same man shall not be *kosmos* again for ten years. If he does act as *kosmos*, whatever judgments he gives, he shall owe double, and he shall lose his rights to office, as long as he lives, and whatever he does as *kosmos* shall be nothing. The swearers shall be the *kosmos* and the *damioi* and the twenty of the city. (trans. Meiggs and Lewis 1969, 2)

Here the *kosmos* would appear to be the Chief Executive Officer of the city, apparently functioning on a one-year term, held at most once per decade. The *damioi* seem to be the financial supervisors of the city (your Chief Financial Officers, if you will), with the "twenty" being a representative of the civic assembly (Meiggs and Lewis 1969, 3).

What a polis did, then, was all the functions of what today we would call a national government, busying itself with matters of law, money, internal and "international" trade and relations, and, of course, warfare. In addition, the polis was involved in many aspects of the public expression of religion, including city festivals and consulting the deities on the city's behalf. As well summarized by Hansen:

> [T]he polis legislates and passes laws, or naturalizes foreigners, or bestows honours on foreigners. In the administration of justice it passes sentences, or inflicts punishments, or arrests somebody, or brings an action on behalf of a citizen, or shelters a refugee, or appoints a panel of jurors. In financial matters it strikes coins, or accepts as legal tender coins struck by other poleis, or collects revenue, or defrays expenses, or takes up a loan, or pays interest on a loan, or enters into a contract, or owes money, or pays a fine, or buys landed property, or pledges some property. In religious matters it organizes a festival, or makes sacrifices to a god, or makes a dedication to a god, or consults an oracle. In foreign policy it sends out envoys and representatives, or enters into an alliance, or goes to war, or sends out an army, or buries the citizens killed in war, or makes peace, or defects from a league or a ruler, or founds a colony. (2006, 113–114)

In their day-to-day lives, then, most Greeks from the Archaic through Hellenistic periods were attached to, and identified with, a polis, whether they lived in the city proper or in one of the villages or farmsteads associated with the walled city. At best, they were citizens, with the males enjoying varying rights depending on their class and the city's constitution, and the women taking part in the religious life of the city. Some, called *perioikoi* ("around the residence") were local residents who had circumscribed civic rights. Many Greeks were resident aliens, generally known as *metics*, mostly deprived of political rights (although not absolved from taxation and conscription) but enjoying the economic benefits of the city. These could be both Greeks and foreigners, and in a very large city like Athens could comprise over a third of the population. The worst off were slaves (pretty much a human constant when you think about it), who could also be either Greeks or, far more likely, foreigners, especially from regions such as Thrace to the north or from as far away as Skythia (modern-day Ukraine).

Attachment to one's polis was often very strong, and a functional synonym of "polis" was "*patris*," literally "fatherland." Thus, the gulf between family loyalty and city loyalty was bridged. The ideal relationship and reciprocating responsibilities between a polis and its citizens/residents were well expressed by Sokrates in the dialogue *Krito*, written by Sokrates's follower Plato. This citizen of fifth-century Athens imagines the city herself with her laws having the following conversation with the philosopher (50d–51c):

"First off, did we not engender you, and through us didn't your father receive your mother and create you? Speak now, to those of us, the laws about marriage: Do you find fault with some aspect of us, that we didn't do well?"

"I find nothing to blame," I should answer.

"But what about the laws concerning the rearing of a baby, and his education, by which even you were educated? Did we laws who regulated these matters not arrange them well, ordering your father to educate you in music and sports?"

"Well, indeed," I should say.

"Well then. Since you were born and reared and educated, could you say that you are not both our child and our slave, both you and your forefathers? And if this is so, then do you think justice between us is based on equality, and that if we attempt to do something to you, that it is just for you to retaliate? There was no such equality between you and your father, or a master, if you happened to have had one, so that having suffered something you might retaliate—hearing bad things, you might answer in kind; hitting back when struck, or many other such things. Considering your forefathers and the laws, then, is it permissible for you, if we should decide to kill you—justly in our opinion—to attempt to the full extent of your ability to destroy us in return, both the laws and your fatherland? And then to say that you are doing these things justly—you, Mr. I'm-all-about-the-truth-of-virtue? Are you really so wise that you have forgotten how your fatherland is to be honored above mother and father and every last one of your forefathers, and is holier, and more revered, and has greater due both among the deities and among rational humans; and how she must be respected and yielded to and adored—your fatherland when incensed even more so than your father? And that you must believe and do what she bids, and suffer if she tells you to, holding your tongue? To be struck or imprisoned, or if she leads you to war to be wounded or killed? It is necessary to do these things, and it is just, and you must not retreat or give ground or leave your post, but in war and in the law courts and wherever else you must do what she commands, your fatherland and your city. Or, you must persuade her in justice. But it is impious to use violence, against father or mother, and most certainly against the patris!"

Love of polis/patris was felt very strongly in ancient Greece, as is attested in poetry, history, and epigraphy. Already in the works of Homer we hear of heroes expressing their love of their homelands, even to the point of preferring home to immortality. Thus Odysseus, "So true is it that nothing is sweeter than a man's own land and his parents, even though he might dwell in a rich house in a foreign land, far away from his parents" (*Odyssey* 9.34–35). In a similar vein, Theognis writes of how nothing is dearer than one's homeland (783–788):

> As for myself, I once went to the land of Sicily,
> And I went to the plains of Euboia rich in vines,
> And to the shining city of Sparta on reed-rich Eurotas,
> And having arrived they all loved me greatly.
> But no pleasure has come to my heart from them,
> Since nothing else is more beloved than one's patris.

This same longing for home was just as keenly felt by the Greek mercenaries fighting for the would-be Persian king Kyros, especially on their long walk home after the failed coup d'état (Xenophon *Anabasis* 3.1.3):

> Thinking such things and being dispirited, few of them ate that evening, and few kindled a fire; many did not come to camp that night, each one just stopping wherever he was, unable to sleep for grief and desire for fatherland, family, wife, and children, whom they thought that they would never see again.

Once again, love of the patris was felt just as strongly as love of the family itself.

For men especially, there could be no greater honor than to fight, and even die, for one's homeland. As the Spartan poet Tyrtaios put it in the seventh century (fr. 10):

> For it is a fair thing when a good man dies
> Standing in the front ranks defending his fatherland.
> But leaving his city and fleeing the rich fields
> Is the most horrid thing of all,
> Wandering with dear mother and old father
> And with small children and wedded wife.

For he is hateful to those around him; he will come upon them
Resembling want and hateful poverty.
He shames his clan and disgraces his shining face;
All dishonor and cowardice follow him.
And if thus there is no concern for such a man,
Or reverence or regard or compassion,
Then with heart let us fight for this land and our children,
Let us die never sparing the spirit!

This same notion of "save the patris or die trying" drove exiled citizens of Corinth to return home to save their city from invading Argives in the fourth century, as recounted by Xenophon (*Hellenika* 4.4.5–6):

> And at first they left as refugees from the territory of Corinth. But when their friends persuaded them, and their mothers and siblings came out too, and those in power promised them under oath that they would suffer nothing bad, then some of them returned home. But seeing the tyrant and seeing the city wiped out—the boundary stones having been removed—and their fatherland being called Argos rather than Corinth, and having to share in the government of Argos, which they didn't want anyway, being less powerful in the city than the metics, some of them thought that this was intolerable. But to try to make the fatherland Corinth again, just as she was even from the beginning, and to make her free again, and so purify the murderers, making use of good order— this would be right. If they could accomplish these things, they would be saviors of the fatherland; if not, it would be a most praiseworthy death, striving for the fairest and greatest good.

Not being expected to be warriors, somewhat less suicidal devotion was demanded of female citizens. This does not mean that women were any less patriotic, but it does mean that women had more opportunities to try to "make nice" between conflicting parties, either internally during civil war or between rival poleis. Most people reading this book are probably familiar with Sophokles's tragedy *Antigonê*, where the Theban princess Antigonê attempts, not entirely successfully, to repair the conflict between her uncle and her brothers (one of whom led a revolt against the other and thus the state itself). In so doing, she also attempted to resolve the conflict between the state, which would not allow a traitor to be buried, and the laws of the deities, who demanded burial for all the dead.

A more historical example was recorded by Plutarch in his essay on *The Bravery of Women* (§13: *The Women of Phokis*). In 355 BCE,

> Back when the tyrants in Phokis had seized Delphi and the so-called Sacred War was being fought between them and the Thebans, the women worshipping Dionysos—called Thyiades—went wandering and wilding about in the night and they unknowingly wound up in Amphissa. Being exhausted

and not yet realizing their situation, they proceeded into the agora and tossed themselves about and so lay down to sleep. The wives of the Amphissans, fearing lest the Thyiades would be abused because of the alliance their city had with the Phokians and the very many soldiers of the tyrants about, all went out to the agora and stood in a quite circle about the sleeping women, not waking them. But when they woke up, the one group of women went to tend to the other and brought them breakfast. In the end they persuaded their husbands to let them escort the women safely back to the border.

Even so, devotion to one's city was so strong that even women are recorded as having fought in defense of their homes. One of the most famous examples was the day in the fifth century when the women of Argos, under the leadership of the poetess Telesilla, successfully defended their city from the Spartans (the SPARTANS!). So much was also recorded by Plutarch in the previously mentioned essay (§4: *The Women of Argos*):

Of all the deeds accomplished for a community by women, the one second to none in honor was that during the conflict between the Argives and Kleomenes, in which the women exerted themselves when Telesilla the poet roused them. She, they say, was of a noble household, but being sickly in body they sent her to the god for healing. An oracle told her to attend to the Muses, and being convinced by the god she devoted herself to song and harmony, and she was thus quickly freed from her suffering. Additionally, she became admired by the women for her poetic talent.

But when Kleomenes, the King of Sparta, killed many before the city (although not the full 7,777 reported by some mythographers!), a daring, divinely-inspired urge arose amongst the women to ward off the enemy from the fatherland. With Telesilla leading, they took up arms and set themselves up in a defensive circle on the city walls, such that the enemy was amazed. They beat off Kleomenes, many falling; and when the other king—Damaratos—as Sokrates says, got inside and took the Pamphylion, they kicked him right out. And so the city was saved. Those of the women who fell in battle they buried on the Argive Road; and for those who survived, they permitted them to dedicate a memorial of their courage to Enyalios [Ares].

Another tale of women defending their land from the Spartans comes from Tegea, and is recorded by Pausanias (8.48.4–5):

There is a statue of Ares in the agora of the Tegeans. It is in high relief upon a stele, and they call it the "Feaster of Women." For at about the time of the Lakonian War, when Kharillos, King of the Lakedaimonians made the first invasion, the women arming themselves lay in ambush on the hill called by us Phylaktris. When the armies came together and displayed many great deeds on both sides, then they say the women revealed themselves and they went and routed the Lakedaimonians, and that Marpessa, called Khoira, outdid in daring the other women. Amongst the Spartans they seized Kharillos himself, and they released him without ransom, as he swore to the Tegeans never again to fight against Tegea. He broke that oath. But they say that the women sacrificed to Ares without the men, keeping the victory celebration for themselves and not sharing the sacrificial meat with the men. In light of these things Ares got his epithet.

If there is joy in dying to defend one's patris, the corollary is the sorrow attendant upon dying and being buried away from it. The most extreme expression of such a sentiment was expressed in the law court speech *Against Eubulides*, written in the fourth century by the Athenian orator Demosthenes. Here the speaker begs the jury not to deprive his mother of burial in her native land, and he even goes so far as to claim that he would willingly commit suicide if it would guarantee that his own death would at least take place in his homeland (57.70):

I am left bereft of a father, but I beseech and beg you in this trial to grant that I may bury my mother in the ancestral tomb, and not to deny me, nor make me a man without a city, nor turn me away from the many people in my household, and so destroy me utterly. For rather than leave these, if they cannot save me, I shall kill myself, so that I might be buried by them in my fatherland.

This may have been a rather extreme example (the man was pleading before a court, after all), but various inscribed gravestones from around the Greek world indicate that burial far from home was a concern even for the dead. Thus a mid-fifth-century grave marker from the Saronic Gulf region reads (*IG* I^3 1503):

Greetings, O Passers-by!
I am Antistates,
son of Atarbos. I lie
here dead
having left the earth of my fatherland.
Antistates, Athenian.

In the sixth century, the Spartan Pleistias died in Athens, leaving behind the following sentiments (*IG* XII,9 286):

Pleistias.
Sparta is my homeland, but in spacious
Athens I was buried, there
having met my fate—Death.

Another foreigner who met his end in Athens was the young Ephesian Pythokles, who died in the fourth century and whose mother came to set up his memorial (*IG* II^2 8523):

Here lies Pythokles, loved by many,
A youth with the surname Satyros.
Child of Herakleidos and his mother Ariastis,
His fatherland is Ephesos, most illustrious of poleis.
Having been buried in this land where he died, it is a great sorrow for friends
And the greatest pain for his sister, whom he left behind.
Ariastis. Pythokles.

And if the demise of young Pythokles was sorrowful, at least one might take away some sobering wisdom from the fate of poor old Orthon the Sicilian (*Greek Anth.* 7. 660):

Stranger, a Syracusan man Orthos commands you:
'Never go out drunk into a wintery night.'
For I had just such a fate, and instead of in my great
City, I lie clothed in a foreign one!

All in all, the polis was for most Greeks a second family, a source of identity, and "the sweetest thing on earth." As summarized by Thomas Heine Nielsen:

Greeks of the Archaic and Classical periods thought of their *patris* almost as a next of kin; it was the sweetest thing on earth; it was the proper place to be buried; it was what they lost by going into exile or regained by their return; it was something for which they would lay down their lives; it was, in short, an object of their love, and Greeks took pride in their *patris*. (2004, 74)

While the Greeks may have been united in their love of their cities, they were also divided in their love of their cities. Then as now, the Greeks had a fierce sense of individualism regarding their hometowns, and identification with polis was always stronger, and much older in Greece, than any sense of extrapolitical community (see later in this chapter). The ancient Greeks had city pride, and how any individual Greek viewed him/herself was in part dependent on how he/she viewed his/her patris. The Greeks were only barely united as a country; civic pride did more to separate and divide the Greeks than to unite them. As the Hellenistic poet Poseidippos put it "There is only one Hellas, but there are many poleis" (fr. 30 PCG).

The city for which we have the most information about city pride is, of course, Athens. All sorts of people lived in Athens: citizen men and women, metics, displaced persons, foreign businesspersons, and the ubiquitous slaves. Over the course of the fifth century especially, Athens became increasingly democratic, as more and more citizen males were admitted into more aspects of city government regardless of their financial situation. Athens took great pride in this. But as a corollary, the more citizens got to do, the more important it became to identify citizens and to limit, as it were, the franchise.

To give a sense of this change: In the sixth century, two of the most important families in Athens were the Peisistratids and the Gephyraí. The former were the family of Peisistratos, who was the tyrant of Athens and father of later tyrants of the city, starting in 545 BCE. The latter family produced Harmodios and Aristogeiton, famous as tyranicides for having killed a member of the preceding family. These were Athenian nobles at their finest (in their own unique ways). Nevertheless, the Peisistratids, rather than emphasizing any Athenian origins, claimed to come from the family of the Homeric hero Nestor in Pylos, as recounted by Herodotos (5.65.3):

> These ones were originally Pylians and descendants of Neleus; from them came both the people of Kodros and Melanthos, who first being foreigners became kings of the Athenians. At the time, Hippokrates memorialized this by giving the name Peisistratos to his son, after the Peisistratos who was the son of Nestor [son of Neleus].

At least they came from a Greek family, and an illustrious one at that. The Gephyraí, as recounted by the same historian: "came, according their own account, originally from Eretria; but I myself looked into the matter and discovered that they are really Phoenicians, descendants of those who came with Kadmos to what is now Boiotia, where they were allotted the district of Tanagra in which to make their homes" (5.57).

So originally, there was some caché in being "exotic," at least for the nobility. Things changed quite a bit in the fifth century. In 451, Perikles of Athens changed the marriage laws such that to be a citizen a person had to have both a citizen father *and* a citizen mother. This made it far more difficult for foreigners to marry into citizenship and for upper-class citizens to marry into foreign nobility. To engage in full citizen rights and prerogatives, citizen males had to prove their citizenship, either by showing where their names were recorded when inducted into their phratries and/or demes (see Chapter 1) or, in less extreme circumstances, showing their bronze citizenship cards (IG II^2 1835–1923; perhaps something equivalent to today's passport or social security card). Unfortunately, there were no such forms of proof for female citizenship, and thus a woman's behavior became the primary criterion on which to establish her citizenship. As one might imagine, life got rather oppressive for Athenian women in the fifth and fourth centuries . . .

In his *Funeral Oration*, delivered over the military dead during the second year of the Peloponnesian War, Perikles described in explicit detail why Athens was worth self-sacrifice (Thuc. 2. 37–42; see sidebar). For Perikles, and probably the majority of fifth-century Athenians, Athens was the School of Greece, the center of the world, the place with the most freedoms and the most consumer goods. There was a strong sense that Athenians were just *better* than everyone else, manifest especially in the fact that they were innately better at most things, including warfare, without needing incessant training.

In this they were most certainly superior to their (then) enemies the Spartans, who were utterly oppressed by their laws and had no lives apart from military training.

Periklean Funeral Oration (Thucydides 2: 37–42)

Our constitution does not copy the laws of neighboring states; we are rather a pattern to others than imitators ourselves. Its administration favors the many instead of the few; this is why it is called a democracy. If we look to the laws, they afford equal justice to all in their private differences; if to social standing, advancement in public life falls to reputation for capacity, class considerations not being allowed to interfere with merit; nor again does poverty bar the way, if a man is able to serve the state, he is not hindered by the obscurity of his condition. The freedom which we enjoy in our government extends also to our ordinary life. There, far from exercising a jealous surveillance over each other, we do not feel called upon to be angry with our neighbor for doing what he likes, or even to indulge in those injurious looks which cannot fail to be offensive, although they inflict no positive penalty. But all this ease in our private relations does not make us lawless as citizens. Against this fear is our chief safeguard, teaching us to obey the magistrates and the laws, particularly such as regard the protection of the injured, whether they are actually on the statute book, or belong to that code which, although unwritten, yet cannot be broken without acknowledged disgrace. Further, we provide plenty of means for the mind to refresh itself from business. We celebrate games and sacrifices all the year round, and the elegance of our private establishments forms a daily source of pleasure and helps to banish the spleen; while the magnitude of our city draws the produce of the world into our harbor, so that to the Athenian the fruits of other countries are as familiar a luxury as those of his own.

If we turn to our military policy, there also we differ from antagonists. We throw open our city to the world, and never by alien acts exclude foreigners from any opportunity of learning or observing, although the eyes of an enemy may occasionally profit by our liberality; trusting less in system and policy than to the native spirit of our citizens; while in education, where our rivals from their very cradles by a painful discipline seek after manliness, at Athens we live exactly as we please, and yet are just as ready to encounter every legitimate danger. In proof of this it may be noticed that the Lacedaemonians do not invade our country alone, but bring with them all their confederates; while we Athenians advance unsupported into the territory of a neighbor, and fighting upon a foreign soil usually vanquish with ease men who are defending their homes. Our united force was never yet encountered by any enemy, because we have at once to attend to our marine and to despatch our citizens by land upon a hundred different services; so that, wherever they engage with some such fraction of our strength, a success against a detachment is magnified into a victory over the nation, and a defeat into a reverse suffered at the hands of our entire people. And yet if with habits not of labor but of ease, and courage not of art but of nature, we are still willing to encounter danger, we have the double advantage of escaping the experience of hardships in anticipation and of facing them in the hour of need as fearlessly as those who are never free from them.

Nor are these the only points in which our city is worthy of admiration.

We cultivate refinement without extravagance and knowledge without effeminacy; wealth we employ more for use than for show, and place the real disgrace of poverty not in owning to the fact but in declining the struggle against it. Our public men have, besides politics, their private affairs to attend to, and our ordinary citizens, though occupied with the pursuits of industry, are still fair judges of public matters; for, unlike any other nation, regarding him who takes no part in these duties not as unambitious but as useless, we Athenians are able to judge at all events if we cannot originate, and instead of looking on discussion as a stumbling-block in the way of action, we think it an indispensable preliminary to any wise action at all. Again, in our enterprises we present the singular spectacle of daring and deliberation, each carried to its highest point, and both united in the same persons; although usually decision is the fruit of ignorance, hesitation of reflection. But the palm of courage will surely be adjudged most justly to those who best know the difference between hardship and pleasure and yet are never tempted to shrink from danger. In generosity we are equally singular, acquiring our friends by conferring not by receiving favors. Yet, of course, the doer of the favor is the firmer friend of the two, in order by continued kindness to keep the recipient in his debt; while the debtor feels less keenly from the very consciousness that the return he makes will be a payment, not a free gift. And it is only the Athenians who, fearless of consequences, confer their benefits not from calculations of expediency, but in the confidence of liberality.

In short, I say that as a city we are the school of Hellas; while I doubt if the world can produce a man, who where he has only himself to depend upon, is equal to so many emergencies, and graced by so happy a versatility as the Athenian. And that this is no mere boast thrown out for the occasion, but plain matter of fact, the power of the state acquired by these habits proves. For Athens alone of her contemporaries is found when tested to be greater than her reputation, and alone gives no occasion to her assailants to blush at the antagonist by whom they have been worsted, or to her subjects to question her title by merit to rule. Rather, the admiration of the present and succeeding ages will be ours, since we have not left our power without witness, but have shown it by mighty proofs; and far from needing a Homer for our panegyrist, or other of his craft whose verses might charm for the moment only for the impression which they gave to melt at the touch of fact, we have forced every sea and land to be the highway of our daring, and everywhere, whether for evil or for good, have left imperishable monuments behind us. Such is the Athens for which these men, in the assertion of their resolve not to lose her, nobly fought and died; and well may every one of their survivors be ready to suffer in her cause.

Indeed if I have dwelt at some length upon the character of our country, it has been to show that our stake in the struggle is not the same as theirs who have no such blessings to lose, and also that the panegyric of the men over whom I am now speaking might be by definite proofs established. That panegyric is now in a great measure complete; for the Athens that I have celebrated is only what the heroism of these and their like have made her, men whose fame, unlike that of most Hellenes, will be found to be only commensurate with their deserts. And if a test of worth be wanted, it is to be found in their closing scene, and this not only in the cases in which it set the final seal upon their merit, but also in those in which it gave the first intimation of their having any. For there is justice in the claim that steadfastness in his country's battles should be as a cloak to cover a man's other imperfections; since the good action has blotted out the bad, and his merit as a citizen more than outweighed his demerits as an individual. But none of these allowed either wealth with its prospect of future enjoyment to unnerve his spirit, or poverty with its hope of a day of freedom and riches to tempt him to shrink from danger. No, holding that vengeance upon their enemies was more to be desired than any personal blessings, and reckoning this to be the most glorious of hazards, they joyfully determined to accept the risk, to make sure of their vengeance and to let their wishes wait; and while committing to hope the uncertainty of final success, in the business before them they thought fit to act boldly and trust in themselves. Thus choosing to die resisting, rather than to live submitting, they fled only from dishonor, but met danger face to face, and after one brief moment, while at the summit of their fortune, escaped, not from their fear, but from their glory. (trans. Crawley 1910)

The Spartans, for their part, saw things a bit differently. They took considerable pride in the fact that they were, in body and soul, subjected to their laws in a very literal sense. The Spartan *nomoi* (which, please remember, means both "laws" and "customs") infringed on every aspect of Spartan life, literally from birth until post-mortem. As far as the Spartans were concerned, this made them better people, more virtuous. Even some better-educated philosophers in Athens saw it this way. For example, Xenophon, in his *Constitution of the Lakedaimonians*, records that (8. 1–2, 10. 4–7):

But really, we all know how in Sparta they are most obedient to the magistrates and the laws. I indeed don't think that Lykourgos trusted the well-running of the state to advance before he got the most powerful men in the city to agree with him. And here's a proof of these things: In other cities the most powerful do not want to seem to fear the magistrates, but they think of this as being slavish. But in Sparta the most powerful submit the most to the magistrates, and they take pride in their own humility, and whenever summoned they run—not walk—to respond, believing that if they lead the way in showing prompt obedience, then the others will follow. And so it is.

And in this thing too doesn't Lykourgos merit great admiration? When he learned that, all over, those who wished to cultivate virtue were not strong enough to improve the fatherland, he required in Sparta that everyone publicly practice every virtue. So just as individuals differ from one another in virtue as they do or do not practice it, so too Sparta is, predictably, distinguished in virtue from all other cities, she being the only one to enforce good conduct. For isn't this a good thing—in other cities they punish someone for harming another; but Lykourgos established no less a penalty if a person didn't openly try to be his best. For he thought, as is reasonable, that some things—enslavement, fraud, theft— only harmed the victims, but that evil and cowardice betray the whole city. And so, as seems reasonable to me, he set up a great penalty for these things. And he decreed that the most important need was to practice civic virtue. For to all those who fulfilled the laws he gave the city, equally, without regard for weaknesses in body or finances. But if someone flinched from carrying out the laws, this man he made clear was no peer of the rest.

It is quite well known that the Spartans took incredible pride in their military training and sense of duty. Most famous, of course, is the epitaph of those 300 Spartans who died defending the pass at Thermopylai from the Persian army (Herodotos 2.228.2):

O, Passer-by! Go tell them at Sparta that
Here we lie, obedient to their word.

Another famous anecdote comes from Plutarch's *Life of Agesilaos* (26. 4–5):

So the allies said that they did not wish to be destroyed, going here and there every year, so many accompanying just a few. At that, then, it is said that Agesilaos, wishing to refute their majority, devised the following. He bade all the allies to sit down mixed up amongst themselves, and the Lakedaimonians singly amongst themselves. Then he called on the potters to stand up, and so they stood; second he called on the smiths, then the carpenters in their turn, and the construction workers, and each one of all the other professions. So then almost all of the allies were standing, but not one of the Lakedaimonians, for it was forbidden for them to work at trades or to learn crafts. Laughing at this Agesilaos said, "You see, men, how many more soldiers we lead out than you?"

(This anecdote appeared in somewhat warped fashion in Frank Miller's *300*, when Gerard Butler, playing the Spartan king Leonidas of Thermopylai fame, cried out to his men, "Spartans! What is your profession?!?!" And they all shouted back something akin to "Hoot!" which apparently was supposed to mean "soldier" or something.)

Spartan men were not the only ones to express civic pride. As Plutarch once again related, when an Athenian women once asked Queen Gorgo (wife and niece of the previously mentioned Leonidas, played by Lena Headey in *300*) why only Spartan women ruled their men, she replied, "Because only we give birth to men."

ETHNICITY

In many ways, the most elusive category of self-identification in ancient Greece was that of ethnicity. There has been much debate in modern scholarship on what actually constitutes "ethnicity," especially since World War II, before which ethnicity was seen as roughly tantamount to "race" and had some very politically incorrect associations. Although matters such as language, religion, dress, and cuisine have their roles to play in the matter of ethnicity as currently understood, it is perhaps best to think of ethnicity as a concept of very extended family, whereby people identify themselves as part of a larger group based primarily on notions of some kind of common ancestor and/or some kind of original homeland. Whether the ancestor is real and how close those ties are to the *Urheimat* are not as important as the sense of community fostered by belief in both. To give a modern example, much of southern Philadelphia ("South Philly") is inhabited by people who self-identify as Italian. These residents are first-, second-, third-, fourth-, and fifth-generation "immigrants," few of whom speak more than a few words of Italian and many of whom could not find their Italian town of origin on a map. To emphasize their Italianess, though, they make a point of eating Italian food (as understood), listening to Italian music (ditto, often Sinatra), cursing in Italian, and watching *The Godfather* frequently. In so doing, they fortify their bonds of ethnicity with each other, thus forging a strong sense of community.

(In the interest of full disclosure, the author would like to point out that she is a South Philly Italian whose first words of Italian were "Shut up, Chatterbox" ["Stai zitto, chiacchierone!" pronounced "zata zeet, a gya-gyeron!" in South Philly] and who has never actually seen *The Godfather* all the way through. La famiglia comes from Formia, on the west coast between Rome and Naples.)

Such ethnic ties existed in ancient Greece, once again based primarily on notions of common ancestors (thus the notion of extremely extended family) and original homeland. What becomes immediately obvious, however, is that both of these criteria—ancestry and "homeland"—are mythological in nature (considering the fact that some of those ancestors are folks like Herakles); as such, a study of Greek ethnicity is in many ways an extension of Greek mythology. Furthermore, these myths can be altered or "corrected" to accommodate changing political circumstances.

Although there were many *ethnê* (plural of *ethnos*) in ancient Greece, the largest ones were the Ionians, Dorians, Akhaians, and Aiolians. Smaller groups included the Dryopes, Phokians, Eleans, and Arkadians. So what, then, would make a person, say, Ionian? Well, first off, the person would probably speak an Ionian dialect of Greek, that dialect spoken in Attika and along the central west coast of Anatolia (modern-day Turkey). As far as Herodotos is concerned, that person would celebrate a religious festival called the Apatouria ("the Trick"), and more likely than not would have a standing invitation to participate in ceremonies taking places at the Panionion ("All Ionians") sanctuary on the north side of Mykalê in Anatolia (Herodotos 1.147).

But what about those two most important criteria: a common ancestor and a common homeland? Well, that's where things can get a bit tricky. If one were to go back to an Archaic-Age document called the *Catalogue of Women*, attributed to Hesiod but actually composed later, probably in the sixth century, one would see that our Ionian should be a descendant of (not surprisingly here) a fellow named Ion, who was the son of Xouthos, who was the son of Hellen, from whom the Hellenes (the Greeks) got their name. Ion's brother's name was Akhaios, father of the Akhaians, and thus we might understand that the Ionians and Akhaians were sibling ethnic groups, much closer in nature and alliances than they were with groups such as the Dorians. However, if one were to consult an alternate family tree as recorded by Euripides, a fifth-century Athenian playwright, in his play *Ion*, one would find that the Ionians, while still the descendants of Ion, have the god Apollo as their grandfather, not Xouthos, who is actually the father of Akhaios and Doros. The Ionians are thus descended from the deities, and one would expect the Akhaians and Dorians to be closer in a familial and political way. At any rate, one thing that is consistent is that Ion himself had four sons—Geleon, Hopletes, Argades, and Aigikores—from whom the Ionians both in Attika and Anatolia derive their tribal names. So to be an Ionian meant to be a descendant of Ion through one of his four sons, regardless of who Ion himself actually was.

What about a homeland? Well, things get tricky here too, especially if our Ionian happens to be an Athenian. Now, once again according to Herodotos (1.147), all Ionians originally came from Athens, or at least Attika (the district for which Athens is the main city). As Herodotos put it, "The name [Ionian] applies to all who originate from Athens and keep the Apatouria festival; all the Ionians, that is, except for those from Ephesos and Kolophon, who are excluded from the rite because of some murder." The idea is that during the Dark Ages, many Greeks from the mainland set out looking for literally greener pastures, and most went to Anatolia. Those in the Ionic dialect–speaking areas were understood to come originally from Athens, taking their festivals (the Apatouria), their tribal names, and their dialect with them.

At first, this would seem to reflect the data provided by Thucydides, (1.2):

> Attika from remote times, being free from faction because of its poor soil, has been inhabited by the same peoples always. And here is a not paltry proof of this statement: Because of displacements to other regions other places did not grow to the same extent. For from the rest of Hellas those most powerful people driven out by war or faction relocated to Athens, it being safe. They became citizens immediately, and made the city so full of people that eventually they had to send out colonies to Ionia, as Attika wasn't large enough.

What Thucydides does, though, is suggest that two separate groups may have come out of Attika to colonize Ionia—indigenous Athenians and refugees who came to Athens, got over-crowded, and then proceeded east. This separation between indigenous Athenians and other such Ionians is then reflected in Herodotos, who preserves a distinct tradition. According to him, the Ionians, as entirely distinct from the Athenians, originally lived in the Peloponnese, south of Attika, and were only chased out by the Akhaians when *they* were chased out of their Peloponnesian homeland by the arrival of the Dorians (see later in this chapter). "These people [the Ionians], according to the Greek account, as long as they lived in what is now known as Akhaia in the Peloponnese, before the coming of Danaos and Xouthos, were called the Pelasgians of the Coast. They took their present name from Ion, son of Xouthos" (Herodotos 7.94).

The Athenians themselves claimed to be autochthonous, meaning that they had always lived in the exact same place, and that they had been residents of Athens since pretty much the dawn of humanity. Some of their myths even claim that at least some of their kings were born from the earth in Athens itself. Thus once upon a time, Hephaistos, the god of arts and crafts, felt a bit randy and tried to rape the goddess Athena. Hephaistos was the husband of Aphrodite, the goddess of sex, and Athena was a sworn virgin and a goddess of warfare, so this was an amazingly stupid decision all around on Hephaistos's part. Nevertheless, he attacked Athena and wound up ejaculating on her thigh. Athena wiped away the semen with a bit of wool and dropped it onto the earth in Athens, where it grew into the child Erikhthonios, one of the primordial Athenian kings. In a very literal sense, the Athenians understood themselves to be almost literally born from the land. So once again, by this tradition Athenians and Ionians are *not* related, in spite of all the common attributes.

Of course, this same tradition also seems to imply that the Athenians aren't exactly Greek either. As the Lydian king Kroisos discovered when he did a study of the Greeks (Herodotos 1. 56–58):

> Asking around he discovered that the Lakedaimonians and the Athenians were pre-eminent, the former of the Dorians, the latter of the Ionians. For these were the primary tribes, being of old the Pelasgian [indigenous] and Hellenic tribes. The one never relocated ever, while the other wandered around extensively. For about the time of King Deukalion [the Dorian tribe] dwelled in the land of Phthia, and in the time of Doros son of Hellen in the land beneath Ossa and Olympia, called Histiaia. When driven out of Histiaia by the Kadmeians, they dwelled in Pindos, called Macedon. Next they moved into Dryopian land, and from Dryops' territory so came into the Peloponnese, as so-called. Now whatever language the Pelasgians spoke, I am unable to say for sure. If it is possible to offer in evidence those of the Pelasgians still now residing in the city of Kreston, above the Tyrhenians, who shared a border there with those now called Dorians (in the area now called Thessaly), and those Pelasgians inhabiting Plakia and Skylax on the Hellespont, who came to live with the Athenians, and as many other Pelasgian cities that changed names, if one might take them into evidence, then the Pelasgians spoke a barbarian [non-Greek] language. If then the whole Pelasgian group was such, then the Attik tribe, being Pelasgian, must have learned the Greek language at the same time as it became Greek. For indeed neither the Krestonians speak the same language as any of its neighbors, nor do the Plakaians, but they spoke the same language as each other, and they make it clear that they brought their type of speech with them when they migrated to their lands—they preserved it. But the Greek contingent—when they became Greeks—has always made use of the same language, as it seems quite clear to me. When they split off from the Pelasgians they were weak, but from their small beginnings they grew into a great multitude of peoples, mostly Pelasgians and other non-Greeks joining with them. Before this it seems to me that the Pelasgians, while barbarians, didn't expand much.

Herodotos later finishes his account of Athenian transformation (8.44.2):

> The Athenians—when the Pelasgians held the land now called Hellas—were Pelasgian, called Kranaoi; when Kekrops was king they got the name Kekropians; when Erekhtheus succeeded to rule they changed their name to Athenians, and when Ion son of Xouthos became chief general over the Athenians, they were called after him—Ionians.

According to this tradition, then, Athenians are Ionians by association, although they were originally members of an indigenous group called the Pelasgians, who were not Greek. Furthermore, they are not descendants of Ion; he was merely one of their generals, thus the name Ionian. Eventually, however, the Pelasgians of Athens learned Greek, adopted other Greek customs, and thus became Greek. Greeks, then, come from elsewhere (see later in this chapter). Athenians are autochthonous, thus not originally Greek, but Greek by adoption and adaptation. So in summary, to be Athenian means to be Ionian or possibly not Ionian, indigenous, Greek or possibly not Greek but Pelasgian, a descendant of Ion, or possibly just one of his soldiers. To be an Ionian indicates that you may be of Athenian origin, Pelasgian origin, or Peloponnesian origin. Whatever works at the time . . .

So, what if you're a Dorian? Well, harkening back to Herodotos's statement presented above (1.56–58), you have moved around a *lot*. You are—congratulations—actually Greek, and you started out in the north, specifically in Phthia, which, as we shall see, was deemed the original homeland of the Greeks generally. You were driven from home by the Kadmeians, named for their king Kadmos who was originally from Phoenicia but whose subjects were not Phoenicians but rather grown-from-the-soil Boiotians (thus autochthonous) and thus called Spartoi ("Sown Men"), not to be confused with Spartans, who are, of course, Dorians, bringing us back to you. You then spent a fair amount of time in Macedon before coming to conquer southern Greece at the fall of the Bronze Age. As such, you did not return to your original home in the north, but rather came to occupy most of the Peloponnese and the island of Crete. What allowed for this stunning military conquest was a brilliant alliance made between the Dorians and a small group of Akhaians who were descendants of Herakles—the Herakleidai.

According to tradition, especially as preserved in Book III of Apollodoros' *Bibliothekê* ("Library"), Herakles once allied himself with King Aigimios, the son of Doros, son of Hellen (see earlier in this chapter about the *Catalogue of Women*), and with him defeated the Lapiths and acquired all of their land. In gratitude, Aigimios the Dorian offered a portion of this land to Herakles, but the strongman declined, being too involved in travel. He asked instead that the land be reserved for his descendants. Considering that Herakles rivaled his father in coital excess, this was probably a bad idea . . . Anyway, the descendants of Herakles were later banished from southern Greece by Herakles's obnoxious cousin Eurystheus. In remembrance of his former ally, Aigimios adopted Herakles's (main) son Hyllas, thus making him a stepbrother to his own two sons Dymas and Pamphylos. Later, when Eurystheus died, Herakles's son Hyllas tried to lead his family back into the Peloponnese, only to find out from the oracle at Delphi that this would not happen for another three generations. So much is recounted by the Tegeans just south of Argos, as recorded by Herodotos (9.26):

> "We have always been deemed worthy of this position out of all the allies, as many as marched out together amongst the Peloponnesians, both anciently and now, from that time when the Herakleidai attempted to return to the Peloponnese after the death of Eurystheus. Then we got the right in this

way: When, along with the Akhaians and Ionians who were then in the
Peloponnese, we, as helpers, took up position in the isthmus against the
invaders. Then it is said that Hyllas announced that it was not right that
the armies endanger themselves by coming together, but rather that from the
Peloponnesian army the one chosen by them as the best should fight him
[Hyllas] in single combat according to agreed terms. And this seemed to the
Peloponnesians to be workable and they cut an oath on the following terms: If
Hyllas should defeat the leader of the Peloponnesians, then the Herakleidai
should retake their ancestral land; but if he were conquered, then the
Herakleidai would depart and lead away the army, and they would not see the
road to the Peloponnese for one hundred years. Of all the allies present
Ekhenos son of Eëropos son of Phygeos was chosen, who was our general and
king, and he fought Hyllas single-handedly and killed him."

So the Herakleidai, the descendants of Herakles, had to wait another hundred
years or so to return, thus pretty much entirely missing out on the Trojan War.
However, when they did return, the old alliance between the descendants of
Hyllas, the son of Herakles, and those of Aigimios, the Doric adoptive father
of Hyllas, was still intact, and they took southern Greece together. Henceforth, the majority of the Peloponnese, as well as Crete and portions of Sicily,
spoke a Doric dialect, celebrated the Karneia and Hyakinthia festivals (much
as the Ionians celebrated the Apatouria), celebrated rites at the Triopion
Sanctuary, and were divided into three tribes—the Hylleis, Pamphyloi, and
the Dymanes—named for the sons of Aigimios and Herakles.

Granted, not everyone liked these new Dorian neighbors, and some emotions were still raw well into the historical period. For example, Kleisthenes,
the tyrant of Sikyon (in the northern Peloponnese) self-identified as an
Argive, thus pre-Dorian, and he chose to humiliate the Dorians in his
territory by changing their tribal names (Herodotos 5.68):

[Kleisthenes] changed the manes of the tribes of the Dorians, so that they tribes
would not be the same amongst the Sikyonians and the Argives. He thus made
total laughing stocks of the Sikyonians, for he swapped in the names of pigs,
asses, and swine (changing the endings), except for his own tribe, of course, to
whom he gave the name of his own rule. So these latter ones were called
Arkhelaoi (Rulers), but the others were Pigmen, Assmen, and Swinemen. The
Sikyonians made use of these tribe names both during the reign of Kleisthenes
and for some sixty years after his death. Afterwards, discussing the matter
amongst themselves, they switched to Hylleis, Pamphyloi, and Dymanes. A
fourth group was established among them called Aigiales, after Aigialeus, son of
Adrastos.

Sometimes, for political reasons, the old distinction between the Dorians (the
descendants of Aigimios) and the Herakleidai (the descendants of Akhaian

Herakles) could be invoked. Thus in the late sixth century, the Spartan king Kleomenes invaded Athens and attempted to walk right up to the temple of Athena on the Acropolis. As Herodotos narrates the event (5. 72):

> For as Kleomenes went up the Acropolis intending to occupy it, he went to the adyton [Holy-of-Holies] of the goddess to consult her. But the priestess rose up out of her throne and going before the doors said to him, "O Lakedaimonian foreigner, go back and do not enter the sanctuary, for it is not permitted for Dorians to enter there." And he said, "O woman, I am not Dorian, but Akhaian."

Nevertheless, the groups were typically more united than distinguished, as Pindar recounted in his *First Pythian Ode* (l. 64)

> Those come of Pamphylos, and the descendants of the Herakleidai,
> Dwelling on the hills below Taygetos, ever abiding by the ordinances of
>   Aigimios—
> Dorians.

Although the Ionians and Dorians were the most popular ethnic groups (see Kroisos earlier in this chapter), there were also many other smaller ethnic groups, and they each had their own tales of self-history and self-definition. Take, for example, the Dryopes. According to tradition, the Dryopes ("Woodpeckers") had originally lived in central Greece, a region specifically called Doris by Herodotos, but they were driven out by Herakles. They dispersed to various islands, including Euboia off the coast of Attika, the Cyclades, and even Cyprus. Later though, Eurystheus, king of Mycenae and rival cousin of Herakles, gave them land in the Peloponnese, including the region of Asinê. So much is recorded by the second-century CE travel guide Pausanias (4.34. 9–11):

> The Asinians from the beginning used to live by Mount Parnassos, bordering on the Lykoritans. Their name [Dryopes], which they preserved even in the Peloponnese, was from their founder Dryops. In the third generation after, when Phylas was king, the Dryopes were conquered in battle by Herakles and were brought to Delphi as a dedication to Apollo. Having been brought to the Peloponnese by the gods' oracle to Herakles, first they lived in Asinê by Hermionê; but being driven from there by the Argives they came to dwell in Messenia, it being given to them by the Lakedaimonians, and when in time the Messenians retook the place, they were not uprooted from the city by them. The Asinians themselves say this about themselves: conquered by Herakles in battle, they agree that their city near Parnassos was captured, but they do not agree that they were prisoners and brought to Apollo. But when their walls fell before Herakles, they abandoned the city and fled to the heights of Parnassos, the next day embarking on ships to the Peloponnese. They say that they went

and supplicated Eurystheus, and because Eurystheus hated Herakles, he gave them Asinê in the Argolid. Only the Asinians of the race of Dryopes take pride in this fact and still keep the name into our own day. Not so with the Euboians in Styra. For they are also Styrian Dryopes from the beginning, but they did not take part in the battle with Herakles, dwelling in a city farther away. But the Styrians disdain to be called Dryopes, just like the Delphians avoid being called Phokians, whereas the Asinians warmly welcome being called Dryopes. And the most sacred of their sanctuaries were clearly made in memory of those which they one consecrated at Parnassos. For the one is their temple of Apollo, and another the sanctuary and old statue of Dryops; they hold the rite for him every year, saying that Dryops is the son of Apollo.

These non-Doric inhabitants of the Peloponnese went out of their way to establish their distinctive ethnic identity. The settlement plan of Asinê, already in the early Archaic Age, was distinct from all others in the local Argive plain, and the inhabitants of Asinê made much greater use of imported Attik pottery than anyone else in the Argolid. Their religious rituals appear to have been unique for the region, making use as they did of circular stone platforms currently understood as aspects of ancestor cult. Such platforms are, once again, unique for the Argolid but have parallels in both Attika and the Cyclades (Hall 1997, 137). For that which concerns death, the people at Asinê were more likely to use cremation when their neighbors continued to inhume. People in nearby Argos and Tiryns buried their dead in a contracted position, typically facing west. In Asinê, skeletons were buried fully extended and facing east (Hall 1997, 137). Obviously, these Asinians were indeed proud of their Dryopean heritage, and they took full opportunity to express their uniqueness in a very physical way.

Perhaps regardless of their various histories, families, and homelands, the various ethnic groups of ancient Greece were seen to have certain "ethnic" characteristics above and beyond things such as dress and food. Much like today, when we think of the Japanese as polite and the Germans as efficient, the Ionians (including the Athenians) were seen as luxurious and innovative, while the Dorians (along with the Herakleidai) were more simple and modest. As Thucydides recounts it in his early history of Greece (1.6.3–4):

> The Athenians were the first both to lay down the sword and, by abandoning this way of life, to switch over to a daintier one. And the old men among them, those of the wealthier sort, only recently stopped wearing linen khitons and golden grasshopper hair-fasteners in their hair, so à la mode in the luxurious lifestyle. From them this fashion spread to the old men of the Ionians—their relatives—and lasted a long time. The Lakedaimonians were the first to make use of the moderate dress which is even now the fashion, and in other things the peers possessing the most basically act as does the majority. They were the first to strip themselves naked and openly and richly to oil themselves after

sports. In the old days even at the Olympics the athletes wore belts about their privates, and it is not many years since they stopped.

Such notions even extended to architecture. The Doric Order, such as the Temple of Zeus at Olympia, is seen as "masculine," with clean, straight lines and a simplicity of decoration, usually narrative in character. The Ionic Order, such as the Siphnian Treasury at Delphi, is more "feminine" and frilly, with swirling capitals, floral decoration, and sometimes even caryatid maidens serving as roof supports!

Such differences in character, as one might imagine, led to some interesting stereotypes and prejudices, as exploited by the Spartan general Brasidas during the Peloponnesian War: "Lakedaimonian men, we come from such a country which is always free due to courage, and that you are Dorians about to fight Ionians whom you are accustomed to beat, well, this is shown quickly enough" (Thuc. 5.9.1).

All ancient Greeks would identify with some ethnic group, be it Dorians, Dryopes, or otherwise. This type of self-identity would be summoned to account for common aspects of life such as why our women wear linen *khitons* (Ionians) as opposed to woolen *peploi* (Doric), or why we speak with a Boiotian accent (Aeolic) as opposed to Arkadian, or why we are smarter than most Greeks (Ionian) or, obviously, more valorous (Dorian). It would in many ways explain our history, accounting for how we came to be descended from Zeus via Apollo (Ionians) or via Herakles (Akhaian Herakleidai), but also how we came to inhabit this land, being long-term migrants (Dorians, Akhaians, Dryopes) or autochthons (Athenians, Boiotians, Arkadians). As such, the idea of ethnicity was woven into the fabric of daily living as Greeks understood their daily customs and their place in the universe.

Nevertheless, the notion of ethnicity in ancient Greece was also easily malleable, being based as it was in mythology, and family lines could be so easily tweaked. Thus the "fraternal" alliance attested between Akhaians and Ionians as attested in the *Catalogue of Women* can turn into a fraternal alliance between Akhaians and Dorians in Euripides. Ultimately, on a public or political level, ethnic identity was seldom as strong as the daily political realia, and what brought peoples together in alliance had far more to do with power and property than old bonds of family and ethnicity. Thucydides was perhaps the most realistic (or, if you prefer, cynical) when it came to this fact, and he seemed to enjoy advertising how much the Greeks would go against ethnic lines in face of *Realpolitik* (7.57):

These are those who fought either against Sicily or alongside the Syracusans, coming either to defeat the land or to save it, standing with each other not according to any sense of justice nor family bond, but as chance or necessity benefitted each of them. The Athenians, being Ionians, happily came against

Dorian Syracuse, and those still using the same language and laws as they did—the Lemnians, Imbrians, and Aiginetans (those who held Aigina at the time), and also those Hestiaians living in Histiaia on Euboia, being their colonists, went out with them. Of the others who fought along with them were their subjects, of those free states who came through alliance, and mercenaries. Of the subject states and those paying tribute were Eretria and Khalkidia and Styria and the Karystians of Euboia; from the islands the Kaians and Andrians and Tenians; and from Ionia the Milesians and Samians and Khians. Of these the Khians did not pay tribute, but provided ships and followed along of their own volition. And the majority of these, being Ionian, were all descended from the Athenians—save for the Karystians who are Dryopes; they were subjects and constrained, but nevertheless were Ionians going after Dorians. With these were the men of Aiolic origin—Methymnians who owed ships, not tribute, and Tenedians and Aimians, who did pay tribute. These Aiolians fought against their Aiolic founders the Boiotians alongside the Syracusans out of necessilty; Boiotians only fought against Boiotians from Plataia willingly out of enmity. Rhodians and Kytherians were both Dorians—the Kytherians were colonized by the Lakedaimonians—but they bore arms along with the Athenians against those Lakedaimonians with Gylippos. The Rhodians, Argives by race, were compelled to fight against the Dorian Syracusans, and also their own colonists the Gelans who were fighting with the Syracusans. Of the islanders by the Peloponnese the Kephalanians and the Zakynthians were autonomous; but being quite hemmed in on their islands, because the Athenians ruled the seas, they followed the Athenians. The Kerkyrians were not only Dorians, but descended from Corinthians, went against the Corinthians and Syracusans, although colonists of the former and family of the latter, claiming constraint but really willingly out of hatred for the Corinthians. And those now called Messenians from Naupaktos and Pylos (held by the Athenians at the time) were taken with them to the war. And the few remaining refugees of the Megarians fought against the Megarians, being Selinutians, as chance would have it. The campaigning of the rest was more voluntary. For the Argives went after the Dorians alongside the Ionian Athenians, not out of any alliance, but rather out of hatred for the Lakedaimonians and out of a straight-out self-interest, while the Mantineans and other Arkadian mercenaries always willingly went against their indicated enemy, and along with the Corinthians they deemed other Arkadians enemies too—for profit. The Cretans and Aitolians both worked for pay, and so it happened that the Cretans who cofounded Gela with the Rhodians came to fight not with their colonists, but against them, for pay. And some of the Akharnanians, both for profit but more so out of friendship with Demosthenes and being allies of the Athenians, served as their allies out of good-will. Now these are bordered by the Ionian Gulf. Of the Italians the Thurians and Metapontans were dragged out to fight by the constraints of revolutionary times. Of the Sicilians were the Naxians, and Katanians, and from the barbarians the Egestans who had summoned [the Athenians], and most of the Sikels, and of those outside of Sicily some of the Etruscans out of a dispute with the Syracusans, and Iapygian mercenaries.

HELLAS

One of the most important things to remember when studying the Greeks is that for the most part, they didn't really think of themselves as being Greek, and certainly not all that much before the fifth century. Our modern sense of the nation-state, with its modern borders, did not apply in ancient Greece, and the fact that the Greeks were incessantly at war with each other should indicate to just what an extent they did not feel all that unified amongst themselves. As Jonathan Hall, the world expert on Hellenic ethnic identity, put it:

> In reality, it is probably the case that for the vast majority of the population of Greece—especially outside Athens and with the exclusion of those who sought employment as mercenaries—the issue of Hellenic identity, let alone how it was defined, was relatively low on the list of self-reflexive priorities. Attachment to one's family, local community, and *polis*, the need to subsist and make a living and the necessity of defending oneself against (Greek) neighbours were concerns that were probably far more important than a putative Hellenicity that frequently had little practical relevance in daily life. (2002, 219)

The Greek world for "Greece" is *Hellas* (thus terms such as "Hellenistic" and "Philhellene" = "lover of Greece"). In modern Greek, the *h* became silent, and thus the modern name for the country is Ellas (or *Ellada* in the accusative).

It is interesting to note just how rarely references to either Hellas or its residents—the Hellenes—appear in the early Greek literature. As is often noted, Homer does not discuss Hellenes. His heroes from Greece are Argives, Akhaians, and Danaans. They are barely a united group, recognizing Agamemnon as a kind of "High King," or at least war leader. But many of the heroes on the Greek side are kings or princes in their own right, and as the conflict between Agamemnon and Akhilleus in Book 1 of the *Iliad* makes clear, the various Akhaian chieftains were not wholly under Agamemnon's authority or control.

When Homer does mention Hellas, it is clear that he is referring to a section of northern Greece, the homeland of Akhilleus specifically. In the Catalogue of Ships in Book 2 of the *Iliad*, the poet mentions (2.681–85):

> Now those who inhabited Pelasgian Argos,
> And lived in Alos and Alopê and Trekhinia,
> And those who held Phthia and Hellas of beautiful women,
> Called Myrmidons and Hellenes and Akhaians,
> Of these and fifty ships was Akhilleus lord.

That Akhilleus had lordship over those fair Hellenic women is emphasized in Book 9, when he claims (ll. 395–397):

> There are many Akhaian women in Hellas and Phthia,
> Daughters of nobles, who guard strongholds;
> I might make any of these my wife, should I wish.

And finally, in death, Akhilleus worries about the aging family he left behind in his domains, asking Odysseus (*Odyssey* 11.494–497):

> Tell me if you have heard anything about noble Peleus,
> Whether he still has honor among the many Myrmidons,
> Or if they dishonor him in Hellas and Phthia,
> On account of his old age in hand and foot.

"Hellas," then, was just another district in the region of Thessaly, associated with, but separate from, Phthia. Its residents are called Hellenes, but also Akhaians and even Myrmidons ("Ant People"). (Okay, according to Hesiod, the story goes that Zeus once created a human army out of ants in Phthia, the same way that in Thebes soldiers grew out of dragon's teeth, thus the name.) When used more generally, Hellas as the north appears in conjunction with the "Argive heartland" to the south to refer to what would now be termed the Greek mainland. Thus Odysseus is famous "throughout Hellas and the Argive heartland" (*Od.* 1.344), meaning all of Greece. Hellas was a region in Greece, but it was not "Greece" yet.

This lack of early unification was evident to the Greeks themselves, at least in the fifth century when it occurred to them that there was something to contrast to the system of (mostly) independent poleis that was the norm throughout most of Greek history. Thucydides begins his account of the Peloponnesian War with just such an observation (1.3):

> And this is not the least sign of the weakness of the ancients, for before the Trojan War it does not appear that Hellas acted together. Rather it seems to me that they did not even all together have the same name of "Hellas"; before Hellen son of Deukalion the title did not exist. But for the most part the Pelasgians had their own names amongst themselves by tribes, while the children of Hellen himself were strong in Phthia; they were brought together for mutual aid throughout the cities, and by association each one eventually came to be called "Hellenes," and in not much time really the name prevailed over all of them. Homer gives the best evidence, for not much after the events of the Trojan War he nowhere calls them all by this name, no one except those with Akhilleus from Phthia, who were the first Hellenes. The others he called Danaans and Argives and Akhaians in his epics. Nor did he call anyone barbarians, since there was not yet a Hellas from which to distinguish them, as it seems to me. Each of those Hellenes, city by city, as many as set out with each other and later were all together named thus, did not act together before the Trojan War due to weakness and a general lack of interaction.

This started to change in the Archaic Age. One impetus was that the region of the original Hellas got involved in some serious supraregional religious politicking. Those Akhaians living in Phthia joined up with their neighboring Lokrians, Malians, Ainianes, and maybe even a few Dorians to regulate the functioning of a sanctuary of the goddess Demeter in the territory of Anthela in the Sperkheios Valley—heartland of the original Hellas of Akhilleus fame. Such a religious organization is called an *amphiktyony*, and this one was called the Pylaian Amphiktyony (so called for the nearby polis of Pylaia, not to be confused with Pylos, in the western Peloponnese!). Eventually, the Pylaian Amphiktyony decided to branch out and acquire/seize control of the far more prestigious sanctuary to their south—Delphi, home of Apollo's oracle and, as far as the Greeks were concerned, the center of the world (there is actually a stone there called the *Omphalos*, deemed to be Mother Earth's bellybutton). Acquiring a more renowned sanctuary required admitting more people into the amphiktyonic organization, and added to these original "Hellenes" and friends were Thessalians, Dolopes, Perraiboi, Magnesians, Phokians, Boiotians, and Ionians. Eventually, Greeks from even farther regions joined the group, including the Spartans from the Peloponnese and representatives from Prienê all the way in Anatolia (Hall 2002, 151–152). All of this seems to have taken place by the end of the seventh century, and certainly no later than the start of the sixth. As more people became allies of the Hellenes, more people started to think of themselves *as* Hellenes.

A second impetus, also religious, took place farther south, at the Panhellenic sanctuary of Zeus at Olympia, home of the original Olympic Games. According to Greek tradition, these games were originally founded by Herakles himself (and later refounded in 776 from which the dating of the Olympiads comes) for the purpose of bringing together the various Greek communities in friendship. So recounts the Athenian orator Lysias (33.1–3):

> Of all the other fine works on account of which, O men, it is proper to remember Herakles, there is also that he was the first to set up this competition, out of good will for Greece. For in previous times the cities were arrayed against each other, but when he stopped the tyrants and staunched those who were outrageous, then he made physical competitions, displays of wealth, and displays of intelligence in the fairest part of Greece, so that we might all gather together at one place for things to be seen and heard. For he deemed the gathering there to be the beginning of friendship amongst all the Greeks for one another.

So once again, the Greeks of the Classical period remembered that their land was only recently recognized as an integral unit (it still could hardly be called "unified"). Once the games recommenced in the historic period, they began to attract competitors from farther and farther afield. In the early eighth century, most victors came from the western Peloponnese, where Olympia is located. By mid-century, the rest of the Peloponnese started showing up, with victors from Corinth and Megara. Starting in the early seventh century (twenty-first Olympiad = 696 BCE), northerners started showing up, with Pantakles of Athens winning the foot race. From this point on, Athenians and Spartans were to account for over half of all Olympic victors for generations. It was also in the early seventh century that the first contender—and victor—from Italy showed up, when Daippos of Kroton won the boxing match in 672. But it was in the sixth century that the Greek Italians and Sicilians really started to make their presence felt. A similar pattern was followed by those from northern Greece—Pagondas of Thebes won the four-horse chariot race in 680, and Kleonidas from the same town won the foot race in 616. But like their western cohorts, northern Greeks came to be increasingly better represented in the sixth century (Hall 2002, 160). As Lysias put it, then, the Olympics were an event involving all the Greeks, thus creating a unifying element, like Delphi, around which the Greeks could form a notion of "Hellenicity."

And the emphasis here really is on Hellenic. The Olympic games, apparently by Herakles's design, were open *only* to Hellenes (i.e., descendants of Hellen). As a matter of fact, over 90 percent of the victors recorded for the first 300 years came from poleis that were either Aiolic, Doric, Ionic, or Akhaian in origin— "Greekness" was still a matter of ethnicity. But ethnicity itself, as we saw, was always open to negotiation, and eventually this was to be the case with Hellenicity as well. So much became apparent when the king of Macedon, Alexander I (not the Great), son of King Perdikkas, wanted to play (Herodotos 5.22.1–2):

> That those who descend from Perdikkas are Greeks, as they themselves say, I happen to know myself and shall especially prove later in my narrative how they are Greeks. Before that, though, even those running the games of the Greeks at Olympia knew them to be so. For when Alexander came to compete and went down for this purpose, those of the Greeks to run against him debarred him, saying that it was not for barbarians to compete in the games, but Greeks. Then Alexander showed how he was an Argive. He was judged to be Greek and, competing in the stadion race, he tied for first place.

Basically, Alexander convinced the Hellanodikai, literally "Greek Judges," that he was a descendant of Herakles and thus Greek. Perhaps more importantly, he made his arguments in the Greek language, for the purpose of competing in a sport where the only reward was an olive leaf crown. This was too distinctively Greek for the judges to ignore, and they let him compete.

Ultimately the Greeks had four Panhellenic games, meeting once every two to four years (see Chapter 4). In addition to the Olympic games held in honor of Zeus, there were also the Nemean games in his honor, the Isthmian games in honor of Poseidon, and the Pythian games held in honor of Pythian Apollo at Delphi, that same Delphi that gave us one of our original cores of Greekness. That notions of games, Greekness, and the amphiktyony were prevalent by the sixth century is manifest in an inscription that Pausanias saw during his excursion to Thebes (Paus. 10.7.6)

> And, as I see it, the dedication of Ekhembrotos is witness to this—he dedicated a bronze tripod to Herakles in Thebes, and the tripod bears this epigram:

"Ekhembrotos the Arkadian, having been victorious in the Amphictyonic
Games, set up this dedication for Herakles, singing songs and laments for the
Greeks."

The problem with having a shared sense of Greekness through such institutions as the Olympic games is that they were inevitably open only to the upper
classes. Travel was slow and expensive in the premodern world, and thus only
those with considerable means could afford to go to the games. This is doubly
so if one wanted to compete: This involved time to train, resources to hire
coaches and assistants, not to mention major purchases such as horses and
chariots! Early Greekness, then, was a type of identity open only to the wealthy elite. So much is made evident in Herodotos's tale of the wooing of Agaristê (see sidebar). Nevertheless, by the end of the sixth century, it was starting
to become evident that Greekness was trickling down to the lower classes,
with members of the merchant classes at least coming to understand their
commonalities if not full-scale unity. An idea of this development comes
across in Herodotos's account of the establishment of the Hellaneion—the
"Greek sanctuary" founded by several island-dwelling Greek communities in
the Egyptian town of Naukratis already in the mid-sixth century (Herodotos
2.178):

Amasis became a philhellene and he did various things for the Greeks, and
most especially he gave to those coming to Egypt Naukratis as a city to live in;
and for those of them not wishing to reside [in Egypt], to those travelers he
gave lands where they could dedicate altars and sanctuaries to the deities. Now
the greatest sanctuary of these, and the most renowned and most used, was the
one called the Helleneion, and these cities built it together: of the Ionians
Khios and Teos and Phokaia and Klazomenai, of the Dorians Rhodes and
Knidos and Halikarnassos and Phaselis, of the Aioleans only those from
Mytilenê. This sanctuary belongs to these, and these cities also furnish the
magistrates of the emporion [trading town]. All other cities as lay claim to this
sanctuary . . . it does not belong to them. Separately the Aiginetans built for
themselves a sanctuary for Zeus, and the Samians one for Hera, and the
Milesians one for Apollo.

Herodotos, of course, still recognizes the ethnic diversity of the various founders, and it is important to note that each community separately founded sanctuaries to their own regional deities. But it is significant that these Greek
merchants in Egypt had enough sense of common Greekness to establish a
sanctuary for common Greek usage—in some ways a shrine to Hellas itself—
and dedications from the site bear inscriptions to "the gods of the Hellenes."
    It was in the fifth century that full-scale Panhellenism really took hold in
Greece, and this was mostly because of the united effort that the Greeks put

The Wooing of Agaristê (Herodotos 6.126–130)

Kleisthenes the Sikyonian tyrant exalted his house, such that it became by far much more renowned amongst the Greeks than it was previously. Now there was a daughter born to Kleisthenes, son of Aristonymos, son of Myron, son of Andreas—her name was Agaristê. Kleisthenes wanted to give her as a wife to him whom he found amongst all the Greeks to be the best. Being at the Olympics and winning in the four-horse chariot race, Kleisthenes made an announcement—whoever of the Greeks deemed himself worthy to be the son-in-law of Kleisthenes was to come by the 60th day or sooner to Sikyon, with Kleisthenes ratifying the marriage one year from that date. Then as many of the Greeks as were proud of themselves and their countries came as suitors. Having made a track and palaistra for them, Kleisthenes maintained them there. Now from Italy came Smindyrides the son of Hippokrates of Sybaris, who was the most effeminate man who came (Sybaris was at its peak at this point); and Damasos son of Siris, son of Amyris called the Wise. These men came from Italy; from the Ionian Gulf came Amphimestos son of Epistrophos of Epidamnos. He came from the Ionic Gulf. An Aitolian came, brother of Titormos who excelled by nature all the Greeks and who fled humankind to the farthest reaches of Aitolian lands; this Titormos was the brother of [the suitor] Malis. From the Peloponnese came Leokedes, son of Pheidon, tyrant of the Argives; that Pheidon who established weights and measures for the Peoloponnesians and who most outraged all the Greeks when he kicked out the Elean gaming officials and himself held the games in Olympia. His son came, and Amiantos, son of Lykourgos of Arkadian Trapezos, and Laphanes from the city of Paios in Azinia, son of Euporion who received, as the story goes in Arkadia, the Dioskouroi in his halls and who from that time was host to all strangers; and Onomastos, son of Agaios of Elis. These are the men who came from the Peoloponnese; from the Athenians came Megakles son of Alkmeon who visited Kroisos [king of Lydia], and also Hippokleides, son of Teisander, foremost of the Athenians in wealth and looks. From Eretria, which was flourishing at the time, was Lysanias; he alone came from Euboia. From Thessaly came Diaktorides of the Skopads, from Krannon; from the Molossians came Alkon. These were the suitors.

When they arrived for the day announced, the first thing Kleisthenes did was inquire about the fathers and the lineage of each. Then keeping them for a year he tested them in regards to manliness and temper and education and character, going to each one both individually and gathered together. And as many of them as were young competed in sports, and most of all he tested them in social company. As long as he maintained them, he took care of everything and entertained them lavishly. And indeed those of the suitors who pleased him most were those who came from Athens, and of these especially Hippokleides, son of Teisander, so judging him for his manliness and because by descent he was related to the Kypselids in Corinth.

And so the appointed day arrived both for the wedding feast and for Kleisthenes's announcement of his decision. Sacrificing one hundred bulls, Kleisthenes feasted the suitors themselves and all the Sikyonians. Then, after dinner, the suitors were contending in music and stories in the midst of the guests. When the drinking progressed, Hippokleides pushed away many of the others and summoned the flute-player there to play a dance tune, and having persuaded the musician, he danced. And as far as he was concerned he danced marvelously, but Kleisthenes, seeing him, took it rather badly. After this Hippokleides stopped for a bit, and then ordered a table to be brought in. When the table arrived, first he danced upon it in Lakonian style, then in Attik, and then he stood on his head on the table and flung about with his legs. [Sounds a bit like break-dancing, really] Kleisthenes at the first and second performances started hating the idea that Hippokleides might become his son-in-law because of the dancing and the impudence of it; but he kept it to himself, not wishing to explode at Hippokleides. But seeing the legs swinging about he could no longer contain himself, and said, "O son of Teisander, you have danced away your wedding." And Hippokleides responded, "Not a concern for Hippokleides!" From this comes the saying. Kleisthenes called for silence, and said in their midst, "Men courting my child, I praise you all, and each of you, if it were possible, I should gratify, neither choosing one of you to single out, nor rejecting the rest. But this isn't possible with only the one daughter, to please you all, so for those of you who will not be taking part in the wedding I am giving a talent of silver each as a consolation prize for courting a marriage with my family and for being away from home. But to Megakles son of Alkmaon I give my daughter Agaristê, according to the laws of the Athenians."

forth in resisting the Persian invasions. The Persians attacked Greece twice in the early fifth century, once under King Darios in 490, when the Athenians and Plataians held them off at the Battle of Marathon, and once again in 480–479 under King Xerxes, when the Battles of Thermopylai and Salamis (among others) took place. Persia was an enormous empire stretching from modern-day Afghanistan to Egypt to Turkey, whereas Greece was a highly dispersed group of people who only barely managed to stop killing each other every few years to compete in sporting events. All things considered, it's pretty amazing Persia didn't crush Hellas like tic-tacs under a steamroller. But it didn't—Greece won and remained independent. And this, more than anything else, is what solidified the notion of Greekness for the Greek population at large.

The idea that the Greeks had a common foe, and won a common victory, gave great impetus to the idea of Hellenism at the dawn of the Classical period. This is not to say that all the Greeks, as we currently understand them, were actually unified during the invasions; Thebes "Medized," capitulated to the Persians, and all of the Greeks on the Ionian coast were already under Persian domination. (The Persian Empire was composed of two closely related ethnic groups, the Persians and the Medes. The Greeks couldn't tell the difference and often used the names interchangeably. Thus the old saying, "One man's Mede is another man's Persian.") Nevertheless, the idea of a common struggle, a *Greek* concern, pervades many of the documents from this period. For example, there is a tale, preserved in no fewer than three separate documents, that records how the women of Corinth prayed to Aphrodite for the sake of the Greek armies during the Invasions:

> . . . the Persian invasions, during which, for the salvation of the Greek army, the Corinthians performed nobly, and Theopompos says even their wives, entering into the sanctuary of Aphrodite (which they say Medea built at Hera's command), prayed to Aphrodite to cast desire to fight the Medes for the sake of Hellas upon their husbands. And even now they say the inscription is there, on the left hand going into the temple:
> "These ones, for the sake of the Greeks and close-fighting citizens,
> stood praying to Kypris divine;
> For holy Aphrodite did not wish to give
> an acropolis of the Greeks to bow-toting Medes".

After the invasions, the various Greek poleis who held off the Persians got together to dedicate a common Greek thank offering to Apollo at Delphi, once again the center of the Greek conceptual universe (remember the belly-button?). This was a gold tripod set atop three bronze intertwined rising snakes, on whose bodies were inscribed the names of the contributing poleis (ML 27):

> These ones fought in the war:
>   Lakedaimonians
>   Athenians, Corinthians, Tegeans, Sikyonians, Aiginaitans
>   Magarians, Epidaurians, Erkhomenians, Phleiasians, Trozanians
>   Hermiones, Tirynthians, Plataians, Thespies, Mykanians
>   Keians, Malians, Tenians, Naxians, Eretrians
>   Khalkidians, Styrians, Waleians, Potideians, Leukadians
>   Wanaktorians, Kythnians, Siphnians, Ambrakians, Lepreatians

From the fifth century on, Greekness came to have less to do with being an Ionian or Aiolian, less to do with being a descendant of Hellen or Herakles, and came to have a lot more to do with being not foreign, especially not Persian. Greeks became obsessed with the *barbaros*, the barbarian, one who did not speak Greek, and much artistic talent went into highlighting the differences between Greeks and barbarians. Obviously what we mainly have is the Greek side of this equation, which, not surprisingly, paints the Greeks in a much better light than their eastern neighbors. The Greek notion was that Greeks, as a people, were more civilized than the "Orientals," braver, smarter, with more self-control and freer lives. Greeks were civilized, integral human beings; Persians were barbaric slaves.

Thus in 472, just a few years after the second invasion, the Athenian playwright Aeschylus, himself a veteran of Marathon, penned *The Persians*, a drama set in Persepolis that portrayed the Persian court when it got the news about the resounding Greek victory, also known as the crushing Persian defeat. Here the Queen Mother Atossa recounts a dream she had, contrasting her own people with those of Hellas (ll. 176–199):

> For many nights dreams have ever
> Been with me, since the very moment my son, having mounted an army,
> Has gone to the land of the Ionians, wishing to destroy it.
> But never yet have I seen such distinct visions
> As what came at night. I shall tell you:
> I fancied two women well-dressed,
> The one adorned in Persian peploi,
> The other in Doric robes, appeared before my eyes.
> In their stature they were far more striking than women now,
> Faultless in beauty, sisters both.
> In country the one dwelled in Hellas,
> Receiving the land as her lot; the other in a barbarian land lived.
> These two, as I seemed to see, engaged in
> Some strife with each other. My son, learning of this,
> Restrained and placated them, and to a chariot
> He yoked them and placed a halter around their necks.
> And the one exulted in these trappings,
> Wearing the reins in her obedient mouth;
> But the other struggled and with her hands tore up
> The chariot harness, and with force she seized
> And shattered the yoke in half, free of her bit.
> My son fell, and his father stands near him,
> Dareios, pitying him. When Xerxes saw him
> He ripped the robes upon his body.

The idea of the weak, slavish, eastern barbarian even came to influence the so-called hard sciences, as medical writers such as Hippokrates tried to explain why Asian geography inevitably resulted in passive, "whipped" Asiatics, while Europeans were just so innately butch (*On Airs, Waters, and Places* 16 and 23):

> And regarding the distinct nature and appearance of those in Asia and those in Europe is the following. Concerning the lack of spirit of the people and their cowardice, that the Asiatics are less warlike than the Europeans and more tame

in character, the seasons are the main cause of this, as no great changes occur either in heat or cold, but they are balanced. For no disruptions of the mind occur, nor changes in the strength of the body, from which things, truly, anger is roused and rashness and courage imported, more so than in a constant state of being. For of all things change is what spurs on peoples' minds, and it does not allow them to keep still. Because of this, it seems to me that the race of Asiatics is weak, and further so because of their laws. For the majority of Asia is ruled by kings. Where people wield no power over themselves, nor are autonomous, but ruled by despots, it is not a concern for them how to prepare for war, but how not to appear warlike. For their risks are not the same. For those who do fight and suffer and die out of necessity for their masters, far from their children and wives and the rest of their friends, all their good and useful deeds aggrandize and support the despots, while they themselves cultivate danger and death. Furthermore, the land of such people must be deserted because of enemies and idleness, such that even if someone was by nature brave and spirited, his mind would be turned away by these laws. Here is a considerable proof of this: As many Greeks or barbarians in Asia who are not ruled by despots, but who are autonomous and suffer on their own behalf, these are all warlike. For the dangers they face are for themselves, and they bear the prizes of their courage and the penalties of their own cowardice. You will find that even the Asiatics differ from one another, some being better, some worse.

The remaining people in Europe differ amongst themselves in size and appearance because of the changes in the seasons, because they are great and many, and the heat strong and the cold severe and the storms many and the droughts frequent, and then there's the wind. From these the changes are many and diverse. From these it also appears that generation in the mixing of seed happens differently in different environments, and it is not the same in summer as it is in winter, nor in wet weather as in dry. From this I believe that the appearances of the Europeans differ more than those of the Asiatics and their sizes differ very much amongst themselves according to city. For there is greater decay of the foetus in its creation in the more volatile seasons, being harsher than the seasons that are more constant. Concerning character the same applies. Savagery and anti-social tendencies and spirit emerge in such a context. For shocks are frequent and instill savagery in the mind, while they obscure gentleness and softness. Because of this, I think that those inhabiting Europe are more spirited than those in Asia. For apathy is ever present in homogenous environments, but in changing ones there are challengers to the body and mind. And from quiet and idleness cowardice grows; but from challenges and hard work comes courage. From this those inhabiting Europe are most warlike, and also because of their laws, as they are not ruled by kings like the Asiatics. For anywhere that people are ruled by kings, there is need to be most cowardly. I said this before. For their spirit becomes slavish and does not wish to risk itself willingly for the sake of another's power. But those who are autonomous—as they run risks for themselves and not for others—they risk and rush into the fray. For they themselves bear the prize of victory. Thus the laws work towards courage not a little.

Figure 5.1
Attic red-figure oinochoe known as the Eurymedon Vase, ca. 450 BCE. Hamburg,
Museum für Kunst und Gewerbe 1981.173. Composite drawing showing both sides
of the vase. (Drawing by Paul C. Butler)

The image of the Greek as opposed to the Barbarian became a dominant
theme in the visual arts as well, both on vase paintings, which are specifically
Athenian in origin, and in the field of architectural sculpture, especially sanctuaries. In some cases, the references to us Greeks versus them Persians was
explicit, to put it mildly, as on the famous red figure vase showing a Greek
youth about to rape a Persian soldier (see Figure 5.1). The inscription on
the vase reads "Eurymedon," which, among other things, means "Wide
Mede." There was no point for subtlety.

More often than not, though, the notion of the eastern barbarian was sub-
limated into mythical, barbaric characters, namely centaurs, giants, and most
especially Amazons. Amazons were an excellent foil for the Persians, as they
combined two conflicting notions that the Greeks had about their neighbors:
they were belligerent, and they were feminine. Since these two qualities were
not supposed to go together (unless one was defending one's polis from Spartans), it highlighted the basic wrongness of the Persians. In the red figure pottery tradition, Amazons came to dress as Persians. Consider, for example, the
garb on the Amazon in this red figure vase with that on poor old buggered
Eurymedon mentioned earlier (see Figure 5.2). Similar motifs appeared in
sculpture. One of the most famous examples of an Amazonomakhy (a battle
with Amazons) decorated the fourth-century tomb of King Mausolus of

Figure 5.2
Attic red-figure oinochoe with Amazon, ca. 450–
400 BCE. Ferrara, Museo Nazionale di Spina
5029. (Drawing by Paul C. Butler)

Halicarnassus (thus a "Mausoleum") of southwestern Anatolia, now in the
British Museum (see Figure 5.3). Once again, the emphasis is on combat
between eastern-style Amazons (note the pointed cap) with noble Greek
warriors.

CONCLUSIONS

In 479 when the Persians made overtures to the Athens to join with Persia
against their homeland, the Athenian representatives declined, and they
offered the following explanation to their Spartan allies (Herodotos 8.144.2):

> For there are many and great reasons which prevent us from doing these things,
> even if we wanted to. First off, and greatest, are the statues and temples of the
> deities which were burnt and ruined; for these we are compelled to take
> vengeance to our utmost rather than come to terms with those who did it.

Figure 5.3
Amazon Frieze from Halicarnassus (modern Bodrum, Turkey), fourth century BCE. British Museum 1847,0424.8. (Drawing by Paul C. Butler)

> Moreover, there is our Greek identity—being of common blood and common language, and worshipping and sacrificing to our deities in common, and our common customs, all of which it would not be right for the Athenians to betray.

When these early fifth-century Athenians had to explain how they were related to other "Greeks" as we would understand the term, they noted blood, speech, religion, and culture. "Blood" refers to family lines, ultimately uniting the Hellenes into the giant family tree of Deukalion and his son Hellen, however the various ethnic groups understood their place on that tree. The Greeks all spoke some dialect of Greek—Ionic, Doric, Aeolic, or Arkadian. There is continued debate on how mutually intelligible these various dialects were, but for Herodotos at least, they were close enough to count as a single tongue, and both Thucydides and Xenophon followed his lead, using the verb *hellenizô* to mean "to speak Greek." Not a dialect, the language. The Greeks, for the most part, worshipped the same deities, or at least the Olympians (see Chapter 7). Granted, they had their own private cults to these various deities, the Eleusinians worshipped Demeter with her daughter Korê, while the Arkadians worshipped her with her daughter Despoina. But the names and the rites were sufficiently similar throughout the Greek world that one could speak of a common religion. As for way of life, well, a simple contrast between the Athenians and the Spartans (see discussion earlier in this chapter) would seem to contradict that notion. But all Greeks professed to love freedom and to value courage and wisdom and temperance, and they sought to compete in athletic contests where the main prize consisted of leaves. This was enough for them, especially in contrast to the Barbarian Other who was slavish and decadent (without ever entirely noting that these two concepts don't really go together—a decadent slave?).

But the concept of an integral Hellas was never as important to the Greeks as any individual polis, where any citizen's true loyalties lay. Fifty years after the Persian invasions, the Peloponnesian War commenced, an all-out battle between Athens with her allies and Sparta with hers. All of Greece, and even Persia, was pulled into the fray. Yet at no point was this deemed a civil war—*stasis* in Greek. The Athenians and Spartans may have had a similar language and religion, but in the long run their lifestyles and their aims were too different, and eventually they found that they could not tolerate each other anymore. The notion of "Greek" was irrelevant; both sides were out to conquer their enemy.

6

Peri Tês Oikoumenês: On the World

EARTH AND FAMILY

The ancient Greeks, as you have no doubt already guessed, lived on earth, and like all peoples they had various ideas about how that earth came into existence. The best known creation tale, and probably the most prevalent amongst the Greeks as a whole, is the one presented in Hesiod's *Theogony*, a late eighth-century poem about the creation of the natural world and the gods who ruled it. According to Hesiod (ll. 116–133, 337–382):

> First of all Chaos came into being, but then
> Broad-bosomed Gaia (Earth), ever the steadfast seat of all
> The immortals who hold the snowy peaks of Olympos,
> And shadowy Tartaros (Hell) in the gloom of broad-pathed earth,
> And Eros (Desire), most beautiful amongst the deities,
> Limb-losener, of the deities and all humans
> He tames the mind in their bosom and other sage counsels.
> From Chaos were born Erebos (Underworld) and black Nyx (Night);
> From Nyx were born Aither (Air) and Hemera (Day),
> Whom she bore having conceived mixing in love with Erebos.
> Earth first bore—peer to herself—
> Starry Ouranos (Heaven), so that he might cover her all over.
> So that he might be an ever steadfast seat for the blessed deities.
> And she bore great mountains, joyful haunts of the deities,
> The nymphs, who dwell in the wooded mountains.
> And she bore the barren sea with swelling waves—
> Pontos—without love's union. But then she
> Lay with Ouranos and bore deep-eddying Okeanos . . .
> Tethys bore to Okeanos the eddying rivers . . .
> And she bore a holy race of daughters, who on earth
> Raise boys to men along with King Apollo
> And the rivers; this task they have from Zeus . . .
> These girls are the oldest born of Okeanos and Tethys,
> And they are many and varied;

There are 3,000 slim-ankled Okeanids
Who are dispersed on earth and the marshy depths,
Serving everywhere alike, shining offspring of goddesses.
And many other rivers flow loudly,
Sons of Okeanos, whom revered Tethys bore.
It is difficult for a mortal man to relate all their names,
But all peoples know the ones by which they live.
Theia was conquered in love by Hyperion
And bore great Helios (Sun) and shining Selenê (Moon)
And Eos (Dawn), who shines on all upon the earth
And the immortal deities who hold the broad sky.

Physical reality, then, was conceived of as an extended family of deities. The first four came into being literally *ex nihilo*—Chaos, Earth, Hell, and Love. The first two were understood to be female, and both could, and did, reproduce parthenogenically. Chaos gave rise to the scary things, such as Night and the Underworld. Gaia, by contrast, created the heavens, mountains, and the surging sea. Then Eros-Love got involved, and everyone, for the most part, began reproducing sexually. Barren Pontos (Sea), born solely from Gaia, was complemented by dear old Okeanos (Ocean, obviously), far more fertile, himself the result of a fertile union. Gaia and Ouranos together gave rise to the Titans, who themselves bore such beings as the sun and moon, the rivers and nymphs (see Chapter 7). Chaos's daughter Night gave birth to Day, as well as Dreams, Love, Sleep, and Death, amongst others. So this is how the world came into being.

Although some ancient natural philosophers, what we would call scientists, seem to have known that the world was spherical (see later in this chapter), this was not the normal understanding. Like many ancients, the Greeks believed that the world was essentially flat. Some, such as Theaitetos from the Platonic dialogue of that name, argued that the world was cube-shaped, flat on top (where we are) but extremely sturdy. After all, what could be sturdier than the earth? (All you astrophysicists and Doctor Who fans can insert your own jokes here.) The more common conception was that the earth was a broad disk surrounded by water—the swirling "river" Okeanos. Underneath this disk, waaaaaay down, was Tartaros—Hell, where the gods bound their immortal enemies. Well above this was Hades/Erebos, where the human dead went, underground but with doorways on earth such as that approached by Odysseus when he went to consult with the dead seer Tiresias. Above the earth was the sky. Originally, Ouranos/Heaven lay right atop earth, a relationship that ended when Gaia got one of their children to castrate their father (there is such a thing as too much sex). After that incident, Ouranos flew far above the earth. As Hesiod put it in his *Theogony* (ll. 722–728):

A bronze anvil falling nine nights and days
From the sky would reach earth on the tenth,

A bronze anvil falling nine nights and days
From earth would reach Tartaros on the tenth.
It is surrounded by a bronze wall. About it night
Pours three-fold about its neck, but above
Grow the roots of earth and the barren sea.

Ouranos was apparently held in place by one of the Titans—Atlas, who held the starry sky upon his shoulders, himself standing at the western edge of the world/disk. This Greek idea probably comes from the Egyptians, who had a long-standing myth of the god Shu (Air) holding up the body of his daughter Nut (Sky) and separating her from his son Geb (earth) because they were having too much sex. The genders of the sky and earth are reversed (as far as the Greeks were concerned, the Egyptians did everything bass-ackwards; see later in this chapter), but otherwise the image is the same.

GEOGRAPHY

The Greeks were absolutely certain that they were located at the center of the world described in the preceding section. As discussed in the last chapter, there was a rock at the sanctuary of Delphi called the Omphalos that was literally believed to be Mother Earth's bellybutton, and thus the center of the universe, or at least the disk. More practically, the Greeks were originally concerned with the Mediterranean, which was really the center of their universe. Since the Bronze Age, the Greeks (and the Minoans before them) had long-range contacts with the various civilizations of the Mediterranean and the Near East. For the Hittites they were Ahhiyawa, mostly likely understood as the kingdom of the Akhaians. They traded with Cyprus for copper, with Egypt for a host of luxury goods, with Italy and Sardinia, and one Aegean-style dagger even made its way to Wessex in England. Trade with these foreign regions slowed down a bit during the Dark Ages that followed the collapse of the Bronze Age, but only a little. Regions of Greece such as the island of Euboia just off the eastern coast of Attika were still trading with the Levant during this period, just as the Greeks themselves were migrating out to make new lives for themselves in places such as Cyprus and Palestine. This outward movement only increased in the Archaic Age, when, starting in the eighth century, the Greeks began colonizing the Mediterranean, founding poleis from Spain to Libya to the Ukraine. The Greeks were always part of a much larger world.

Many aspects of this larger world were already well understood as early as the Homeric epics, as the various Akhaian, Argive, and Danaan heroes traveled and interacted with "strangers in strange lands" on their way home from the Trojan War. Although the average Greek, regardless of wherever he or she lived, was mainly focused on the very local geography of homestead and

polis, the epics provided an important window into the larger world. As would
be the case throughout Greek history, this "larger world" was a fascinating
combination of what in modern times we would call reality and the fantastic
—a universe of islands, monsters, mountains, and occasional giant ants. For
no one was this more true than Odysseus, who took close to a decade to get
home from Troy and whose travels included, among other places, the entry
to the Underworld (making, say, Cyprus seem relatively tame). Regardless of
some of the more fantastic aspects of his travels (islands of Cyclopes and rav-
enous whirlpools), there is quite a bit of discussion of the "real" geography
experienced by the early Archaic Age Greeks. So much is recounted by
Odysseus in his lying tale to Eumaios, where our hero delivers what was deemed
to be a reasonable account of his travels (*Od.* 14. 233–320, excerpted):

> Quickly my household increased, and so
> I became mighty and revered amongst the Cretans.
> But when indeed broad-faced Zeus proclaimed that
> Hateful journey, which loosed the knees of many men,
> Then they urged me and illustrious Idomeneas
> To lead forth ships to Ilion, nor was there any remedy,
> No way to refuse—the voice of the people was adamant.
> There for nine years fought the sons of the Akhaians;
> In the tenth, having destroyed the city of Priam, we came
> Home on ships, but a god scattered the Akhaians.
> But for wretched me counselor Zeus devised evils,
> For I stayed a month enjoying my children
> And my wedded wife, and my possessions. But then
> My heart led me to sail to Egypt.
> Ships were readied, with godlike companions . . .
> On the fifth day we came to fair-flowing Egypt,
> The double-oared ships. I moored in the Egyptian river.
> Then, indeed, I bade my trusty companions
> To stay there with the ships to guard them,
> While I sped off scouts to go to the lookouts.
> But they yielded to hubris, led by their own force,
> And quickly they plundered the lovely fields of the Egyptians,
> Leading away their wives and small children,
> Killing the men. Quickly the outcry reached the city.
> Those hearing the uproar came at shimmering dawn
> And the whole field was full of soldiers and horses
> And flashing bronze . . .
> But Zeus himself in his mind wrought this plan for me;
> O how I wish I died and followed my fate that
> Day in Egypt, for trouble still welcomed me.
> Immediately I took off the well-wrought helmet from my head
> And the shield from my shoulders, and I cast away the spear from my hand.
> Then I went before the king's horses

And grasping the king's knees I kissed them. And he delivered me and
   pitied me,
And seating me in his chariot he took me to his home as I shed tears . . .
I stayed there for seven years; I acquired many
Possessions amongst the Egyptians, for everyone offered them to me.
But when my eighth year came circling around,
Then indeed a Phoenician man came, knowing trickery,
Greedy, who wrought many evils for people.
He persuaded my mind to leave, to go
To Phoenicia, where his house and possessions lay.
I stayed with him for a full year.
But when the months and days wore out,
Quickly the year rolled about and the seasons passed,
He took me on board his sea-going ship to Libya,
Plotting lies that I might bring cargo with him,
But really so that there he might sell me and fetch a welcome price.
I followed him on the ship, suspicious, out of necessity.
The ship sailed with a fine, keen north wind,
Midway above Crete. But Zeus plotted destruction for them.
When then we left Crete, with no other land in sight,
But only sky and sea,
Then the son of Kronos set dark clouds
Upon the hollow ship, the sea below us grew dark.
Zeus in one go thundered and tossed lightning at the ship,
And the ship was entirely destroyed, being struck by Zeus' lightning,
Filled with sulfurous fumes. All abandoned ship . . .
Nine days I was borne; on the tenth night a great wave
Rolled me onto the dark land of the Thesprotians.
There the king of the Thesprotians—heroic Pheidon—
Took me in, no ransom asked. For his dear son came across
Me worn out by cold and exhaustion; he led me to the house
Having pulled me up by the hand.
About me he placed a cloak and robe as clothing.

The Greeks of the early Archaic Age, then, lived in a world with well-
established connections with Anatolia (Troy), the Levant (Phoenicia), and
northern Africa (Egypt and Libya). Even Italy and Sicily appear in the hero's
journeys, the straight between them being the lairs of Skylla and Charybdis.
Although these regions were rarely of concern to most peoples, the prevalence
of the Homeric epics guaranteed that any Greek anywhere knew tales of
Egyptians, Phoenicians, and others, often with many aspects of reality
(warfare, trade, piracy, etc.).

The process of colonization, prevalent especially in the eighth through
sixth centuries, brought the Greeks increasingly into an even larger world.
Although places like Egypt and Phoenicia remained prevalent in the Greek
worldview, farther territories started to appear in their daily consciousness,

such as Skythia to the north (modern Ukraine) and Libya to the south. Furthermore, there grew an interest in the residents of these "new" territories, and hand-in-hand with the increased knowledge of the world went a fascination with the residents of these far-off lands. A text known as the *Catalogue of Women* (erroneously attributed to Hesiod) dating to the sixth century already gives a fascinating world geography (*Oxyrhynchus Papyrus 1358 fr. 2,* ll. 8–35):

> (The Sons of Boreas pursued the Harpies) to the lands of the Massagetae [Africa] and of the proud Half-Dog men, of the Underground-folk and of the feeble Pygmies; and to the tribes of the boundless Black-skins and the Libyans. Huge Earth bare these to Epaphus—soothsaying people, knowing seercraft by the will of Zeus the lord of oracles, but deceivers, to the end that men whose thought passes their utterance might be subject to the gods and suffer harm— Aethiopians and Libyans and mare-milking Scythians. For verily Epaphus was the child of the almighty Son of Cronos, and from him sprang the dark Libyans, and high-souled Aethiopians, and the Underground-folk and feeble Pygmies. All these are the offspring of the lord, the Loud-thunderer. Round about all these (the Sons of Boreas) sped in darting flight . . . of the well-horsed Hyperboreans [Northerners]—whom Earth the all-nourishing bare far off by the tumbling streams of deep-flowing Eridanus . . . of amber, feeding her wide-scattered offspring—and about the steep Fawn mountain and rugged Etna to the isle Ortygia and the people sprung from Laestrygon who was the son of wide-reigning Poseidon. Twice ranged the Sons of Boreas along this coast and wheeled round and about yearning to catch the Harpies, while they strove to escape and avoid them. And they sped to the tribe of the haughty Cephallenians, the people of patient-souled Odysseus whom in aftertime Calypso the queenly nymph detained for Poseidon. Then they came to the land of the lord the son of Ares . . . they heard. Yet still (the Sons of Boreas) ever pursued them with instant feet. So they (the Harpies) sped over the sea and through the fruitless air . . . (trans. Evelyn-White 1914, 603–605)

By the early fifth century, the Athenian playwright Aeschylus could present a circumnavigation of the eastern world, as told to the heroine Io as she fled the wrath of Hera (*Prometheus Bound,* 707–735, 790–815):

> First from here, having turned east,
> Traverse the untilled fields.
> You will come to the nomadic Skythians, who live in thatched homes
> Upon upraised, wheeled wagons,
> Furnished with far-darting bows.
> Do not approach them, but leave their land,
> Your feet keeping close to the sea-sounding shore.
> To the left dwell the iron-working
> Khalybes, against whom you must guard yourself,
> For they are savage and not welcoming to strangers.
> You will come to the river Hybristes, aptly named,

Which you shall not cross, for the crossing is not easy
Until you come to the Caucus itself; seeing
Its peak, there the river pours out its force
From its bluffs. You must go over its star-reaching peaks
And take the southern path. There you will come to the army
Of the man-hating Amazons, who dwell in Themiskyra
Around Thermodon, where is
The rugged jaw of the sea of Salmydessa—
Harsh-welcomer of sailors, mother-in-law of ships.
The Amazons will welcome you well and help you on your way.
You will come to the Kimmerian Isthmus
By the narrow gates of the harbor,
Which you must bravely leave
And proceed to the Maiotikon Straights.
Amongst mortals ever after there will be a great tale
Of your journey, and the straights will be named for you—
Bosporos. Leaving Europe you will come to the
Continent of Asia. . . .
When you have crossed the stream between the two lands,
Towards the flaming, sun-trodden east,
Crossing the roar of the sea until you come
Before the Gorgon Plain of Kisthenes, where
The Phorkides live, ancient maidens three,
Swan-shaped, sharing one eye in common,
One tooth; the sun does not behold them
With his beams, nor the moon by night ever.
Nearby are their three winged sisters,
Snaky-haired Gorgons, hateful to mortals.
No mortal who sees them continues to breathe.
I tell you to guard against such things.
But hear another wretched marvel:
You must guard against the Grypas, the
Sharp-mouthed, silent dogs of Zeus, and
The one-eyed, horse-riding Arimpaspian people
Who live about the gold-flowing stream of the Plutonian Ford.
Do NOT go among them. You will come to a distant land,
A dark race, who lives at the sun's source.
There is the Aithiops River.
Follow its banks until you come to
The waterfall; there from the Byblian mountain
The august Nile sends forth its potable flow.
The Nile will lead you to the Delta
Nilotis, where Io, it is foretold for you
And your children to found a distant colony.

The combination of colonization, foreign trade, and scientific pursuits of
the late Archaic and Classical periods inevitably brought new understandings

of the universe. Although the idea of world-as-disk-in-Ocean held on until well in the Common Era (to the great annoyance of scholars such as Herodotos, Aristotle, and Ptolemy), by the fifth century, the Greeks understood that that disk was subdivided into three primary land masses—Europe, Asia, and Libya (aka Africa)—along with a host of islands, all somewhat organized around a central sea (the Mediterranean) and bordered at least on the west by water and apparently on the south by desert (the Sahara). Along with the interest in foreign peoples grew a very practical interest in the physical realia of foreign lands, what we would deem true geography today. The first "modern" description of world geography was probably written by a fifth-century geographer-ethnologist named Heketaios of Miletos, whose works do not survive. They were influential, though, and inspired the works of Herodotos, whose *Histories* were an important factor in how the Greeks of the Classical period and beyond came to understand the composition of the world. By combining the work of previous scholars (such as Heketaios) with travel reports and his own observations, Herodotos functionally wrote the Classical Greek understanding of the inhabited world, called the *oikoumenê* (literally "inhabited"). Among other things, though, Herodotos is known for being an excellent storyteller, and sometimes his reports of foreign lands betray more than a hint of the fantastic. So much is certainly obvious in his descriptions of the edges of the oikoumenê, those places that it was possible to know anything about, as described in Book Three of his *Histories* (see *Herodotos* sidebar). A more "practical" description appears in the fourth book of his *Histories* (4.36–42) (you can decide for yourself which one is more interesting):

> I laugh seeing the maps of earth that many draw these days, and not one with any sense. They draw the ocean flowing around the earth, which is round like a compass drawing, and they make Asia equal in size to Europe. For I shall show in just a few words the size of each of them and how each should be drawn.
>
> The Persians live down to the southern sea, called the Red Sea. Living above them towards the north wind are the Medes; past them are the Saspeires, past them the Kolkhians up to the north sea, into which the Phasis River flows. These four nations inhabit the regions from sea to sea. From there heading west two land masses stretch out from each other to the sea, which I shall relate. The one land mass going north from the Phasis extends to the sea along the Pontus and Hellespont until it reaches Sigeion on the Troad. The same land mass going south from the Myriandric Gulf lying by Phoenicia stretches along the sea up to the Triopian promontory. Thirty different nations inhabit this promontory. This is the one land mass. The other land mass starts in Persia and stretches to the Red Sea; this is Persia, followed by Assyria, and after Assyria Arabia. It ends (not really "ending," just a turn of phrase) in the Arabian Gulf, to which Dareios brought a canal from the Nile. Now from the land of the Persians up to Phoenicia the land is broad and vast, the land mass extends along this sea from Phoenicia to Palestinian Syria and Egypt, to its end.

Only three nations live here. These are the things westwards of the Persians in Asia. The things inland of the Persians and Medes and Saspeirans and Kolkhians, those things towards the dawn and rising sun: There lies the Red Sea, to the north the Caspian Sea and the Araxes River, flowing east. Asia is inhabited up to India; the land from there is deserted to the east, nor is anyone able to say what's there. Such is the nature of Asia. Libya is on a different land mass, for Libya extends out from Egypt. The Egyptian part of the land mass is narrow: there are 10,000 fathoms from this sea [the Mediterranean] to the Red Sea, equaling some 1,000 stades. From this narrow part the territory called Libya happens to be very broad.

I am amazed at those who have gone through and divided Libya and Asia and Europe—for the differences between them are not small; for in length Europe stretches along both the others, and in width nothing seems to me to be worthy of comparison. Libya reveals itself to be surrounded by water, except that part bordered by Asia. We know this from when Neko, King of Egypt, first demonstrated it. When he finished digging the canal extending from the Nile to the Arabian Gulf, he sent out Phoenician men on ships, ordering them to sail through the Pillars of Herakles up to the northern sea and thus return to Egypt. Setting out from the Red Sea the Phoenicians sailed the south sea. Whenever autumn came about, they turned landward and planted the land, in whatever part of Libya they sailed to, and there they waited out the harvest. Having gathered the grain they set sail, so that two years passed, and in the third they rounded the Pillars of Herakles and arrived in Egypt. And they tell me—it's not likely, but maybe plausible to others—that sailing around Libya they kept the sun to their right.

Herodotos, Book 3.98–116

To the east of the Indian country is sand. Of all the people of Asia whom we know—even those about whom something is said with precision—the Indians dwell nearest to the dawn and the rising sun; for on the eastern side of India all is desolate because of the sand. There are many Indian nations, none speaking the same language; some of them are nomads, some not; some dwell in the river marshes and live on raw fish, which they catch from reed boats. Each boat is made of one joint of reed. These Indians wear clothes of bullrushes; they mow and cut these from the river, then weave them crosswise like a mat, and wear them like a breastplate. Other Indians, to the east of these, are nomads and eat raw flesh; they are called Padaei. It is said to be their custom that when anyone of their fellows, whether man or woman, is sick, a man's closest friends kill him, saying that if wasted by disease he will be lost to them as meat; though he denies that he is sick, they will not believe him, but kill and eat him. When a woman is sick, she is put to death like the men by the women who are her close acquaintances. As for one that has come to old age, they sacrifice him and feast on his flesh;

but not many reach this reckoning, for before that everyone who falls ill they kill. There are other Indians, again, who kill no living creature, nor plant anything, nor are accustomed to have houses; they eat grass, and they have a grain growing naturally from the earth in its husk, about the size of a millet-seed, which they gather with the husk and boil and eat. When any one of them falls sick, he goes into the desert and lies there, and no one notices whether he is sick or dies. These Indians whom I have described have intercourse openly like cattle; they are all black-skinned, like the Ethiopians. Their semen too, which they ejaculate into the women, is not white like other men's, but black like their skin, and resembles in this respect that of the Ethiopians . . .

Other Indians dwell near the town of Kaspatyros and the Paktyic country, north of the rest of India; these live like the Baktrians; they are of all Indians the most warlike, and it is they who are sent for the gold; for in these parts all is desolate because of the sand. In this sandy desert are ants, not as big as dogs but bigger than foxes; the Persian king has some of these, which have been caught there. These ants live underground, digging out the sand in the same way as the ants in Greece, to which they are very similar in shape, and the sand which they carry from the holes is full of gold. It is for this sand that the Indians set forth into the desert. They harness three camels apiece, males on either side sharing the drawing, and a female in the middle: the man himself rides on the female that was harnessed as soon as possible after having given birth. Their camels are as swift as horses, and much better able to bear burdens besides . . . Thus and with teams so harnessed the Indians ride after the gold, being careful to be engaged in taking it when the heat is greatest; for the ants are then out of sight underground. Now in these parts the sun is hottest in the morning, not at midday as elsewhere, but from sunrise to the hour of market-closing. Through these hours it is much hotter than in Hellas at noon, so that men are said to sprinkle themselves with water at this time. At midday the sun's heat is nearly the same in India as elsewhere. As it goes to afternoon, the sun of India has the power of the morning sun in other lands; as day declines it becomes ever cooler, until at sunset it is exceedingly cold. So when the Indians come to the place with their sacks, they fill these with the sand and drive back as fast as possible; for the ants at once scent them out, the Persians say, and give chase. They say nothing is equal to them for speed, so that unless the Indians have a headstart while the ants were gathering, not one of them would get away. They cut loose the male trace-camels, which are slower than the females, as they begin to lag, one at a time; the mares never tire, for they remember the young that they have left. Such is the tale. Most of the gold (say the Persians) is got in this way by the Indians; they dig some from mines in their country, too, but it is less abundant.

The most outlying nations of the world have somehow drawn the finest things as their lot, exactly as Greece has drawn the possession of by far the

best seasons. As I have lately said, India lies at the world's most distant
eastern limit; and in India all living creatures four-footed and flying are
much bigger than those of other lands, except the horses, which are smaller
than the Median horses called Nesaean; moreover, the gold there, whether
dug from the earth or brought down by rivers or got as I have described, is
very abundant. There, too, wool more beautiful and excellent than the
wool of sheep grows on wild trees; these trees supply the Indians with clothing. Again, Arabia is the most distant to the south of all inhabited countries: and this is the only country which produces frankincense and myrrh
and casia and cinnamon and gum-mastich. All these except myrrh are difficult for the Arabians to get. They gather frankincense by burning that
storax which Phoenicians carry to Hellas; they burn this and so get the
frankincense; for the spice-bearing trees are guarded by small winged snakes
of varied color, many around each tree; these are the snakes that attack
Egypt. Nothing except the smoke of storax will drive them away from the
trees. The Arabians also say that the whole country would be full of these
snakes if the same thing did not occur among them that I believe occurs
among vipers. Somehow the forethought of God (just as is reasonable)
being wise has made all creatures prolific that are timid and edible, so that
they do not become extinct through being eaten, whereas few young are
born to hardy and vexatious creatures. On the one hand, because the hare
is hunted by every beast and bird and man, therefore it is quite prolific;
alone of all creatures it conceives during pregnancy; some of the unborn
young are hairy, some still naked, some are still forming in the womb while
others are just conceived. On the one hand there is this sort of thing, but on
the other hand the lioness, who is so powerful and so bold, once in her life
bears one cub; for in the act of bearing she casts her uterus out with her cub.
The explanation of this is that when the cub first begins to stir in the
mother, its claws, much sharper than those of any other creature, tear the
uterus, and the more it grows the more it scratches and tears, so that when
the hour of birth is near seldom is any of the uterus left intact. So too if
the vipers and the winged serpents of Arabia were born in the natural manner of serpents life would be impossible for men; but as it is, when they cop-
ulate, while the male is in the act of procreation and as soon as he has
ejaculated his seed, the female seizes him by the neck, and does not let go
until she has bitten through. The male dies in the way described, but the
female suffers in return for the male the following punishment: Avenging
their father, the young while they are still within the womb gnaw at their
mother and eating through her bowels thus make their way out. Other
snakes, that do no harm to men, lay eggs and hatch out a vast number of
young. The Arabian winged serpents do indeed seem to be numerous; but
that is because (although there are vipers in every land) these are all in Arabia and are found nowhere else.

The Arabians get frankincense in the foregoing way, and casia in the following way: when they go after it they bind oxhides and other skins all over their bodies and faces except for the eyes. Casia grows in a shallow lake; around this and in it live winged creatures, very like bats, that squeak similarly and make a fierce resistance; these have to be kept away from the eyes in order to take the casia. As for cinnamon, they gather it in an even stranger way. Where it comes from and what land produces it they cannot say, except that it is reported, reasonably enough, to grow in the places where Dionysus was reared. There are great birds, it is said, that take these dry sticks which we have learned from the Phoenicians to call cinnamon and carry them off to nests stuck with mud to precipitous cliffs, where man has no means of approach. The Arabian solution to this is to cut dead oxen and asses and other beasts of burden into the largest possible pieces, then to set these near the eyries and withdraw far off. The birds then fly down (it is said) and carry the pieces of the beasts up to their nests, while these, not being able to bear the weight, break and fall down the mountain side, and then the Arabians come and gather them up. Thus is cinnamon said to be gathered, and so to come from Arabia to other lands. But *ledanon*, which the Arabians call *ladanon*, is produced yet more strangely than this. For it is the most fragrant thing produced in the most malodorous; for it is found in he-goats' beards, forming in them like gum among timber. This is used in the manufacture of many perfumes; there is nothing that the Arabians burn so often as incense.

Enough of marvels, and yet the land of Arabia gives off a scent as sweet as if divine. They have besides two marvellous kinds of sheep, found nowhere else. One of these has tails no less than nine feet long. Were the sheep to trail these after them they would suffer by the chafing of the tails on the ground; but every shepherd there knows enough of carpentry to make little carts which they fix under the tails, binding the tail of each sheep on its own cart. The other kind of sheep has a tail a full three feet broad. Where south inclines westwards, the part of the world stretching farthest towards the sunset is Ethiopia; this produces gold in abundance, and huge elephants, and all sorts of wild trees, and ebony, and the tallest and handsomest and longest-lived people. These then are the most distant lands in Asia and Libya. But concerning those in Europe that are the farthest away towards evening, I cannot speak with assurance; for I do not believe that there is a river called by foreigners Eridanus issuing into the northern sea, where our amber is said to come from, nor do I have any knowledge of Tin Islands, where our tin is brought from. The very name Eridanus betrays itself as not a foreign but a Greek name, invented by some poet; nor for all my diligence have I been able to learn from one who has seen it that there is a sea beyond Europe. All we know is that our tin and amber come from the most distant parts. But in the north of Europe there is by far the most gold. In this matter again I cannot say with assurance how the gold is produced, but it is said that one-eyed men called Arimaspians steal it from griffins. But I do not believe this, that there are one-eyed men who have a nature otherwise the same as other men. The most outlying lands, though, as they enclose and wholly surround all the rest of the world, are likely to have those things which we think the finest and the rarest. (trans. Godley)

As far as the early Greeks were concerned, the Pillars of Herakles—the Straits of Gibraltar—were the end of the oikumenê. As James Romm, an expert on ancient Greek notions of geography, put it:

Indeed, since the Pillars or Columns of Heracles—the name usually associated with the twin rocks standing astride the Straits of Gibraltar—afforded the only known connection between the familiar Mediterranean and alien Ocean, they became a vivid symbol for the gateway or barrier between inner and outer worlds. For the most past they stood in the Greek imagination as a forbidding *non plus ultra*, a warning to mariners not to proceed any further. (1992, 17)

For Pindar, it was a symbol of the extreme, as he praised Theron of Akragas in his *Third Olympian Ode* (ll. 43–45):

If water is best, and gold most revered of possessions,
Now Theron arriving at the extremes of excellence reaches
By his own virtue the Pillars of Herakles. The land
Beyond is untreadable for the wise, and
Untreadable for the foolish. I shall not follow there; I would be an idiot.

The fact that Greeks could not go there (Phoenicians did, by the way) did not mean that there were no speculations as to what lay beyond the Pillars of Herakles. Just as we believe(d) in a magical place east of the sun and west of the moon (GPS coordinates for Never Never Land) and that Mars was inhabited by little green men (but apparently not women, so we have no idea how they reproduced), the Greeks of the Classical period at least believed there was a great island in the great sea beyond the Pillars. A fourth-century text called *On Marvelous Reports* gives a description of this land beyond the Pillars, as discovered, of course, by the Phoenicians/Carthaginians (84, 836b30–37a7):

They say that in the sea outside the Pillars of Heracles an uninhabited island was discovered by the Carthaginians, many days' sail from shore, which has all kinds of trees, and navigable rivers, and a marvelous variety of other resources. When the Carthaginians began going there often on account of its fruitfulness, and some even emigrated there, the Carthaginian leaders decreed that they would put to death anyone who planned to sail there, and got rid of all those who were living there, lest they spread the word and a crowd gather around them on the island which might gain power and take away the prosperity of the Carthaginians. (trans. Romm 1992, 126–127)

For the Greeks, this island was called Atlantis (named for the Titan holding up the sky at the western edge of the world), lying in the great sea beyond the Pillars (which, in case you were wondering, is how it got the name Atlantic.) As described by the eminent philosopher Plato himself in his dialogue *Timaios* (24e–25b):

For the sea there was once navigable, for an island was before the straits called, as you say, the Pillars of Herakles. And the island was larger than Libya and Asia combined; from it it was possible for travelers to go to the other islands, and from these islands to the whole mainland opposite, which went round that veritable ocean. For such things as we say are within the straits—they appear to be a harbor with a narrow entrance. But *that* is a real ocean, and the land extending all around it most rightly might be called a continent. On that island of Atlantis there was a great and wondrous confederation of kings, wielding power over the whole island as well as many other islands and parts of the mainland. Of the lands within the straits they also ruled Libya up to Egypt, and Europe up to Etruria. This entire dynasty was gathered into one body, and in a single coup they once attempted to enslave your land, ours, and every territory within the straits.

Atlantis, or the ocean past it (????) was the farthest imaginable land to the west of the Greek oikoumenê. The farthest folks to the imaginable north were the Hyperboreans, literally those "Above the North Wind." Like most semi-imaginary peoples living at the edges of reality, the Hyperboreans were thought to be especially blessed and happy, much like the residents of Tír na nOg, or El Dorado. Pindar, in his *Tenth Pythian Ode*, relates (ll. 29–44):

Neither by ship nor going on foot might you find
The amazing road to the assembly of the Hyperboreans.
Amongst them once Perseus feasted, leader of the people, coming to their
    homes,
An illustrious hecatomb of donkeys he found them sacrificing
To the god. Their continual revels
And praises does Apollo enjoy
The most; he laughs seeing the erect outrageousness of the beasts.
The Muse is not absent
From their paths. But everywhere choruses of maidens
And lyres and shouts and keen flutes whirl about;
Heads bound with golden laurel, they revel joyously.

Neither illness nor destructive old age overcomes
The sacred race; separate from labors and wars
They live, fleeing harsh Nemesis.

For his own part, Herodotos was a tad more "practical" in his description, explaining how the Greeks ever came to know of such northerly people in the first place. Apparently, the Hyperboreans were especially dedicated to the deities Apollo and Artemis, and they themselves made the effort to bring offerings to these siblings at their great sanctuary on the island of Delos (Herodotos 4, 32–35, excerpted):

Concerning the Hyperborean people neither the Skythians say anything nor any of the others living in that area, except perhaps the Issedonians, and it seems to me that they don't say much either. For if they did, so would the Skythians, just as they both talk about the one-eyed people. But there is a passage from Hesiod about the Hyperboreans, and one from Homer in his *Descendants*, if indeed that epic was really done by Homer. By far the Delians have the most to say about them, saying that the sacred objects tied up in wheat straw are borne from the Hyperboreans and arrive in Skythia; from the Skythians then they are always received by the next neighbors down the line, who carry them as far west as the Adriatic. From there they are sent on southwards, first to be received by the Greek Dodonians; from them they go down to the Melian Gulf and continue forward to Euboia. City after city sends them to Karystos, skipping Andros. For they say the Karystians bring them to Tenos, and the Tenians to Delos. In this way they say that the sacred objects now get to Delos. But originally the Hyperboreans sent two girls to carry the sacred objects, whom the Delians named as Hyperokhê and Laodikê. Together with these girls, for their safety, the Hyperboreans sent five men of the cities as escorts, whom they now call Perpherees, who have much honor in Delos. But when those sent back to the Hyperboreans never returned back home, being upset if it should always happen that they never get back those they sent out, they changed the practice and now carry the sacred objects bound in wheat straw to the borders, and they enjoin upon their neighbors to send them from themselves to the next tribe down. And thus they say the objects sent get to Delos . . . And these things indeed I know that they do for those same maidens who came from the Hyperboreans and died in Delos—both the girls and the boys of the Delians cut their hair. The girls before marriage cut off a tress and wrap it around a spindle and place it on the tomb (the tomb is within the Artemision precinct on the left, where the olive tree grows); the Delian boys wrap the hair around some green shoot and they lay it on the tomb. The maidens have this honor amongst the inhabitants of Delos. These same people also say that both Argê and Opis, Hyperborean girls, came by way of the same peoples to Delos even before Hyperokhê and Laodikê. These other girls brought to Eileithyia tribute in exchange for a swift birth, and they say that Argê and Opis came together with the deities, and that they give them other honors on their behalf.

So much for the north. The far-off, semimythical, inevitably blessed and eternally happy people to the far south were the Ethiopians. These residents of Libya (aka Africa) were already presented as favorites of the deities in the works of Homer. In Book 1 of the *Iliad*, Thetis must wait twelve days before making her request to Zeus, as he just "went off to the Ocean River to feast with the Ethiopians, loyal, lordly men; and all the gods went with him." Likewise it is only because Poseidon was visiting them in the *Odyssey* that Athena was able to rescue Odysseus from Kalypso (*Od.* 1, 22–26):

> But Poseidon was visiting the far-off
> Ethiopians—divided in two—farthest of men;
> Some at the setting of Hyperion's son, some at his rising,
> Sharing in the hecatomb of bulls and rams,
> There seated enjoying the feast.

More "factual" information of course comes from Herodotos, who relates a tale of what happened when some Persian spies went to learn about these Ethiopians living south of Egypt. As an intermediary/translator revealed (3. 23–24):

> Asking the king of the Fisheaters about their life and lifestyle, he said that most of them live to 120 years, some even longer, and that their diet was boiled meat and their beverage of choice was milk. When the spies showed surprise at the span of life, he brought them to a spring—bathing in its waters made one shimmer, just as if it were olive-oil. And it emitted a scent like violets. The water of this spring was so delicate indeed—so said the spies—that nothing was able to float upon it, neither wood nor any of the things lighter than wood, but everything sank to the bottom. This water, if it is true what they say, would be the reason that they are so long-lived. Departing from the spring he led them to the jail—there all the men were bound in golden shackles. Amongst these Ethiopians bronze is the rarest and most valued of all things. Having seen the jail they also saw the table called "Of the Sun." After this, finally, they saw their coffins, which are said to be made from a transparent stone used in the following manner: Whenever they desiccate a corpse, either in the Egyptian or other fashion, having powdered the whole body with chalk they adorn it, making it resemble the appearance as much as possible. Then they erect a hollow stele made from the transparent stone (which they make with much well-wrought chiseling). The corpse is visible from inside the stele; neither does any bad odor emanate out, nor anything else unpleasant, and it totally looks like the corpse itself. They keep the stele at home for one year, offering it the best of everything and the first fruits and making sacrifices. After this they take it out and erect the stelai around the city.

Such were the limits of the oikumenê as the Greeks understood them. Granted, most Greeks still believed that the inhabited world was bounded by Okeanos on all sides, and places like Ethiopia were simply within the boundaries of the great river. But other thinkers, such as Herodotos and Aristotle, were a tad more skeptical. They were at least willing to admit that they had no real idea of what existed at the farthest extremes of the world, past the waters and deserts. They could go as far as Atlantis to the west, the Hyperboreans to the north, and the Ethiopians to the south. India was the farthest known region to the east (see *Herodotos* sidebar), and when he got there, Alexander the Great was certain that if he just went a little farther he would reach the eastern streams of Ocean. I can't imagine how he would have reacted to the notion of China. As we shall see farther along, some later philosophers actually came to believe that the earth was spherical and that there was a whole other oikoumenê in the "southern hemisphere." But very few people listened to them.

FUN WITH FOREIGNERS

And so the farthest boundaries of the world had wonderful, fascinating places where you, the average Greek, couldn't go. It was like Tolkien's Western World, where the Elves and Ring Bearers could retreat when magic left the world. Or Rivendell, a nonexistent spot in New Zealand that the New Zealand tourism bureau kept having to explain wasn't real to all the people trying to book tours there after Peter Jackson's *Lord of the Rings* trilogy came out. You can, however, go to Hobbiton. Really. They left up the set as a tourist attraction, so while you can't go to Rivendell, you can to the Shire. This was never a problem for George Lucas . . .

Anyway, within these far-off boundaries of the oikoumenê were the places and peoples the Greeks actually dealt with on a daily basis—Skythia, Egypt, Italy, Sicily, France, and Spain. Much of Sicily and southern Italy were colonized by the Greeks, such that the Romans' name for this area was Magna Graecia—Greater Greece. As such, they would not really be considered "foreign." The situation in places like France or Skythia, though, was a bit different. In the former, the Greeks had an important colony at Massalia/Marseille, which was the hub of a very brisk trade in Gaul and north up even into Scandinavia (apparently the favorite Greek import was wine). This trade, plus their colonies in Italy, brought them into frequent contact with foreigners such as Celts and Etruscans. A similar situation developed in the far northeast, where Greeks living in Greek colonies lived side-by-side with foreigners such as Skythians, Kolchians, and, of course, Amazons.

As perhaps with all peoples, the Greeks' understanding of foreigners was a combination of the fantastic (it's not just for the borders!), the realistic, and the somewhat derogatory. Here I shall present three case studies of Greek relations with foreign peoples—both in terms of their actual interactions and in the amusing stereotypes that emerged from these interactions. As in modern times, the quotidian realities seldom bore much in common with the perceptions of the average man in the agora.

Egypt

Greece has had contact with Egypt since the Early Bronze Age, before Greece was even Greece. The Bronze Age Minoans of Crete traded with the Egyptians, who depicted these "Keftiu" on their wall friezes wearing distinctively Minoan garb and carrying distinctively Minoan pottery. Artisans from the Aegean decorated the Hyksos palace at Avaris (modern Tell el-Daba'a), and it was the Egyptian pharaoh Ramses who battled Mycenaean refugees in the Levant, who later became the Biblical Philistines. After this Time of Troubles, trade relations between Egypt and Greece cooled off a bit but resumed with a fervor in the seventh century, partially because Persia to the east was making life extremely difficult for Egypt. The Greeks were natural allies. East Greek pottery started showing up in Egypt by the mid-seventh century, and it was during this period that the Greeks established for themselves a trade city at Naukratis in the Delta. Thus the Greeks had a kind of permanent residence in traditionally xenophobic Egypt. At Naukratis they established various temples, including the Hellaneion discussed in Chapter 5, as well as sanctuaries to Hera, Aphrodite, and the Dioskouroi (Kastor and Polyduktes, aka the Gemini). The power of Aphrodite was certainly strong in Naukratis, to judge from various anecdotes told of her in the Greek tradition. According to a story preserved by Athenaios, himself a Hellenic resident of Egypt in the third century CE (*Deipnosophistai*, 15, 675f–676c):

> During the 23rd Olympiad Herostratos, a citizen of ours, making use of trade and sailing about the various lands, arrived at Paphos on Cyprus, and purchasing a small idol of Aphrodite, a span in height and of old-fashioned craftsmanship, went bearing it to Naukratis. And while approaching Egypt a sudden storm fell upon him and he didn't know where on earth he was; all the sailors fled to the image of Aphrodite and besought her to save them. And the goddess (for she was friendly with Naukratis) suddenly made the area before her full of fresh myrtle and a sweet scent filled the ship, while previously those sailing despaired of safety, being really sea-sick and retching profusely. And when the sun appeared they saw their anchorage and arrived at Naukratis. Herostratos set out from the ship along with the idol, and also bearing the miraculously appearing fresh myrtle; he dedicated them in the sanctuary of Aphrodite. He sacrificed to the goddess and dedicated the idol to Aphrodite, and summoning about the hearth of this sanctuary those who came with him and his closest neighbors, he gave them each a crown from this myrtle, which he then called "Naukratitis."

In a slightly different vein, Herodotos records that Aphrodite was extremely generous with the prostitutes who plied their trade in this town, especially a particularly famous Naukratian prostitute named Rhodopis ("Rosy-Face") (2.135):

> Rhodopis came to Egypt brought by Xantheus the Samian, but once arrived she was released from her profession for a lot of money by Kharaxos of Mytilenê, son of Skamandronymos and brother of Sappho the poetess. Thus Rhodopis was liberated, and she remained in Egypt and was so utterly charming that she acquired a huge fortune, such as it would be for Rhodopis . . . The hetairai in Naukratis are quite lovely, for the very woman about whom this story is told became so famous that all the Greeks learned the name of Rhodopis. And after this in Naukratis it was the name "Arkhidikê" that became the subject of song throughout Greece, although less so than her more notorious companion. Kharaxos who freed Rhodopis went back home to Mytilenê, where Sappho mocked him severely in song. And now I shall stop about Rhodopis.

In the early sixth century, the Pharaoh Psammetikos, founder of the 26th Dynasty, made use of Greek mercenaries, extending the Greek presence all the way south into extreme Upper Egypt to the borders of Nubia. Here many Greeks carved their names into the famous temple of Abu Simbel, preserving evidence of their presence to the modern day. One series of such "amateur" inscriptions, dating to 591 BCE and inscribed on the left leg of a colossal statue of Rameses II, reads (ML 7):

> When King Psammetikhos came to Elephantine, those who sailed with Psammetikhos son of Theokles wrote this; and they came above Kerkis as far as the river allowed; and Potasimto had command of those of foreign speech and Amasis of the Egyptians; and Arkhon the son of Amoibikhos wrote us and Peleqos the son of Eudamos.
> Helesibios the Teian.
> Telephos the Ialysian wrote me!
> Python (son of) Amoibikhos.
> Krithis wrote me!
> Pabis the Qolophonian with Psammata.

Later that century, the general Amasis fought against Ionian and Carian mercenaries in his coup d'état against King Apries. After his victory, he employed those same mercenaries as his personal corps, installing them in the central Egyptian town of Memphis. At Saqqara, the necropolis associated with Memphis, evidence of an early blending of Greek and Egyptian cultures is apparent in a funerary stele, now in the British Museum, which shows a typical Egyptian funerary motif on the top of the stele (the deceased worshipping

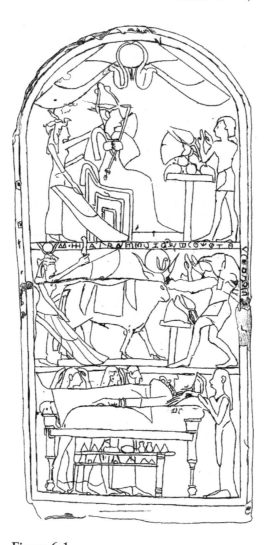

Figure 6.1
Grave stele of a Carian woman from Saqqara,
Egypt, sixth century BCE. British Museum
67235. (Drawing by Paul C. Butler)

Osiris), while the bottom register shows a typically Greek funerary scene, with
females mourning the dead. The whole thing is complemented with a Carian
[Western Anatolian] inscription (see Figure 6.1). Soon another Greek emporion was established in the Delta at Daphnê, modern Tell Defenneh, and
these three sites—Naukratis, Memphis, and Daphnê—served as long-
standing Greek residences into the Common Era.

The Greeks had high reverence for the Egyptians. They believed them to be the oldest civilization in the world and that they taught civilization to the Greeks. For example, according to Herodotos, it was Egypt that gave Greece its religion (2.52, 58):

> Originally the Pelasgians used to sacrifice to their gods always praying to them
> —as I know from hearing it at Dodona—without naming any of them; for they
> had not yet heard of any names. They called their deities "deities" (*theous*) from
> the fact that they set (*thentes*) all things in order and maintained them thus.
> When much time had passed they learned from Egypt the names of most of the
> deities, but only much later that of Dionysos. And after some time passed they
> consulted an oracle at Dodona about the names, for this oracle was believed to
> be the oldest of the oracles in Greece, and at the time the only one there was.
> When the Pelasgians asked the oracle in Dodona if they should adopt the
> names which came from the barbarians, the oracle replied that they should use
> them. From this time on they sacrificed using the names of the deities. Later
> the Greeks got the names from the Pelasgians. Festivals and processions and
> parades—the Egyptians were the first of humankind to have these things; the
> Greeks learned them from them. Here's a proof of this: The Egyptian rites seem
> to have been done for a very long time, but the Greek ones only quite recently.

Along with its extreme age, the Greeks attributed great learning to the Egyptians, and there is a long list of Greek sages and philosophers who at least visited Egypt, and some actually settled down and lived there for several years. Two of the so-called Seven Sages of Greece learned wisdom in Egypt—Thales of Miletos, father of algebra and geometry who, using long-standing records of astronomical events as recorded in the Near East, was the first known Westerner accurately to predict a solar eclipse; and Solon of Athens, father of the Athenian democracy, who lived in Egypt for 10 years after revising the Athenian constitution (he figured he'd hear less kvetching in Egypt). Pythagoras, who gave us the Pythagorean Theorem, visited Egypt, as did Demokritos of Abdera, father of atomic theory. Even Plato spent some time in Egypt after the execution of Sokrates, learning from the Egyptian priests in the stead of his Athenian mentor. Clearly, Egypt was *the* center of learning as far as the Greeks were concerned. Even the Athenians, who prided themselves as being the School of Hellas, deferred to Egyptian scholastic superiority (and, believe me, that is really saying something, like a New Yorker admitting someplace on earth is better than New York).

The flip side of Egyptian superiority was the fact that Egyptians were weird. As far as the Greeks were concerned, the Egyptians did, literally, *everything* backward. Egypt was the consummate anti-Greece. Persia, of course, was the anti-Greece for things like nobility and machismo; Egypt was the anti-Greece for life in general. As recorded once again by our Father of History (2.35–36):

The Egyptians, both in terms of their own distinct climate and their river, which has a different nature than the other rivers, stand as the complete opposite of other humans in terms of customs and laws. Among them the women go about and keep shop; the men stay home and weave. Others weave pushing the weft up; the Egyptians down. Men carry loads on their heads; women on their shoulders. Women pee standing up; men sitting down. They defecate in the house and eat outside in the roads, explaining that one must do shameful necessities in hiding, non-shameful ones openly. No woman serves as priestess to any deity, either male or female; men serve all of their gods and goddesses. To care for one's parents is not required of anyone (male) who does not wish it; it is required of all daughters even if they don't wish it. Priests of the deities elsewhere grow long hair; in Egypt they shave. For other peoples the custom for mourning is to cut the hair if those most closely related; the Egyptians, upon a death, allow their tresses to grow, both on the head and on the chin; otherwise they are clean-shaven. Living takes part for other peoples apart from animals; the Egyptians live together with their animals. Others live on wheat and barley; it is the greatest disgrace for the Egyptians to make anything from those, but they make flour from spelt, which various among them call spelt [two words in Greek, one in English here]. They knead dough with their feet; clay with their hands, which they also use to pick up dung. Others leave their genitals as they are, except those who have learned from the Egyptians, who circumcise. Each man has two articles of clothing; each woman only one. The sail rings and ropes others place outside; the Egyptians inside. The Greeks write letters and calculate numbers from left to right; the Egyptians from right to left; and in doing these things they say they're going rightwards; the Greeks leftwards. They use two different writing systems, and they call the one sacred [hieroglyphics] and the other mundane [demotic].

Some of these observations are inaccurate: The Egyptians did have priestesses, and I'm reasonably sure that their women at least squatted to pee. Much is accurate, however, including the details about circumcision and that their priests were traditionally clean-shaven. This general backwardness of the Egyptians was virtually proverbial in Greece. In his *Oedipus at Kolonos*, Sophokles virtually quotes Herodotos's brief ethnography of inversions when discussing Oedipus's sons (ll. 337–345):

Oh, those two entirely resemble the laws, nature,
And way of life in Egypt!
For there the men stay at home
Weaving, while their partners
Outside ever pursue their livelihood.
Those two, O children, who should truly labor thus,
Stay at home tending house, just like girls,
While you two in their place undertake together
These hardships.

The number one Egyptian backwardness that bugged the Greeks was the Nile River itself. First off, it flowed backward, south to north rather than north to south like every other river they knew of. Second, and even more perplexing, was the fact that the Nile flooded in the summer, when all other rivers shrank. Clearly, there was something very wrong with the Nile. Herodotos dedicated several paragraphs to various theories concerning this phenomenon, but none of his presented hypotheses were quite so spectacular (in the sense of being simultaneously utterly insane and essentially accurate) as the idea that emerged in the fourth century. Basically, the Greeks (and Romans after them) came to believe that the source of the Nile was literally on another plane of existence. As James Romm explains it:

> Beginning with Aristotle, Greek geographers speculated about a second habitable world in the southern hemisphere matching the *oikoumenê* in the North. The supposition that such a world existed was based . . . on the then-emerging picture of a large and spherical earth divided into climatic zones. It had long been theorized that the *oikoumenê*, stretching roughly from the arctic circle to the Tropic of Cancer, constituted a single habitable zone bordered by two uninhabitable ones; more recently the new science of earth measurement had demonstrated that this entire landmass took up only a small portion, certainly less than half, of the global surface. The conjunction of these two hypotheses then gave rise to the third, that is, that a congruent *oikoumenê*, stretching from the Tropic of Capircorn to the antarctic, formed the mirror image across the equator of the one formed by Asia, Africa, and Europe. Whether the two habitable worlds were separated by sea . . . or by an intolerably hot stretch of desert, was open to debate; but in either case the two worlds were cut off from each other with equal finality. (1992, 129–130)

This anti-oikoumenê was known as the Antikhthones, literally "antiearth." Concerning the backward nature of the Nile, Romm continues:

> Eudoxus [of Knidos, as he claimed he learned from Egyptian holy men] reasoned that since the Nile rose in summer and fell in winter, the opposite of the pattern followed by other rivers, its waters must originate in the southern hemisphere where summer and winter were reversed. It was only a short step from this theory to an assumption that the Nile's source lay in an antipodal continent, separated from the *oikoumenê* not only by the equator but by Ocean as well. The problem of how the river could then reach the *oikoumenê* was solved by means of an underground channel passing beneath Ocean, the same sort of conduit that was thought to connect the spring Arethusa in Sicily with its source in mainland Greece. (1992,150)

It is important to understand that such reasoning was not the norm of the average man in the agora in Greece. Invoking the Antikhthones was the ancient equivalent of invoking Higgs boson to explain the matter-energy continuum (just Google it). What was important for most people was that Egypt was one of the more revered places in the oikoumenê and utterly different from us. Deep down, this probably ought to say something profound about the Greek psyche.

Etruria

One of the first Greek colonies established in the eighth century was on the island of Ischia off the west coast of central Italy. Soon the Greeks moved landward and established themselves on the mainland at Cumae. As a result, the Etruscans, the inhabitants of northern-central Italy, were one of the first Western groups with whom the Greeks had extensive contact. The Etruscans were a highly civilized people in the original meaning of the term—they excelled in urban planning and architecture, and they already had long-term connections with other peoples in the western Mediterranean, notably the Carthaginians to the south. Their language has yet to be fully deciphered (they wrote mainly on perishable materials, which have, over the past 2,000 years, perished, so there is dismally little material to work with), but it is clearly not Indo-European and thus not part of the giant linguistic family that includes, among other tongues, Greek. As non-Greek speakers, the Etruscans were, technically, barbarians, as explained at the end of the last chapter.

But the Etruscans were too civilized to be barbarians. As Larissa Bonfante, a world expert on the Etruscans put it, "For the Greeks, the Etruscans were technically 'barbarians', non-Greeks. But considering their literacy, technical advances, aristocratic society, their civilized, city-centered, luxury filled way of life, and the pull they exerted for Greek traders and immigrants at various moments of Greek history, it seems clear that the Greeks considered the Etruscans to be closer to the Homeric Phaeacians than to the Western Cyclops" (2002, 43). The Etruscans were very good for the Greek economy, engaging in trade especially at the port towns of Cerveteri (ancient Caere) and Tarquinia. They were avid importers of Greek, and especially Attik, pottery, and most intact Greek vases that one sees in museums come from Etruscan tombs rather than Greek settlements. Greek-style pottery came to be so popular in Etruria that many Greek potters and painters simply relocated westward, setting up workshops in Vulci, Cerveteri, and Tarquinia, amongst other areas. In addition to pottery, the Etruscans adopted (and adapted) many aspects of Greek culture, notably the alphabet (which they then exported northward so that an originally Phoenician writing system came to express not only Greek, Latin, and English, but even became Nordic runes), monumental architecture and sculpture, narrative art, artistic nudity, and the ritual of the *symposion* (see Chapter 2). All in all, except for a strange language, the

Etruscans were remarkably similar to the Greeks in many respects, and Etruria became an increasingly easy place to move to when political situations in the Greek east induced emigration.

The influence was not one-way, though. The Greeks for their part imported their own aspects of Etruscan culture. Most notable is the influx into Greece of Bucchero ware, the distinctively Etruscan shiny black pottery. The Corinthians were especially fond of it, and by the fifth century, it became customary to show Dionysos himself drinking wine out of an Etruscan-style *kantheros* (wine-cup). Eventually, the Etruscans from Cerveteri dedicated their own treasury at the sanctuary of Apollo at Delphi, that bastion of consummate Greekness (see Chapter 5).

On a daily basis, Greeks and Etruscans had the majority of their interactions in the economic sphere. In addition to the mad importation of things Greek into Etruria, both populations traded extensively in the western Mediterranean, especially in ancient Gaul (modern France) and Spain. Here they traded and worked both with each other and with local residents such as the Emporitans mentioned later in this chapter, but also the Celts of the interior and the Phoenicians, those Mediterranean merchants extraordinaire. We are fortunate to have preserved a few personal documents dating from the fifth century recording business arrangements. One example is a business contract written on lead and discovered at the site of Pech Maho in Languedoc. The contract is bilingual, an Etruscan version complemented by Ionian-dialect Greek. Although the Etruscan, for reasons mentioned previously, is not entirely legible, the Greek text reads:

> So-and-so (*perhaps* Kyprios) bought a boat [from the] Emporitans. He also bought [three (?) more] (*i.e. from elsewhere*). He passed over to me a half share at the price of 2 1/2 *hektai* (*each*). I paid 2 1/2 *hektai* in cash, and two days later personally gave a guarantee. The former (*i.e. the money*) he received on the river. The pledge I handed over where the boats are moored. Witness(es): Basigerros and Bleruas and Golo.biur and Sedegon; these (were) witnesses when I handed over the pledge. But when I paid the money, the 2 1/2 *hektai*, -auaras, Nalb..n. Heronoiios. (trans. Chadwick 1990, 165)

The Emporitans are the residents of Emporion (literally "trading town") now known as Ampurias in eastern Spain, (the eastern-most colony established by the Greeks). Here was found another business-related document, a letter written in the Ionic dialect on a lead leaf recording transport arrangements for wine. Unfortunately, the letter is not incredibly intact, but the gist of the matter comes through easily:

> [Greetings to . . .]
> You must take care to be at Saiganthê, and if . . .
> . . . for the Emporitans, but not for the passengers . . .

. . . more than twenty, and wine, not for . . .
. . . that the cargo that was at Saiganthe and which Baspedas purchased
. . . set to sea to transport the merchandise also in . . .
. . . at. . .what should we do with all this . . .
. . . and invite Baspedas to tow you . . .
. . . ask if there is someone who can tow up to . . .
. . . of our (cargo/boat); and if there are two, which send two . . .
. . . but make sure he is responsible; and for his own part, he wishes . . .
. . . he shares half, but if he is unwilling . . .
. . . he stays there and sends me a letter telling me how much . . .
. . . as quickly as he can . . .
. . . These are my requests. Be well! (trans. Grego and Santiago 1988, 13)

The eternal problem of transporting one's wares to market . . .

There is, of course, a certain irony in the study of Greek-Etruscan relations. Basically, the two societies were just a tad too close in terms of culture and clientele, and this resulted in both fierce competition between the two groups and a number of interesting misconceptions. For example, regarding competition, the Greeks could be, understandably, peeved when economically outstripped in the western Mediterranean markets. Those who best you in overseas trade are, of course, pirates (not that you're bitter), and just as the Homeric Greeks tended to cast the Phoenicians (their primary eastern Mediterranean business rivals) as greedy, mercantile pirates, so too the P-word came to accrue to the Etruscans as well. Already they had this stereotype in the Archaic *Hymn to Dionysos*, which relates how Etruscan (Tyrsenian) pirates tried to abduct the god (ll. 1–15):

About Dionysos, glorious son of Semelê,
I shall turn my mind, as he appeared by the shore of the barren sea,
Upon a jutting promontory, resembling a young man
In the prime of youth. His lovely hair flowing around,
Dark; a cloak he had about his strong shoulders,
Purple. Soon pirate men on a well-oared ship
Came swiftly over the wine-dark sea,
Etruscans. An evil fate led them. They, seeing him,
Nodded to each other. Quickly they leapt out; quickly they seized him
And put him on board, rejoicing in their hearts.
For he appeared to be a son of god-reared kings,
And they wished to bind him in painful bonds.
The fetter was not strong; the willow ties fell right off
Of his hands and feet. He sat smiling
With his dark eyes.

Eventually Dionysos turned them into dolphins, so it all worked out okay in the end.

The closeness, but not exactness, of cultural institutions also colored Greek perceptions of the Etruscans, especially as concerns the symposion. As discussed in Chapter 2, no respectable Greek woman attended the symposion —it was a drinking party enjoyed by men, boys (mainly the wine-pourers), and various types of prostitute. By contrast, the Etruscans invited their wives to take part in the festivities—the drinking party was enjoyed by both sexes equally. This boggled the minds of the Greeks, who could not fathom the concept of a decent woman going to a symposion, and thus they figured (rationally, right?) that all Etruscan women must simply be whores. And if all of your women are whores, what does that say about your society in general? The fourth-century historian Theopompos knew the answer, as recorded by Athenaios in his *Deipnosophistai* (12.517d–18b):

> Theopompos in the 43rd chapter of his *Histories* says that it is the custom among the Etruscans to share the women in common. The women care very much for their bodies and often exercise in the nude, both with the men and sometimes amongst themselves. For it is not shameful for them to be seen naked. And they dine not alongside their own husbands, but with whomever happens to be present, and they toast whomever they wish. They are heavy drinkers and quite good-looking. The Etruscans rear all the children born, not knowing who the father of any of them is. They live in the same manner as those who rear them, taking a lot of drink and consorting with all the women. It is no shame for the Etruscans not only to do these things in public, but even to be seen on the receiving end, for in that land it is their way. And they so thoroughly do not consider it shameful that they even say, whenever the master of the house is making love, should someone inquire for him, that he is experiencing so and so, shamefully naming the act. Whenever they get together with companions or family, they do as follows: First, when they have stopped drinking and are about to go to bed, the servants lead in among them—lamps still blazing—sometimes hookers, sometimes quite handsome boys, and sometimes women. When they have enjoyed these, then again young men at their peak—they consort with these. They make love while having these gatherings in full view of each other, or more often having set up screens amongst the beds, constructed of reeds with cloaks cast over them. And they avidly consort even with their wives, but even more so with boys and youths. For there are many good-looking ones amongst them, because they live daintily and soften their bodies. All those barbarians living in the west pluck and shave the body; and amongst the Etruscans many businesses and artisans provide this service, just like barber shops here. When they enter these places, they reveal themselves in every way, ashamed neither before onlookers nor those passing by. Even many of the Greeks living in Italy follow this custom.

So there you have it. The Etruscans were trading partners and competitors, suppliers of Bucchero and buyers of Attik-wares, literate drinkers and wild-orgy mongers who apparently had no shame about going full Brazilian in public. Of course, those Italian *Greeks* weren't much better . . .

Skythia

The Greeks made an intensive colonization of the lands around the Black Sea especially in the seventh and sixth centuries, mainly starting out from metropoleis along the Ionian coast. By 500 BCE, there were important Greek cities at Berezan, Histria, Apollonia, Pontika, Sinopê, Trapezos, and Amisos, most showing a material culture related to that of the poleis of Miletos and Ephesos, and the islands of Samos and Khios. In addition to these pots and pans, the cults of the Black Sea region continued to betray Ionian/Anatolian influence: cults to Apollo and Ephesian Artemis were prominent in the epigraphy, and in later years dedications were even made to the Phrygian Mother goddess Kybelê.

As was the case in the west, the Greek settlers lived side-by-side with local populations, notably the Thracians, Getae, Skythians, Tauroi, Maeotians, Kolkhians, Mariandyni, and Khalybes, many of whom, of course, had their own subgroupings. When the Greeks first settled in these frigid northern climes, they adopted the architectural practices of their indigenous neighbors. In contrast to the courtyardcentric homes that were prevalent in Greece proper, these domiciles focused on minimalism and warmth. Specifically, they were mostly underground and could be either round or rectangular, with only a sloped roof appearing above ground level. At Berezan, some 200 such underground residences have been excavated, and they are the only evidence of architecture of any kind at that site from the late seventh to the end of the sixth centuries (Tsetskhladze 2002, 137; see Figure 6.2). There were no temples, or stoas, or apparent agoras. The Greeks certainly did not lose their sense of Greek identity, however, and from the fifth century and later, the Greek settlements around the Black Sea came to resemble other more traditional Greek poleis, with the features of temples, walls, stoas, and more traditional Greek houses. The dugout domiciles of the early Archaic period might be contrasted with those from the end of the sixth century, which, in typical Greek fashion, were composed of several rooms around a large central courtyard (see Figure 6.3).

Although the nature of trade relations between the indigenous inhabitants of the Black Sea region and the Greeks is still in debate, there appear to have been close relationships between the indigenous and Greek populations. According to Herodotos, the city of Gelonos was settled by a combination of Greeks (called Gelonoi) and a local population called the Budinoi. Herodotos makes it clear that the two groups are utterly distinct in culture—the Gelonoi being somewhat more civilized farmers—but the historian also points out that many Greeks were oblivious to these distinctions and could not tell a Greek from a northerner (4.108–109):

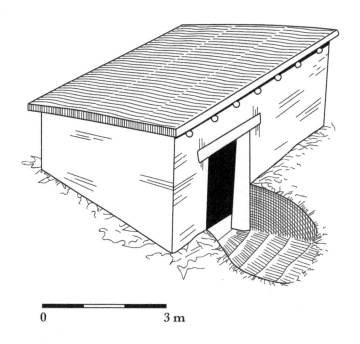

0   3 m

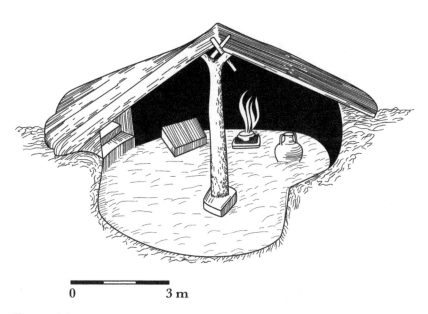

0   3 m

Figure 6.2
Greco-Skythian pit houses of the late seventh to early sixth centuries BCE.
(Illustration by Tina Ross, after Kryzhitskii 1993, 44, fig. 17)

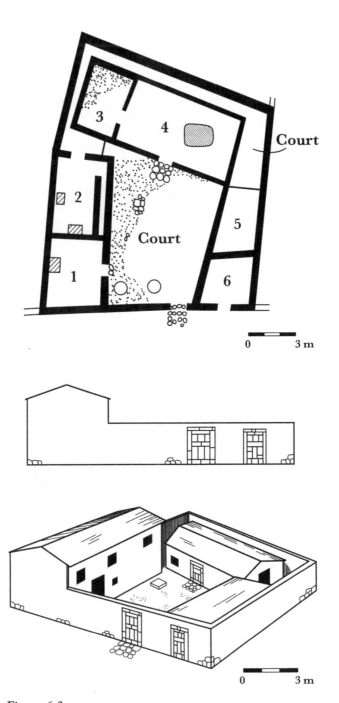

Figure 6.3
Berezan houses of the late sixth century BCE. (Illustration by
Tina Ross, after Solovyov 1999, 69, fig. 52)

The Budinoi—being a great and populous nation—are all blue-eyed and very ruddy. They city situated amongst them is wooden; the city's name is Gelonos. The size of its wall is 130 stades per side, and it is wood to its full height, and the houses are also wood, and the sanctuaries. For there are sanctuaries there of Greek deities, constructed in Greek fashion, and statues and altars and temples in wood. And for Dionysos they celebrate festivals every other year. For the Gelonoi are originally Greeks; having spread out from the emporia they live amongst the Budinoi. And they use a language that is part Skythian, part Greek. The Budinoi do not use the same language as the Gelonoi, nor the same lifestyle. For the Budinoi are autochthonous and nomads and are the only ones in the area who eat lice [or possibly pine cones], while the Gelonoi work the land and eat grain and tend gardens; they are unalike in appearance and coloring. The Gelonoi are called Budinoi by the Greeks, but this is incorrect.

The idea of such cohabitation as between the Greek Gelonoi and the native Budinoi was tempered by the idea that northerners kept their own customs and could even be actively hostile to foreign ways. The flip side of the Gelonoi/Budinoi narrative appeared a few passages earlier in Herodotos's narrative, when he recalled the fate of a half-Skythian, half-Greek king named Skyles (4.78–80):

Among the other children born to Ariapeithes, King of the Skythians, was Skyles; but Skyles was born of his wife from Istrina, who was by no means native—his mother herself taught him the Greek language and letters. Some time later Ariapeithes died through the treachery of Spargapeithes, King of the Agathyrsoi. Then Skyles took the kingship and his father's wife, whose name was Opoiê. This Opoiê was a native; from her was born Orikos, child of Ariapeithes. Although king of the Skythians, Skyles was never really pleased with the Skythian lifestyle, but rather was drawn to the Greek culture which he learned from his upbringing. So this is what he did . . . Whenever he should lead the Skythian army to the city of Borysthenes (they say the Borysthenians themselves are Milesians), whenever Skyles went there, he would leave the army outside of the city, while he himself would go within the walls and would shut the gates, remove his Skythian clothing, and dress in Greek garb. So dressed he would socialize, with neither spear-man following nor anyone else. (They guarded the gates, lest someone of the Skythians should see him in this attire.) And he made use of the other aspects of Greek life, and he made offerings to the deities according to the Greek customs. Once he had spent a month or more thus, he changed back into Skythian garb. He did these things often, and he had a house built in Borysthenes, and he married a local wife of the town. When disaster took him, it happened on the following occasion. He desired to be initiated into the rites of Dionysos Bakkhos. A great portent occurred for him when he was about to begin the rite. He had a large and lavish walled house in Borysthenes (the one I mentioned just a bit ago), which was covered all around with white stone and sphinxes and griffins. The god struck it with lightning, and it was totally burnt. But Skyles engaged in the rite even in spite of this. Now the Skythians ridiculed the Greeks because of the Bakkhic rites, for they said it is not reasonable to seek out a god who makes people crazy. So when Skyles was initiated into the Bakkhic rite, one of the Borysthenites hurried over to the Skythians and said, "You laugh at us, O Skythians, because we rave with Bakkhos and receive the god. Well now the god himself has also taken your king, and he raves with Bakkhos and goes wild under the god's influence. If you don't believe me, follow, and I shall show you." The foremost of the Skythians followed, and the Borysthenite led them and secretly brought them up a tower. When Skyles was going along with the thiasos and the Skythians saw him raving with Bakkhos, it was a very great misfortune for him, for they went out and signaled what they saw to the entire army. So after these things, when Skyles went out to his own people, the Skythians set up his brother Oktamasades [as king], he being the son of Tereus' daughter; and they rose against Skyles. Oktamasades then cut off Skyles' head. This the Skythian laws demanded for those who illicitly adopted foreign customs; this then they give as penalty.

The Greeks always saw the inhabitants of Black Sea regions as rather barbaric. And not barbaric like the Persians. As discussed at the end of the last chapter, Persian barbarism consisted of over-refinement, an excessively high level of civilization, and the fact that they invaded Greece and nearly won. Northern barbarism was more like what we tend to think of today as barbarism—folks in furs wielding clunky but sharp weapons, eating things raw, living on horses, and having excessive lice. Conan the Barbarian was a Kimmerian, a close neighbor of the Skythians, if that means anything. To give a sense of Greek perceptions of these northern barbarians, consider Herodotos's description of the Tauroi (4.103):

The Tauroi use the following customs: They sacrifice to the Maiden those sailors and those they seize of the Greeks whom they went to sea against, in the following manner. Starting the rite they bash the head with a club. Some say that they toss the body down a cliff (for the cliff stands by the sanctuary), then they impale the head. Others agree about the head-bashing, but they do not say that they toss the body from the cliff, but rather bury it in the ground. The same Tauroi say that the divinity to whom they sacrifice is Iphigeneia the daughter of Agamemnon. This is what they do to enemy men they conquer: Each one cuts off the head and carries it from the house; then impaling it on a large wooden stake he stands it high above the house, mainly over the chimney. They say they hang them up there to guard the house as a whole. They live from plunder and war.

And it is clear that the notions presented in the *Histories* did pervade Greek society generally. The preceding description about the sacrifice of shipwrecked sailors is repeated in the opening speech of Euripides's Iphigeneia when she was among the Tauroi (*Iphigenia among the Taurians*, ll. 26–41):

Coming to Aulis and suffering above the pyre
High up I was raised, bled out with a blade.
But Artemis stole me away, giving a deer in exchange
For me to the Akhaians; through the bright air
She brought me here, and settled me in the land of the Tauroi,
Whose land barbarian Thoas rules for
The barbarians, whose swift foot is equal to wings—
He got his name for this swift-footedness.
In these temples she made me priestess,
Where the goddess Artemis enjoys the customs,
Festivals fair in name only—
But I keep silent on other matters, fearing the goddess.
For I sacrifice—it being the law—before the city,
The man who has come down from Greece.
I begin, but the slaughter is the concern of others,
Horrid things within the goddess's temple.

Pay no attention to the fact that the Greeks were sacrificing Iphigeneia herself at the start of this little narrative. The point is that the Tauroi are barbaric, showing no Greek *xenia* to strangers, rather killing them in honor of a deity.

By far the most fascinating residents of the Black Sea region were the Amazons: We are still obsessed with them. As noted at the end of Chapter 5, the main reason that the Greeks were so obsessed with the Amazons was their innate wrongness: Females were not supposed to be belligerent, and yet this was a "race" of innately warrior women. In the arts, they came to be strongly associated with the Persians and Medes—those belligerent effeminates!—but in other aspects of Greek culture, they fascinated as ethnographic and even biological subjects. The early medical writer Hippokrates recorded in his *On Airs, Waters, and Places* (17):

In Europe there is a Skythian nation which dwells around the Maiotis Mere, and which is different from the other nations. They are called Sauromatai. Their women ride horseback and shoot bows and hurl javelin from horseback and fight enemies, so long as they are maidens. They do not lose their virginity until they have killed three enemies, and they do not cohabitate until they sacrifice the lawful rites. She who takes a man to herself stops riding horseback, until necessity compels a full-scale expedition. They do not have a right breast, for to those yet small children the mothers take a burning bronze implement and place it on the right breast and burn it off, so that they might halt its growth and send all the growth and strength to the right shoulder and arm.

A far more detailed narrative comes, of course, from Herodotos (4.110–117):

This is what is said about the Sauromatians. When the Greeks were fighting the Amazons (the Skythians call the Amazons Oiorpata; the name can be

taken in Greek to mean "man-killer," for they call "man" "oior," while "pata" is
"to kill"), then the story goes that the Greeks, having won in the Battle of
Thermodon, sailed off with three ships, taking along as many Amazons as they
could capture alive. But when they embarked the Amazons attacked them and
cut down the men. But they didn't know how to sail, or use oars, or sails, or
rowing. So, when they cut down the men, they were carried along by wind and
wave, and so they came to the Maiotis Mere by Kremnos. The Kremnians live
in the land of free Skythians. There the Amazons disembarked from the ships
and proceeded to the inhabited region. Having first come across a herd of
horses, they seized them, mounted, and raided the Skythian properties. The
Skythians were unable to understand what was going on, for they knew neither
the language nor the clothing nor the nation, but they were utterly at a loss
regarding whence the Amazons had come. They figured that they were young
men, and they fought against them. The Skythians got hold of the corpses after
the battle, and thus they discovered that they were women. Deliberating on
this it seemed better to them no longer to kill them in any way, but rather that
they should send their own youngest men to them, as many of them as there
were women, and they were to camp near them and do whatever the women
did. If they chased them, not to fight, but to flee; when they ceased, to go back
to camping near them. The Skythians devised these things because they
wanted to have children with the Amazons. So the young men went back and
followed their orders. When the Amazons learned that they approached with
no evil intentions, they were pleased, and every day the two camps drew closer
to each other. Just like the Amazons, the young men had nothing except for
weapons and horses, and so they lived the same way as the women—hunting
and pillaging. Come noontime the Amazons did as follows: They broke up into
groups of ones and twos, dispersing apart from each other when "nature called."
Learning this the Skythians did the same thing. And when one of the men was
alone with one of the women, he drew near her, and the Amazon did not draw
away, but allowed it. And it was not possible for them to converse (for they
couldn't understand each other), so with her hand she said to come the next
day to the same place, and to bring another, signaling the "two," and she would
bring another woman. The young man then went back and told these things to
the rest. On the next day he went to the same spot, and he brought a comrade.
And he found the Amazon and a second waiting. The rest of the young men
learned of these things, and they hooked up with the rest of the Amazons.
After this, they united the two camps and lived together, each man having the
woman with whom he first had sex. The men never could learn the language of
the women, so the women adopted the men's. When they could understand
each other, the men said to the Amazons, "We have parents and property. Let
us therefore now no longer live this way, but return home to live. And we shall
have you as wives and no others." And the women said to them, "We are not
able to live alongside your women, for we don't have the same customs as they
do. We shoot archery and hurl javelins and ride horseback—we don't learn the
womanly arts. Your women don't do any of these things we've described, but
they only do the womanly arts while remaining in the wagons, not going out to
hunt or anything else. We shall not be able to get along with them. But if you

wish to have us as wives—and this seems to be most just—go to your parents and take your share of the possessions, and then come and we shall dwell amongst ourselves." And the young men were persuaded and did just this. When they took the portion of the possessions allotted to them, they returned back to the Amazons, and the women spoke to them thus, "Fear and dread have hold of us, while we are dwelling in this land, where we have stolen you from your fathers and where we have wrought so much havoc. But since it seems good to you to have us as wives, do this with us: Come let us emigrate from this land and go dwell across the Tanais River." And the young men were persuaded. Crossing the ford at the Tanais and heading east, they proceeded for three days along the Tanais, then another three from the Maiotis heading north. Arriving in this land they settled there and live there even now. And the women still follow the old ways of the Sauromatians, and they routinely go hunting on horseback, either with or without the men. And they routinely go to war and wear the same clothes as the men. The Sauromatians use the Skythian language, although degraded from the pure form, for the women never did learn it correctly. Concerning marriage they do this: No maiden marries before she has killed a man of the enemy. Some of them even die old spinsters, not being able to fulfill the law.

From a feminist perspective, one might suggest that the Greeks ultimately accepted and even welcomed the notion of the Amazon because, in the end, these warrior women could be tamed by marriage. As Hippokrates noted, they gave up the warrior lifestyle upon marriage, and Herodotos is quite explicit that not only can they not sail ships (the ancient equivalent of a female driver, I suppose), but they are happy to engage in carnal relations with suffi- ciently handsome young men. They still fight, unlike Hippokrates's Amazons, but they do not fight their men, and they married and had children, and this was what ultimately mattered.

Perhaps the most interesting understanding of the Skythians came from Hippokrates. Typically, these northerners were understood to be rugged, brutal, and hardy, having to survive as nomads in a place not exactly known for its nice weather. For Hippokrates, though, the defining characteristic of Skythian nomadism was their reliance on transportation vehicles, specifically wagons and horses. To put it simply, the Skythins simply did not walk enough, and this led to all the same health issues that we complain about today regarding a sedentary lifestyle. (*On Airs, Waters, and Places* 18 and 20–21):

The desert called "Skythian" is a plain, meadowy and open and relatively well watered, for there are large rivers which pour out water from the plains. The Skythians who live there are called nomads, because there are no houses, but they live in wagons. These wagons are at least four-wheeled, some six-wheeled. They are covered all about with felt. And they have been constructed just like two- or three-room houses. These felts are waterproof, snowproof, and windproof. Teams of two or three oxen, without horns, pull the wagons. They don't have horns because of the cold. In these wagons the women reside. The men ride on horses. They are followed by their herds—these being cows and horses. They stay in the same place for a while, as long as there is sufficient pasturage for their flocks. When there isn't, they move on to the next place. They eat boiled meat and drink horse milk. And they eat *hippakê*, a cheese made from mare's milk . . .

I shall offer a significant proof of their exceptionally wet [feminine and weak] nature. For you will find the majority of the Skythians—and all the nomads—stunted in the shoulders and arms and wrists and chest and hips and loins, for no other reason than the wetness of their nature and its softness. For they are unable either to draw a bow or cast a javelin from the shoulder because of the extreme wetness and limpness. Whenever they are cauterized, the majority of the water dries up from the joints, and they become more sinewy, and their bodies better nourished and better articulated. Their bodies grow flabby and stout, first off because they don't use swaddling clothes as in Egypt; they don't use this custom because of the horse-back riding, so that they might be well-seated. Then there's the sitting issue. For the men-folk, when they are unable to ride horseback, they sit most of the time in the wagon and make scant use of walking because of the wandering and driving about. The women-folk are amazingly flabby and stout in appearance. The Skythian race is ruddy because of the cold, not being exposed to the sun's rays. The whiteness of their skin is burned by the cold and becomes ruddy.

Fertility is incompatible with such a nature. For the men have no great enthusiasm for sex because of the wetness of their nature and the extreme softness and cold of the innards, from which qualities a man is least capable of lust. Plus, being jostled about on horseback makes them weak vis-à-vis intercourse. For the men then these are the alleged causes. For the women it's obesity and dampness. For their wombs are unable to hold fast to the embryo. Nor is their monthly purging sufficient, but little and short-lasting, and the mouth of the uterus is closed because of the excessive fat, and thus cannot receive the embryo. They are apathetic and fat, and their innards cold and soft. Because of these constraints the Skythian race is not fertile. And the maid-servants furnish an excellent proof of this—for they no sooner go to a man than they have one in the womb, because of the well-exercised and lean nature of their flesh.

CONCLUSIONS

It must be noted that much of our evidence for the world outside of Greece, other than what derives from the epic poets Homer and Hesiod, comes from the literati, the upper-class, well-educated, well-traveled types such as Hero-dotos and Dr. Hippokrates. As such, we are getting a very specific view of the non-Greek world, a world that was utterly outside of the daily lives of the average Greek. But one must remember that in "Greece"—the mainland, islands, Ionia, Magna Graecia—many Greeks had opportunities to hear, and even read, such narratives. And it is evident that there was a trickle-down effect involved. The highly literate Euripides experienced in some way the works of Herodotos, whose description of the Tauroi then wound up in a play performed before the citizenry of Athens. One way or another, these various understandings of the foreigners beyond the borders circulated amongst the various Greeks.

And we must always remain cognizant that not all Greeks lived in "Greece proper." Many, many Greeks lived in colonies and trade centers side-by-side with Etruscans, Egyptians, Skythians, and Phoenicians. These people did experience "foreigners" on a daily basis and were themselves "foreigners." For the Greeks living "abroad," these peoples were trade partners, spouses, clients, and friends, and interactions in such a milieu were probably very similar to living in a multicultural city today. Consider Jerusalem, where people are constantly communicating in Hebrew, Arabic, and English, and you can tell if a store is run by a Muslim, Jew, or Christian based on what days it is closed for the "weekend." But this side-by-side living did not then, as now, necessarily eventuate accurate understandings of such people back in the homeland. In spite of anything they might hear from relatives in the Bosporan Kingdom, many Greeks were probably surprised to learn that all Skythians weren't fat, just as most Americans can't quite seem to understand that just because you're an Arab doesn't mean you're a Muslim.

Most importantly, one must remember that what is presented here is not so much (or only) an account of the foreign peoples with whom the Greeks had contact as it is an account of how the Greeks perceived these foreign peoples, with all the misconceptions and goofy prejudices involved. This is not reality, but perception. To all Egyptians, Etruscans, and Skythians ("Hello, fellow Budinoi!") I offer my apologies for any potential offense incurred.

7

Peri Hierôn: On Sacred Matters

AN IMPORTANT INTRODUCTION TO THE IDEA OF GREEK RELIGION

It is exceptionally rare in the modern day and age that a person can approach Greek religion without the ton of baggage dropped onto her/him by the currently prevalent, text-based, monotheistic religions. Common attitudes are that the Greeks didn't actually have religion, merely mythology (a statement I got from my mother-in-law many years ago); or that their "religion" was as superficial as their gods were petty and irrational. As expressed in the otherwise excellent book by Robert Garland *Daily Lives of the Ancient Greeks*, "Arrogant, fickle, cruel, and treacherous, the Olympians have been aptly described as superhuman in power and subhuman in morality. . . . The difference between the Olympian deities and, in particular, the Christian God, who has been likened to an inoffensive celestial social worker of indeterminate gender, could hardly be more extreme" (1998, 134). Or as Dave Barry once put it (humorously, but probably pretty close to most modern understandings):

> Back in ancient Greece and Rome they had gods all over the place, and it was no fun at all being a mortal, as you know if you ever read any myths:
> "One day two young lovers, Vector and Prolix, were walking in a garden. This angered Bruno, the god of gardens, so he turned Vector into a toad. Saddened, Prolix picked up her lover and squeezed him to her bosom, which caused him to secrete a toad secretion upon her garment. This angered Vito, the god of fabric, who turned Prolix into an exceedingly unattractive insect. Saddened, Vector hopped to his lover, which angered Denise, who was the goddess of municipal water supply and just happened to be in the neighborhood, so she hit them both with a rock." ("He Knows Not What He Writes")

Regardless of the ideologies currently attendant on a modern deity most commonly known as "God the Father" in common parlance, what is

important to understand here is that ancient Greek religion was neither irrational nor superficial, and neither were its gods. Quite to the contrary, the
beliefs and rites of the Greeks held deep spiritual significance and served
important psychological functions. Their deities were far more concerned
with humanity than many modern critics would admit or necessarily understand. In short, ancient Greek religion was just as reasonable and meaningful
as any religion can be, and there are very good reasons the Greeks adhered to
it. Allow me to give a quick but (hopefully) meaningful demonstration
of what I mean, both in terms of modern misunderstandings and ancient
realities.

Most people have read, or at least know about, the story of Oedipus, that
Theban fellow who inadvertently killed his father and married his mother,
as was prophesied long before his birth. Having grown up an adopted prince
in Corinth after his biological parents (reasonably, really) exposed him at
birth, Oedipus abandoned home the moment he heard about the awful proph-
ecy. Of course, this led him right to his father traveling the other way, leading
to a dispute, leading to an ultimately fatal but necessary self-defense on the
part of Oedipus. Upon arriving in Thebes, he defeats a monster and is given,
as a thank you gift, the hand of the queen in marriage. Over a decade passes
before a plague hits Thebes, leaving Oedipus tearing his hair out trying to figure out how to save his people. The answer lies with an irascible old prophet
who knows the solution but pointedly refuses to tell Oedipus, using the
ancient Greek equivalent of *"You want the truth? You can't handle the truth!"*
Oedipus has a conniption fit, eventually learns the truth, has another fit,
and blinds himself. There are a few variations to the story (as there are in most
Greek myths, due to the localized and oral nature of the tales). In the most
famous version, Oedipus blinds himself then banishes himself from Thebes.
According to another version, he stayed in Thebes for a while before being
banished by his sons. In yet another version, he remained the blind king of
Thebes for life. Whatever. Eventually he discovers that his corpse will be a
blessing for whatever community has it buried on its land: That community
will never lose a war with Thebes, based on the power and blessing of the
now defunct Oedipus.

What inevitably comes up in mythology class is the question: Why was
Oedipus punished? It is always assumed that Oedipus was being punished for
something. Usually it's his anger, which students (and teachers) assume is an
example of *hubris*. Really, that was one hell of a tongue-lashing he gave
Tiresias the prophet, right? Must be hubris. Okay, granted, that happened *after*
the plague had already set in, so apparently the gods were punishing him (and
all of Thebes because, of course, the Greek gods were bitchy and irrational,
right?) because he was the sort of person who would display this kind of
hubris. It was an example of that "tragic flaw" most people are sure Aristotle
was talking about. Except that, technically, the "punishment" really begins

with the patricide and rather awkward marriage alliance, and all this was prophesied before Oedipus was even conceived! So to get at the answer of why the Greek gods punished Oedipus, the typical student of Greek relig. . . er, mythology has to assume that the gods were mean and petty enough to condemn a person before he even existed, and that they were utterly vicious in carrying out their torments. All of you who have heard this explanation, please raise your hands.

Time to reevaluate. The main problem with the Oedipus story as given is that it begins *in media res*. Not in the middle of Oedipus's tale, as one typically hears, but in the middle of the tale itself, which begins with Oedipus's father Laios. Who once raped a boy, the son of his *xenos*. So we have a man who violated the xenos relationship, the same crime that started the Trojan War (see Chapter 3), by committing what in modern times we would call child molestation. These were both seen as bad by the ancient Greeks, who were neither irrational nor morally bankrupt. They were especially condemned by the Greek gods. As punishment, Apollo—the immortal representation of all Greek boys—told Laios that he had forfeited any rights to a family of his own. If Laios had a son, a descendant to carry on the family and household, that son would kill him, marry and reproduce with his mother, and destroy the family line. In short, if you can't control your sexuality, you shan't be allowed to use it legitimately, either. All in all, a relatively modest punishment for a rather heinous crime.

But Laios can't control his sexuality. He does marry in spite of the reproduction injunction. He does have a son (not like he could have planned for the sex of the child, but anyway . . .). The curse, the punishment for his crime, is set into action. Oedipus was not being punished—Oedipus *was* the punishment.

For his own part, Oedipus did nothing wrong. He was apparently a model son. Upon hearing that he would hurt his family, he banished himself from what he thought was his natal home. He killed that stranger on the road in self-defense (also indicating that, years later, Laios still had a problem personality). He saved Thebes and graciously acquiesced to their request to become their king, being their savior and all. He was a loving husband (yeah, you can shudder here) and father, and a very attentive king. If he had a temper, well, how would anyone react when told that he is too petty to hear the cure for the plague killing everyone he loves? That's not hubris, that's normal. Anyone behaving differently is probably a sociopath.

So why then was there a plague, I hear you ask. Because self-defense or not, by killing someone Oedipus rendered himself ritually impure, known in Greek as a *miasma*. This impurity seeped into the entire community, causing plague. To end the miasma-induced plague, Oedipus had to be purified, plain and simple. The problem, really, was that to get the full information about this, and especially the part about how he didn't just kill a random stranger but his own father (a *serious* miasma), all the truth about his parentage, and current family life, had to come out. What is odd in this scenario is that it took so long for the miasma to reach this effect; Oedipus had been married for at least a decade by this point. It would seem that the deities were being rather gracious to Oedipus, allowing him to enjoy at least some domestic bliss before having it all ripped away from him because of the curse on Laios (remember him? the child molester?). If Oedipus had managed to keep his cool, things still might have turned out reasonably well for him. Okay, so his wife/mother committed suicide; it's not like they wouldn't have divorced anyway. And yes, he blinded himself. But he was also king of two cities, Thebes and Corinth, and he could have passed one along to each of his sons, were it not for the curse on Laios. Oedipus's sons appear to have inherited their grandfather's problem personality. They started a civil war that got both of them killed, leading to the death of their sister Antigonê and what at least appears to be the abandonment of their sister Ismenê. Apollo's curse came to fruition: the house of Laios was exterminated. But we must notice that the deities did what they could to shield Oedipus, the hapless victim of all of this. He got to enjoy several years of peaceful kingship and fatherhood. According to the oldest version of the story as preserved in Homer, he lived to a ripe old age as the king of Thebes. Even after death he was accorded honor: The deities made him a hero who received a minor cult and protected those who, in his final days, protected him.

So do we all got that straight? *Laios* was the bad guy; he was a child molester, and the gods punished him because the gods to *not* approve of such behavior. Oedipus was the punishment, and the deities gave him the best life they could under the circumstances because he was, ultimately, innocent and a good guy, and the gods reward good behavior. Most examples of the deities being petty actually come down to an example of a human acting like an idiot. Greek religion was not irrational.

POLYTHEISM: THE GODS AND GODDESSES OF THE GREEKS

The ancient Greeks worshiped a plethora of different divine beings. At the top of the hierarchy were the Olympian deities, a host of gods and goddesses who inhabited Mt. Olympos in northern Greece, the highest mountain in the area and perpetually encased in clouds. Just below them on the divine social hierarchy were the gods of the underworld—Hades and Persephonê. In many respects, they were just as highly revered as the Olympians, although humans were, perhaps, just a touch more afraid of them, and they had far fewer temples and rituals. Next came the deities who lived in nature. These could include powerful primordial deities such as Okeanos (Ocean) and Tethys, water deities; Gaia, the earth herself; the Furies, goddesses who punished crime; or the Hesperides, the daughters of Atlas (who holds up the vault of heaven) who live at the western edge of the world. All bodies of water were understood to be divinities in their own right; rivers were typically understood to be male, and springs and fountains female (reflecting the standard Greek understanding that males were more active than females). There were some exceptions, though: the most powerful river in the Greek imagination was Styx, a goddess highly revered by Zeus. Somewhere between divine and mortal were creatures such as nymphs, who were embodied in the natural world, inhabiting trees and bodies of water; satyrs, who were a cross between humans and goats or horses; and centaurs, human-horse hybrids. Such beings had superhuman powers, attributes, and life spans, but they could die eventually, and thus were distinct from the ever-living deities.

A good way to think about it is that the world was infused with divinity. Every tree and fountain had an inhabitant and protecting spirit. Every aspect of the world—be it the sea, death, or the art of weaving—had a deity overseeing it and looking after the people involved with it. Everything had a patron, from grapes to sheep to children to kings.

The Olympians

The most popular deities in the Greek pantheon were, of course, those Olympians. Technically, a lot of deities lived on Olympos, more than just the standard "12" people tend to talk about. The "12" consisted of Zeus, Hera, Poseidon, Demeter, Hestia, Athena, Artemis, Apollo, Aphrodite, Hermes, Ares, Hephaistos, Apollo, and Dionysos, or, to put it another way, 14. Sometimes the "12" included the Kharites, the goddesses of beauty; the Horai (seasons); the nine Muses who governed the arts, and even the demi-god Herakles. Basically, there was never any real consensus as to who, exactly, the 12 were, although the first 13 listed in this paragraph (removing Dionysos from the equation, or possibly even Hestia) are the commonest approximation. Other divinities who inhabited Olympos include Ganymedes, the former Trojan prince who was abducted by Zeus, immortalized, and made the gods' cupbearer; Eros, the god of love; Dikê, the embodiment of Justice who attended on Zeus; Nemesis, another goddess of justice; and even Sleep. Rather than picturing Olympos as a single room with 12 (or 14) thrones, it is better to think of it as a luxury resort with several houses, elegant landscaping, and a fancy dinner hall featuring many thrones, drinking amenities, a dance floor, and so on.

The somewhat fractured Greek culture promoted by the Greek landscape provided for highly localized pantheons. In some cases, this means that Greeks in one area worshipped deities that no one else did. This was certainly the case for very localized deities such as rivers and lakes, not to mention the local nymphs (more on these later in this chapter). It was also so for local heroes, who protected their territories (such as Oedipus mentioned earlier). But even the Olympians were understood and worshipped differently in different regions of Greece. Different *poleis*, while holding all the Olympians in high esteem, had closer attachments to some deities than to others. Athens, of course, was particularly attached to Athena. Hera held sway in Argos, Samos, and Olympia, only being joined by her husband at that last site in later years. Corinth was the city of Aphrodite, even if the Isthmos was more closely associated with Poseidon. In contrast to these more civic deities, Eileithyia (goddess of childbirth), for example, was worshipped in the birth bower.

There are numerous books out there that give excellent (and sometimes not so excellent) introductions to the Greek pantheon. A wonderful resource is Jennifer Larson's *Ancient Greek Cults: A Guide* (2007), as well as the website www.theoi.com. So I am not going to do the standard presentation of Greek Deity: History: Areas of Influence here. Rather, I include here a selection of case studies of the ways different deities functioned in the Greek psyche and society. Some cases are Panhellenic, others apply more to one sex than the other, some pertain to exclusive sects. In any event, I believe such an examination provides a better presentation of how the Greeks *experienced* their religion and maintained their relationships with their deities than a listing of gods with attributes.

Hestia

The least written about member of the Greek pantheon is Hestia, whose name means "hearth." She appears only six times in the extant literature (for her presence in Pindar's *Eleventh Nemean Ode*, see Chapter 4). First, she is the oldest of the Olympians in Hesiod's *Theogony* (l. 454), although having been thrown up in reverse order, she is also the youngest. A fuller description of her is given in the *Homeric Hymn to Aphrodite* V, where she is described as one of the three goddesses immune to the powers of the goddess of sex (ll. 22–32):

Hestia, whom crooked-minded Kronos first sired,
But also the youngest by the will of aegis-bearing Zeus,
A revered lady, whom Poseidon and Apollo courted.
But she did not want this; she quite insistently refused.
She swore a great oath which has indeed gone fulfilled—
Grasping the head of aegis-bearing father Zeus—
To be a virgin for all her days, that fair goddess.
To Hestia father Zeus gave a fine gift instead of marriage,
And in the midst of the house she arrives and sits before the fire.
She receives honor in all the temples of the gods
And amongst all mortals she is the most revered of the deities.

Furthermore, there is a short *Homeric Hymn* to her (24):

Hestia, you who attend to the sanctuary of far-shooting
King Apollo in most holy Pytho,
Soft oil ever drips from your tresses.

Come to this house, having one heart with cunning Zeus,
And bestow grace upon my song.

Hestia's association with, and even identification as, the hearth is no trivial matter. As the source of controlled fire, the hearth formed both the physical and ideological core of any Greek communal entity, be that a house, a temple, or a city. At the political level, a city's main hearth was located either in the prytaneion (city hall, see Chapter 4) or the agora. When new colonies were established, fire from the mother city's main hearth was used to light the hearth of the daughter city, thus establishing a political-familial link between the two poleis (Sourvinou-Inwood 2000, 25). As such, Hestia had an important job in the formation of new political identities.

As the goddess of the hearth, Hestia was also automatically associated with every Greek sanctuary. Ancient Greek sanctuaries had three necessary components: a temenos, an altar, and a temple. The temenos is the area "cut out" and dedicated to a deity; it is the sanctuary proper. The altar is where burnt sacrifices took place, the most important element of Greek worship. Different things might be burnt upon an altar. Animal sacrifice was common (see Chapter 3 and later in this chapter), but bread and incense could also be burnt to the deities. Aphrodite's most famous sanctuary at Paphos was known for having no blood whatsoever spilled upon it. The temple, or *naos*, was optional, so much so that sometimes the Greeks didn't even bother finishing them, and the gods were left with no roofs over their heads. But the critical thing was the altar, and the altar was nothing more or less than the seat of Hestia, the place of fire. As such, every cult ritual that involved burning something to a deity inevitably involved her. She was literally mortals' conduit to divinity, and one could not approach the gods without revering her in the process. Although the least mentioned deity in the literature, Hestia was inevitably the most worshipped.

As the goddess who formed relationships, Hestia was vitally important in the Greek household. It was she who inducted new children into the family through the *amphidromia*, a ritual wherein fathers walked (or ran, although I imagine the mothers would have screamed at them for this) around the hearth holding a new baby, thus incorporating the infant into the family. Babies not so inducted were viewed as strangers and could be exposed without guilt. New slaves were brought to the family hearth to cement their inclusion in the family household. Finally, it was Hestia who formed marriage alliances. After a feast at the bride's house, the bride was taken to her husband's house and brought to the hearth. Here she was fully inducted into her husband's family, and the newlyweds were showered with small fruits and nuts as a symbol of future fertility (something akin to our throwing rice). The marriage was finalized by Aphrodite in the bedroom, of course.

As the goddess most involved with familial transitions, Hestia was ultimately a protectress of home and family. In Euripides's *Alkestis*, when the

queen is about to die, she goes to the hearth and addresses Hestia
(ll. 163–169):

> Mistress, as I proceed beneath the earth,
> For the last time I shall beseech you in supplication,
> To care for my orphaned children, to join my son in
> Marriage to a dear wife, my daughter to a noble husband.
> Nor let them, as their mother was destroyed,
> Die as children, before their time, but happily
> Give them a joyful life in their fatherland.

Hestia was of crucial importance in the daily lives and religious outlook of
the ancient Greeks. She was omnipresent, holding sway in the sanctuary of
every deity and having a place of prominence in every house, family, and city.
She was the most worshipped goddess of ancient Greece, as recounted in her
second *Homeric Hymn* (29):

> Hestia, who in the high halls of all the immortal
> Deities and of earth-dwelling men too
> Has an everlasting seat and foremost honor;
> She has a fair prize and right. For without you
> Mortals cannot revel—where does one not begin the libations
> Of sweet wine, first and last, to Hestia?

Demeter and Persephonê

One of the most beautiful and meaningful pieces of literature to emerge
from ancient Greece is the *Homeric Hymn to Demeter* (see this chapter's
appendix), discovered in a barn in Moscow in 1777. If you ever use the
expression "Stranger things have happened" and someone asks you to name
one, this is a pretty good example. Really, a barn in Moscow. Anyway, go read
the text (it's not that long) and then come back for an analysis.

There are a number of ideas that one must keep in mind when trying to
understand this story. The first, and perhaps most difficult to get through to
a modern audience, is that *Hades is not evil.* People are somewhat reasonably
afraid of death, and in the modern world, we tend to equate Hades with the
devil, sometimes merely on a subconscious level. As a result, Hades gets a *lot*
of bad press in the modern media, as you know if you have ever seen *Percy
Jackson and the Olympians*, Disney's *Hercules*, *Clash of the Titans*, and/or *Wrath
of the Titans*, assuming that these are actually different movies. As a result,
people reading the *Hymn* are not all that inclined to like him to begin with.
Add to this the fact that it appears that his main role in the story is kidnap-
per/child molester, and we seem to have one hell of a villain.

Step back from this notion for a few minutes. Here's another thing to consider. Ancient Greece was both patriarchal and patrilineal, that latter term

meaning that sons inherit from fathers and that the family is based on a long line of property descending down the male line. Problems emerge if a family has no sons, only daughters. The standard way of dealing with this in ancient Greece was to marry off such a daughter, called an *epikleros* or *patroukhos*, to her closest male relative on her father's side (you may remember this fact from this book's introduction). Thus girls marry first cousins or even paternal uncles. Persephonê is an only child (assuming that you do not count half-siblings, in which case, being the daughter of Zeus, she has a million-billion siblings), making her, technically, an epikleros. It is thus an ideal scenario for her to marry a close male relative on her father's side, to wit, her uncle Hades. Hades is wealthy, loyal to his wife, and, as his argument to her as to why she should remain with him shows, treats his wife as a rational being. Hades is a good husband; and Persephonê emerges from the story of her marriage in a very good situation indeed. On the one hand, she is Queen of the Dead. Since everyone dies, it means that she holds sway over all of humanity, just as Hades explained it. As the returning daughter of Demeter, she gets to travel between the world of the living and the realm of the dead (one of the very few deities able to do so), enjoying the benefits of both worlds. Persephonê made a *very* good match; the story has a happy ending.

So why does the story rub people the wrong way? It is because the process of everything happening correctly (daughter being married off to good husband by father) still causes a lot of pain, mainly to the females in the story. Persephonê is ripped away from her childhood to become the wife of a stranger, and not only does Dad not come to save her, he was actually in on it! Demeter has little to no say in the fate of her own offspring and is left bereft when her child becomes an adult. Her child literally dies to her. What seems so tragic to us is that goddesses are experiencing what humans, and especially women, must go through all the time (death, losing children, having no control). And it is in dealing with these experiences that the true beauty of the myth emerges.

Demeter learned from her experiences. Specifically, she learned what it means to be human and to lose a child to death. Deities, being immortal, do not die, so they rarely have to worry about child mortality. Those deities, and there were very many, who had mortal children already knew that this was in the cards for them. Zeus could eventually accept that his son Sarpedon would die on the fields of Troy, just as Thetis could build up inner resources for the eventual death of Akhilleus. Demeter was blindsided. Persephonê was fully immortal, the daughter of Zeus; she was not supposed to die. But being married to Hades and moving to his realm was the equivalent of dying for a deity, since, traditionally, no god but Hermes travelled between the realms. So on the one hand, Persephonê's marriage to Hades was like a death for her, at least to those who remained above. Demeter learned the true meaning of death.

On the other hand, by having a daughter marry and move away, Demeter experienced what all human mothers experienced with their daughters—loss. If a girl married the man next door, there could still be close contact between mother and daughter. But if the girl moved far away, there would be few occasions for mother and daughter ever to see each other again. Thus for woman, marriage could feel like death. This, thought Demeter, was unacceptable, and she did something about it.

The remedy to patrilocal marriage (where brides leave their natal home to move in with their in-laws) was the Thesmophoria, one of the most widespread festivals held in honor of Demeter and Persephonê. This ritual was practiced exclusively by women, usually married citizens (although there may have been exceptions) throughout Greece. In Athens, it took place in October or early November; in Delos and Thasos, it occurred in late Summer (Cole 1996, 203). From the scraps of literary evidence, epigraphy, and archaeology we have, we can determine a fair amount about the ritual's physical manifestation. In Athens, the women congregated near or on the Pnyx, the site of the men's Assembly. Thus women took over male space during the ritual, fencing off the area to protect their activities from male eyes. The ritual lasted three days. The first day was the *Anodos*, or "Road Up," referring to the women's arrival at the Pnyx. The second day was the *Nesteia*, or "Fasting," when the women sat on branches on the ground and did not eat all day. Not much is known about the going-ons of this day, but two possible elements— obscene language and the drinking of pennyroyal—have been related to the *Hymn*, (ll. 192–211):

> But unwilling [Demeter] waited, her fair eyes cast down,
> Until indeed wise Iambê set down for her
> A well-built seat, and upon it she cast a silvery fleece.
> There sitting she held her veil before her with her hands.
> A long time she sorrowed in silence, seated upon the stool,
> Nor did she great anyone by word or motion.
> But unlaughing, eating neither food nor drink,
> She sat wasting for longing of her deep-girdled daughter,
> Until wise Iambê joked with her,
> Pleasing the reverend lady with many wily jests,
> Causing her to smile and laugh and her heart to be glad.
> She indeed later pleased her moods.
> To [Demeter] Metaneira gave a cup of honey-sweet wine,
> Having filled it; but she declined it, for she said it was not right
> For her to drink red wine.
> Then she bade them give her water
> And barley mixed with soft pennyroyal to drink.
> And [Metaneira], preparing a drink, brought it to the goddess, as asked.
> Greatly reverend Deo received it for the sake of the rite.

The last day of the festival was the *Kalligeneia*, or "Beautiful Birth," which celebrated the return of Persephonê. This was the time for a massive, celebratory picnic on the part of the celebrants, in some ways reflecting the reunion between Rhea, Demeter, Persephonê, and Hekatê at the end of the *Hymn*. And, in truth, that's what the festival really was—a reunion. All husbands were legally obliged to send their wives to the Thesmophoria, so it was a massive, annual, all-female family reunion throughout Greece. In celebrating the rites of Demeter and Persephonê, the women who were separated from each other by patrilocal marriage could once again be together, overcoming the "death" of marriage for at least a few days. Demeter knew how it was: She made it better.

The same goes for death. By definition, the immortals do not die. They get a bit bent out of shape when their mortal children die (and there was a certain tendency to blame Aphrodite for causing gods to mate with mortals in the first place), but death was, for the most part, out of their area of concern. One may perhaps liken it to pampered Hollywood stars not really thinking that much about starving Cambodian refugees. Then one day, a perceptive Hollywood star goes to Cambodia, sees a starving refugee, and freaks out. That was Demeter's experience with death. Being a kind and, one might say, proactive sort of deity, Demeter chose to do something about it. Because ultimately, those mortals were really nice to her when she was in a bad way, and she wanted to do something to show her gratitude. So Demeter improved death. As the *Hymn* relates (ll. 473–482):

> And [Demeter] going to the law-bearing kings
> Showed to Triptolemos, to horse-driving Deokles,
> And Eumolpos the powerful and Keleos leader of the host,
> The conduct of her worship and described her rites to all,
> To Triptolemos and Polyxenos and Deokles,
> Holy rites which in no way might be transgressed nor
> Revealed nor spoken of, for a great awe of the deities
> Restrains the voice.
> Happy is he who among earth-dwelling men has seen these.
> But the one uninitiated, who has taken no part in these rites,
> Never has an equal portion after death, down in the shadowy gloom.

Demeter, along with her daughter Persephonê, Queen of the Dead, created a ritual that allowed mortals to have a better afterlife. Called the Eleusinian Mysteries, they existed at least as early as the sixth century BCE (to which dates the *Hymn*), but there is at least some archaeological evidence to suggest that the rites were much older, possibly even Bronze Age. In these rites, people, anyone who spoke Greek and could afford to go, even slaves, went to Eleusis and took part in a several-day long ceremony that functionally initiated them into the Eleusinian cult. Not much is known about the rituals, since "awe of the deities restrains the voice," or, put another way, they were a secret. But it appears that initiates somehow took part, at least emotionally, in the experiences of Demeter and Persephonê, and they were somehow personally introduced to the goddesses. After death, then, Persephonê remembered the person as someone who pleased her by taking part in her rites, and she gave her/him a better afterlife. Such a blissful afterlife was described by the Athenian playwright Aristophanes in his play *The Frogs* (ll. 440–456):

> Go forth now to the goddess's sacred circle, playing in the
> Flowery grove, for those taking part in the holy festival.
> And I go with all the maidens and women,
> Where they keep the all-night-revels for the goddess, bearing
> the holy light.
> Let us go to the rosy, flowery meadows,
> Our path the most beautifully danced,
> Playing, whom the happy Muses lead along.
> For only on us shines the sun, the joyous light,
> Being initiates.

Feeling bad for the plight of humanity, Demeter created heaven.

Dionysos

The cults of Demeter and Persephonê were Panhellenic. All women celebrated the Thesmophoria, and people from all over the Greek world were initiated into the Eleusinian Mysteries. Myth has it that even Herakles was inducted, after being purified by Medea. Somewhat more rare were the Orphic rites of Dionysos, although they, too, offered hope for a better afterlife.

Orphism, as the name implies, was attributed to the mythic poet Orpheus, son of Apollo and Kalliopê, who lived one generation before the Trojan War. Orpheus reputedly composed—actually wrote—several books of metaphysical philosophy concerning the origins and natures of the gods, the creation of humanity, and the path to a just life and blissful afterlife. Orphism espoused metempsychosis (reincarnation) and the idea that morality in this life effects the quality of one's later (after)life. According to Orphic theology, and in contrast to the more "standard" tales of Hesiod, Zeus once had sex with his mother Rhea. She gave birth to Persephonê, with whom Zeus also had intercourse. Persephonê bore Dionysos, who immediately achieved "favorite son" status with Zeus. Although Zeus kept the child well guarded, Hera convinced the Titans to kidnap and murder the child. This they did, and ate him! Only his heart was preserved by Athena, who gave it to Zeus. When Zeus found out about all this, he smote the Titans with a lightning bolt. From their ashes, humans were formed. The human body, then, is composed of dead, evil gods. However, those Titans still had Dionysos, their last meal, running through their veins, and thus Dionysos is also present in all humans, providing the immortal aspect of the soul. In many respects, this theology runs contrary to Greek ideology, where the gods are understood to be pointedly *immortal*. The idea of humanity being created from the blood and body of an evil, ex-deity, however, is present in Near Eastern cosmogonies like the *Enuma Elish* and *Atrahasis*, and it appears that some of Orphism derives from eastern ideologies.

One idea deriving from this myth is that humans are, by their very creation, evil and guilty of Dionysos's death. Humans consist of evil flesh (Titans) that imprisons a divine soul (Dionysos). Dionysos's mysteries purge humanity of this guilt, overcoming the evil flesh and setting humanity into accord with divinity. The books of Orpheus establish how to do this, consisting of prescriptions for daily living as well as specific rituals used to expunge impurity. Being mysteries, of course, we know little about the rituals. Even though some philosophers like Plato scorned them and the "priests" who enacted them, the rites received enough reverence not to be spoken of except very indirectly. The general understanding is that, as with the Eleusinian Mysteries, some re-creation of the Dionysos story was re-enacted (probably *not* eating a baby, though), leading to catharsis and expiation of guilt (Guthrie 1993, 206). Concerning the daily living, we know a bit more. Orphics disdained the flesh, the material aspect of humanity formed from the "sinful" Titans. The Orphic lifestyle, then, was ascetic and nonsensual, and it attempted to purify the flesh to bring one into closer union with the divine. Vegetarianism was practiced, and there was an interesting prohibition on eating beans as well.

The ultimately goal of Orphism was communion with the divine, an event which must occur upon death and the final shedding of the evil flesh of humanity. Even in death, though, the initiate needed help in attaining bliss, lest she/he get reincarnated back into the human condition. To help the recently deceased, the Orphics buried their dead with "instructions" to navigate the afterlife. Often these were composed on sheets of gold, and they have come to light in Hellenistic burials from Crete, Italy, and Thessaly (Meyer 1987: 101). A text from Thessaly reads:

> I am parched with thirst, and perishing.
> But drink of me, the ever-flowing spring on the
> right, (where) there is a fair cypress.
> Who are you? Where are you from?
> I am a child of Earth and of starry Heaven, but my
> race is of Heaven (alone).
> (trans. Meyer 1987, 101)

The texts from Crete are almost identical:

> I am parched with thirst and am perishing; but (give) me to drink from the ever-flowing spring to the right; there! The cypress. "Who are you?" "Where are you from?" "I am the son of Earth and Starry Sky." (trans. Tzifopoulos 2010, 12)

Orphism was rare in ancient Greece (you'd be amazed how difficult it is to get people to go vegetarian). Nevertheless, it offered people an explanation as to why life could be so hard and people so cruel. Psychologically, it even gave people an "out": my innate evil isn't really my fault—it was those Titans, and ultimately Hera. Just as with the story of Adam and Eve, then, people could locate a distant reason for their "original sin" and find some way to blame it on a woman. Perhaps more importantly, though, the Orphic lifestyle and rites gave people a way to correct the problem. In life they could overcome the evil tendencies of the flesh, and in death they could find purity and peace.

Zeus

Zeus's name means "Sky Father," and this in many ways sums up his char-acter. In truth, the sky element isn't as important as it sounds. At the great division of the world between the three older, male Olympians, Zeus got the sky, Hades the Underworld, and Poseidon the sea (everyone, even the god-desses, shared the Earth). There is much to be said for these two latter domains. There's a *lot* of stuff in the sea, likewise the underworld. Plus, as head of the Underworld, as noted previously, you eventually get dominion over anything mortal, which is a good 99 percent of reality. By contrast, the sky is relatively empty. One must remember that the Greeks did not imagine their deities living in a celestial heaven like many people do today; the sky was not "heaven." The main benefit of the sky was that it gave perpetual high ground in case of a fight, and it was linked to Zeus's favorite weapon, the thunderbolt (i.e., lightning). So the association with the sky mainly had a lot to do with Zeus as warrior, which was actually a rather minor element of his persona. Otherwise, Zeus could be thought of as a rain deity, but, once again, this was a minor aspect of his persona.

Far more important was Zeus as Father. Zeus rarely bears any title like "king," but his rule over reality is summed up in his title "Father of Men and Gods." He certainly did have quite a number of children, seeing as how he would have sex with pretty much anything (typically blaming Aphrodite for his lack of self-restraint). Actually, for the most part, Zeus never had sex with his own children, so there was a one-generation buffer zone that also went for his own mother. Otherwise, he was in the sack with his aunts, sisters, grand-daughters, and other random males and females in the mythology. It was not difficult to trace one's lineage back to Zeus. Furthermore, Zeus's son Herakles had similar proclivities, so it was also easy to trace one's lineage back to Hera-kles, and thus to Zeus. Zeus was father of his people in a very real sense in the Greek understanding.

But there was more to Zeus's fatherhood than mere lechery. The Father of Men and Gods took a strongly paternal attitude to his human worshippers and demanded good behavior from them. Like a good father, Zeus inculcated morality and ethics, and punishments from Zeus were correlated with bad behavior on the part of mortals. This is succinctly expressed in the first book of the *Odyssey* when the gods are gathered on Olympos, chatting (ll. 28–43):

> Among them began to speak the father of men and gods,
> For he remembered in his heart noble Aigisthos
> Whom the far-famed son of Agamemnon killed—Orestes.
> Remembering him he spoke then to the immortals,
> "Oy! How indeed mortals now blame the deities!
> For they say that evils come from us. But it is they
> Themselves through their own follies who have pain beyond fate,
> As even now Aigisthos beyond fate married the
> Wedded wife of Atreus' son, whom he killed on homecoming,
> Knowing it was utter destruction. We ourselves told him,
> Having sent Hermes, wide-seeing, Argeiphontes,
> Not to kill him nor to court his wife,
> 'For from Orestes son of Atreides would be payment
> When he grew up and desired his own land.'
> So said Hermes. But these good things did not
> Persuade the mind of Aigisthos, and now he has paid for everything!"

Very important in Greek literature and society was Zeus's role as protector of strangers (*xenia*, discussed at greater length in Chapter 3). It was Zeus who guaranteed the protection of travelers and who demanded that strangers, no matter how lowly (or regal), receive hospitality. As the swineherd Eumaios explained it to Odysseus, when the latter was in disguise as a travelling beggar (*Od.* 14, 56–59):

> Stranger, it is not right for me, even if a lesser man than you should come,
> To dishonor a stranger. For all strangers and beggars
> Are from Zeus; our gift to them is small but dear . . .

A popular motif emerged in later years, especially in Roman times, of Zeus and Hermes (the god of travelers, *inter alia*), traveling in disguise amongst humans to see how they would be treated. In one of the most popular versions of the tale as recounted by Ovid in his *Metamorphoses*, the gods arrive in a town and are universally rejected, shown no hospitality whatsoever. They finally make their way to a small farmhouse owned by an old couple named Baukis and Philemon. The old couple brings them in, cooks up a meager but tasty meal for the strangers, and makes them feel right at home. Zeus and Hermes were pleased, and graciously kept the wine jug full over the course of dinner. When the farmer couple noticed the miraculously refilling wine, they realized that their guests were gods, fell onto their knees in worship, and immediately (and quite unsuccessfully) tried to catch their guardian goose to offer in sacrifice. The gods spared the goose, and instead made Baukis and Philemon a priestess and priest and offered to grant them a wish in exchange for their kindness. The couple asked that they might die at the same time so that neither would have to live without the other. This the gods granted, although it occurred much later, for the gods gave them long, prosperous lives. More immediately, Zeus and Hermes flooded the town and drowned the inhabitants for their lack of xenia (hospitality). This motif of the wandering deity testing hospitality extended well into Medieval times, with similar tales told of Saint Peter or of a wandering wise rabbi.

More immediately in the Greek experience, this punishment of bad behavior/bad xenia could have rather extreme consequences, with the primary example in the Greek repertoire being the Trojan War. In truth, the ancient Greeks had certain problems understanding the Trojan War. The war, or at least *a* Trojan war, probably did take place at the end of the Bronze Age. The archaeological site identified by Heinrich Schliemann as Troy showed multiple layers of destruction, and references in the Hittite documents to a Wilusa (Ilios) indicate that it may have been a hub of trade and commerce, thus a target in times of crisis. So the tradition of a war at Troy can at least in part be ascribed to memory. The *reason* for the war that the Greeks got, though, was not one of trade embargo or international politics, but one of marital infidelity—the Trojan prince Paris (also called Alexandros) ran off with the Spartan queen Helen, who was currently married to Menelaos, Paris's xenos (host). And so a war raged for over 10 years, a whole bunch of people died, Troy was destroyed, and its population was killed or enslaved. Even the Greeks thought that this was a bit much, and they occasionally came up with alternate explanations that made more sense. For example, Herodotos, in the second book of his *Histories* (2.115–118), recounts a story that Helen never actually made it to Troy. She and Paris were blown off course and shipwrecked in Egypt, where the pharaoh, hearing their story, indignantly refused to let Helen leave but insisted that she wait in Egypt until Menelaos came to collect her. On the one hand, it made a bit more sense to the Greeks that the Trojans would have given back Helen if they had her, and that such a protracted war would never occur for such a mundane reason. On the other hand, even in the midst of examining alternate theories, Herodotos still falls back on the same basic ideology that pervades all understanding of the "Rape of Helen": Paris violated xenia. And xenia was sacred to Zeus. In Herodotos's account, it was Pharaoh Proteus who embodied the will of Zeus, punishing Paris (while still showing enough xenia himself not to harm his shipwrecked guest). In other accounts, though, Zeus acted far more directly, and as the chorus of Old Men put it in Aeschylus's *Agamemnon* (60–62):

Just so he sent the sons of Atreus
Against Alexandros, mighty
Zeus Xenios, because of a many-manned woman.

The justice of Zeus was seldom quite so harsh, but justice inevitably was what was at issue. Zeus demanded a certain level of good behavior on the part of the Greeks, and there were negative consequences for violating those demands.

Artemis

In modern times, one of the most common complaints leveled against the Greek gods is that they worked against each other. By following the will of Zeus, for example, you wind up annoying, say, Hera, who then punishes you. Humanity is seen as a helpless pawn in the grand scheme of a polytheistic universe in which it was impossible to please all of the deities all of the time, and innocent humans got caught in a kind of divine cross-fire.

Once again, this isn't entirely accurate. As stated previously, most examples of apparent divine irrationality are actually examples of human idiocy. More specifically, the wrath of multiple deities might be understood to emanate from human bad actions that have multiple consequences. Let us consider, once again, the case of the Trojan War just discussed. As noted, the Greeks understood that the Trojan War resulted from a breach of xenia: The guest Paris abducted the wife of his host Menelaos. As Zeus oversees xenia, he demanded that the violator be punished, and thus the Trojan War. This war, however, would eventuate the death of many children and the enslavement of many women, all of whom were innocent of Paris's crime. Another deity felt sorry for them—Artemis, the protectress of women and children—and so she added her own wrinkle to the story: She demanded that Agamemnon, Menelaos's brother and the leader of the Greek expedition, sacrifice his daughter Iphigeneia to her. In so doing, he would have a direct appreciation for the misery he would be enacting upon his enemy; one might call it an object lesson. Technically, this put Agamemnon into one heck of a bind. If he doesn't kill his daughter, the war cannot proceed and the will of Zeus cannot be enacted, with all that that implied. However, if he does sacrifice his daughter, then he sacrifices his daughter. This is a prime example of the divine cross-fire frequently cited.

Nevertheless, it is worthwhile to stand back and reconsider what is happening. First of all, the wills of the deities are in fact not contradictory here. Menelaos is required to avenge the abduction of his wife, and Agamemnon is required to sacrifice his daughter. So long as Agamemnon follows the wishes of Artemis, all can proceed relatively smoothly. The problem from the modern perspective (not to mention Iphigeneia's) is that it doesn't seem fair. It is unfair that a little girl die at the hands of her father (or any way) when neither he nor she did anything wrong. The action is perceived as a punishment, one that is wholly unmerited.

Rather than punishment, though, it is better to think of Artemis's demand as a lesson. The war, as discussed, results from a human crime. Paris misbehaved. Paris is a prince, ergo not just he but his entire kingdom suffers for his action (part of the downside of being royal—nothing you do just pertains to you). Wars, however, take a very human toll on both sides, especially on civilians. For the most part, Homer's Greeks were free from such collateral damage—the war was not taking place in their territory; their families were safe. But rather than letting the Greek war leaders be immune to the humanitarian disasters wrought by warfare, Artemis forces the war leader to experience what he is about to enact himself—the bloodshed of innocent children. In modern times, we might argue that having experienced first-hand the suffering of a child, his own child, Agamemnon might show some pity for the innocents whom he is about to conquer or at least understand on a very personal level the agony that he is inflicting. Artemis was working on behalf of her "constituents," those most vulnerable to war.

And, for what it's worth, most versions of the story have Artemis save Iphigeneia in the end, replacing her with a deer to be sacrificed as she takes the girl to the Ukraine to serve as her priestess. In such a capacity, Iphigeneia was eventually able to rescue her shipwrecked brother and return to Greece, where she came to be worshipped at Brauron alongside Artemis. Iphigeneia the victim became Iphigeneia the heroine, receiving divine honors. Iphigeneia's parents were emotional wrecks, of course, but Iphigeneia herself turned out okay.

Another example, involving both Artemis and Aphrodite, gives a similar result. The Athenian hero Theseus had a son named Hippolytos, who was ancient Greece's version of Peter Pan. Hippolytos did not want to grow up, which, in ancient Greece, consisted of getting married, having children, and becoming a politically active citizen. Hippolytos hated women and the thought of marriage; he preferred to remain in the domain of Artemis, spending his time in the wilds, hunting all day, and eschewing sexuality. His intense devotion to Artemis the Virgin was paralleled only by his hatred of Aphrodite, goddess of sex. Obviously, he was asking for trouble. To punish him for his disrespect, Aphrodite caused his stepmother Phaidra to fall in love with him. On the verge of death, she confessed her love to her nurse, who passed the word along to Hippolytos, who threw a conniption fit. In distress, Phaidra killed herself, leaving behind a message for her husband that Hippolytos had tried to rape her. Then it was Theseus's turn to have a fit, and he cursed his son, who was banished and got dragged to death by his chariot horses, the ancient Greek equivalent of dying in a car crash. All things considered, it's a great soap opera story—forbidden desire, the sense of "dying" of love, betrayed secrets, lies, and a father so out of touch with his own kid he actually believes that Hippolytos, the poster child for frigidity, would rape someone. There is definitely something to be said for getting fathers more involved in raising their children.

Other than entertainment value, though, the story does much more than apparently exemplify some divine pettiness on the part of Aphrodite and a remarkable lack of concern on the part of Artemis. No society can support a child who refuses to grow up. For Greek society to function, people had to take on adult responsibilities, and these included marriage and the rearing of the next generation. To despise Aphrodite is to despise adulthood, along with its inherent delights and duties. Hippolytos, then, was an object lesson for the Greeks—Peter Pan will not be tolerated: Grow up. Artemis could not protect him because ultimately he should not be protected. Artemis is protectress of those in the process of transformation. She protects and helps rear children who are becoming adults and girls who are becoming women (at menarche, marriage/defloration, and parturition). Artemis looked after the young Hippolytos as he grew, but he reached the age where the goddess was supposed to hand him over to Aphrodite. He refused to go. There was little else to do but let him perish and become a lesson for the Greeks. In Athens, he came to be worshipped alongside Aphrodite, and girls going to be married made offerings to his shrine. Those fulfilling the dictates of Artemis and Aphrodite, and Greek society in general, were reminded of one who refused to bear this burden and perished.

In Defense of Hera

With the possible exception of Hades (see earlier in this chapter), no ancient Greek deity has been so maligned as Hera. A shrew, a bitch, spiteful and vindictive, she is held up as all that is wrong with womankind. There even appears to be a certain tendency to feel sorry for poor old Zeus, who is stuck being married to this queen of Harpies.

As with all aspects of ancient Greek religion, it is worthwhile to take another look at Hera, to try to understand what she meant for her worshippers. She is, in so many ways, the epitome of womankind, being the quintessential wife in the Greek pantheon and imagination. Many aspects of her cruelty and bitchiness can be easily understood as a manifestation, writ large, of woman's power contrasted with male authority. ("Power" is, quite simply, the ability to achieve one's desired ends, be that moving a rock or overthrowing a government. "Authority" is the socially recognized right to have and wield power. All people have some degree of power, even a two-year-old who manipulates through whining. In many societies, authority rests mainly or exclusively with men.) As king of the gods and father of gods and men, Zeus wields ultimate authority. As his wife, Hera has some authority over gods and men, but, technically, none over her husband. To control him, she must use her power. The only time she needs to use this power is when she is working against his wishes. Because Hera occasionally has an agenda different from her husband's, and because Zeus will commit adultery with anything with an orifice, Hera must make frequent use of this power, and she is often successful. From a male perspective—just about the only perspective we get from the ancient world—this makes her a bitch, one whose power trumped her husband's authority.

Hera's power, especially as seen in contrast to that of Zeus, is typically feminine, at least from a male perspective (see above: the only one we get). Principally, she uses her sexuality against Zeus. This is particularly manifest in Book 14 of the *Iliad*, the scene of the so-called *hieros gamos*, or "Sacred Marriage," when Hera seduced Zeus, had sex with him, and lulled him to sleep so that the rest of the gods could take part in the war against Zeus's wishes (see the *Hieros Gamos* sidebar). In Book 15, when Zeus woke up again, he was, needless to say, rather irked at his wife. However, he also chose to recount his various marital infidelities while supposedly seducing her, so he need not elicit much of our sympathy.

Hieros Gamos (*Iliad* 14, 292–353)

Quickly Hera approached Gargaron, summit
Of lofty Ida. Cloud-Gathering Zeus saw her.
When he saw her, lust wrapped around his wise mind
As much as the first time they mingled in love,
Going to bed, unnoticed by their dear parents.
He stood before her and spoke a word and addressed her,
"Hera, what possesses you to come here, down from Olympos?
You have no horses nor are come on a chariot."
And plotting Lady Hera replied to him,
"I come seeking the ends of the bountiful earth,
Ocean, origin of the deities, and mother Tethys,
Who well reared and cherished me in their home.
I'm off to see them, and I shall end their endless quarrel.
Because for a long time now they've held off from each other
In love and the bed, since anger filled their hearts.
The horses stand at the foot of many-springed Ida;
They will carry me over land and sea.
But now I have come here directly from Olympos because of you,
Lest you get angry with me later, if without telling you
I should go to the home of deep-whirling Ocean."
Replying to her Cloud-Gathering Zeus said,
"Hera, there is time to head out later;
But come let us two turn to the well-made bed in love.
For never has desire for goddess or woman so conquered
My heart, pouring into my chest,
Not even when I made love with the wife of Inion,
Who bore Perithoös, counselor equal to the deities;

Nor with fair-ankled Daneä, daughter of Akriseos,
Who bore Perseus, illustrious among all men;
Nor that time with the daughter of far-famed Phoinix,
Who bore me Minos and godly Rhadamanthys,
Nor that time with Semelê, or with Alkmenê in Thebes—
She bore the child stout-hearted Herakles,
While Semelê bore Dionysos, a joy for mortals;
Nor with Demeter, lovely-haired queen;
Nor with glorious Leto; or even with you yourself,
As now I desire you and sweet lust seizes me."
And plotting Lady Hera answered him,
"Most dreadful son of Kronos, what on earth are you saying?
If now you desire to mingle in love in bed
On the peaks of Ida, everyone will see!
How would it be if someone of the eternal gods should see us two
Making love, and then goes amongst all the deities and tells them?
I couldn't go home again
Coming from *that* bed; it would be so embarrassing.
But if you really want to, and love has filled your heart,
There is a bedroom, which your own son Hephaistos built,
Fitted with close set *doors* on the door frames.
Let's go there to sleep, since now the bed is so pleasing."
And Cloud-Gathtering Zeus answered her saying,
"Hera, fear not—neither any gods nor men
Will see; I shall cover us up with such a cloud
Of gold, not even Helios will see us through it,
Whose light is most piercing when spying."
Then the son of Kronos took his wife in his arms.
Under them the divine earth sprouted forth newly blooming foliage,
Dewy lotus and crocus and hyacinth
Dense and soft, which lifted them from the ground.
In this they lay, surrounded by a cloud
Fair and golden; sparkling dew fell from it.
Thus the father quietly slept upon Gargaron peak,
Conquered by love and sleep, holding his wife in his arms.

Another, typically feminine, source of Hera's power was her ability to give birth parthenogenically (without male contribution). Considering that one of Zeus's main concerns was to avoid siring a son stronger than he who could thus overthrow him, this was a serious threat to hang over his head. The most vicious creature Hera created this way was the monster Typhaon, as recounted in the *Homeric Hymn to Apollo* (ll. 306–307 and 340–354):

Fierce and grievous Typhaon, scourge to mortals,
Whom once Hera bore when angry at Father Zeus
. . . .
So speaking she struck the earth with her broad hand,
And life-bearing Gaia was moved. And she seeing
This was glad in her heart, for she knew it would come to perfection.
From this time for one fruit-bearing year
Neither did she come to the bed of wily Zeus,
Nor to her ornate throne, where formerly
She sat speaking shrewd counsels to him.
But she remained in her prayer-filled temples
Enjoying her rites, cow-eyed Lady Hera did.
But when the months and days of the fruitful
Year were completed and the seasons came around,
She bore one resembling neither gods nor men,
Fierce and grievous Typhaon, scourge to mortals.
Immediately cow-eyed Lady Hera took him and
Gave then one evil to another; Python received him. . .

Somewhat less threatening was her parthenogenic birth of Hephaistos, as recorded by Hesiod in the *Theogony* (ll. 927–929):

Hera, without mixing in love, gave birth to
Illustrious Hephaistos, being angry and annoyed with her spouse;
He surpasses all who hold the heavens in artistic skill.

As the son of the Queen of the gods, but not the King, Hephaistos sided with mom against dad one too many times (probably equaling one time total): Zeus hurled him from Olympos, rendering the god permanently lame. Lesson learned, but the birth of Hephaistos did, nevertheless, send the message that Hera could generate her own allies, if necessary. And eventually, one of them would get lucky. Zeus watched his step.

It is interesting, if perhaps distressing, to note that other than Hephaistos, Hera's champion, Hera is the only Olympian against whom Zeus uses violence. All the other deities were, apparently, sufficiently cowed by even the threat of his power, but not the cow-eyed goddess. When Hera was overly excessive in her persecution of Zeus's favorite mortal son Herakles, Zeus responded by handcuffing his wife and hanging her from the vault of heaven with anvils tied to her ankles. Any deity who tried to rescue her was thrown forcefully to earth, dazed (*Iliad* 15, 17–22). It is perhaps an awkward reflection of the ancient Greek family that sometimes dad needed the threat of domestic violence to keep mom in check. So much for male authority.

One must keep in mind, though, that there was much, much more to the marriage of Hera and Zeus than conflict. There were very good reasons Zeus married Hera, and not just because she was beautiful and he was thinking with the wrong organ. Most importantly, Hera was intelligent, and Zeus relied on her for good advice. So much is hinted at in the *Hymn to Apollo* above, where the poet claims that:

> From this time for one fruit-bearing year
> Neither did she come to the bed of wily Zeus,
> Nor to her ornate throne, where formerly
> She sat speaking shrewd counsels to him.

Hera's counseling skills come across in high relief in the *Iliad*, when Zeus must deal with the possible death of his mortal son Sarpedon. When trying to decide whether to rescue his beloved son, Hera offers the following advice (Bk. 16, ll. 440–458):

> Cow-eyed Lady Hera answered him,
> "Most august son of Kronos, what kind of word do you utter?
> He being a mortal man, long ago doomed by fate,
> Do you wish to free him from horrid-sounding death?
> Do it. But not all of us other deities will approve.
> And I'll tell you something else; keep this in mind:
> If you send Sarpedon, living, to his home,
> Think, might not someone else of the gods then also wish
> To send a dear son from the harsh battle?
> For many sons of the immortals fight around the
> Great city of Priam. You will stir a dread grudge in them.
> But if he is dear to you, and your heart pities him,
> Then let him, in the harsh battle,
> Be subdued at the hands of Patrokles son of Menoitios.
> But when indeed his soul and life have departed,
> Send Thanatos [Death] to carry him, and sweet Sleep,
> To broad Lykia, taking him home.
> There his brothers will bury him, and his kinsmen,
> With a tomb and stele. For this is the boon of the dead."
> So she spoke, and the father of men and gods did not disobey her.

Sometimes the father of men and gods deliberately tried to provoke her, instigating a minor marital spat. Even in these cases, though, Hera and Zeus typically emerged seeing eye-to-eye, a fact often facilitated by Hera's stroking of Zeus's ego. Thus, in Book Four of the *Iliad*, Zeus, knowing how much Hera wants the Greeks to demolish Troy, muses out loud about establishing peace between the two and thus ending the war. The results are, perhaps, predictable, with an eventual reconciliation of wills and egos, and a concern to lead the rest of the family peacefully (ll. 25–64):

> "Most august son of Kronos, what kind of word do you utter?
> How do you wish to render vain and fruitless my effort,

And the sweat I sweat with toil, my horses weary
While I summon the host, evil things for Priam and his children?
Do it. But we other deities shall not approve of you."
Cloud-gathering Zeus, greatly vexed, answered her,
"Mad Woman! What sorts of evil things did Priam and
His children do to you, that now you so vehemently desire
To destroy the well-wrought citadel of Ilion?
If you, entering the gates and great walls
Were to eat Priam and his children alive
And the other Trojans, then perhaps you would appease your anger.
Do as you wish; let this quarrel not hereafter
Become a source of strife between us for you and me.
But I'll tell you something else, and you keep this in mind:
Whenever I then eagerly want to destroy a city
Where men dear to you live,
Don't try to put off my anger in any way; but let me.
For I have given this to you contrary to my heart.
For those cities dwelling under the sun and starry heaven,
Cities of earth-bound humans,
Of these sacred Ilion is so highly honored,
And Priam and his people, deft with spears.
For my altar is never bare of a well-balanced feast,
Or a libation, or fat—for we receive these as our prize."
The cow-eyed Lady Hera replied to him,
"There are three cities most dear to me—
Argos and Sparta and broad-pathed Mycenae.
Destroy them, whenever they are hateful to your heart.
I shall not stand up for them nor begrudge you.
For if I should deny you, not let you destroy them,
I would not accomplish much, since you are so much stronger.
But it is necessary to fulfill my anger and not leave it unfinished.
For I too am a deity, my race the same as yours,
And crooked-minded Kronos sired me the eldest,
Greatest twice over, by birth and because I am called your wife,
And you rule over all the immortals.
But now we shall yield to each other in this,
Me to you, you to me. Then the other immortal
Gods will follow . . ."

In all ways, Hera was Wife personified. As the embodiment and protectress of marriage, she was a stabilizing force in human civilization, the unifying force of the familial unit, and thus at the heart of the *oikos*-based Greek society. As a female, she was inevitably subjugated to her husband and had to find her own means of getting her way when disputes arose. Her main weapon was her sexuality (she didn't cook)—she could seduce Zeus's brains out, and she could threaten him with undesired offspring. But more often than not, she was a source of help and guidance for her husband, who ultimately preferred domestic harmony. When Thetis first approached Zeus about giving honor to her son, Zeus's first words were (*Iliad* Bk. 1, ll. 518–19):

> These indeed are ruinous works; what you say will set me quarreling
> With Hera, who will chastise me with reproachful words.

Much like Demeter, Hera gave the women of ancient Greece a deity who understood their predicaments and provided a role model for empowered action.

On a Philosophy of Divine Justice

In the end, one of the most fascinating things that the ancient Greeks understood about their gods was that they were dispensers of both good and evil. Basically, Zeus and colleagues gave everyone some share of joy and hardship, and that was simply how reality worked. This was how Akhilleus comforted Priam after the death of Hektor (*Iliad* 24, 527–533):

> For two pithoi [large, clay jars] of gifts rest on Zeus' floor,
> Such as he gives—one of evils, the other of blessings.
> Zeus delighting in thunder gives them mixed—
> At one point one falls in with the bad, at another with the good.
> But when he gives to one from that of sorrows, he makes a wretch,
> And his wretched misery extends throughout the earth,
> And he goes about honored neither by deities nor mortals.

When Odysseus—naked, exhausted, and starving—first met the princess Nausikaä, she reminded him that (*Od.* 6, 188–190):

> Olympian Zeus himself bestows joy to mortals,
> To good and to bad, as he wishes to each,
> And surely he has given this to you, so you must endure it.

Likewise, the Eleusinian princess Kallidikê ("Fair Justice") explained to Demeter, appearing as an old woman far from home (*Hymn to Demeter*, ll. 147–148):

> Dear Mother, we humans must endure patiently the gifts of the gods, perforce,
> for indeed they are much stronger . . .

The beauty of this way of seeing things is that it eschews an *inevitable* connection between suffering and guilt. That is to say, although people who do idiotic things often suffer for their stupidity, this does not mean that everyone who suffers is guilty of something. It is merely the way of life that everyone receives good and bad in some measure. Such an ideology has the potential for leading to greater compassion for the suffering of others, as it negates (or at least tempers) the idea that the sufferer must deserve what he or she got. This stands in contrast to, say, a Victorian ethic that sees the poor as inferior and evil (which is why God made them poor), or a Hindu notion that suggests that people evil in one life come back in a lower caste in the next life. Furthermore, the Greek ideology renders moot the modern question of "Why do bad things happen to good people?" by indicating that a person's morality is not necessarily linked to his or her circumstances in life. The question is irrelevant. Sometimes sh** just happens.

Some Non-Olympians: The Nymphs

In addition to the major deities of the Greek pantheon, the Greeks also worshipped a number of "smaller" divinities, beings who were less powerful than, say, Aphrodite, but who could still wield considerable influence over the lives of mortals. The benefit of such entities is that while less powerful than the Olympians, they were also closer to humanity on a daily basis. In such a way one might compare them to saints: less powerful than God Almighty, but infinitely more approachable. Such beings in the ancient Greek pantheon included heroes and heroines, former humans who were empowered upon death by the deities for their actions in life (once again, much like saints); river lords; and nymphs. We shall consider this last group here.

The word *nymphê* has a number of meanings in ancient Greek, mostly related to each other to one extent or another. The word can mean "bride," specifically a girl who has just married but has not yet born her first child (at which point she becomes a *gynê*). It could also refer to a young bee, the clitoris, the tip of a plough, or even a puppet. In a religious context, the word usually refers to a female nature spirit, in many ways the female equivalent of the river gods. These nature nymphs inhabit different aspects of the natural word. Springs, those sources of fresh water, are the homes of naiads, while trees, and especially oaks, are homes to dryads and hamadryads. Typically, nymphs are daughters of water gods, ranging from the great world river Okeanos (and who are thus called Okeanids) to the offspring of smaller creeks, such as the Ilissos in Athens. Nymphs are especially interesting as they are the only females in ancient Greece who had complete sexual liberty and autonomy— they could have sex whenever and with whomever they wished, a right not even afforded to the Olympian goddesses. As a result, the major role of nymphs in much Greek mythohistoriography is "national" mother—many poleis or islands trace their origins to an eponymous nymph who, having mated with a god or hero, gave birth to a founding hero. Thus the island of Aigina was named after the nymph Aiginê (daughter of the river Asopos), who mated with Zeus and bore Aiakos, ancestor of both Akhilleus and Ajax.

Much political (as in, relating to the polis) identity was wrapped up in the identity of one's national nymph-mother, and it is not surprising that nymphs feature prominently on coinage, where, say, the face of Aiginê identified coinage from Aigina, just as Abe Lincoln marks a penny as coming from the United States.

But the nymphs were also relevant on a more personal level. As inhabitants of the wild places, it was they who looked after those marginal members of society who spent more time in the woods and by the rivers than those fancy city-dwellers in their man-made agoras and theaters. Their springs provided water for weary travelers, their trees shade on hot days, and their caves shelter for shepherds and their flocks. Their considerations were not taken for granted, and many dedications were offered to the nymphs by a very grateful rural populace. Thus the Hellenistic poet Anytê penned for one grateful client who made an offering to these goddesses (*Gr. Anth.* 16.291):

> For bristling-hair Pan and the rustic Nymphs set
> The shepherd Theudotos a gift under the bluff,
> Because when he was greatly afflicted by the scorching heat
> They gave rest, holding out honey-sweet water with their hands.

Likewise Leonidas of Tarentum wrote the poem accompanying the gift of a cup (*Gr. Anth.* 9.326)

> Cold water springing down from the two-fold rock,
> Greetings! And rustic statues of Nymphs,
> And fountain springs, and in the waters these fine
> Thousand little dolls of you, O Maidens,
> Greetings! Aristokles the wanderer, right where I dipped
> My cup, quenching myself, did I give it as a gift.

The reference to "thousand little dolls" probably refers to the dedication of such votives at the nymphs' shrines. Small female statuettes were common dedications, and articulated dolls (such as those mentioned in Chapter 1) were also found in votive contexts.

Not everyone who used nymph water drank it, though, as is attested on a dedication to the nymphs and all the deities made by a group of Athenian launderers (*IG* II/III 2493):

> The Launderers, having made a vow, dedicated to the nymphs and to all the gods: Zoagoras son of Zokypros, Zokypros son of Zoagoras, Thallos, Leukê, Sokrates son of Polykrates, Apollophantes, Euporionos, Sosistratos, Manes, Myrrhinê, Sosias, Sosigenes, Midas.

The image itself has two registers. On the top are three nymphs being led by Hermes to the face of the great river Akheloös while Pan sits behind them playing his pan pipes. Below are Demeter and Persephonê facing a bearded hero with a horse. The imagery shows not only the reverence for the nymphs (above), but also the close connection between the river spot where the launderers worked and the rites of Demeter and Persephonê, whose initiates bathed in this river.

Generally, though, as noted previously, the main dedicants to the nymphs were poor folk who lived in the marginal parts of society, be they shepherds, launderers, or farmers. Most gifts to the nymphs were humble and rarely featured the literary inscriptions that grace the votives mentioned above. In her work on nymph cults, Jennifer Larson noted that what dedications survived were generally of the poorer sort:

> The cave sanctuaries were more likely to receive frequent small offerings (flowers, libations) than periodic expensive ones. For the most part, the votives in nymph caves are of poor quality. The ceramics tend to be the cheapest available, valuable metal objects, although found regularly, are a very small proportion of the offerings. There is also an unusual tendency . . . for the clientele to create their own, homemade votives and to add "amateur" rock-cut features and rupestral inscriptions to the caves. Though some local and chronological variation is inevitable, the cult of the nymphs both at cave sites and other types of sites seems to have been conservative, preserving throughout the Hellenistic period the same basic motifs first found in Homer. (2001, 228)

The kinds of things people offered to the nymphs were chea. . . er, inexpensive ceramics; terracottas featuring nymphs, satyrs and silens, Pan, comic actors, and animals, birds, and even fruit; musical instruments; animal skins; and even painted plaques. One such plaque, from the Saftulis cave sanctuary near Sikyon, shows a group of three women, a boy leading a sheep, and a male lyre player approaching an altar. The painted text names two women—Euthydika and Eukholis—and the expression "dedicated to the nymphs." It appears to be a standard scene of sacrifice (see Figure 7.1).

Both the iconography and the epigraphy give evidence that sacrifices were offered to the nymphs in addition to small votive offerings. Such sacrifices could occur in the nymphs' own sanctuaries and sacred places, or, perhaps more commonly, in the sanctuaries of other closely related deities such as Hermes, Apollo, or even Asklepios. One such inscription from the island of Kos shows that along with sacrifices, some people thought it customary to toss offerings directly into the nymphs' watery homes, much as today people toss coins into fountains (*LSCG*, #152):

> Philistos, son of Aiskhines, said: Whoever sacrifices in the sanctuary of Asklepios to the nymphs, let him sacrifice on the altars, but nobody is to throw either a cake or anything else whatsoever into the springs in the sanctuary. If anyone does throw something in, he must purify the sanctuary of the nymphs as is customary. (trans. Larson 2001, 205)

Figure 7.1
Euthydika votive plaque, paint on wood, ca. 540 BCE. From Pitsa Village, Corin-thia. National Archaeological Museum, Athens, Greece, Inv. 16464. (Gianni Dagli Orti/The Art Archive at Art Resource, NY)

One of the reasons it was so important to keep the springs clean was that they, like the nymphs and, of course, Asklepios, had an important role to play in healing. This was one of the nymphs' most important functions, showing that the connection between springs and miraculous healing has a very old pedigree. Pausanias mentions one such healing spring at Triphylia in the region of Elis. Here (Paus. 5.5.11):

> There is in Samikos a cave not far from the river, said to be of the Anigis Nymphs. He who has whiteness or leprosy enters there, and first he sends himself down to pray to the Nymphs and to promise some sort of sacrifice, and after that he wipes clean the illness from his body, crossing the river he leaves his disgrace in the water, and he emerges healthy and clear-skinned.

Another healing spring was located by the Aetna volcano in Sicily. Here an old woman commissioned an epigram to accompany her thanksgiving gift (Gr. Anth. 6.203):

> The old spinster, lame of feet,
> Hearing good things of the healing water,
> Came creeping with a staff of oak,
> Which propped her up, she being lame.
> Pity seized the Nymphs, who have the watery home
> Of their father swirling Symaithos
> On the mountainside of bellowing Aetna.
> And her lame leg the hot spring of Aetna made sound.

For the Nymphs she left her cane, for them
Who undertook to send her off unsupported, and they
Rejoiced in the giving.

There was certainly quite a lot to like about the nymphs. They were beautiful, sexually liberated, only occasionally stole pretty boys to take as lovers,
helped raise children, and healed. It is not surprising, then, that some people,
men especially, became obsessed with them. One such man was Arkhidamos
the Theran, who in the fifth century moved to Attika and right into the
nymph cave at Vari, where he dedicated his life to the nymphs. Over the
course of at least a decade, Arkhidamos decorated the cave with stairs, rock-
cut pictures, inscriptions, and even a self-portrait. He explained his behavior
in an inscription: "Arkhidamos the Theran, a nympholept [one rendered virtually mad by the nymphs], at the instructions of the nymphs, worked out this
cave" (Larson 2001, 14). Arkhidamos communed with the goddesses; in
modern times, we might call him a fanatic.

A similar devotion occurred in the Kafizin cave on Cyprus in the third century. A man named Onesagoras, a native Cypriot, was the primary member of
a group that showed a singular devotion to the nymph of the cave. They
made, literally, hundreds of dedications to her, often of pottery and other such
common items, but excavators found a gold diadem in the cave that certainly
belonged to the nymph. In the various inscriptions on the objects dedicated
by Onesagoras, he calls the nymph his sister and his daughter, and he once
even seems to refer to himself as her suitor. Other epithets of the nymph are
"Mistress of the mountains," "Mountain ranging," "Listener" (an aspect of deities who listen and respond to prayers), and "Vow-Loving." The majority of
the dedications in the cave belong to less than a decade, indicating that the
cult belonged to Onesagoras and his group specifically, rather than the community at large. The nymphs had very passionate followers.

In the end, being strongly local, nymphs more than any other divinities
were the one who represented home. In Book 13 of the *Odyssey*, when Odysseus finally gets home to Ithaka, the hero praises the local naiads first in his
prayer of thanksgiving (*Od.* 13, 356–360):

Naiad Nymphs, daughters of Zeus, I never
Thought to see you. But now with kindly exultation
I greet you. And I shall give gifts, just like before,
If the gracious, booty-bringing daughter of Zeus lets me
Live myself, and rears up my dear son.

Religion in Action: Performing Piety in Ancient Greece

One of the primary differences between ancient Greek religion and the
modern religions of the book is that there was no concept of orthodoxy. There

was no authority who determined whether what you believed about the gods was accurate. Technically, the notion of belief was not a major concern. It was generally assumed that you believed in the same deities as everyone else in the much the same way as everyone else, and there were only rare and specialized cases where this might be disputed. Otherwise, what was really important religion-wise in ancient Greece was praxis—the physical manifestation of religion. Dionysos probably did not care so much if you thought of him as having a beard or not (in the art, he actually gets younger over time), but he was concerned that you recognize him as being a deity and respond by celebrating his rites appropriately. You need not love Aphrodite as much as Artemis (or vice versa), but you better show both of them sufficient respect and attend to their worship as necessary.

Public Worship

Fortunately, much religious praxis in ancient Greece was fun. They had no six-hour-long Easter services. There was no month of fasting sun-up to sundown. No one had to confess how many times a week he masturbated. On a daily basis, religious praxis mostly involved offering the deities their due at mealtime, much like a modern family might say grace. On the large scale, the Greek deities liked to be feasted and entertained, and the Greeks were more than happy to oblige.

The most common form of worship in ancient Greece was sacrifice (see Figure 7.2). Typically, this was of an animal, be it a small bird or fish (for those short of funds) to as many as hundreds of animals at a time. Sometimes merely incense or grains were burnt upon an altar, but blood-sacrifice was the norm. The thing that is odd about this is that the Greek deities didn't eat human food. Human food is dead, and the ever-living gods were *not* about to put some dead, rotting thing into their bodies, thank you very much. The gods ate ambrosia, which literally means "immortal." So, you might ask, what is the point of sacrifice? Part of the answer may lie in a human need to expiate the guilt incurred with killing a living creature. All animals must kill in order to eat and thrive. While no one gets worked up over the death of, say, a rutabaga, there is definitely an aspect of guilt involved in killing an animal. Most religions have a sanctioned means of expiating this guilt. In the Judeo-Christian ideology as stated in *Genesis*, God gave humans permission to eat animals after the Flood, when, let's face it, the crops were pretty much destroyed (minus the highly nutritious kelp crop, which apparently didn't play a huge role in ancient Jewish cuisine). In some Eskimo cultures, the bladders of slain animals must be preserved. Then in a ritual, the bladders are released back into the sea, freeing the animals' souls so that they can return to life. For the Greeks, killing an animal could be fully justified only by killing it for a deity. Thus the sacrifice is done in honor of a god/dess, who is inevitably beyond reproach, and humans just happen to get a meal out of it as well.

Figure 7.2
Sacrifice to Athena, black-figure amphora, cir-
cumference 105 cm, h. 47 cm (52 cm with
cover), ca. 550–525 BCE. From Vulci, Italy.
Antikensammlung, Staatliche Museen, Berlin,
Germany, Inv. F 1686. (Antikensammlung,
Staatliche Museen, Berlin, Germany/Johannes
Laurentius/Art Resource, NY)

That's the next important aspect of sacrifice—party. A large-scale sacrifice
is basically a giant barbeque held in one or more deities' honor. The animal is
killed at the altar, flayed, butchered, and cooked, at which point all participants in the ritual feast with and entertain the attending deity/ies. The main
point is to please the deity, for whom a sacrifice is functionally dinner theater.
So much is recounted in one of our earliest descriptions of such a sacrifice as
preserved in the first book of the *Iliad*. Apollo had sent a plague to punish
the Greek army for insulting his priest and kidnapping the priest's daughter.
Forced to relent, the Greeks agreed to release the girl. To make amends
to Apollo, the contingent brought the girl home and held a sacrifice in
honor of the god, while the priest prayed for their collective well-being
(ll. 447–474):

Quickly they set up the sacred hecatomb
For the god, one after another, about the well-built altar;
They washed their hands and then took up the sprinkling barley.
For them Khryses made a great prayer, raising his hands,
"Hear me, Silver Bow, who rules in strength Khrysê
And holy Killa of Tenedos.
In the past you heard my prayer
And honoring me you smote the host of the Akhaians.
And so now accomplish my desire,
And ward off the dreadful plague from the Danaans."
So he spoke praying, and Phoibos Apollo heard him.
And then they prayed and scattered the barley.
First they drew back and slaughtered and flayed [the victims],
Then butchered the thighs and covered them with fat,
Double-folding it, and laid raw flesh upon them.
The old man burnt them on a stake, gleaming wine he poured
On top. The young men near him held forks in their hands.
But when the thighs were burnt and they ate the entrails,
They chopped up the other parts and spitted them,
And they carefully roasted them, and drew them all off the spits.
And when they finished their efforts and readied the feast,
They feasted, nor was any heart denied a fair portion.
But when they put away their desire for drink and food,
The young men filled the kraters with drink,
Which they distributed to all the cups to begin.
Then all day they supplicated the god with song,
The Akhaian youths singing a lovely paian,
Singing to the Far-Worker. And he rejoiced in his chest hearing it.

Sacrifice could also take place on a far more modest and quotidian scale. In his *Works and Days*, the poet Hesiod recommends (ll. 338–341):

At other times supplicate with libations and sacrifices,
Both at bed-time and the coming of holy light,
So that they will have for you a happy heart and mind,
So that you may buy the land-plots of others, not another yours.

Most commonly, though, sacrifices were a family event, although what might constitute "family" could vary considerably. For the daily sacrifices mentioned by Hesiod, close family took part, and the ritual was typically led by the oldest male member of the family. So close-knit were such familial rituals that participation in them could count as evidence of familial status, as occurred in a lawsuit in Athens (Isaios 8, 15–16):

Moreover we have other proofs to provide on these matters, so that you will know that we are [children] of Kiron's daughter. For such things are to be expected of children from his daughter: He never, ever offered any sacrifice without us, but if he should sacrifice something small or large, we were always present and we sacrificed with him. And not only were we summoned for these things, but he even brought us to the country Dionysia, always, and we watched with him and sat by him at all the festivals we went to with him. And when sacrificing to Zeus Ktesios, about which sacrifice he was most zealous and neither admitted slaves nor free strangers, but he himself did everything by himself, and we joined in those and we handled the sacred things and helped out and did all the other stuff with him, and he prayed to grant us health and good possessions, as is reasonable, as he was our granddad.

On a grander scale, sacrificial events were arranged by the *genê* (sing.: *genos*), what we might call today a clan or extended family. Such rituals would take place not at home, but at the receiving deity's sanctuary, where the sacrifice was performed on the deity's altar. Normally a priest or priestess (depending on the specific cult of the specific deity) would perform or at least oversee the rite. Thus a fourth-century inscription from the Athenian Acropolis recounts (*LSCG #31*):

> Gods.
>   Philton says to sacrifice offerings to Poseidon and to Erekhtheus, the sacred things received for the good luck of the Council and the people of Athens and the members of the tribe of Erekhtheus. The priest sacrifices according to the old ways and the oracle—an ox, a bull, and a full-grown sheep. He will spend whatever funds there are. He will arrange on behalf of the Erekhtheus tribe contests in the festival . . . The managers will manage the festival according to the written regulations.

Here we see again the combination of sacrifice and festival that the Greek used to entertain their deities.

In the absence of an official cult functionary, "lay" people could enact the ritual themselves, merely offering a token payment to the official priest(ess). So much is recounted in a fourth-century inscription from the island of Kos, pertaining to the cult of Herakles (*LSCG 119*):

> Whenever the genos sacrifices, give to the priest of Herakles the tongues and entrails and forearms and a double portion of meat and the skin. If an individual should sacrifice, he will give to the priest the tongues and entrails and forearms and a double portion of meat. Let the sacrificer call out for a priest, but if the priest is not present, let someone qualified offer sacrifice in the priest's stead. . . . After the event return the paraphernalia to the priest. Likewise for the other priests, as many as have bought priesthoods according to the regulations.

A major part of the sacrificial festivities, and religious praxis in general, was the *pompê*, literally a parade or procession to whatever ritual was taking place. Some such processions were massive, multiday affairs, such as the two-day procession from Athens to Eleusis at the start of the Eleusinian Mysteries. During this event, initiates walked over 20 kilometers, bathed in public, washed piglets, were ritually insulted by clowns, and literally partied all night. The pompê was a highly structured event, with strict regulations as to who was to take part, where they were to walk, and what they were to carry. One of our most detailed descriptions comes from a second-century inscription from Magnesia in Turkey pertaining to the cult of Artemis (*LSAM* 32):

> The official Crown-Bearer together with the priest and the priestess of Artemis Leukophryenê will in perpetuity lead the procession in the month of Artemision on the twelfth day, and sacrifice the designated bull. In the procession will also be the council of elders, the priests, the magistrates (both elected and appointed by lot), the ephebes, the youths, the boys, the victors in the Leukophyrenê games, and the victors in the other crown-bearing games. The Crown-Bearer, while leading the procession, will carry *xoana* [wooden statues] of all twelve gods in most beautiful attire and will erect a round structure in the agora by the altar of the twelve gods, and he will lay out three couches of the finest quality and will also provide music: a shawm-player, a syrinx-player, and a lyre-player.

Similar details come from a fourth-century inscription from Eretria (*LSCG* 92, 35ff):

> The demarkhs arrange the *pompê* in the agora, where the sacred things are sold: first are the state property and the prize, then the selected objects, then things pertaining to the private citizens, if someone wishes to join the procession. All the musical competitors join the procession, so that the procession and sacrifice will be as lovely as possible. They will inscribe the decree on an erected stele and place it in the sanctuary of Artemis, so that the sacrifice and music competition for Artemis will endure thus for all time, as long as Eretria is free and thriving and autocratic.

As both inscriptions make clear, music was a common element of religious rituals, as were both musical and athletic competitions (see Chapter 4). Many competitions featured both athletic and artistic events, while others focused on one or the other. All over the Archaic Greek world poets like the Homeridai recited original hymns to the deities in such competitions. In Athens from the sixth century, two great civic celebrations—the Greater Dionysia and the Lenaia—were occasions when playwrights and producers competed to produce the best dramas in honor of Dionysos. The Panathenaiac Festival featured both musical and athletic competitions. Here rhapsodes competed to perform the best recitations of Homer, while runners raced for prizes of amphorae filled with precious Athenian olive oil.

The truly great competitions, though, were the Panhellenic Four: Olympic, Nemean, Isthmian, and Delphic. The Olympic Games are the earliest, dating to 776; a common means of reckoning time in ancient Greece was to tell in which Olympiad an event took place. Competitions included poetry and song, foot and chariot racing, boxing, wrestling, and the pankration, which was a no-holds-barred fighting event during which competition got so vicious that at one of the Olympics, victory went to a guy who actually died in the ring. The competitions were segregated by sex. The main events at the Olympics were for men; women had separate competitions at the Olympic *Heraia*. However, in the chariot races, victory went to whoever raised the horses, and in the early fourth century, the Spartan princess Kyniska won the Olympic four-horse chariot competition.

To win at the games brought great social status, both to the individual and his/her polis (much like the Olympics today). Honor was the main prize. Victors at the Panhellenic games got leafy circlets to wear on their heads (laurel for the Delphic Games, celery for the Nemean), poetry composed in their honor by such illuminati as Pindar, and the right to dedicate pictures or statues of themselves at the sanctuary. In some poleis, like Athens, victors got free dinner at city hall.

One can see a good example of all of these elements of public worship coming together in a three-day long festival in Sparta called the Hyakinthia, held in honor of the hero Hyakinthos and the Olympian deity Apollo. According to the historian Polykrates as preserved in the third-century CE work *Deipnosophistai* by Athenaios (4.139d–f):

> Polykrates in his *On the Lakedaimonians* relates that the Lakonians accomplish the sacrifice of the Hyakinthia over the course of three days, and because of the mourning which takes place for Hyakinthos they neither crown themselves for the feasts nor bring in bread nor give other pastries with side dishes, and they don't sing paians to the god or anything else of the sort that they do in the other sacrifices. But with much good order they dine and depart. In the midst of the three days is a colorful spectacle with great and noteworthy festivals. For the boys play kithara while wearing high-belted khitons, and they all sing to the flute along with a plectrum running the chords in anapestic rhythm, singing to the god with a sharp pitch; and others cross through the theater on decorated horses. And full choruses of young men enter and sing some of the national songs, and dancers mingling amongst them do the old moves along with flute and voice. And some of the maidens are carried on wicker carriages that are elaborately prepared, while the others parade in yoked chariots in competition, and the whole city bustles and is in delight for the spectacle. That day they sacrifice a full complement of offerings, and all the citizens feast their acquaintances and their individual slaves. No one refrains from the sacrifice, and it happens that the city empties for the event.

Private Piety

Although it is basically impossible to get into the personal thoughts of the ancient Greeks, we do know a bit about how they individually practiced religion, at least as far as concerns issues such as prayer and promises to the deities. The public sacrifices mentioned earlier were just that, public, but even in these public arenas, there was recognized space (so to speak) for private petitions. Certain texts indicate that there were moments in group activities when individuals could personally address the deities. Thus a rather familiar-sounding inscription from fourth-century Oropos reads (in part) (LSCG 69, 25ff.):

> When he is present, the priest will pray over the offerings and place them on the altar. When he is not, the sacrificer will do this, and during the sacrifice each person prays individually.

At other times, groups were led in prayer by a designated herald, as is recounted by Thucydides of the Athenians about to depart on the (disastrous) Sicilian Expedition (6.32):

> At that time silence was signaled by trumpet, and the customary prayers before send-off were made, not by each ship individually, but all together led by a herald. And having mixed the wine in the kraters among the whole army, both those on board and the arkhons poured libations with drinking cups of silver and gold. They prayed together, both the throng of citizens on land, and if anyone else there wished them well. Having sung the paian and finished the libation they set off.

By far the best evidence for personal prayers in ancient Greece is votive inscriptions, the dedicatory poems that accompanied objects that the Greeks promised and gave to their deities in thanksgiving for prayers fulfilled. Sometimes we have the objects themselves that bear the inscriptions, such as a marble statue base dedicated by the woman Mikythê in Athens (IG I³ 857):

> Mikythê dedicated to Athena this statue, having promised a tithe on behalf of both her child and herself. Eupliron made (it).

Other times the inscriptions were preserved in anthologies, such as Book Six of the so-called Greek Anthology. Here we find some of the most illuminating sentiments of the ancient Greeks.

> (#24) To the Syrian Goddess his fishing net worn out in vain
> Heliodoros dedicated in the porch of this temple;
> Pure of any caught fish it is, but in it lots of
> Seaweed caught on the well-moored anchorage.
>
> (#39) The three Samians—Satyrê and Herakleia and
> Euphro, daughters of Xouthos and Melitê,
> The one the much whirling servant of the spidery warp—
> A spindle, not without the long distaff;

The other the busy comb of the thick-woven peploi—
Loud-sounding! The third her basket delighting in wool.
With these they had a long working life, Lady
Athena—your workwomen dedicated them to you.

(#40) The two oxen are mine, they are made of grain. Be gracious, Demeter,
Receive them out of barley, not from the herd.
Let the two real oxen live, and fill the land
With grain, granting in turn rich grace.
For your truth-loving field-laborer is already eighty-four
Dear years old,
He never reaped Corinth [wealth], nor ever tasted
harsh, starving poverty.

(#59) To the Paphian garlands, to Pallas the lock of hair,
To Artemis a belt Kallirhoê dedicated;
For she found the suitor she wanted, and had a temperate
Youth, and having children bore boys.

(#280) Timareta before her marriage dedicated her tambourine, her
Beloved ball, her hair-guarding snood,
And her dolls to [Artemis] Limnatis, girl to girl, as is fit,
And the dolls' dresses to Artemis.
Daughter of Leto, set your hand over the child Timareta,
And purely save her purity.

(#178) Receive me, Herakles, the holy arms of Arkhestratos,
So that resting before the polished porch
I might come into full old age, listening to dance and song.
May the hateful contest of Enyalios [Ares] bugger off!

(#94) To you this hand-beaten drum;
And shrill-voiced, hollow-rimmed cymbals;
And double, horn-sounding flute, on which once
He shouted for joy, whirling his neck about;
And the double-edged, blood-letting axe—
To you, lion chariot Rhea, Klytosthenes
Dedicated, his wilding feet having grown old.

Of course, there were also the other kinds of prayers, more commonly
referred to as curses. One such curse, dated to the third century BCE, was discovered inscribed on a strip of lead in Athens:

I shall bind Sosiklea and her possessions and her actions and her thoughts. May
she become hateful to her friends. I shall bind her beneath empty Tartaros in
cruel bonds, and with the aid of Hekatê under the earth. Sosiklea [cursed].
Bitto [curser]. Dedicated to the Maddener Furies. (trans. Lefkowitz and Fant,
1992, no. 416)

Such texts have come to light from Attika, Boiotia, Cyprus, Epiros, Euboia, Italy, and Sicily. Some are as early as the fifth century, but cursing seems to have gotten more popular starting in the Hellenistic period.

The Greeks had two postures associated with prayer. The main one, when praying to the deities, was standing erect with either one or both hands held up to the heavens. Aristotle took this posture for granted when he wrote that "All of us humans stretch out our hands to the sky when praying" (*De Mundo* 400a16). A variation on this posture occurred when one was praying to more infernal deities, in which case the hand(s) would be stretched out palm down. Kneeling was not normal for prayer, although it was used when supplicating a human, and the clasping of hands before the body did not enter the prayer physical vocabulary until the Middle Ages, when it replicated the posture taken by a vassal swearing fealty to his lord.

Religion in Groups: Thiasoi and Orgeones

Between public, polis religion and private piety were the "clubs," groups of people in Greece who formed formal alliances to worship a specific deity or two, or possibly a local hero and/or heroine. Such clubs had different names in ancient Greece, but the most common were *thiasoi* (and its variant *thiasotai*) and *orgeones*. Originally, a thiasos (sing.) is the name of the group of roughly identical individuals who accompanied a deity, such as the maenads of Dionysos, or, later, Artemis with her nymphs. As such, a club indicated its devotion to the deity. The original meaning of orgeon is still in debate, but it may have something to do with the word *orgia*, the mania involved in the cult of Dionysos. Such clubs existed at least since the sixth century, as attested in one of the laws decreed by Solon, an early sixth-century Athenian lawgiver (*Digest* 47.22.2): "If a people or phratries or *orgeones* of heroes or *gennetai* or messmates or funerary associates or thiasotai or pirates or traders make arrangements among themselves, these will be binding unless forbidden by public decree" (trans. Kloppenborg and Ascough 2011, 55). However, they became increasingly more common in the Hellenistic and Roman periods for two main reasons. One was that the Greeks came to live more and more frequently with foreigners. Many resident merchants, slaves, and the like came to live in Athens especially in the Classical period, and these folks wanted to be able to worship their traditional deities. The Greeks were accommodating and permitted the construction of sanctuaries and temples of "foreign" deities such as Isis and Astarte (whom the Greeks understood to be an eastern version of their own Aphrodite). Likewise, the Greeks, following in the wake of Alexander, spread out into the world in greater numbers than ever before. This leads to the second reason. With the ease of mobility afforded in the Hellenistic age, the traditional structures of the polis started to break down. Communities that were once based on long-lived households in one area suddenly discovered that their young men, with or without their families, could

easily go to seek their fortunes in, say, Syria or Afghanistan. As both household and polis structures broke down, Greeks came more and more to need
alternate forms of corporate identity. Rather than having close bonds to, say,
a fellow Athenian, he/she might self-identify as a worshipper of Bendis, or perhaps the Mother of the Gods.

Although the various clubs were unique in their own ways, they did each
share certain common attributes. Typically, they had a minor hierarchy whereby
the club was led by an appointed supervisor (*epimeletes*, literally "one who concerns himself with"), a treasurer (*tamias*), and a secretary (*grammateus*). There
were also priests and/or priestesses, depending on the nature of the cult. The club
members were bound to each other in a number of functions, especially helping
each other bury their dead and coming to each other's aid in times of legal crisis.
So much is evident on a late fourth-century inscription from the Piraeus, the
most important port in ancient Athens (*IG II^2 1275*):

> . . . If someone . . .
> . . . .
> . . . of the Thiasoi members. If one of them should die. . . . either son or . . . or
> father or someone very close to the member's family, having died they will go to
> the funeral, both them and all their friends, and should someone be wronged,
> they will, both them and all their friends [go help], so that all will know that we
> are pious both to the deities and to our friends. To those who do these things,
> may there be many good things, and as well for their descendants and ancestors.
> Whenever the thiasos-members ratify the law, may nothing prevail over it. If
> someone should say or do something contrary to the law, there will be an
> accusation against him for anyone so wishing of the thiasos-members, and if he
> convicts him, they will fix the penalty as seems good to the association.

Additionally, and quite importantly, the various club members spent a *lot* of
time giving each other awards for things. A very typical example, dating to
302 BCE, once again comes from the Piraeus (*IG II^2 1261A*):

> In the arkhonship of Nikokles.
> This seemed good to the thiasos-members. Since Stephanos the armorer,
> having become supervisor, cared for all of the association's affairs with all due
> diligence and strove admirably and continually on behalf of the association,
> and he conducted the procession of the Adonia according to the ancestral
> customs. For good fortune, it has seemed good to the thiasos-members to praise
> Stephanos the supervisor for his zeal and valor to the association of the thiasos
> and to crown him with an olive wreath, and to give him ten drakhmai.
> Crowned by the association he dedicated this [stele of] Demeter Homoia of
> the association.

A similar if more fragmentary example, dating to the late third century, reads
(*Agora* 16:235):

Since Hierakleia . . . wife of Antigeneides of Lamptreos was chosen by lot as priestess the year Euandros was arkhon, and both well and piously carried out her priesthood and offered the proper sacrifices and zealously did the remaining . . . she cared for the gods' bedding with all alacrity and enthusiasm, and she tended to the members of the orgeon assembly . . .

The day-to-day management and activities of such organizations were, like the honorifics given above, literally written in stone, and thus we have a pretty good idea of how a number of them functioned. As the inscriptions make quite clear, the thiasoi/orgeones were quite democratic in organization. Positions such as epimeletes were generally rotational, and some offices, such as priest or priestess, were both temporary and assigned by lot. Most of the honorifics were given after a successful term in office.

Like all organizations, money was an important factor in the functioning of the club, and dues were carefully assessed and recorded, as were fines and expenditures. Rules and regulations existed not only to organize the hierarchy, but to establish how the deity/hero/ine would be worshipped, how much it should cost, who was responsible for what, and who took what benefits from the club events. An excellent example of all these factors is presented in an early third-century inscription from the Athenian agora, which records the events surrounding the merger of two separate orgeones, one dedicated to the hero Ekhelos, and one to The Heroines (*Agora* 16:161):

Lysias son of Periandros of Plotheus said:
  Good Fortune. Thus seemed good to the orgeones. So that the association of sacrifices be kept faithfully for all time for the association which is by Kalliphanos' place and that of the Hero Ekhelos, to inscribe those owing anything to the association upon a stone stele and to erect it by the altar in the sanctuary, both the principal and interest, as much as each one owes. And to inscribe the old decrees on the stele. And to care for . . . the inscription and the erection of the stele and to calculate whatever these things will cost for the association. This seemed good to the orgeones. The Hestiator will sacrifice the sacrifice on the 17th and 18th of Hekatombaion. He will sacrifice first a piglet to the Heroines, then to the Hero a full-grown victim, and then prepare a table [of offerings], then on the last [of the month] a full-grown victim to the Hero. He will calculate whatever this will cost, and he will not spend more than the income. Let him distribute the meat to the orgeones present and half as much to their sons, and to the women of the orgeon, the free women an equal portion and half as much to the daughters, and a half share for one female attendant. Let him give the woman's share to her husband . . .

It was generally good to avoid being a deadbeat, as the sum total of your debt, both principle and interest, was carved into a nice, permanent stone stele and erected right by the altar for all to see *forever*. (Think about it: We still have them.)

One of the earliest foreign deities to receive a cult with accompanying club was Bendis, a Thracian nature goddess in many ways similar to Artemis. There appear to have been two separate clubs in honor of this goddess in Athens, one composed of resident Thracians mostly living at the port, and one of Athenian citizens. As a result, the Athenian people got a full complement of Bendis celebrations, which were apparently quite lively. The earliest description comes from Plato's *Republic*, which begins, appropriately enough, at the inauguration of just such a festival at the Piraeus (*Republic* 1.327a–328a, excerpted):

> Yesterday I went down to the Piraeus with Glaukos son of Ariston to offer prayers to the goddess and likewise wishing to see the festival and in what fashion they celebrate it, seeing as how it was the first time they held it. And indeed the procession of the country-folk seemed quite fine to me; and yet it appeared to be less done up than the one the Thracians held. Having prayed and seen everything, we turned back to the city. Then Polemarkhos son of Kephalos spied us from a distance heading homeward, and he ordered his slave-boy to run and ask us to stay a bit . . . and a bit later Polemarkhos also came, as well as Adeimantos—Glaukos' brother—and Nikeratos son of Nikias, and some others coming from the parade. Then Polemarkhos said, "O Sokrates, you fellows seem to me to be starting for the city."
>
> "Nor do you suppose badly," I said.
>
> "So then you haven't heard, you don't know?"
>
> And Adeimantos said, "Really? You don't know that there will be a lamp race this evening from horseback for the goddess?"
>
> "From horseback?" I said. "Well! That's new! Will they have torches and pass them to each other while competing on horseback? Is that what you mean?"
>
> "Precisely!" said Polemarkhos. "And they will have an all-night festival which is worth seeing; we shall set out after dinner to see the all-nighter. And we shall be with several of the young men there and chat. So stay."

It would seem that in the third century, these two groups merged, based on a third-century inscription from the Piraeus that describes the early foundation of the cult, how it was approved by Zeus's oracle at Dodona, and how the cult and club were integrated into the city's religious life (*IG* II^2 1283):

> Gods.
>
> Erected in the arkhonship of Polystratos on the 8th of Hekatombeion. At an official assembly, Sosias son of Hippokrates said: Since the Athenian people have granted to the Thracians alone of the various ethnic groups land tenure and the right to dedicate a sanctuary according to the oracle at Dodona, and to have a procession from the hearth of the prytaneion, and now the elected ones in the city are preparing the sanctuary—they think it is necessary that they be well-disposed towards each other. To this end may the orgeones appear

obedient to the city's law which bids the Thracians to lead the procession to the Piraeus; and to those orgeones in the city, once again, may they be well-disposed. Good Fortune. It seemed good to the orgeones that the procession—as they should decide it, those gathering in the city—this procession will thus proceed from the prytaneion to the Piraeus, in the same procession as those from the Piraeus, and the supervisors for the Pireaus will undertake to provide sponges in the Nymphaion and plates and water and wreaths, and in the sanctuary a breakfast just as they prepare for themselves. Whenever there are sacrifices the priest and priestess will pray, in addition to the prayers they pray for the orgeones who are in the city, in the same way, so that when these things happen the whole ethnic group might be of one mind, and the sacrifices take place to the gods, and as many other things pertaining to the ancestral customs of the Thracians and the laws of the city, and so all will be fair and pious for the whole group vis-à-vis the deities. And concerning another matter, it will be for those, if someone should wish to approach the orgeones, he will have first access after the sacred rites, and if someone of the orgeones in the city should wish to join those orgeones, it is permissible for them, and to receive a portion of the produce without payment, for life . . .

Festivities aside, the orgeones of Bendis dealt with the realia of day-to-day cult just as did all the other groups, collecting dues, tending to a sanctuary, and assessing penalties for inappropriate behavior. The fun side of Greek religion always had to be managed with laws, by-laws, and some degree of bureaucracy (*IG* II^2 1361, late fourth century, Piraeus):

As many as are inscribed on the stele or their descendants.

If someone of the orgeones who have a share in the sanctuary should sacrifice to the goddess, they shall sacrifice free of charge. If some private individual should sacrifice to the goddess, he will give to the priestess: for an infant animal: 1.5 obols and the skin and the whole right thigh; for an adult animal: 3 obols and the skin and the same thigh; for an ox: 1.5 obols and the skin. He is to give the sacred portions of females to the priestess, of males to the priest. It is not permitted to sacrifice anything by the altar in the sanctuary, or one will owe 50 drakhmai . . . So that the house and sanctuary might be repaired, the rent from the house and the sale of water is to be spent on the repairs of the sanctuary and house and nothing else, until the sanctuary and house should be repaired, unless the orgeones vote on something else . . . to the sanctuary . . . To leave the water for the resident so that he might use it. If someone should propose to put to vote counter to this law, let him owe 50 drakhmai to the goddess, both the one proposing, and the one putting to vote, and may they not take part in the association. And the supervisors will inscribe on a stele this silver owed to the goddess. The supervisors and holy-officiants will have an assembly and colloquium in the sanctuary concerning the association on the second of every month . . . They will give to the holy-officiants for the sacrifice two drakhmai—each of the orgeones who has a share in the sanctuary—in the month of Thargelion, before the 16th. Whoever lives in Athens and is healthy who does not contribute, let him owe two sacred drakhmai to the goddess. So that there might be as many orgeones of the sanctuary as possible, it is permitted for anyone who wishes to contribute . . . drakhmai to be a member of the sanctuary, and have his name inscribed on a stele. Those inscribed on the stele are approved by the orgeones and their names are given to the secretary in Thargelion.

Death

The ancient Greeks had the same problems with death as everyone else: Everyone did it, and no one really understood it. The most basic understanding of the afterlife, comparable to modern notions of heaven and hell, was that after death, people went to Hades, the realm of the dead, where they had an exceptionally boring eternal existence. By far the best descriptions of the experience of Hades, and death generally, come from Homer's *Odyssey*. In Book 11 of the *Odyssey*, Odysseus and his crew (or what's left of it) must travel to the threshold of Hades to consult the dead prophet Tiresias (the same guy as mentioned earlier in this chapter in the section on Oedipus). One of the first people Odysseus meets is his own mother, who gives him a crash course on the afterlife. First she explains how to get to Hades (*Od.* 11.155–159):

"My child, how did you come under the murky gloom
While living? It is difficult for the living to see.
For it is in the midst of great rivers and dread streams,
Ocean most of all, which one cannot cross
On foot, not unless one has a well-built ship."

Later when Odysseus tries to hug his mother, he gets another lesson on the nature of death (*Od.* 11.204–222):

So she spoke, but I went thinking in my mind
To grasp the spirit of my dead mother.
Three times then I rushed forward, and my heart pressed me to take her;
Three times she flew out of my hands like a shadow or a dream,
And a sharp pain grew great in my heart,
And I spoke winged words to her:
"My mother, why don't you stay when I want to hold you,
Although in Hades, can't we even throw our arms
Around each other and have our fill of cold lament?
Is august Persephonê stirring up a phantom
That I might grieve even more wretchedly?"
So I spoke, but my revered mother answered me:
"O my dear child, most ill-fated of men,
It is nothing Persephonê, daughter of Zeus, does to beguile you,
But this is the custom of mortals once someone has died.
For sinews no longer hold the skin and bones,

> But these things are tamed by the fierce force of the blazing fire
> When first the heart leaves the white bones,
> But the spirit flutters off like a dream."

Death, then, was when the *psykhê* (see Chapter 1) left the body. The psykhê had a continued existence in Hades, but in the absence of physical pleasures (or physical anything), that existence was deemed dull and ultimately unfulfilling. The best declaration to this effect came from Akhilleus, the one hero in Greek mythology who was functionally able to choose the time and nature of his own death. Although he opted to die young so as to avenge his friend Patrokles, he rather came to regret his decision later, as he recounted to Odysseus (*Od.* 11.488–491):

> Do not console me for dying, Shining Odysseus.
> I should wish to be a serf toiling for another man,
> Alongside one without land, one with no great livelihood,
> Than to be king of all the perished dead.

The basic understanding was that the psykhê was escorted to Hades by Hermes Psykhopompos ("Soul-Leader") once the body was buried. Yet again our best description of this process appears in the *Odyssey*, when Hermes escorts the souls/ghosts of the recently slain suitors to their literal final destination (24.1–14):

> Kyllenian Hermes summoned the spirits
> Of the suitors; he held his wand in his hands,
> Fair, golden, with which he charms the eyes of men
> When he wishes, and with which he wakes the sleeping.
> Rousing them with this he led, and the blithering dead followed.
> As when bats fly out of the inner recess of a wondrous cave,
> Twittering, when one has fallen off
> A rock clustering, and they cling to one another.
> So the blithering ones went forth together. And gracious Hermes
> Led them down dank paths.
> They went by flowing Ocean and the white rock;
> By the gates of the sun and the realm of dreams
> They went. Quickly they arrived in the meadow of asphodel;
> There spirits dwell, images of the dead.

Hermes was not necessarily a frightening creature in this aspect, as one might expect. If anything, he seemed to have a good bedside manner when dealing with the recently deceased, and artistic depictions portray him as kindly and patient.

By the fifth century at the latest, Kharon the Ferryman appeared in the Greek domain of the dead. An early fifth-century inscription from Phokis reads: "Hail Kharon, no one slanders you even when they are dead, you who release many men from toil" (trans. Garland 1985, 55). The earliest extant reference to giving the dead coins to "pay the ferryman" appears in Aristophanes's comedy *Frogs* (269–272), where Kharon charges Dionysos two obols for crossing the river of death, even though Dionysos had to do all the rowing himself. By the Hellenistic period, people were buried with coins for just this purpose.

Already by the time of Homer the notion was in place that the corpse must be buried in order to enter Hades. Even though existence in Hades was dull, it was apparently better than the alternative, which was existence trying to get into Hades and failing. Patrokles reprimanded Akhilleus for taking so long to bury him for just this reason (*Il.* 23.71–76):

> You sleep, and you are forgetful of me, Akhilleus.
> You didn't neglect me living, only now that I'm dead.
> Bury me, so that I might most quickly cross the gates of Hades.
> The souls, images of the dead, keep me distant,
> Nor do they let me mingle with them beyond the river.
> Alone I wander before the wide gates of Hades' home.

Not everyone experienced boredom in Hades. Some people were tortured mercilessly. Such was the fate of those who really pissed off the deities, such as Sisyphos, who once kidnapped Hades, and Ixion, who tried to rape Hera (note the earlier statement about much divine justice involving human idiocy). Odysseus describes seeing a number of these wretched souls from the threshold of Hades (*Od.* 11.604–629):

> And I saw Tityos, son of glorious Gaia
> Lying on the ground. He lay nine plethora long.
> Two vultures on either side of him devoured his liver,
> Penetrating his entrails. He could not hold them off with his hands.
> For he dragged off Leto, glorious spouse of Zeus,
> When she went to Pytho via lovely Penopeus.
> And I saw Tantalos there, suffering greatly;
> He stood in a lake which reached to his chin.
> He seemed to be thirsty, for he could grasp nothing to drink—
> Just as often as the old man bowed, striving to drink,
> Just so often the water was lost, gulped back up, and about his feet
> The black earth appeared, the daimon drying it up.
> And trees with lofty leaves pouring forth fruit top to bottom—
> Pears and pomegranates and shining apples,
> And sweet figs and olives bloomed.
> Whenever the old man strove to reach them with his hands,
> Ever the wind blew them into the cloudy shadows.
> And I saw Sisyphos there, suffering greatly,
> Lifting a huge stone with both hands.
> Truly he pushed against the stone with hands and feet,

Shoving it up that hill. But when he was about to
Push it over the top, then an overpowering force would cast it back,
And again he would roll that shameless stone from the plain.
Then he, stretching, would shove it back, sweat
Pouring from his limbs, dust rising from his head.

Other than these rather extreme examples (accosting a *goddess!*), there is little evidence in Homer that there was reward or punishment for one's life in the underworld. All the dead just hung around, twiddling their thumbs. By the fifth century, however, the notion of postmortem judgment does seem to enter into the Greek conception of death. So much is directly stated by Pindar in his *Second Olympian Ode* (ll. 57–74):

... There immediately the helpless minds of the dead
Pay the penalty—sinful acts in this realm of Zeus
Someone judges beneath the earth, giving sentences with harsh necessity.
But always in equal nights, equal days
They have sunlight, a life without toil
The Good receive, not working earth with force of hand,
Nor the water of the sea for a shallow livelihood. But alongside the honored
    ones
Of the deities, those who respected good oaths dwell tearless
Forever. But others endure pains unbeholdable.
Those who have endured three times
Remaining in either place, keeping the soul from all unrighteousness,
Travel the path of Zeus unto the tower of Kronos.
There Ocean breezes blow about the isle of the blessed,
Flowers of gold blaze,
Some on the shore of glorious trees, some the water nourishes.
With chaplets and garlands of these they wreath their hands
According to the straight judgments of Rhadamanthys.

The reference to the "tower of Kronos" alludes to one of the earliest Greek conceptions of what we might term heaven—the Elysian Fields. Unlike modern non-Calvinistic notions of heaven, though, not everyone could get into the blissful afterlife; it was reserved for very specific categories of people. One of these categories consisted of the race of heroes, the fourth race of men according to Hesiod's *Works and Days* (ll. 166–170):

To them Father Zeus, son of Kronos, gave a living and abode
Far from humans in which they dwell, at the ends of the earth.
And there they live with carefree hearts
On the island of the blessed by deep-swirling Ocean;
Joyous heroes, for whom honey-sweet fruit
The fruitful land bears thrice a year—blooming.
Far from the immortals; Kronos rules over them,

For the father of men and gods released his bonds.
Honor and glory equally accompany these last ones.

Another man who got a blessed afterlife was Menelaos, the husband of
Helen. As a matter of fact, his "afterlife" was so blessed that he didn't even
have to die first—he just went right to his final "reward." This is related
in the *Odyssey*, Book 4, when the Old Man of the Sea tells Menelaos
(ll. 561–570):

For you it is not ordained, O Menelaos, fostered by Zeus,
To die in horse-pasturing Argos and to follow death,
But to the Elysian Fields and the ends of the earth
The immortals will lead you. There is blond Rhadamanthys,
Where the easiest life exists for humans,
Never is there snow, nor great winter storms nor shadows ever,
But always Ocean sends forth gentle breezes of the blowing
West Wind to refresh humans.
This because you have Helen and are son-in-law to Zeus.

An additional description of the Elysian Fields comes, once again, from
Pindar (Dirge 129+130):

For them below the sun's strength shines, while it is night here.
In meadows of red roses their park is shaded
By an incense tree weighted down with golden fruit . . .
And some with horses and sports, some with draughts,
Some with lyres enjoy themselves, and by them has
Bloomed the full flower of joy.
A lovely scent moves throughout the land,
Ever mixing incense with fire upon the altars
Of the deities—visible far and wide.
Opposite from there petty rivers of murky night
Spew forth endless shadow.

By the sixth century at the latest, Mystery initiates as described earlier in
this chapter in the sections on Demeter and Dionysos also could look forward
to a joyous afterlife. One might say that the Greeks grew more hopeful about
death over time. From an experience of irredeemable, unrelenting boredom,
there emerged more and more ways to get a shot at eternal bliss.

One of the more ironic things about death is that all of our information
about it comes from living people. This not only means that all of our data
are horribly suspect, but that these data are inevitably influenced by the concerns and predispositions of the living. For example, in spite of the fact that
the dead are disembodied psykhai wholly deprived of a physical existence, as
described by Odysseus's mother, the Greeks were nevertheless still rather

Figure 7.3
Hero and Heroine Relief. Lakonian gravestone
with enthroned pair, Late Archaic, marble, 72 by
65 by 21 cm, ca. 540 BCE. From Krysapha,
Lakonia. (Antikensammlung, Staatliche Museen,
Berlin, Germany/Jürgen Liepe/Art Resource, NY)

certain that the dead needed things like food and clothing. And so there
existed rituals to bring food, wine, and even clothing to the dead at certain,
regular intervals. At the least, this was done once a year, either by family
members, or, with the more highly honored dead, by the state. Thus the Plataians remarked to the Spartans during the Peloponnesian War (Thuc. 3, 58,
4): "Look at the tombs of your fathers who were killed by the Persians and are
buried in our country; every year we have done them honor at the public
expense, presenting them garments and all the proper offerings, bringing to
them the first fruits of everything which at the various seasons our land has
produced; and these offerings were made by us as friends and from a friendly
country, as allies to our old comrades in battle" (trans. Crawley 1910).

The idea that the dead enjoy feasts in the afterlife appears in multiple
funerary plaques known by the German name *Totenmahl*, literally "Feast of
the Dead." These low-relief sculptures, which first appear around 400 BCE
and have been found in Attika, Sparta, Argos, Corinth, Boiotia, Aitolia,
Poteidaia, Melos, Delos, Thasos, Samos, Asia Minor, and Italy, show the
deceased reclining (if male) or seated (if female) and enjoying a bite to eat
or a fine glass of wine (see Figure 7.3).

The dead also seem to need clothing. This was brought very much to the fore by an incident that Herodotos recorded concerning Periandros, the second tyrant of Corinth (5.91e):

> . . . One day Periandros stripped naked all the women of Corinth on account of his wife Melissa. For he sent a messenger to the Thesprotians by the Akheron River for a necromancer so as to inquire about the property of a friend, and Melissa [dead at the hands of her husband] said that she would neither point out nor relate where the goods lay in the land, for she was cold and naked because they buried her with clothes that were unburnt, ergo useless to her. And to prove that what she said was true, she mentioned that Periandros tossed loaves of bread into a cold oven. This was then related to Periandros, and the latter comment was meaningful to him, since he had had sex with Melissa's corpse. As soon as the messenger gave him this message, Periandros sent all the Corinthian women to the temple of Hera, and they went to the "festival" decked out in their finest apparels. But Periandros, having placed spearmen in ambush, stripped them all at once, both free woman and servant, and bore the clothing to a hole and burnt them, calling upon Melissa. Having done these things and having sent a second time to the necromancer, the ghost of Melissa told him where in the land he had put his friend's property.

Much of our information about the physical needs of the dead come from the grave goods buried with them. Such burial gifts were very much influenced by time and place, as sumptuary laws were passed at different times in different areas of Greece, often limiting what could or could not be placed in a grave. Fashion was also a deciding factor: In the early Iron Age, families often flaunted their wealth by burying their dead with rich goods. Later, it became more fashionable to flaunt one's family's wealth through dedications in a temple, where it could be seen for many generations. Thus, grave goods fluctuate quite a bit, which has far more to do with the concerns of the living than the perceived needs of the dead.

Some graves/tombs were utterly amazing, more along the lines of what one would expect from Egypt rather than from Athens. As stated previously, such tombs were more likely to come from the early period, when wealthy graves were all the rage. One such example is the so-called Tomb of the Priestesses from Eleutherna, Crete. This was a building reaching 7.5 feet in height and 9 by 10.5 feet in area. The center of the room preserved a stone table, while the northern and western walls preserved large amphorae originally containing liquids such as wine and oil. Between the table and the amphorae were numerous bronze objects, including cups, lamps, a scale, and several ceramic vases. Most importantly, the tomb contained the remains of approximately four female skeletons, all bearing similar genetic traits and thus probably related. The women were buried adorned with golden jewelry, bead necklaces, scarabs, earrings and bracelets made of gold, silver, quartz, amber, and a glass-like substance known as Egyptian Blue. Buried with the women were several bronze objects of apparent religious usage, including a bronze bull, a saw, and a small ladle, all implements associated with sacrificial and libation rituals. The combination of wealthy artifacts and ritual goods sent to the hereafter with a family of obviously important women led to the hypothesis that these women were a family, even a dynasty, of priestesses, sent to the afterlife with the tools of their trade and marks of their status (Bonn-Muller 2010).

In more mundane circumstances, adults were often buried with practical or representative items, perhaps a spindle for a woman or a sword (ritually bent and "killed") for a man. If the family held a ritual feast or drink at the grave during the funeral, dishware might accompany the deceased in the grave. Certainly the most touching grave goods were those found with children. Toddlers might be buried with a favorite toy or feeding bottle. In Athens specifically, children who died before they were old enough to have their first taste of wine at the Anthesteria festival were buried with a miniature *chous*, a tiny juglet containing just enough wine for a three-year-old.

In addition to the goods in the graves were the markers above the graves. Once again, these could vary considerably based on region. In Sparta, for example, by the laws of Lykourgos only men who died in battle and women who died in childbirth could even have marked graves. Elaborate grave markers existed in Archaic and early Hellenistic Athens (between which times sumptuary laws prevented the erection of lavish grave markers). Typical were marble stele; later, marble grave markers shaped like *lekythoi* (tall, slim oil jugs) came into fashion. These stele and giant lekythoi were decorated by family members, usually women, who were expected to attend to the graves of kinfolk. Stele were decorated with colorful ribbons, bread was brought to the site (once again, the dead gotta eat!), and libations of wine and oil were poured upon the graves (see Figure 7.4). The oil was brought in lekythoi, which is how that vase shape came to be so closely associated with the grave, and, amusingly, with women!

Ultimately, of course, the living really had little idea of what death was all about, and opinions varied. This uncertainty was perhaps best expressed by Sokrates at his trial, after he found himself condemned to death. Musing on his fate he spoke (*Apology* 40c–41c):

> Let us consider in this way too what great hope there is that death is a good thing. For death is one or the other of two things. For either to die is to be nothing or to have no perception of anything; or—as they say—it happens to be some change and a migration of the soul from someplace here to someplace else. Now if it's perceiving nothing, like sleep when someone should sleep seeing no dreams, then death would be an amazing boon. For I would think that if someone had to choose that night in which he slept so soundly that he saw no dreams, and the other nights and days of his own life, and compared

Figure 7.4
Attic white-ground lekythos with grave decoration scene, fifth century BCE. (Drawing by Paul C. Butler)

them with that night, and thinking about it he had to consider how many better and sweeter days and night he lived in his life than that night, I should think that not only some random individual, but even the Great King [of Persia], would find few nights and days better than that one. If then death is thus, I say it's a boon. For then all of time appears to be no more than a single night.

Now if death is like moving from here to someplace else, and what they say is true, how all the dead are there, what greater good than this is there, O men of the jury? For then someone arriving in Hades, free from those claiming to be judges, will then find the real judges, such as they say judge there—Minos and Rhadamanthys and Aiakos and Triptolemos and others, as many of the demi-gods who were just in their own lives. Now, is that really a bad change? And moreover, to meet Orpheus and Mousaios and Hesiod and Homer—how much would any one of you give? I should wish to die often if this is true! And for me myself this would be an amazingly good pass-time there: whenever I should encounter Palamedes and Telamonian Ajax, and if someone else of the old ones died through an injustice, to compare my experience with theirs—and I don't think that this would be unpleasant; and best of all, I might cross-examine them and question them there, just like I did here in life—who of them is wise and who only thinks so, or not. How much, men of the jury, would you give to question him who led the whole army to Troy, or Odysseus, or Sisyphos, or the multitude of men or women one might mention, to talk with them there and be with them and question them with limitless joy? Because, really, those there don't kill you for it. For those there are happier than those here, and spend their remaining time immortal—if what they say is true.

One could certainly argue that Sokrates was an eternal optimist. Far less so was the Hellenistic poet Kallimakhos, who mooted in his 13th *Epigram*:

"Did she indeed die because of you Kharida?" "If you mean
Arimma child of Kyrenaios, it was because of me."
"O Kharida, what are the things below?" "Lots of darkness." "What roads upward?
"Lies!" "And Ploutos [Hades]?" "A myth." "We are undone!"
These words of mine are true. If you want something sweet,
A big bull of Pellaios to Hades!

Whereas the pragmatist Alkaios sang:

Drink and be drunk with me, Melanippos. Do you
Think when you have crossed the great fuming river,
You will ever return from Hell to see the clean
Bright light of the sun? Do not strive for wild hopes.
Even the son of Aiolos, King Sisyphos, wisest of men,
Thought that he had eluded death. But for all his brains
Fate made him recross Akheron, and the son of Kronos

Assigned him a terrible trial below the dark earth.
Come, I beg you not to brood about these hopeless
Matters while we are young. We shall suffer what must
Be suffered. When the wind is waiting in the north,
A good captain will not swing into open sea. (trans. Barnestone, 62–63)

If nothing else, the ancient Greeks understood that death was inevitable, often unfair, and certainly heartbreaking. No better expression of these sentiments can be offered here than the epitaph of Xenokleia, who lived in fourth-century Attika (*IG* II^2 12335):

Kind Xenokleia.
Xenokleia, the daughter of Nikarkhos,
having left behind two young girls perished completely,
piteous, suffering because of the death of her child Phoinix,
who died eight-years-old on the high seas.
He who does not know lamentation—he, Xenokleia, does not
Pity your fate. You, having left behind two young girls
For love of a dead child, who has an open
Tomb, lying in the murky sea.

THE HOMERIC HYMN TO DEMETER

I begin to sing of fair-haired Demeter, Holy Goddess,
herself and her slim-ankled daughter, whom Aidoneus[1]
seized; broad-browed, deep-thundering Zeus gave her
unbeknownst to Demeter of the golden sickle and shining fruit.
She was playing with the deep-bosomed daughters of Ocean,   (5)
plucking flowers—roses and crocuses and fair violets
of the meadows, as well as soft iris and hyacinth,
narcissus too, which Gaia grew as bait for the fair-bosomed girl
by the plans of Zeus, pleasing the Receiver-of-Many.[2]
The wonder gleamed, a wonder for all to see—   (10)
immortal deities and mortal humans.
From its roots one hundred heads grew forth,
and it smelled most sweet; all the wide sky above
and all the earth laughed, as well as the salty swell of the sea.
She, being truly amazed, grasped with both hands   (15)
to pluck the lovely plaything. But the broad-pathed earth gaped open
upon the Nysian Plain, whence sprang out the Much-Receiving King[3]
with immortal horses, the son of much-hymned Kronos.
Having seized the unwilling, wailing girl, he
drove off in the golden chariot. She cried out at the top of her lungs,   (20)
beseeching her father, highest and best son of Kronos.
No one of the immortals nor of mortal humans
heard her voice, nor the olive trees with their shining fruit,
save only the daughter of Perses, ever of youthful spirit,
outside of her cave—shining-veiled Hekatê,   (25)
and King Helios, shining son of Hyperion.
They heard the girl crying for her father Kronides.[4] But he was
sitting all alone far from the gods, in his much-besought temple
receiving fine sacrifices from mortal humans.
At the suggestion of his brother Zeus, he led away the unwilling girl,   (30)
the Many-Named Receiver-of-Many,
with immortal horses, the much-sung son of Kronos.
As long as the goddess saw the earth and the starry sky
and the swift-flowing, fishy sea
and the light of the sun, she still hoped   (35)
to see her dear mother and the race ever-living deities,
so long hope enchanted her so grieving mind.
Mountain peaks and the depths of the sea resounded
under her immortal voice; her revered mother heard it.
Sharp pain seized her heart, and about her tresses   (40)

---

[1]Hades.

[2]Also Hades.

[3]Yep, Hades again . . .

[4]"Son of Kronos," Zeus.

she donned an ambrosial veil, and with her dear hands
she cast a blue shawl about both shoulders,
and then she rushed like a bird-of-prey, raving
over land and sea, but no one wanted to tell
her the truth, neither deities nor mortal humans,   (45)
nor did any omen birds come as trusty messengers.
Nine days then did revered Deo[5] go about over land
bearing shining torches in her hands,
and she tasted neither ambrosia nor sweet nectar ever,
being so grieved, nor did she bathe.   (50)
But on the 10th day when glistening Dawn emerged,
Hekatê came to her, bearing a torch in her hands,
and greeting her she spoke:
"Revered Demeter, season-bearer, of shining gifts,
has someone of the heavenly deities or of mortal men   (55)
seized Persephonê and broken your heart?
For I heard a voice, but I didn't see with my eyes
who it was. I'm telling you the whole truth."
So spoke Hekatê. And the fair-haired
daughter of Rhea didn't answer her at all, but swiftly   (60)
she darted off with her, bearing flaming torches in her hands.
She came to Helios, light of gods and humans.
She stood before his horses and this goddess of goddesses spoke:
"Helios, if you truly revere me as a goddess, if ever indeed
I, either in word or deed, have cheered your heart—   (65)
I bore a girl, a sweet child fair of face,
whose cry I heard through the barren air
as she was abducted, but I didn't see it with my eyes.
But, since truly you look down upon the whole earth and along the sea
with your beams from the shining air,   (70)
truly tell me about my dear child, if somehow
someone took the unwilling girl by force when my back was turned,
carrying her off, someone of the gods or of mortal men."
So she spoke, and the son of Hyperion answered her with a word:
"Fair-haired daughter of Rhea, Queen Demeter,   (75)
you will know, for indeed I greatly revere and pity you,
suffering like this over your slim-ankled child. No one
of the immortals is guilty, save for cloud-gathering Zeus,
who gave her to Hades to be called his blooming bride—
his own brother! And he has led her under the murky gloom   (80)
having seized her, crying greatly, with his horses.
But, goddess, cease this terrible lamentation; nor should you
maintain in vain this boundless anger. He's not an unseemly
son-in-law among the immortals, Aidoneus of the Many-Names,
your own brother and family. As far as honor goes   (85)

---

[5]Demeter.

he received during that first great tri-partition of the world as his share
to be ruler of those with whom he dwells."
So speaking he called to his horses; and with a "Tally-Ho!"
they swiftly drew the fleet chariot like lithely-winged birds.
A dreadful, harrowing grief came upon Demeter's heart;   (90)
she was infuriated with cloud-gathering Kronides.
She abandoned the gathering of deities and left blessed Olympos,
and she went to the cities of men and the rich earth
disguising her face for a long time. No one of mankind
recognized her, nor did any deep-bosomed women.   (95)
First then she came to the house of wise Keleus,
who was at that time the ruler of fragrant Eleusis.
She sat by the road, grieving in her dear heart,
by the Maiden's Well, where the citizen women drew water
in the shade. An olive tree grew above.   (100)
She resembled an old woman, one barred
from childbearing and the gifts of garland-loving Aphrodite.
Such women are nurse-maids to the children of law-giving kings
and the care-takers in their resounding houses.
The daughters of Eleusinian Keleus saw her   (105)
as they were coming to draw water, so that they might bring
it in bronze buckets to the dear house of their father.
Four of them, like goddesses, having a youthful bloom—
Kallidikê and Kleisidikê and lovely Demo,
and Kallithoê, who was the oldest of them.   (110)
They didn't recognize her—it is difficult for mortals to see the deities.
Standing close by she uttered a winged word:
"Who are you, Old Lady, and from where among men of old?
Why have you gone far away from the city and not come to the houses?
There are women in shadowy halls there   (115)
of your own age, just as old as you, even, and younger,
who would welcome you in both word and deed."
So she spoke; the revered one of the goddesses answered her thusly:
"Dear children, whoever you are of womankind,
greetings. I shall tell you. To tell you the truth would not be improper. (120)
Doso is my name; my revered mother gave it to me.
Now then, I have come from Crete upon the broad back of the sea
against my will, taken by force;
pirates led me here. They, then,
traveled by swift ship to Thorikos. There the women   (125)
disembarked onto the mainland *en masse* as well as the men,
and they prepared dinner by the ship's prow.
But my heart did not desire a tasty supper.
Secretly hastening across the dark land
I fled those arrogant commandos, so that they   (130)
might not carry me off unransomed.
And so wandering I arrived here, I don't know where I am,

what land this is or who is here.
But may all who have homes on Olympos
give you husbands, and may you have children,   (135)
as parents wish. But pity me, girls.
Tell me clearly so that I might understand,
truly, dear children, to whose house might I go,
of a man or a woman, so that I might find work
in good faith? Such work as might be done by an old woman?   (140)
Maybe even cuddling a new-born baby in my arms
I could nurse him well, and I could care for a house,
and in the innermost of the lovely rooms I could fluff up the lord's bed
and teach the women their tasks."
So spoke the goddess, and immediately the maiden girl replied to her— (145)
Kallidikê, Keleus' fairest daughter:
"Dear Mother, we humans must endure patiently the gifts of the gods, perforce,
for indeed they are much stronger.
But I'll tell you these things clearly, and I'll name
the men of influence and honor   (150)
who protect the people and the city towers
by counsel and straight judgments.
There's shrewd Triptolemos and Diokles
and Plyxenos and noble Eumolpos
and Dolikhos and our own heroic father.   (155)
All of these have wives who care for their homes.
Not one of them, seeing your face,
would scorn you or turn you from the house,
but they will receive you, for you're god-like in appearance.
If you wish, wait a bit, and we'll go to our father's house   (160)
and ask our deep-bosomed mother Metaneira
about all of this. She might ask
you to come to our place and not go to the others' houses.
She has a dear son being raised in the well-decked halls;   (165)
If you would rear him and bring him to the full bloom of youth
anyone of womankind would easily grow jealous seeing you,
such things would Mom give you for your nannying."
So she spoke, and the goddess nodded her head, and they carried off the
shining water pails and went off proudly.   (170)
Quickly they came to their father's great house, and quickly they told
their mother what they had seen and heard, and immediately she
told them to go hire her for copious wages.
And like deer or calves in spring,
frolicking in the meadows, sated at heart with pasturage,   (175)
so did they, holding the folds of their lovely dresses,
dart along the wagon-traveled valley; about their shoulders
their tresses danced like crocus flowers.
They arrived near the road where they left the noble goddess previously,
then they led her to the house of their dear father.   (180)

But Demeter, sorrowing at heart, stood behind
with her head covered, down to the goddess's slim feet
hung a deep-blue gown.
Right away they came to the house of divinely-raised Keleus.
They went through the portico where their revered mother   (185)
sat by a pillar of the well-wrought wall,
holding a child on her lap, a young sprig, and they ran to her.
But Demeter stepped with her feet onto the threshold, while her head
touched the ceiling; the doorway was filled with holy divinity.
Reverence and piety and pale fear grasped Metaneira,   (190)
and she rose from her couch and asked her to have a seat.
But season-bearing Demeter of the shining-gifts
did not wish to sit upon the shining seat,
but silently she waited with her fair eyes cast down
until indeed trusty, wise Iambê set down for her   (195)
a well-wrought stool and cast upon it a shining fleece.
Sitting there she held her veil before her in her hands.
Long Demeter sat silently, grieving upon the stool,
not greeting anyone by word or by deed,
but unlaughing, tasting neither food nor drink   (200)
she sat grieving for her deep-bosomed daughter
until trusty, wise Iambê, jesting
with many sly jokes, pleased the revered Holy One,
and she smiled and laughed and kept a happy heart.
(Even later Iambê pleased her moods).   (205)
Metaneira gave her a cup full of honeyed wine,
but she declined, for it was not pious, she said to her,
to drink red wine. Demeter asked Metaneira
to give her a mixture of barley and water and soft pennyroyal to drink.
And she prepared the concoction and presented to the goddess
    as asked.   (210)
Receiving it for the sake of the rite very revered Deo . . .
Fine-belted Metaneira began to speak to her:
"Greetings, Lady, since I don't suppose you are born of base parents,
but noble. Reverence and grace befit your eyes
as even those of justice-bearing kings.   (215)
But we humans suffer in sorrow the gifts of the deities by necessity,
for a yoke lies upon the neck.
But now, since you have come here, such things as I have will be available.
Care for this child of mine, late-born and against all hope
the deities gave him, very dear to me.   (220)
If you should rear him to the full measure of youth,
easily anyone of womankind seeing you
would be jealous, such rewards shall I give you for your nursing."
Well-crowned Demeter then answered her:
"And you, Lady, many greetings! May the deities grant you good things.   (225)
I shall receive the child wisely, as you ask,

to raise him, and never do I think that by the folly of his nanny
will witchcraft hurt him, nor the "Woodsman,"[6]
for I know a very good antidote to the "Woodsman,"
and I know a good safeguard against baleful witchcraft."   (230)
Having thus spoken she received him to her holy bosom
with her immortal hands; his mother rejoiced in her mind.
So she cared for the shining son of wise Keleus—
Demophoön—whom well-belted Metaneira bore
in the halls. And he grew like a divinity,   (235)
neither eating grain nor suckling his mother's milk,
for by day fair-crowned Demeter
anointed him with ambrosia as if he were born of a deity,
and breathing on him sweetly she held him at her bosom.
At night she would hide him in the fire's power like a fire brand   (240)
unbeknownst to his dear parents. And to them he became a great wonder,
as he grew so quickly, for he resembled the deities in appearance.
And Demeter even would have made him ageless and immortal
if well-belted Metaneira foolishly one night
had not spied her out while looking out from the fragrant chamber.   (245)
She shrieked and struck both thighs
in fear for her child and got hysterical at heart,
and in her distress she cried out in winged words:
"My child, Demophoön, this guest hides you in the full flames
and sets grief and baleful sorrow upon me!"   (250)
So she spoke wailing; the goddess of goddesses heard her.
Then fair-crowned Demeter, growing enraged,
took the dear child—unhoped for, whom Metaneira bore in the halls—
from the hearth with her immortal hands and placed him on the ground,
took him from the fire, livid at heart,   (255)
and at the same time she addressed well-belted Metaneira:
"Idiot humans! Morons! Not perceiving
your coming fate either for good or bad!
Now you by your own stupidity have been irreparably damaged!
For know by the oath of the deities, by the water of the relentless Styx, (260)
immortal and ageless all his days
I would have made the dear child, and granted him imperishable honor.
But now he won't escape death nor fend off his fate.
But at least undying honor will be with him forever, because on my knees
he crawled and slept in my arms.   (265)
But soon as the years circle about by seasons
the children of the Eleusinians will come against each other
in war and in dread battle cry, always, for all days.
I am honor-bearing Demeter, she who is greatest
among immortals, a boon to mortals, and a bringer of joy.   (270)
Now build me a great temple, and set up

---

[6]Hades yet again.

an altar by it—all the people by the steep city
and the Kallikhoros wall above the projecting hill.
I myself shall reveal my rite, so hereafter
you may please my mind when offering holy sacrifice." (275)
So speaking the great and holy goddess changed
from her old woman appearance. Beauty fluttered all about her,
a lovely scent emerged from the folds of her gown,
splendorous light shown far and wide from the immortal skin
of the goddess, gold hair flowed down her shoulders. (280)
The well-wrought house was filled with light like lightning.
She walked out of the halls. Immediately Metaneira's knees went slack,
she was speechless for a long time, nor did she
remember to pick up the dear child from the ground.
But his sisters heard his piteous voice, (285)
and they rushed down from their well-covered beds. One of them
taking up the child in her hands snuggled him to her bosom,
while another revived the fire. Another stood up their mother on soft feet
and led her from the fragrant room.
Gathering about the fretting child they bathed him (290)
lovingly; but his heart wasn't soothed,
for lesser nurses held him now.
All night they supplicated the illustrious goddess,
shaking with fear; but when Dawn shined forth
they related everything to powerful Keleus (295)
as the goddess—fair-crowned Demeter—had ordered.
And he, summoning the many people to an assembly,
ordered a rich temple to be constructed for fair-haired Demeter
and an altar upon the projecting hill.
And right quickly they obeyed his commands
and built it, as ordered. Demophoön grew like a divinity. (300)
And when they finished and rested from their labor,
each one went home. But blond Demeter
sat inside far from all the other Blessed Ones
and dwelled in sorrow for her deep-bosomed daughter.
A most dreadful year upon the much-nourishing earth (305)
she made for men—and worse! The earth did not
yield up its seeds, for well-crowned Demeter hid them.
In vain did oxen drag the curved ploughs through the fields;
much white barley was cast fruitlessly upon the earth.
And now she would have destroyed all the race of speaking humans (310)
with harsh famine, and she would have deprived
those with homes on Olympos of gifts and honors and sacrifices
if Zeus has not pondered and debated in his heart.
First he sent golden-winged Iris to summon
fair-haired Demeter, lovely of form. (315)
So he spoke, and she obeyed dark-clouded Zeus son of Kronos
and sped down to earth on swift feet.

She came to the walled town of fragrant Eleusis;
she found blue-cloaked Demeter in the temple
and addressed her in winged words: (320)
"Demeter, Father Zeus of undying wisdom summons you
to join the race of ever-living deities.
Please go! Let my word from Zeus be fulfilled!"
So she spoke, imploring, but Demeter's heart was not persuaded.
Again then the father sent out, one after another, the ever-living, blessed
　　deities,   (325)
going to her one after the other.
They implored her and gave many very beautiful gifts
and honors, whichever she might want to take among the immortals.
But no one was able to persuade her heart
raging in her breast; she firmly rejected their words.   (330)
For she said she would never set foot on fragrant Olympos
nor release the fruit of the earth
before she saw with her own eyes her broad-faced daughter.
And so when deep-thundering, broad-browed Zeus heard this
he sent gold-wanded Argeiphontes[7] to Erebos   (335)
so that, persuading Hades with soft words,
he'd get holy Persephonê to emerge from the murky gloom
into the light among the divinities, so that her mother,
seeing her with her own eyes, would relent in her anger.
Hermes was not disobedient, but quickly he dove under   (340)
the earth's depths, leaving the seat of Olympos.
He came upon the King of the house inside,
seated on the bed with his hallowed wife,
who was sorely missing her mother. She, far away
from the works of the blessed gods plotted her harsh plan.   (345)
Standing close by, powerful Argeiphontes spoke:
"Dark-haired Hades, ruler of the departed,
Father Zeus sent me to lead up noble Persephonê
from Erebos to those above, so that her mother,
seeing her with her own eyes, might relent   (350)
her anger and dread wrath against the gods. For she plots a great deed—
to destroy the feeble race of earth-dwelling humans,
hiding the grain under the earth, and depriving the immortals of their honors.
She's really angry, won't mingle
with the gods, but far away in her fragrant temple   (355)
she sits in the walled city of Eleusis."
So he spoke. Aidoneus, king of those below, smiled
with his brows, nor did he disobey the command of King Zeus.
Quickly he bade wise Persephonê:
"Go, Persephonê, to your blue-robed mother,   (360)
having a gentle mood in your heart and breast for me,

---

[7]Hermes.

nor feeling exceedingly dejected on other matters.
I'm not a bad husband among the immortals,
being a brother of Father Zeus. Being here
you shall rule over all, as many as live and crawl,   (365)
and you'll possess fantastic honors among the immortals.
There will be payment for all days for wrong-doers,
for those who do not supplicate your mood with sacrifices,
offering guiltlessly, making proper gifts."
So he spoke, and wise Persephonê rejoiced, swiftly jumping up with joy.
    But he   (370)
gave her a pomegranate seed to eat, honey sweet, secretly,
guiding it nimbly about her, so that she might not remain for all days
beside revered, dark-robed Demeter.
Then many-named Aidoneus equipped his immortal horses
before him with golden reins.   (375)
And she entered the chariot, beside her powerful Argeiphontes,
taking the reins and whip in his dear hands,
drove through the halls, nor did the horses gallop slowly.
Quickly they made the long trip, neither sea
nor river nor grassy dale   (380)
nor hills held back the on-rush of the immortal horses,
but they cut through the deep air above them as they went.
And the driver stopped them there, where well-crowned Demeter was
before her fragrant temple. And she, seeing them,
sprang out like a wild woman in the shady glen.   (385)
Persephonê, for her part, when she saw with her fair eyes
her mother, she jumped from the chariot and left
the horses to rush forward, falling on her neck in embrace.
While still holding her dear child in her hands,
Demeter's heart quickly felt some horribly dread panic.   (390)
She let go of her dearest and addressed her in a word:
"Child, you didn't eat any food while you were below, did you?
Speak, don't hide it, so we both may know.
For if not, you, coming from beside hateful Hades,
might dwell with me and your father, the dark-clouded son of Kronos, (395)
being honored by all the immortals.
But if you ate, you'll return again under the depths of the earth,
living there a third of the seasons of the year,
the other two with me and the other immortals.
And whenever the earth blooms with every type of sweet-smelling
    flower,   (400)
then up from the murky gloom
again you will rise, a great wonder to deities and mortal humans.
Say how he seized you under the murky gloom
and what type of trick he played on you, the powerful many-named one?"
And most lovely Persephonê replied to her: (405)
"Well then, Mom, I'll tell you the whole truth.

When luck-bringing, swift messenger Hermes came for me
from Father Kronides and the other heavenly ones
to bring me out of Erebos, so that, seeing me with your own eyes,
you might relent your anger and harsh wrath against the immortals,   (410)
immediately I leapt up for joy. But he secretly
fed a pomegranate seed to me, a sweet morsel,
against my will and by force he made me eat it.
And likewise, I'll tell how, seizing me by the crafty plotting of Kronides,
my father, he whisked me off, bearing me underground.   (415)
I'll recount everything, as you asked.
We were all then in the lovely meadow,
Leukippê and Phaino and Elektra and Ianthê
and Melitê and Iakhê and Rhodeia and Kallirhoê
and Melobosis and Tykhê and flowery Okuroê   (420)
and Khryeis and Ianeira and Akastê and Admetê,
Rhodopê and Plouto and luscious Kalypso
and heavenly Styx and lovely Galaxaurê
and fight-rousing Pallas and arrow-shooting Artemis.
We were playing and picking lovely flowers with our hands   (425)
among gentle crocus and iris and hyacinth
and rosebuds and lilies, wonders to see,
and narcissus, which the wide earth grew like crocus.
And I was plucking them with great joy. Then the earth
gaped open; from her rushed out the powerful king of many names.   (430)
He bore me under the earth in a golden chariot,
I was completely unwilling. I cried out in a loud voice.
These things I tell you in sorrow are the whole truth."
Then all day, having sympathetic hearts,
they soothed each other in heart and mind,   (435)
embracing each other—They ceased sorrowing at heart.
Great joy did they receive and give to each other,
and Hekatê of the shining veil approached them
and gave the revered daughter of Demeter a big hug,
and from this time Queen Hekatê was Persephonê's attendant
        and companion.   (440)
After this deep-thundering, broad-browed Zeus sent a messenger to them—
fair-haired Rhea, to lead blue-robed Demeter
back to the race of deities, and to tell them he promised
to give her honors, those she would choose among the immortal deities.
And he agreed to her that the girl would   (445)
spend one third of the circling year under the murky gloom,
the other two thirds with her mother and the other immortals.
So he spoke, nor did the goddess disobey Zeus' tidings.
Swiftly she darted down from the summit of Olympos.
She came to Rharion, once a nourishing plain,   (450)
before, but lately not all that fertile, but fallow;
it stood all fruitless. There the white barley was hidden

by the contrivance of fair-ankled Demeter. But later,
in time, it would be luxuriant with slender stalks
of the growing season, while the rich furrows in the plain (455)
would grow heavy with shoots to be bound with sheaves.
There first Rhea set foot from the barren air.
Joyously they saw each other, rejoicing at heart.
Rhea with the shining veil addressed her:
"Come, child, deep-thundering, broad-browed Zeus summons you (460)
to come among the race of deities, and he promises to give you honors,
whichever ones you desire from the immortal deities.
He has agreed for your daughter that over the circling year
she spend one third under the murky gloom
and two thirds with you and the other immortals. (465)
So he promised to fulfill it, for he nodded his head.
But come, my child, and obey, do not remain angry long with dark-clouded
    Kronides.
And, quickly!, grow nourishing grain for humans."
So she spoke, nor did well crowned Demeter disobey.
Quickly she brought forth grain in the fertile fields, (470)
all the wide earth was heavy with leaves and flowers.
And she went to the justice-bearing kings
to reveal to Triptolemos and horse-driving Diokles and
Eumolpos the powerful and Keleus leader of the people
holy rites and to explain all her mysteries (475)
to Triptolemos and Polyxenos and Diokles
about her holy rites, which never can be transgressed nor revealed
nor uttered, for some great reverence of the deities restrains the voice.
Fortunate is anyone of earth-dwelling humans who has seen these.
But the one who is uninitiated has no share, nor an equal (480)
fate does that one have under the murky gloom once dead.
And when the goddess of goddesses established all these
she went to Olympos, to the assembly of the other deities.
There they dwell with Zeus delighting in thunder,
holy and revered. Very fortunate is anyone whom these two (485)
love sagely among mortal humans,
quickly they send to him, at the hearth of his great house,
Ploutos, who gives wealth to mortals.
But come, Lady, shining-gifts, season-bearing Deo, Queen
of fragrant Eleusis, having the (490)
people of sea-girt Paros and rocky Antron.
You and your most beautiful daughter Persephonê,
grant me a happy life for my song.
And I shall remember you in another song.

Bibliography

Barnard, M. 1958. *Sappho: A New Translation*. Berkeley, CA: University of California Press.

Barnstone, W. 1988. *Sappho and the Greek Lyric Poets*. New York, NY: Schocken.

Bonfante, L. 2002. "The Greeks in Etruria." In Karageorghis (ed.), 43–58.

Bonn-Muller, E. 2010. "Dynasty of Priestesses." *Archaeology Archive*. Retrieved March 1, 2010, from http://archive.archaeology.org/online/features/eleutherna/

Burnett, A. P. 2005. *Pindar's Songs for Young Athletes of Aigina*. Oxford: Oxford University Press.

Calame, C. 2001. *Choruses of Young Women in Ancient Greece: Their Morphology, Religious Role, and Social Functions*. New York, NY: Rowman and Littlefield.

Calame, C. 1999. *The Poetics of Eros in Ancient Greece*. Princeton, NJ: Princeton University Press.

Calder, L. 2011. *Cruelty and Sentimentality: Greek Attitudes to Animals 600–300 BC*. Oxford: BAR International Series 2225.

Campbell, D. A. 1982. *Greek Lyric I: Sappho and Alcaeus*. Cambridge, MA: Harvard University Press.

Carson, A. 1996. "The Justice of Aphrodite in Sappho I." In E. Greene (ed.), *Reading Sappho: Contemporary Approaches*. Berkeley, CA: University of California Press, 226–232.

Chadwick, J. 1990. "The Pech-Maho Lead." *Zeitschrift für Papyrologie und Epigraphik* 82, 161–166.

Cole, S. G. 2000. "Landscapes of Artemis." *Classical World* 93, 470–481.

Cole, S. G. 1996. "Demeter in the Ancient City and its Countryside." In S. E. Alcock and R. Osborne (eds.), *Placing the Gods: Sanctuaries and Sacred Space in Ancient Greece*. Oxford: Clarendon Press, 199–216.

Cole, S. G. 1981. "Could Greek Women Read and Write?" In H. P. Foley (ed.), *Reflections of Women in Antiquity*. Philadelphia, PA: Gordon and Breach, 219–245.

Crawley, R. 1910. *Thucydides: The Peloponnesian War*. London: J. M. Dent.

Dillon, M., and L. Garland. 2000. *Ancient Greece: Social and Historical Documents from Archaic Times to the Death of Socrates*. London: Routledge.

Edelstein, E. J., and L. Edelstein. 1998. *Asclepius: Collection and Interpretation of the Testimonies*. Baltimore, MD: Johns Hopkins University Press.

Empereur, J.-Y. 2002. "Les Grecs en Égypte." In Karageorghis (ed.), 23–42.

Evelyn-White, H. G. 1914. *Hesiod, Homeric Hymns, Epic Cycle, Homerica*. Cambridge, MA: Harvard University Press.

Fisher, N. 2011. "Competitive Delights: The Social Effects of the Expanded Programme of Contests in Post-Kleisthenic Athens." In N. Fisher and H. van Wees (eds.), *Competition in the Ancient World*. Swansea: Classical Press of Wales, 175–219.

Foley, H. 2003. "Mothers and Daughters." In Neils and Oakley (eds.), 113–137.

Garlan, Y., and O. Masson. 1982. "Les Acclamations Pédérastiques de Kalami." *Bulletin de Correspondence Hellénique* 106(1), 3–22.

Garland, R. 1998. *Daily Life of the Ancient Greeks*. Westport, CT: Greenwood.

Garland, R. 1995. *The Eye of the Beholder: Deformity and Disability in the Graeco-Roman World*. Ithaca, NY: Cornell University Press.

Garland, R. 1990. *The Greek Way of Life: From Conception to Old Age*. Ithaca, NY: Cornell University Press.

Garland, R. 1985. *The Greek Way of Death*. Ithaca, NY: Cornell University Press.

Godley, A. D. 1920. *Herodotus: The Persian Wars*. Cambridge, MA: Harvard University Press.

Golden, M. 2003. "Childhood in Ancient Greece." In Neils and Oakley (eds.), 13–29.

Golden, M. 1981. "Demography and the Exposure of Girls at Athens." *Phoenix* 35, 316–331.

Greene, E. 2002. "Subjects, Objects, and Erotic Symmetry in Sappho's Fragments." In Rabinowitz and Auanger (eds.), 82–105.

Grego, E. S., and R. A. Santiago. 1988. "La letter grecque d'Emporion et son context archéologique." *Revue archéologique de Narbonnaise* 21, 3–17.

Guthrie, W. K. C. 1952. *Orpheus and Greek Religion*. Princeton, NJ: Princeton University Press.

Hall, J. M. 2002. *Hellenicity*. Chicago, IL: University of Chicago Press.

Hall, J. M. 1997. *Ethnic Identity in Greek Antiquity*. Cambridge: Cambridge University Press.

Hansen, M. H. 2006. *Polis: An Introduction to the Ancient Greek City-State*. Oxford: Oxford University Press.

Hanson, A. E. 1990. "The Medical Writer's Woman." In D. M. Halperin, J. Winckler, and F. Zeitlin (eds.), *Before Sexuality: The Construction of Erotic Experience in the Ancient Greek World*. Princeton, NJ: Princeton University Press, 308–338.

Harrison, T. 2003. "The Cause of Things: Envy and the Emotions." In Konstan and Rutter (eds.), 143–163.

Henderson, J. 1996. *Three Plays by Aristophanes: Staging Women*. London: Routledge.

Holmes, B. 2010. *The Symptom and the Subject: The Emergence of the Physical Body in Ancient Greece*. Princeton, NJ: Princeton University Press.

Jeffrey, L. H., and A. Morpurgo-Davies. 1970. "ΠΟΙΝΙΚΑΣΤΑΣ AND ΠΟΙΝΙΚΑΖΕΝ: BM 1969. 4–2. 1, A New Archaic Inscription from Crete." *Kadmos* 9, 118–154.

Jordan, D. 2000. "A Personal Letter Found in the Athenian Agora." *Hesperia* 69(1), 91–103.

Karageorghis, V. (ed.). 2002. *The Greeks Beyond the Aegean: From Marseilles to Bactria.* New York: Alexander S. Onassis Public Benefit Foundation.

Kloppenborg, J. S. and R. S. Ascough. 2011. *Greco-Roman Associations: Texts, Translations, and Commentary.* Berlin: De Gruyter.

Konstan, D. 2006. *The Emotions of the Ancient Greeks: Studies in Aristotle and Classical Literature.* Toronto: University of Toronto Press.

Konstan, D., and N. K. Rutter (eds.). 2003. *Envy, Spite and Jealousy: The Rivalrous Emotions in Ancient Greece.* Edinburgh: Edinburgh University Press.

Lambert, S. D. (ed.). 2011. *Sociable Man: Essays on Ancient Greek Social Behaviours in Honour of Nick Fisher.* Swansea: Classical Press of Wales.

Lang, M. 1977. *Cure and Cult in Ancient Corinth: A Guide to the Asklepeion.* Princeton, NJ: American School of Classical Studies in Athens.

Larson, J. 2007. *Ancient Greek Cults: A Guide.* New York, NY: Routledge.

Larson, J. 2001. *Greek Nymphs: Myth, Cult, Lore.* Oxford: Oxford University Press.

Lear, A., and E. Cantarella. 2008. *Images of Ancient Greek Pederasty: Boys Were Their Gods.* New York, NY: Routledge.

Lefkowitz, M. R., and M. B. Fant. 1992. *Women's Life in Greece and Rome: A Source Book in Translation.* Baltimore, MD: Johns Hopkins University Press.

Malkin, I. (ed.). 2001. *Ancient Perceptions of Greek Ethnicity.* Cambridge, MA: Harvard University Press.

Meiggs, R., and D. Lewis. 1969. *A Selection of Greek Historical Inscriptions: To the End of the Fifth Century BC.* Oxford: Clarendon Paperbacks.

Meyer, M. W. 1987. *The Ancient Mysteries: A Sourcebook of Sacred Texts.* Philadelphia, PA: University of Pennsylvania Press.

Miller, S. G. 2004. *Ancient Greek Athletics.* New Haven, CT: Yale University Press.

Miller, S. G. 1991. *Arete: Greek Sports from Ancient Sources* (2nd and expanded ed.). Berkeley, CA: University of California Press.

Miller, S. G. 1978. *The Prytaneion: Its Function and Architectural Form.* Berkeley, CA: University of California Press.

Morgan, Morris Hicky. 1914. *Vitruvius: The Ten Books on Architecture.* Cambridge, MA: Harvard University Press.

Neils, J., and J. H. Oakley (eds.). 2003. *Coming of Age in Ancient Greece: Images of Childhood from the Classical Past.* New Haven, CT: Yale University Press.

Newmyer, S. T. 2010. *Animals in Greek and Roman Thought: A Sourcebook.* New York, NY: Routledge.

Newmyer, S. T. 2007. "Animals in Ancient Philosophy: Conceptions and Misconceptions." In L. Kalof (ed.), *A Cultural History of Animals in Antiquity.* Oxford: Berg, 151–174.

Nielsen, T. H. 2004. "The Concept of *Patris* in Archaic and Classical Sources." In T. H. Nielsen (ed.), *Once Again: Studies in the Ancient Greek Polis.* Copenhagen: Franz Steiner Verlag, 49–76.

Page, D. 1955. *Sappho and Alcaeus: An Introduction to the Study of Ancient Lesbian Poetry.* Oxford: Clarendon.

Plant, I. M. 2004. *Women Writers of Ancient Greece and Rome: An Anthology.* Norman, OK: University of Oklahoma Press.

Pomeroy, S. B. 2002. *Spartan Women*. Oxford: Oxford University Press.

Potts, S. 2011. "Co-Operation, Competition and Clients: The Social Dynamics of the Athenian Navy." In S. D. Lambert, (ed.), 45–66.

Rabinowitz, N. S. 2002. "Excavating Women's Homoeroticism in Ancient Greece: The Evidence form Attic Vase Painting." In Rabinowitz and Auanger (eds.), 106–166.

Rabinowitz, N. S., and L. Auanger (eds.). 2002. *Among Women: From the Homosocial to the Homoerotic in the Ancient World*. Austin, TX: University of Texas Press.

Romm, J. S. 1992. *The Edges of the Earth in Ancient Thought*. Princeton, NJ: Princeton University Press.

Sage, M. M. 1996. *Warfare in Ancient Greece: A Sourcebook*. London: Routledge.

Shapiro, H. A. 2003. "Fathers and Sons, Men and Boys." In Neils and Oakley (eds.), 85–111.

Sourvinou-Inwood, C. 2000. "What is *Polis* Religion?" In R. Buxton (ed.), *Greek Religion*. Oxford: Oxford University Press, 13–37.

Stafford, E. 2011. "Clutching the Chickpea: Private Pleasures of the Bad Boyfriend." In S. D. Lambert (ed.), 337–363.

Sternberg, R. H. 2005. "The Nature of Pity." In R. H. Sternberg (ed.), *Pity and Power in Ancient Athens*. Cambridge: Cambridge University Press, 15–47.

Stewart, A. 1997. *Art, Desire, and the Body in Ancient Greece*. Cambridge: Cambridge University Press.

Tod, M. N. 1985. *Greek Historical Inscriptions*. Chicago, IL: Ares.

Tsetskhladze, G. R. 2002. "Greeks beyond the Bosporus." In Karageorghis (ed.), 129–166.

Tzifopoulos, Y. 2010. *Paradise Earned: The Bacchic-Orphic Gold Lamellae of Crete*. Washington, DC: Center for Hellenic Studies.

Van Straten, F. T. 1981. "Gifts for the Gods." In H. S. Versnel (ed.), *Faith, Hope, and Worship: Aspects of Religious Mentality in the Ancient World*. Leiden: Brill, 65–151.

Vernant, J.-P. 1991. *Mortals and Immortals: Collected Essays*. Princeton, NJ: Princeton University Press.

Wentworth Thompson, D. 1952. "History of Animals." *Aristotle: II*. Chicago, IL: University of Chicago Press, 7–158.

West, M. L. 1993. *Greek Lyric Poetry: A New Translation*. Oxford: Oxford University Press.

Index Locorum

Subject Index

About the Author

STEPHANIE LYNN BUDIN is an ancient historian who focuses on ancient Greece and the Near East. Her published works include *Images of Woman and Child from the Bronze Age* (Cambridge University Press, 2011), *The Ancient Greeks: New Perspectives* (ABC-CLIO, 2004), *The Myth of Sacred Prostitution in Antiquity* (Cambridge University Press, 2009), and *The Origin of Aphrodite* (CDL Press, 2003), as well as numerous articles on ancient religion and iconography. She has delivered papers in England, Ireland, Germany, Sweden, Cyprus, Israel, Japan, and Canada, as well as throughout the United States. She lives in New Jersey with her husband and bunnies.